POLITICS OF DISCOURSE

HISTORIA

POLITICS OF DISCOURSE

The Literature and History of
Seventeenth-Century England

Edited by

Kevin Sharpe
and
Steven N. Zwicker

UNIVERSITY OF CALIFORNIA PRESS
Berkeley   Los Angeles   London

University of California Press
Berkeley and Los Angeles, California

University of California Press, Ltd.
London, England

Copyright © 1987 by Kevin Sharpe and Steven N. Zwicker

"Andrew Marvell, Oliver Cromwell, and the Horatian Ode," by Blair Worden,
copyright © 1984 by Cambridge University Press.

Library of Congress Cataloging in Publication Data

Politics of discourse.

  Bibliography: p.
  Includes index.
  1. English literature—Early modern, 1500–1700—
History and criticism.   2. Politics in literature.
3. Politics and literature—Great Britain.   4. Great
Britain—Politics and government—1603–1714.   5. Great
Britain—History—Stuarts, 1603–1714.   6. Literature and
history.   I. Sharpe, Kevin.   II. Zwicker, Steven N.
PR438.P65P64   1987   820'.9'004   86-19153
ISBN 0-520-05829-1 (alk. paper)
ISBN 0-520-06070-9 (pbk)

Printed in the United States of America

1 2 3 4 5 6 7 8 9

Contents

Preface and Acknowledgments

Like most scholarly works, this volume had its origin in questions and problems. At a time when one of the editors was grappling with the status of literary texts as primary historical evidence and the other was engaged in elucidating political contexts of Restoration literary texts, they found themselves on leave at the same place and in frequent discussion of similar questions. The outcome of these discussions was the clear sense that we were dealing with common problems and a growing realization that these were problems that had, for the most part, fallen between the disciplines of literature and history, tackled by neither.

The politics of all modes of discourse—sermon and polemical pamphlet, fable and history, poem and play—is a subject that still awaits both its historians and its critics. From our sense of the need for a broader and more comparative discussion this volume emerged. Of course, a comprehensive study of discourse cannot be accomplished within the confines of a single volume. For the study of the politics of discourse in the seventeenth century must embrace low culture—the ballad and the broadsheet—as well as high culture, and all the genres of prose—legal treatise, parliamentary speech, homily, and proclamation—as well as poetry. Our study at present is not only limited by the scale of the subject and the confines of space but was determined too by the kinds and degree of attention that have hitherto been paid to seventeenth-century literature. The politics of drama has been relatively well explored; other modes of discourse that we are not accustomed to thinking of as "literature" have as yet attracted no such critical attention. Our focus, then, is upon high culture and principally upon poetry, not because they embrace all our concerns but because here the most innovative work is currently in progress which may elucidate those broader concerns. It is our hope that this collection may stimulate and suggest an approach to further literary and historical study of other realms of seventeenth-century discourse.

Kevin Sharpe would like to thank Anne Barton, Jonathan Goldberg, David Norbrook, Stephen Orgel, and David Riggs for their helpful discussions, hospitality, and encouragement, and Dr. Cedric Brown of Reading University and the English Department of Washington University, St. Louis, for opportunities to deliver earlier versions of his essay. Steven Zwicker would like to thank Gerald Izenberg and Richard Davis of the History Department at Washington University for conversation and discussion over a number of years and for their participation in the Literature and History Program at Washington University; and Derek Hirst, David Bywaters, and Charles Newman for helpful comments. Both editors would like to express their thanks to the School of Historical Studies, The Institute for Advanced Study, Princeton, and especially to John Elliott, for providing a period of uninterrupted research; and to Allen Mandelbaum and Stanley Holwitz for their enthusiasm and support for the project. And both would like especially to thank Judy, Laura, Benjamin, Jonathan, and Aaron for comfortable circumstances, patience, and the diversions that preserved what remained of sanity during the completion of the introduction in St. Louis.

St. Louis
1985

Kevin Sharpe
Steven N. Zwicker

1

Politics of Discourse: Introduction

Kevin Sharpe and Steven N. Zwicker

The literature and history of seventeenth-century England have scarcely been neglected. The Stuart age has attracted critical and historical scholarship of remarkable quantity and quality. The appeal of this era is not difficult to understand. Few centuries could rival the literary genius of Shakespeare and Jonson, of Milton and Marvell; few historical periods are marked by more decisive events and struggles. No age has produced a literature of political theory more original, more varied, or more formative. The richness and complexity of the literature, the history, and the political theory have necessitated and produced close and specialized study. We may feel that we know more of this century than any other. But ironically, the very power of such specialized investigation has fragmented the central concerns of the century and distanced us from its most distinctive characteristic, for the creative genius of this century and the force of its history and political discourse owe much to the very interdependence of politics and culture. What inspired the literary imagination also shaped the course of events. Who can doubt that Milton's poetry and civil war politics were alike exegeses of Scripture, that both were meditations on holy writ, or that in general Scripture was the language of both literature and politics?

Scripture was by no means the only language common to the aesthetic and civic realms. The classics and the law, for example, bequeathed their languages to all spheres of discourse. The discovery of such idioms and vocabularies and the plotting of their histories might be described as a recovery and reconstitution of languages, and such an enterprise requires the skills of both historian and critic.[1] At

1

first sight languages might seem scarcely in need of recovery. The literary critic, after all, has long addressed the complexities of metaphor, of paradox and ambiguity; and historians have adopted the very language of the seventeenth century, "court" and "country," "puritan" and "cavalier," in their analyses of politics and society. But to confine metaphor and ambiguity to literary significance alone and merely to appropriate seventeenth-century language as explanatory device is not adequately to study the languages or to locate them in their histories. For the history of languages reveals whole vocabularies of inherited allusion and contemporary associations; it demonstrates when and for what reasons languages acquired polemical thrust. The historical study of language reveals the idioms and commonplaces of culture and discourse; it enables us to hear the subtle inflections and manipulations, the ironic turns and inversions of these idioms. To become sensitive to the full range of linguistic stances and associations and to discern their oscillations across the decades of the century and all its modes of discourse must be the common objective of historical and critical inquiry.

Scholars have shown themselves to be sensitive to nuances of language in literary texts. To isolate what we delineate as literature, however, and to apply to it special techniques of study is to divorce that literature from other modes of discourse and to impose upon seventeenth-century culture our own categories and classifications. We sharply distinguish histories from epics, sermons from pamphlets, creative from critical writing, the imaginative from the documentary. In so doing we fragment what was a common culture partaking of shared languages.[2] At the beginning of the seventeenth century literature was humane letters; it embraced history and ethics, religion and politics. To isolate literature is not only to deprive its language of the power of these associations but also to deny the political its highest polemical mode. *Paradise Lost* was written at the nexus of religion and politics; its spiritual language is freighted with political argument. The poem articulated political values. At one level then, Milton must be read as the greatest protagonist of the "good old cause." At no level can he be fully appreciated without a sense of his polemical engagement.[3]

Criticism has tended to contrast the aesthetic and the political. We think of genius and partisanship as at odds; great art as the sphere of the sublime. "Culture" demarcates an area of autonomous pursuits and sensibility, a realm beyond and above the political. We evaluate the greatest writers as those least fettered by their age. Such appraisals have too often announced Shakespeare's detachment from Tudor politics; and they have too often presented Milton's poetry as a retreat from political concerns.[4] The intention of Milton and Shakespeare to engage political argument will remain a matter of interpretation. What is incontestable is that their languages were perforce political and necessarily conveyed political meanings. There is an important sense in which no seventeenth-century literature is not also political.

For a study of the politics of culture cannot confine itself to an author's intentions. As John Pocock has argued, the history of languages must be concerned not only with acts intended by an author but also, and as importantly, with the various meanings and associations that could have been received by his or her audience.[5] Restoration adaptations of Shakespeare provide some evidence of the meanings that could be found and performed with his texts within the compass of the seventeenth century.[6] Some of these performances accorded with Shakespeare's intentions, but others undoubtedly did not. We may even say that some unwittingly misunderstood or even willfully misinterpreted and misapplied the meanings of his text. Such misunderstandings and misapplications are an important part of our subject; at points they are more revealing cultural documents than what we might regard as faithful interpretations. They demonstrate the conceptual freedom possible within the language. To contemplate such liberties brings us close to the deconstructive reading of modern criticism. What separates us from this approach, however, is our insistence that interpretation take place within the meanings capable of being performed within the confines of seventeenth-century discourse. Our deconstruction, that is to say, demands a reconstruction of the languages of Stuart England.

Language, or, more accurately, languages are the media of what we now think of as literature and, more broadly, of all those texts and documents, letters, speeches, treatises, sermons, statutes, and proclamations from which the historian customarily reconstructs the past. The study of these languages therefore illuminates the history of cultures and in some cases may, from this distance, enable us to rediscover lost territories within that history. Such study should also enable us to locate and hence to explicate from new perspectives what are now regarded as its central literary texts. The archaeology of languages is therefore both a historical and a literary science; it may enable us to study layers of intellectual and social history, of literary articulation and reception, of intent and interpretation, that have eluded study conducted within the boundaries of one field or another. Indeed, to transcend such boundaries is to bring us closer to the seventeenth century, for in this age—the age of *litterae humaniores*—neither the enterprise nor the vocabularies of literature and history were conceived as distinct or independent. The history of language may, then, facilitate understanding of a world in which historians and poets spoke a common discourse and addressed common concerns.

Languages have both a long historical continuum and a precise and particular location in time. We speak, after all, the language of Shakespeare and Donne, but in so doing we do not evoke or communicate their associations and values; nor can we inflect that language with the multiplicities of meaning and nuance of early Stuart culture. There can be no doubt about this distance; we may, however, be less sensitive to the space that separates those we think of as near contemporaries. Dryden spoke Shakespeare's language, of course, but it is clear that he did not thereby convey Shakespeare's meanings. Words may be constant while their meanings undergo change. Hence the history of language must be the history of both long continuities and short periods of time. For linguistic change may be both gradual and abrupt; it may reflect the slow pace of cultural change or the sudden urgency of historical event or crisis. And in turn language may not only reflect change, it may also enact it. Linguistic change enables slow shifts of perception within a society; it may also galvanize existing modes of thought into a force of radical change. When we study long-term cultural changes and when we examine particular and cataclysmic historical events, certain key words forcefully and inevitably present themselves. We may think of *property, order, liberty, authority, privileges,* and *rights;* such words are barometers of the long term. They are also, however, expressions of specific meanings in and shifts of meaning over relatively short periods.[7]

Indeed, it may be the very words that both endure and undergo important shifts of meaning that are the most illuminating indicators for the historian of politics and culture. *Politics* and *culture* are themselves excellent examples. For the historian of the seventeenth century, the study of such terms poses important questions and yields fruitful suggestions about some of the central shifts in this age. *Culture* to us defines a distinct sphere, an area of life outside the political, above the commonplace, both distinct and superior. The arts, literary and plastic, are its central constituents; its membership is an elite. The seventeenth century shared none of these assumptions.[8] The word *culture* enters our language with religious associations. By the early seventeenth century it is a synonym for *cultivation;* first in the literal sense (horticulture, agriculture) and second in the sense of nurture and improvement—of the man as well as his environment.[9] Culture, in other words, is synonymous with all learning: political understanding, knowledge of Scripture, familiarity with the classics, training in the law, education. Even a superficial look at the word underscores not the distinctiveness of literary and artistic culture but its integration with all knowledge, with social and civic life.

A study of the word *culture* points to a perception of the relationship between art and society quite different from our own but continuous through the seventeenth century. This is an important layer of investigation, but the history of languages may enable us to go further, to ascertain important continuities of discourse that may illuminate subtle but fundamental shifts of perception and belief. Historians of the English Renaissance encounter the word *commonweal* at every turn. It is a word that not only describes but exemplifies the polity, a polity uniting its members in an ethical and political union for the common good. The commonweal embraces the whole; the word demonstrates the unitary vision of politics at the close of the sixteenth century. The word remains in currency throughout the seventeenth century, but after the civil wars and certainly after the Restoration we discern a decline and suspect a tone of archaism in its use. More commonly we read of *commonwealth* and more specifically we read of *commonwealthsman*, deployed now not as the language of a unified world of values and politics but as a stigma delineating faction and even treason.[10] The *Oxford English Dictionary* informs us that in 1683 a pamphlet denounced the French Protestants as "commonwealthsmen and traitors."[11] The juxtaposition of terms illustrates not only a shift in meaning but the fundamental reversal of association. It may lead us to suspect an equally fundamental shift in political vision and attitudes.

One of the most important shifts of political vision in the seventeenth century is the gradual recognition of "politics" as a distinct sphere.[12] Again, the history of the word may be our most valuable indicator. In the early seventeenth century the word is found most often as part of the vocabulary of classical inheritance and more particularly as the title of Aristotle's treatise. This is sufficient to remind us that what we understand as politics—the struggles for power, different and rival policies and programs—were seldom articulated in that society. By the end of the seventeenth century this is less clearly the case. The word *politician* retains its pejorative sense, of schemer or Machiavel; but in practice political maneuverings and even programs had become a fact of life, and linguistic usage has begun to acknowledge it, albeit tentatively.[13] Jonathan Swift showed no sign of apology when he informed a correspondent in 1710 that he had spent an hour with Sir Robert Harley "deep in politicks, where I told him the objections of the October Club." Politics has become a respectable facet of life. Our three terms, then, illustrate quite different continuities and changes: one continues to shift meaning across the decade; one goes out of existence by the late seventeenth century; one enters the language of respectability only in its closing years. These and other such words might become valuable documents of broader historical change.

To the political historian of the seventeenth century, the most obvious change is the emergence of party politics. After the Exclusion Crisis and certainly in the wake of the Glorious Revolution, politics centers on "the rage of party."[14] Few would publicly have welcomed the development; the enduring idea of commonweal still led men to disclaim party as personal and factional interest.[15] Despite such disclaimers, however, the historian may discern not only the emergence of party but its acknowledgment; moreover, party has been enshrined not only in political institutions but in local society, civic culture, and social habits.[16] In London most obviously, social life was in part organized around political affiliations: the Kit-Cat Club, the Green Ribbon Club, and the Calves-Head Club provided both social venues and political headquarters.[17] The labels "Whig" and "Tory," of course, do not begin to do justice to the complexity of political organization or political behavior at the close of the seventeenth century: differences within parties, the struggle for office, local suspicions of the center, enduring commitments to one national interest—all these complicate any simplistic picture of two parties. But by the close of the seventeenth century, party must serve as the starting point for any discussion of such complexities. Dispute and fragmentation, once anathematized as the roots of dislocation, have now become the norms of political and social life.

Before the civil war, such a polity could have been contemplated only with horror and fear. The commonweal expressed one unified world of values; the very concept denied the fragmentation of politics and the idea of party. This is not to deny the existence of rival factions or, indeed, of different political positions; nor is it to argue that contemporaries were incapable of recognizing them. The terms *court* and *country*, *puritan* and *cavalier*, after all, suggest a diversity of political groupings—even, some might suggest, ideological positions.[18] But court and country at this point are not the language of party; they are articulations of ideals for the whole commonwealth, not representations of rival programs within it. Fundamental attitudes toward government were shared, not contested. The civil war might at first seem to render incomprehensible the early Stuart vision or ideal of a unified polity. On the contrary, the civil war is the finest demonstration of that perception. Men came to blows because they could not accommodate differences. After the civil war stability and order required the acknowledgment of diversity, the acceptance—indeed legitimization—of differences, and, finally, a political system fashioned and ordered by them.

The history of these developments may once again be divined through the study of languages. The word *party* itself, for example, illustrates and informs such a history. Originally a synonym for *part*, inconceivable outside the whole, it becomes by the end of this century the delineator of independent and contesting groups. The early seventeenth century would have been familiar with the legal usage ("party to a case"), but this itself underscores the sense of a unified politics, inseparable from custom and law.[19] Some Jacobean Englishmen, like Francis Bacon for example, certainly understood a political meaning of the word *party*, not least because he was familiar with Italian. But not until the 1650s do we find the word commonly associated with the taking of sides in political contest.[20] "To party" now meaning "to take sides" may have been borrowed from military usage; a party man is the label of a military unit, a "partisan" that of his weapon. It is instructive that at the end of the century the military association met its demise. Parties as political labels lost their associations with military violence. The changes in meaning and association may themselves suggest a political shift, from violence to verbal contest; they may suggest the civilization of political behavior. In this context it is intriguing that our most common modern usage, "a pleasurable social gathering," enters the language at the end of the seventeenth century, when the associations of party with physical contest have begun to fall away. The sociability evoked by the word may underscore the acceptance of political grouping and disagreement as a fact of national life.

Language, then, may be one of the most yielding documents for the historian of cultural and political change. But language is not only the passive indicator of social development, it may also effect social and political change. From no age is this more demonstrable than from the seventeenth century. It was a fundamental tenet of Renaissance humanism that language participated in authority; rhetoric is, after all, a study of the power of language and an essential for the education of a statesman. Language is seen to be possessed of power. The English interest in philology at the end of the sixteenth century indicates a concern with words not only as representations but as historical realities possessed of authority.[21] To William Camden the historian as to Ben Jonson the poet, no conviction was more fundamental than their belief that the name *was* the thing.[22] Names revealed truths and conveyed authority. For this age language represented power. And power, in turn, depended on language. A government that lacked a standing army and a police force rested upon articulations and perceptions of authority. Rhetoric and governance could not be dissociated. All political life derived its legitimacy from a set of authorizing languages. And it is crucial to recognize that there was an agreed set of languages: the languages of Scripture and the classics, of history and precedent, of custom and law.

These languages have their own histories. They remain in continuous use throughout the seventeenth century, but they undergo important shifts and changes as authorizing vocabularies. The changes, more than the continuities, reveal transitions in the legitimization of authority. From the civil war onward these changes often reveal contest for legitimate authority. After the outbreak of war contending factions strive to appropriate the shared languages of authority for their own particular cause. For all the Puritan trumpeting of godly politics, neither Royalist nor Roundhead could have contemplated battle without the authorizing force of Scripture.[23] Both fought for one law, both appealed to custom and precedent, both even claimed to be fighting for one king—that is, both claimed legitimacy from the same vocabularies. After civil war and interregnum, this is less clearly the case. This is not to argue that Whig and Tory, court and country were prepared to dispense with these vocabularies, but it is to suggest, we believe, that there is a greater willingness to manipulate these vocabularies, to employ them as tactical stances rather than as normative languages. Clearly, tactics is what Dryden had in mind at the opening of *Absalom and Achitophel* in the strategic, perhaps unlikely appropriation of David's story for the style of Charles II's court.[24] Scripture had not lost its prophetic authority either in Dryden's poetry or in his age, but the absolute rule of Scripture has been compromised. Other languages have grown in strength and even acquired ascendancy. The Roman model has political meaning throughout this century; after the Restoration, and especially in the last decades, it seems to acquire preeminence. This is one of the ideas we mean to convey when we speak of Augustan England.[25] Fluctuations in the status of these political languages are determined by the course of events. After the sectarian anarchy of the godly cause, those who sought to force change could appeal to Scripture only with the greatest caution. It is no accident that we speak of Classical Republicans.[26] And no less significantly, many of those who sought to justify the events of 1688 appealed to reasoned argument rather than to history or precedent. By the end of the century, we might suspect, reason itself has become an authorizing language.[27]

The acquisition by politics of its own rationality marks one of the most important developments of the century. Reason of state, the language of Machiavellian politics, aroused only fear and incomprehension in the citizens of a Christian commonwealth. In early Stuart England Machiavelli was the embodiment of evil; for these men politics was inseparable from ethics and religion.[28] The gradual emancipation of politics from these other commonwealths is an important chapter in the history of secularization.[29]

Although the role of religion in engendering the conflict remains a subject of controversy, none of us can doubt that the English civil war was the crisis of a state in which religion and politics could not be separated. Yet the civil war, the supreme illustration of their integration, was paradoxically the crucial step in their separation. The English civil war taught the dangers of a politics defined by religion, and the drive toward toleration came, in part, from the recognition of those perils. An acute political actor such as John Dryden was anxious to unravel the interdependency of religion and politics, to promote their separation. Dryden's religious texts mark a conscious and purposeful distance from the language and politics of zeal, and in this respect his poetry is separated by more than chronology from the poetry and values of John Milton. Milton's poems are the great texts of scriptural authorization and godly politics. We cannot fail to discern in Milton's verse a tone which by the 1660s often rang with anachronism. Politics has marked off its own world. Milton's poetry has deeply polemical concerns, but the poet himself has been banished from the public world of politics.

Milton's anachronism was not merely a matter of personal tone. Though Dryden's near contemporary, in his religiosity Milton seems to speak to us from within the civil war and, in his insistent moralizing of politics, from even earlier decades. In this respect he brings us closer to Jonson than to Dryden. In the early seventeenth century the ethical and political spheres were conceived as inseparable; the languages of what we might call the private and public spheres were interchangeable and interdependent.[30] Jonson's is the most insistent, the most abrasive articulation of the ethical basis of the political. But Jonson's was not an isolated or a dissident voice; he spoke from within, not outside, the political community. And his "sons" inherited his ethical values and political vision. The Caroline poets cannot be understood as merely his stylistic heirs; they were also expositors of Jonson's ethical and political vision.

For the poets no less than for the priests and politicians, the civil war was a contest between the forces of Good and Evil. The most bitter conflicts are fought within those communities that enshrine in their values moral absolutes. We may then be tempted to posit a connection between the retreat from violence in the late seventeenth century and the decline of religious and moral absolutism. If such a model were to be constructed, it would have to include the polarization of politics and the rise of party. For the very existence of party licenses diverse political values. Party authorizes relative values—better and worse—rather than absolute positions—right and wrong. The history of party may be a subtext in the gradual separation of ethics from politics.

The emancipation of politics from ethics and religion may have made possible the emergence of what we delineate as "the aesthetic." Michael McKeon writes of the "replacement" of religious by literary spirituality. Literature has not, of course, ceased to engage with politics, religion, and ethics; but perhaps literature has begun to occupy within these realms territory that will become independent, even autonomous. As we have seen, throughout the seventeenth century the word *literature* embraced all "polite or humane learning" (*OED*): civics and ethics, critical as well as creative writing. We may date the idea of an independent literary career only from the eighteenth century.[31] The first example of our own, more narrow definition comes from Samuel Johnson.[32] And it is in Johnson's age that we find not only the first clear recognition of a sphere of "literature" but as well the creation of its most consciously autonomous mode: the novel.[33] The very basis of the novel is a distinct literary spirituality unimaginable in the seventeenth century.

The novel, however, takes us well beyond our concerns. Our history of languages has introduced three principal themes: polarization, secularization, and the shift from moral absolutism to moral relativism. The chronology, interrelationships, and causes of these developments await their historian and cannot be investigated here. But the literary scholar no less than the political historian cannot doubt that at the center of all their histories stands the English civil war. For the civil war forced the recognition and legitimization of division; it revealed the dangers of a scriptural politics; and it necessitated the emergence of a moral relativism. The civil war bequeathed polemical styles and manners; the memory of the wars stalked the rest of the century, its culture as well as its politics. The importance of the civil war to the political and cultural history of the seventeenth century remains a subject of controversy.[34] In attempting to understand its impact, literature, with its subtle and powerful articulations of political languages, must play a central role.

Literary texts are not merely evidence of cultural and political change, they are themselves part of that history. And the stories of genre, mode, patronage, production, marketplace, and reception are chapters of political and social history as well as subjects for critical inquiry. There is a history of literature, but it is a history that cannot be separated, as we have come increasingly to understand, from the other histories of the seventeenth century. The conventional "history of English literature," like the historian's once-favored chapter on "the spirit of the age," has come to seem unacceptably parochial and naive. This, of course, is hardly a novel pronouncement, but there are still areas we regard as essentially of literary concern that require relocation within other histories of their age.

We think of genre as perhaps a purely literary subject, but the formation of genre and the history of the consciousness of literary genres is part of a history of perception.[35] The early seventeenth century produced what we now call country house poems, but Jonson could hardly have been aware of such a genre when he wrote *Penshurst*; similarly, the heroic drama and the Restoration comedy of manners are explanatory categories for the critic, but they had no meaning for their first authors. This is not to deny that the seventeenth century possessed a complex sense of genre and a sophisticated language for generic distinctions, but to recognize that, as Barbara Lewalski has shown us, models for generic determination often came from sources—the Bible, for example—that were cultural and political perhaps more than literary texts.[36] Donne and Herbert conceived of themselves as devotional writers, not as metaphysical poets. And the devotional mode is the location in which properly to study them. The history both of the creation of genres and of the awareness and manipulation of genres is a literary subject, but its exposition is part of social and cultural history.

There is, then, a history of those genres that the seventeenth century inherited and bequeathed—satire and lyric, for example—to the theoretical understanding of which the century made its own contribution. There is also a history of those genres that the century created, sometimes recognized, but did not always delineate and describe. Epic and fable are classic illustrations of the first of these; the country house poem and the so-called advice-to-painter genre are examples of the latter. The history of epic for this age begins with Spenser's *Faerie Queene* and closes with Dryden's *Virgil*. It was practiced with and generated theoretical discussion of remarkable sophistication.[37] Epic, as form and perceived genre, has a long and continuous history in this century. The continuity of form should not, however, mask the powerful changes in the tactical deployment of epic, the strategic meaning of generic choice, or the impress of political circumstance on the shaping and handling of its conventions and gestures. The decision by Spenser, Milton, and Dryden to take up the epic mode, the circumstances and very moment of that election, and their respective choices of national, cosmic, and Roman materials for the epic project illustrate our propositions and suggest the richness of this subject. When we turn from elite to popular culture, the same proposition can be demonstrated. The fable is a distinct literary genre, and yet for all its antiquity and continuity, as Annabel Patterson demonstrates, an appreciation of the mode in the seventeenth century necessitates an understanding of selection, application, and interpretation.[38]

A quite different history must be written for those genres that emerge or decline within the century. The country house poem is a genre peculiar to this century, more exactly the special property of the first half of the century. To describe the life of the genre is also to document the relations of social orders, the interdependencies of court and country, and the ethics of political activity and retirement across these fifty years.[39] The disappearance of the genre may begin to tell us much about the demise of an entire world. In the second half of the century we may discover another example. The emergence of the advice-to-painter poem may tell us something about the political and social role of the artist in the reign of Charles II; its shift from panegyric to satiric deployment suggests the impact of political polarity and polemical needs on literary forms.[40] The adoption of the advice-to-painter poem for quite different and contrary purposes reminds us that there are many tones, voices, languages, and idioms possible within one genre, that genre itself does not dictate or explain substance and stance. We are just beginning to appreciate, for example, that within the masque, a quintessentially courtly mode, lay the possibility for criticism and complaint as well as compliment.[41] To recognize the various languages and stances within genres is to indicate complexities that can question patterns and labels. Yet, of course, classification is one of the prerequisites of study, and at the close of the seventeenth century a remarkable and novel kind of classification has begun to take place: the formation of literary canons.

Throughout this century prominent and distinctive literary personalities gathered about them admirers and disciples; the positions of Ben Jonson and the self-appointed "sons of Ben" nicely exemplify this tradition. By the end of the century certain authors and, perhaps more important, selected texts have begun to acquire a commanding literary authority. The formation of a canon is one aspect of the emergence of a distinct literary sphere, of the creation of literary institutions and literary careers. Such distinctiveness did not divorce literature from politics; indeed, the literary canon was formed by political needs as much as by evaluations of purely literary merit. The role of Shakespeare on the Restoration stage, the celebration of his "native" genius, expresses a polemical need for an English authority as a counterweight to French cultural models. Polemical determination of literary reputation takes us even further than such broad national considerations. The emerging political parties sought in commanding literary figures an authentication of their political positions. In doing so they, in turn, enshrined certain authors and invested them with political authority. It was more than coincidence that the first edition of the poetry of Marvell, that protagonist of country politics from Hull, was published at the time of the Exclusion Crisis. And who can doubt that the sudden republication of *Paradise Lost* on the eve of the Glorious Revolution and Toland's magisterial *Life* and edition of carefully selected prose owed much to the Whigs' desperate quest for authentication?[42] Ironically, the author of *Eikonoklastes* had himself become an icon.

Literary reputations raised by political motives, enshrined in editions and biographies themselves not free of political bias, outlived immediate political crises; they remained to influence the canon. Until 1688, Dryden was published as the foremost Tory poet; by then he had acquired sufficient literary authority to sustain a reputation throughout adverse political times. The ascendancy of the Whigs, however, may have confined earlier works, "Cavalier poetry" or Caroline court masques, to an oblivion from which they have been rescued only in recent times. To acknowledge the creation or enhancement of literary reputation by political needs and interests may cause our own aesthetic sense some discomfort; to the seventeenth century it would have been a commonplace. Literary careers could be and often were determined by powerful political connections. Nowhere is this more obvious than in the history of patronage.

Patronage in early modern England was the cynosure of all political and social relationships. To see literary relations as part of the system of clientage is to chart the history of literary production, to add a dimension to our understanding of literary genre, and to open new perspectives on literary texts.[43] From the Earl of Leicester in Elizabethan England to the Earl of Dorset at the close of the seventeenth century, the great aristocratic figure endures as the model for literary as well as other patronage. Such protection and favor were dispensed variously, raised differing expectations, and implied varying obligations. We think of the powerful magnate and his literary client—the Earl of Leicester and Edmund Spenser—but most patrons had more than one literary dependent and many literary figures had more than one patron. As Lewalski has shown, the Countess of Bedford maintained a string of poets. For Donne her patronage was crucial; for Jonson it was peripheral. In Donne's verse she became the center of a symbolic system; for Jonson she was a respected but distant figure.

Under the Countess of Bedford's patronage and with Donne's impress, the verse epistle as a mode of praise was transformed. Donne canonized the Countess of Bedford as a "saint," but even that image did not contain her. From the praise of other poets, in other literary modes and roles, from Daniel and Jonson, in masques and festivities, she fashioned for herself and projected a spectrum of images and roles.[44] She employed patronage as a tool of "self-fashioning."[45] Patronage was not, however, an instrument exclusive to the patron. The client also fashioned and authorized his own moral universe through this system. Often he sought specific patrons and anchored his verse in positions and policies. At times he sought from great names no more than the validation of his own deep moral convictions. The verse epistle is praise of a patron; but with Jonson we often feel that the patron is simply an instrument for the projection of the poet's own profound moral convictions. For us the word *patronage* evokes images of subordination and servility; in the seventeenth century it was a system of mutual obligations and benefits even if not a relationship of equals. Patronage, then as now, was an effort to acquire cultural authority. What needs remarking is that the acquisition of authority through patronage was sought and obtained by poet as well as patron.[46]

During the course of the seventeenth century the opportunities within the system of patronage increased, the modes of patronage broadened, and new sources of maintenance opened. The story of patronage that at the beginning of the century may be written entirely around the great patron must by the end of the century also include the marketplace. For during the closing decades of the century, the instruments of commercialization became firmly established. Book subscription to support literary works, the establishment of the London season and a defined London society, the broadening fashion for cultural sophistication, the beginnings of provincial capitals, and the inception of the literary journal began to make possible the literary career independent of aristocratic patronage. This was not an unqualified emancipation, of course. The marketplace imposed its own strictures, and authors dependent on commercial success had always to remain conscious of its requirements. One of the new features of the marketplace was political journalism and political propaganda. This is one way in which the polarization of politics saw the diversification of literary modes; the newspaper as a polemical and literary medium was essentially a product of the civil wars, and by the 1680s and 1690s the battle of the books had become largely the rage of party. This is not to suggest that the political subsumed the literary or confined its modes or universal concerns to the polemical pamphlet or the needs of the moment. Few would argue that *Absalom and Achitophel* is the creature only of party. But it is to insist that at the end of the century no less than at the beginning, for all the diversification of its modes, patronage remains central to literary production. And to acknowledge the continued force of patronage is to recognize how broadly and deeply literary production is politicized in this age.

Patronage is but one of the political circumstances of literary production in this age, a century in which what we too often regard as exclusively literary matters—genre and mode, language and style—are determined in part by political considerations. The very choice of mode and genre often carried political meaning; the handling of conventions and vocabularies was a matter of polemical concern. The most obvious example is that verse which calls itself "Poems on Affairs of State." Here polemical need is expressed in every gesture. In literature less obviously partisan, works located less in the minutiae of party politics, the political may often be as important and intrinsic. Recently we have become aware of the extent to which the masque is a political as much as a literary genre. Its most immediate political argument is an encomium of the ideals of the court.[47] Moreover, within the convention lay the possibilities for more particular, more diverse, and even more critical statement. Even in those works and genres that announce themselves above politics, sublime and spiritual in character and intention, we can detect the pressure of political circumstance. The epic stands traditionally as the loftiest of literary modes, the form raised highest above what is transient, commonplace, and contested in human affairs. But the election to write epic could itself be a political act. Those who found themselves in a condition of exile, defeat, and deprivation may have sought in the triumphal gestures of the epic refuge from and defiance of the victory of their enemies. It may be no accident that Davenant in exile in the 1650s, Milton proscribed in the 1660s, and Dryden wistfully contemplating the fate of his master in the 1690s, all sought comfort, transcendence, and justification in the epic mode.[48] Those who would sustain defeated causes as their enemies consolidate power must write with discretion and art. Their purpose may be defiance, but their language must be oblique. Ambivalence and obliqueness as linguistic conditions have a long history in this century.[49]

Metaphysical poetry is defined by ambiguity and multivalence, but multivalence is more than linguistic agility. For Donne and Herbert wit was not mere verbal repartee; it was a central vehicle for the conveyance of moral and philosophical truths. The capacity of literary languages in the seventeenth century to sustain multiple levels of meaning was not confined to the paradoxes of metaphysical poetry.

Private languages sustained quite public argument; love poetry, for example, could articulate political as well as personal relationships.[50] The discourse of the masque in Caroline England is that of Platonic love. It is allegorical; it is rarefied; it may be oblique and require explication. But prefatory explanations of the "argument,"—in Jonson's words, "to make the spectators understanders"—are evidence that its purpose was to communicate, not to conceal.[51] Literature in the first half of the seventeenth century participated in a commonwealth of understanding. The civil war shattered that commonwealth. The very fact of war necessitated the language of code and cypher; the divisions of civil war and the eventual rise of party created differentiating meanings and vocabularies; the excesses of that war and the anarchy of millenarianism tainted certain languages with associations now anathema. Finally, the fear of renewed conflict and the heat of party fostered a language of healing and moderation, a language that often concealed quite radical intentions and positions. Our sense that the Glorious Revolution was the politest deposition in European history is a recognition of both the use and success of such concealment. At the close of this century men may have reconstructed a common discourse, but it was no longer the language of a unified polity. The *Horatian Ode* stands exactly at midpoint in our history of linguistic multiplicity; it is a brilliant example both of conveyed ambiguity and paradox and of concealment and disguise.

One language may not only speak to several meanings, to public as well as to private concerns, but it may also resound or echo with earlier vocabularies and texts and convey earlier significances. This subject has often been studied under the heading of "influence." However, the idea of influence is too narrow to contain the complexity of inheritance and allusion; it implies too conscious an act of adoption and rearticulation. That Herbert read Donne and intended to echo and allude to him is undeniable, but we would wish and are able to go further. We cannot be certain that Marvell had read Machiavelli; yet Marvell's concerns, his engagement with issues central to Machiavelli's politics, and especially the cast of his language argue a powerful Machiavellian presence in Marvell's text, a presence which his contemporaries could hardly have failed to discern.[52] Machiavelli's *Discourses* and *Prince* had become subtexts in the political culture of the seventeenth century. They coexisted and at times had to contend with other such subtexts—with Arthurian legend, with the literature of romance, with Petrarch and Boccacio, and with Magna Charta and histories of ancient Rome. Such subtexts were a common inheritance; they could, of course, be appropriated polemically and manipulated selectively. And they were the more polemically and selectively handled as division inclined men to languages capable of confrontation and exclusion. The language of Classical Republicanism by the late 1680s had all but become the preserve of a party. A subtext once common property had become exclusive.

To consider allusions and echoes and their capacity to select and exclude audiences is to address the intractable problem of reception.[53] Even when we can identify and delineate an audience—the courtly spectators of the masque, for example—we can reach few conclusions about the effect of meanings and allegories. In the many more frequent cases in which audience can only be inferred from language, any argument about intention and reception is in danger of becoming circular. Even within shared vocabularies or common idioms, however, the selection of a phrase, the handling of syntax, even the slightly unusual application of mode to moment is often instructive as to the particular as well as general meanings being conveyed. When particular languages and subtexts are selected and applied, at certain historical moments, the study of discourse may qualify us to identify both purpose and audience. In so doing it may deepen and extend our interpretation of the text.

Historians are not unaccustomed to using literature as historical evidence. Quotations from Shakespeare and Jonson, passages from Milton's great prose or Rochester's scurrilous verse have often been paraded to illustrate the Elizabethan world picture, the cast of Puritan religiosity, the libertine excesses of the Restoration court. Literature, that is to say, has been plundered for examples that reinforce arguments already determined from more serious historical documentation: from state dispatches and letters, from proclamations and parliamentary diaries. But this is hardly to study literature as history. Indeed, it is to deny the status of literary texts *as* primary historical evidence. Like the poll book or the parish register, the poem is a historical artifact, fully capable of yielding data about its society. Poems and plays, of course, are imaginative, fictional creations, but the fictitious should not be contrasted with the factual, for within the fictive realm lie romance and fable, utopia and political theory—some by the end of the century might have said faith itself.[54] Once we recognize the imaginative as a cultural product we may begin to see its rich potential as historical evidence. Poetry deepens and complicates our historical understanding of politics as well as of values and culture. The truly historical reading of literary texts leads not to the mere illustration of historical argument but to the reinterpretation of the past. The poems dedicated to the Countess of Bedford, her patronage of both courtier and Puritan, the godly sobriety and brilliance of her public images undermine rather than illustrate the explanatory categories of court and country, Puritan and Cavalier. A poem so delicately poised as Marvell's *Horatian Ode* insists that we consider the difficulty of choices during the English civil war. At times poems seem to embody shifts and prophesy new orders. "As so often, it is the poet who divines the transition."[55]

Literature, however, not only divines the important changes in history but can mold, accelerate, and even enact them. That history in which we may most obviously see literary texts performing actions is, of course, literary history. The shaping force of the *Faerie Queene* can be felt in Milton's conception of a Protestant epic;[56] the personal authority of Jonson's ethical and lyric voice echoes through Cavalier poetry. Literary scholars have long studied such enactments as convention and influence, but such a conception of the action of literary texts confines their force to the realm of the aesthetic and fails to acknowledge their force in other histories. We have only begun to appreciate how, for the early modern period, representations of authority were not easily divorced from power itself. The images of Elizabeth as the omnicompetent goddess Astraea may have been vital in sustaining the authority of Tudor monarchy at a time of instability and foreign threats.[57] Whatever its status as historical truth, the *Eikon Basilike* must have its place in any history of the Restoration.[58] In an age that distinguished less clearly than our own the authentic from the fictive, the aesthetic from the political, the literary—indeed, the imaginative—could fashion the course of events. And the literary text might so fashion at each, or every, moment of its history: with first circulation in manuscript or performance on the stage, at the time of publication and dissemination, in subsequent editions and reissues, through critical reaction, and the history of critical response. *Paradise Lost* was coolly received in 1667; on the eve of the Glorious Revolution Tonson's new edition enjoyed immense success.[59] In the early years of the Restoration it could hardly influence events. In 1688, Milton's text reinforced and authorized the revolutionary cause.

Literature could shape political events because it spoke political languages. It may be that concentration upon the aesthetic properties of literature has dulled our sensitivity to those languages. Their rediscovery and reintegration into literary texts may help us better to understand contemporary reception—how, for instance, Milton was so differently received in 1667 and 1689. To raise such questions, moreover, is to open new aesthetic as well as political dimensions. To discern, as did Pocock, the eschatological in Hobbes's vocabulary is to recognize the role of religion in the concept of order of a philosopher once deemed irreligious, or at least the role of religion that contemporaries might have discovered in Hobbes's philosophy.[60] Similarly, to become sensitive to the millenarianism of Marvell's *First Anniversary* is newly to understand the complex patterning of the poem, to appreciate the role of Marvell's narrator as angel of the apocalypse and to sense in the delicate qualifications of that apocalyptic language the poet's own doubts and hesitations over the prophetic order.[61] When we learn to read the languages—all the languages—of an author we may truly begin to comprehend his own acts and perceptions of creative writing. Only by studying the history of languages can we appreciate why Milton did not distinguish between the sphere of the spirit and the state and the radical force of his refusal to make that distinction.[62] Only through a sensitivity to linguistic performance and association may we see the love lyric as a mode addressing public and political concerns.[63] *Macbeth* we appreciate as one of the greatest tragedies of the Renaissance stage. To discover, as David Norbrook does, that it addresses the ideological issues and controversies of Scottish history and historiography is not to diminish the tragedy but to add to our understanding of the polemical within the universal and so to enhance our appreciation of the text.[64]

We are accustomed to regarding particular concerns as inimical to the universal. "Great literature," we have been too often taught, is that which rises above contemporary concerns—it is not of an age but for all time. But awareness of the circumstances in which a poem or play was written and an understanding of the topical and polemical intentions of a work should enrich rather than impoverish our reading. For the universal and philosophical are not detached from the particular; they rise from it. The verse epistles of Ben Jonson provide a fine illustration. Though addressed to individual courtiers on particular occasions—a marriage, a bereavement, or an elevation—Jonson's verse epistles are the vehicles of the poet's own moral vision of ethical and political values which it would not be an exaggeration to describe as a philosophy.[65] Jonson's name should be sufficient authority to argue that even the great texts of literature must be located within their histories. What distinguishes the great text is not its distance from particular circumstance but its address to and transformation of historical circumstance. Indeed, both as polemical and as aesthetic product, the great texts are those which simultaneously engage particular and universal concerns. And it may be that texts which draw on contemporary languages and depend on contemporary associations also rearrange existing vocabularies in order to articulate new positions, refashioning the patterns of contemporary language and meaning in the process. Machiavelli wrote the language of classical political theory and of humanism, but the vocabulary of the classics and of humane letters was never quite the same again.[66]

The great text is that which exemplifies its age and refashions it. Only when we appreciate the commonplace idioms and contemporary associations of language, the ethical and political values and taboos enshrined in words can we understand just how the great texts address, question, and then reshape all future considerations, even all future discourse on an issue. To urge, as we have done, that Shakespeare and Jonson, Hobbes and Milton, Marvell and Dryden be repatriated within their age is not to confine them to the past; it is to release them into the rich complexities of their historical moment.

2

Texts as Events: Reflections on the History of Political Thought

J. G. A. Pocock

The playwright Tom Stoppard was once heard to deliver a lecture entitled "Theatre as Event or as Text?" He declared in its course that he wrote his plays to be performed by actors, and that when scholars discovered all manner of layers of meaning in the published texts, he felt as if his baggage was being unpacked by customs officials and he was saying, "Well, I've got to admit it's there, but I don't remember packing it." Fair enough. It is implicit in the act of publishing the text, however, that a play is performed more than once and that the text exists even when the play is not being performed. Furthermore, it is a basic rule of historical method that more meanings can be found in a text, or in any document, than the author intended to convey when he wrote it; and this is why (to pursue the dramatic analogy a little further) a play can always be performed one more time, enacting a different set of meanings than the time before.

So when Stoppard insists that it is rarely to the point to ask the author "what does that mean?" an obvious corollary is that it is always possible for the actor performing or the critic reading the text to find meanings in it which the author did not know were there and which have not been enacted or discerned before. The text now becomes a matrix or holding pattern within which a series of widely differing events can and do occur. This is one of several reasons why authors, actors, and critics usually hate one another heartily; but the author, who has created the text and made the events possible, is entitled to be surprised at—but not necessarily entitled to object to—any event that may be performed within it. There may be cases in which he can and must say, "Look, that's really off-limits; with this text you just cannot do that"; but these are only limiting cases, and it is not clear that the author has a greater right to say that than any actor or critic may have.

I will now apply some of these reflections to the history of political thought. The phenomena we study under that name consist in the first place largely of texts—that is, of more or less coherent written or printed texts preserving their verbal content over long and unfinished periods of time—and many (though not all) of these texts are believed or known to have had authors about whom we know a lot or a little, as the case may be. Political thought is studied by scholars who practice various disciplines: critics, philosophers, theorists, historians, and so on. It is about historians that I want to write here, being one myself, but I need to say something about their relations with scholars practicing other disciplines. I will be discussing these matters within the framework provided by the notions of text and event, though most of my emphasis falls on the suggestion that text and event for the historian are nearly the same thing: that the text is an event as well as a framework within which further events occur.

Quentin Skinner, in *The Foundations of Modern Political Thought*,[1] lays down the premise that what is needed by historians is a history of political thought constructed on genuinely historical principles. He implies that histories of political thought are often constructed on principles that are not genuinely historical, and I return to that aspect of the question in my closing sentences. For the present let us consider what such a genuinely historical history must be. Let us propose— what may not be adequate for all purposes—that for the historian history consists of actions, events, and processes. Events happen as the result of actions by persons; the actions are performed and the events happen in contexts that make them possible and (to the historian) intelligible; but they modify these contexts in ways that make other, differing actions and events possible and intelligible. This is part, though not all, of what is meant by processes. To French historians today, of course, this would sound like *histoire evénementielle;* they would want to draw attention to the *longue durée,* to the type of infrastructure that makes events possible but changes so slowly that one must doubt whether it is modified by the events at all. The reply to this is that if one is writing a history of texts, one is writing a history of sophisticated verbal performances that are certainly events. To go deeper is to enter a history of languages and *mentalités* that do not consist of texts but into which texts—such as the Bible, the Koran, or the Six Classics—do seem to enter and produce profound modifications. To go yet deeper is to enter a world of grammars and deep structures and to encounter the question of whether such structures have a history or only a *longue durée*. And the true *longue durée* consists of material and geophysical conditions that may or may not pertain to the history of consciousness; even Marx could take it no deeper than the act of production. So let us return to that admittedly sophisticated and elitist world in which the actions of authors produce texts and modify the contexts and structures they do reach. This is the level at which a program in history and literature must desire to operate.

At this level a text can and must be seen as both an action and an event. To quote Skinner again, the first necessity in constructing a truly historical history of political thought is to equip ourselves with means of knowing what the author was *doing* when he wrote the text.[2] This matter is not as simple as it may sound, however. To begin with, it does not reach that depth to which Stoppard was pointing when he said the author did not know himself what he was doing, and that when it was brought to his attention later he did not remember doing it or even recognize himself as having done it. Knowing is not doing, and to know what an actor (even oneself) was doing is not the same thing as doing it.

At this point it may be objected that the dramatist is writing a text for actors to perform, whereas the theorist may be writing a text for contemplatives to read. But this may not make much difference. I write long, complex theoretical treatises and histories, and my experience is exactly the same as Stoppard's when he claims that an author discovers what he is writing in the act of writing it and often does not know what he is writing until he sits down to write. As I wrote these sentences, I had only the vaguest notion what was coming next. The experience of authorship seems exactly the same in this respect in both cases, and I have always believed there is something naive and philistine in the distinction often made between creative writing (which is always about images and fictions) and critical writing (which is always about facts). Furthermore, I doubt how far one can really press the distinction between the actor performing and the reader reading. As students of literature, we are familiar with the idea that reading a text can be a complex action, and as students of history, we need—as I shall try to show—to think of the reader as an actor in the same historical sequence as the author.

So to *know* what the author was doing when he wrote the text is not to repeat the author's experience in *doing* it; it is to reconstitute the experience in terms designed to make it intelligible to the historian, and this is certainly not what the author was aiming to do. I have never met anyone who wrote in order to communicate with historians in the future, and I do not suppose I ever shall. As we reconstitute the author's actions, then, it is in order to watch him performing it, not to repeat the performance ourselves; we write about it in the third person, not the first, and perhaps this is what the distinction between creative and critical is really about. I could use words like *entfremdung* and *alienation* at this point, but it would probably be better if I did not. Third-person reconstitution of the author's action, however, necessarily involves looking at it in ways and saying things about it that would not have, could not have, and did not need to become apparent to the author himself—finding things in his baggage, to use Tom Stoppard's imagery, which he did not put there or know he had. If we could read what historians will say about us, we would probably be even more astonished, though perhaps less outraged, than we are when we read reviews of the books we write. And that is saying a good deal, because the review is one starting point (only one) of the book's history.

We set out to reconstitute the author's performance, to study the text as event (something happening) and as action (something done); but third-person reconstitution is aimed at providing coordinates, at situating the action in the midst of conditions and circumstances that will help us understand, first, what the action in fact was and, second, why and how it was performed. The author may not have needed to know what these were, but we do. This is where the emphasis shifts from text to context, and also—to use terminology borrowed from Skinner[3]—from intention to illocution and perlocution. In both the first (Stoppard/author) and the third person (Skinner/historian), we know that the author did not begin by acquiring a set of intentions and proceed to acquire a set of words with which to carry them into effect. He found out what he meant to write only in the act of writing it. This places illocution at the center of the picture and perlocution in the next frame. We study the text in order to see what it says, what effects the words constituting it actually carried out (or, if we are cautious, may have carried out); and this means that we know more about the intentions it did perform than about other intentions which it might have performed but did not.

If this were the whole of the story, however, it would follow that we knew the author only from the text. Often this is not the case; we know a lot more about the author from other texts he wrote, his correspondence, his friends' recollections, the police files on him—and from the knowledge we have as competent historians of the social and historical universe he inhabited, knowledge not identical with his own because we can obtain it only by reconstitution. All this information enables us to form hypotheses about (1) intentions and actions he may have performed without our noticing them at first reading; (2) intentions and actions he may have performed without noticing them himself; (3) intentions and actions he might have performed but did not; and (4) intentions and actions he could not possibly have performed or tried to perform, whatever our misguided colleagues may urge to the contrary.

Now we know that to situate the text (and the author) in a context is necessary in order to reconstitute the text as a historical event; and because we have a diversity of information concerning its (and his) universe, we face the problem of deciding how this context is to be constructed, how its component parts are to be selected from the diversity of historical information at our disposal. To historians of the school to which Skinner and I (among others) belong, it seems evident that the primary component of this context has to be language. There exists a language, or a complex of more than one language, with which things can be said or illocutionary acts performed, within which (it is the next step to add) they must be performed. The primary context within which the speaker or author and his speech or text are situated must be that of the language he speaks. Here, of course, an argument can develop. A Vulgar Marxist may appear and point out (rightly) that language itself is formed within a context of social relations, so that (he adds wrongly) it is possible to know the context of social relations and infer the character of language from them. To study language as if it operated autonomously, the Marxist will say, is idealism or something nasty like that. The reply is that of course language takes shape from its social context, but we do know by now that it is not just a mirror. The trick is to see in what ways language indicates the context in which it is formed and in what ways it does not; what signs it contains that point directly at the phenomena of social relations, what signs that point at them indirectly, and what signs that point away from the phenomena of social relations as historians may perceive them. (The historian must now decide what to make of that.) To do all this, the language-oriented historian adds, one must infer the egg from the chicken; if one wants to know how language indicates society, one must look at the language and see how it works—what it told those who used it about their society and what it did not. And if one wants to know how a speaker's or author's illocutionary act was concerned with things going on in his society, one must go through this same mediatory structure: the language context. What will continue to part the language-oriented historian from the intelligent Marxist (the Vulgar Marxist having been left in his wallow) is that the latter will want to pursue the language-society relationship, whereas the former, for whom the relation between language and illocution comes first, will want to discuss the language as

a historical phenomenon that operated autonomously enough to provide the primary (not the only) set of conditions within which the
illocution was performed. The history of political thought becomes
primarily, though not finally, a history of language games and their
outcomes.

The historian's reconstitution of the context that makes the text,
as action and event, intelligible now becomes a matter of reconstituting the languages in which certain illocutions—those defined as
existing for the purposes of political thought—were carried out, and
of discerning what the individual text, author, or performance did
with the opportunities offered and the constraints imposed by the
languages available to it. A number of interesting problems arise here,
some of them historical and some of them theoretical. To take the
former first, what are these languages of which I speak in the plural,
and how does one reconstitute them? About thirty years ago I wrote
a book, *The Ancient Constitution and the Feudal Law*,[4] which set something of a fashion for this sort of method, and I have been practicing
it ever since. In the early modern period (1500–1800) it is especially
useful to say that there was not just one specialized language of
political thought—such as the idiom of Christianized Aristotelian philosophy, which many considered the paramount language for these
purposes—but a number of them; and that these were located in and
derived from the activities of a number of specialized professional
groups: in England not only the still-scholastic academics who kept
the medieval and Aristotelian idiom going but the common lawyers,
the established clergy, the dissentient and radical Puritans, the specialists in classical rhetoric whom Thomas Hobbes believed were
largely to blame for the civil war, and so on. It was Edmund Burke,
so far as I know, who was the first to point out the historical importance of the fact that the English talked about their liberties in the
common-law language of real property. Historians of political
thought, at least in the early modern period, spend much of their
time reconstructing these languages and reconstructing the performances of texts, by pointing out that they were performed in this or
that language or combination of languages. Because this is still a fairly
recently perfected archaeological technique, it is still common to find
that one has made some exciting discovery in it; as that Thomas
Hobbes was doing eschatology,[5] John Locke natural jurisprudence,[6]
Edmund Burke common law or paper-money theory,[7] and so on. And
this may still be surface archaeology, not carried out by any sophisticated technique of excavation. The author's use of this or that language may not be indirect or concealed but perfectly explicit; it may
simply have been neglected by scholars who have been trained to

look only for forms of thought considered important for reasons sometimes not historical at all. The merit of the technique I am describing
is that it obliges the scholar to ask what languages people in the past
really spoke, and what forms of thought they considered important,
and so to reemphasize previously neglected answers to the Skinnerian
question, "What were they actually doing?"

"Languages" such as these are not, of course, "languages" in the
same sense as Latin or English, but specialized idioms existing in
Latin or English and sometimes translatable from one to the other. It
seems inadequate to call them "vocabularies"; that term sounds rather
too lexical. I am following Burke in calling them "languages," but
possibly they should be called "idioms" or "rhetorics" instead. Those
I have described so far may be called "institutional languages," meaning that they were the idioms used by powerful corporations of intellectual specialists: scholastics, rhetoricians, common lawyers, and
so on. It is possible, however, to detect the presence of "languages"
by other means and see them as existing in other ways. In *The Machiavellian Moment*'s early chapters[8] I tried a problem-situation approach.
I asked, "In what idioms did people deal with a certain intellectual
problem: that of the sequence of events in secular time?" Here is the
answer I came up with: "in three idioms: those of custom, grace and
fortune." Now there might be a rough-and-ready professional differentiation among these three: custom was a lawyer's word, grace a
theologian's, fortune a rhetorician's. But that was not of much interest
when I wanted to exhibit the presence of all three idioms in the
writings of Machiavelli, who was neither a jurist nor a theologian but
much closer to being a rhetorician—which is one reason why he does
more with the concept of fortune than with the other two. What I
was then in a position to suggest was that Machiavelli belonged to a
culture limited to these three idioms for dealing with the problem,
but that he selected and rearranged from the modes of speech available to him in such a way as to produce extraordinary changes in
them.

But languages sought out by methods such as that tend to become
increasingly implicit, and the historian faces increasingly severe problems in demonstrating that they were really there. An "institutional"
language is rendered much easier to detect by the existence and activities of the institution within which it is spoken; it will be relatively
self-conscious, and there may even be a secondary literature about
how it should be spoken. One that is implicitly present, as a kind of
sublanguage or idiom within generalized "ordinary language," will
be a good deal harder to verify. In *The Machiavellian Moment* I was
obliged to show that idioms and modes of speech resting on custom,

grace, and fortune—which later helped to generate a rhetoric of virtue, corruption, and commerce—could be detected in the writings of the people I had under study, and that they were employed consistently (i.e., consistently with the characteristics I had ascribed to them) and also consciously. One does this essentially by learning to speak the language in question and then showing that some author in history was speaking it also. Obviously, however, you must confront the query, "How do you know you have not invented the language and read it into the text? If you are a historian, as distinct from some other sorts of reader, you are not allowed to do that." Here you must produce the best available evidence for the autonomous existence of your language in history. The more authors you can show to have made use of it the better. If you can show them arguing with one another in it, so that it produces different results and grows and changes in the course of usage, better still; and if some Monsieur Jourdain should appear in your history who says, "We seem to be talking in such and such an idiom, whose characteristics are such and such," and such as you have said they must have been, you get up and dance around the room. This does not happen very often, and sometimes you must face the fact that you are sitting on the fence that divides the historian from other kinds of readers, in which case you must be very careful what you say.

We have now moved from saying that texts are events to saying that languages are the matrices within which texts as events occur, and our history has become less a history of individual performances and acts of authorship than a history of languages, or (as David Hollinger has put it)[9] one of continuities of discourse. We have reconstituted a context, or a series of contexts, in which the text as event may be rendered intelligible, thus permitting us to read a whole series of meanings into the text—as many as there are idioms or languages in which it may be seen as performing. A really complex text, occurring in a really complex historical situation, may be seen as performing polyvalently: not only will there be several continuities of discourse (another term is levels of meaning) within which it may be read and seen to have acted but it may be seen as performing all manner of cunning games as it moves from one level to another. No student of literature needs to be told what I mean here. If we have succeeded in demonstrating that the continuities of discourse were historically actual, that they were recourses of language available for use, and modified by use, over periods of historic time, then we have escaped the reproach that we are merely reading them into the record; that we are dishonest customs searchers planting in the baggage of Tom Stoppard's author the concealed goods we claim to have found there.

All we are telling the author (should he be still alive to hear us) is that he was operating in more continuities of discourse than he knew at the time. And if he has told us that he did not know what continuities of discourse he was operating in, he has told us that he knew he did not know what we have just told him. He has, of course, also told us that he did not need to know at the time; that he did not need to know what he was doing—in Skinner's use of the phrase—in order to do it; that he did not need to go about like an Owl of Minerva looking over his shoulder. Well, we know that, because we are the Owls; but as soon as he has finished his act, he became one of us—like Monsieur Jourdain.

There seem to be two main senses in which texts are events and make history. One is that they are actions performed in language contexts that make them possible, that condition and constrain them but that they also modify. Texts, whether individually or cumulatively, act upon the languages in which they are performed: as they perform they inform, injecting new words, facts, perceptions, and rules of the game; and, whether gradually or catastrophically, the language matrix becomes modified by the acts performed in it. A text is an actor in its own history, and a polyvalent text acts in a multiplicity of concurrent histories. This is complex enough, but it is actually one of the easier shapes in which to conceive a history of public discourse. If I were ever to write a long-term history of political thought in Britain, it would probably be organized in terms of the rise, change, and decline of the various idioms in which that activity from time to time has been conducted.[10] This, however, would certainly be attacked as failing to do justice to the magnitude of the great masters and their masterpieces; and certainly Thomas Hobbes, say, and Jonathan Swift are bad men to reduce to the status of performers in any finite number of circus rings. You cannot write a history in terms of the great texts; but there is a sense in which the great texts are difficult to reduce to history. This is because they continue to be read and used by people who are not historians.

The second sense in which texts make history is that texts have readers and outlive their authors. The author, in creating the text, creates the matrix in which others will read and respond to it. Readers, however, are like the actors as well as the critics in the dramaturgical analogy with which I began—in fact, it seems important at this moment to call the reader an actor in the sense that he is one in a historical process. No text is ever read exactly as its author intended it should be read; there is a sense in which the reader reenacts the text, and this never happens twice in exactly the same way. The dramatist aims principally at providing occasions for actors to reenact what he gives them; but the people Malvolio calls politic authors aim immediately at affecting the consciousness of other actors in political society: they are engaged in rhetoric, which is traditionally the most political form of speech. The dramatist may pursue the same aims but in a form more complex than rhetoric. But the readers' consciousness is no less active than the author's; they respond to him—which is why the concept of "influence" has fallen out of critical use—and they preserve the independent activity of their consciousness by reading him as they intend, which may or may not be how the author intended to be read. Students of literature know that text-reader relationships are complex and unpredictable affairs; students of "the history of ideas" may need to be reminded that they are a very large part of what they are studying.

It may be said that reading is an act of translation: I translate your message into my understanding of it. But if I do so in ways that effect no modification of the language you used, there is no change in the matrix within which we both act. It is another matter if I effect such a modification by illocutionary performances of my own. All I may do in such a case, however, is to continue, without interrupting, the history of the language in which your text was written. It is another thing again if I read you so as to translate your text into terms of some other of the languages or idioms in which our society conducts its discourse—which, in the situation of polyvalence, will be going on all the time. True, some idioms are remarkably resistant to translation and use their impenetrability as a means of gaining ascendancy over other idioms. It was notoriously difficult to present the thought of common lawyers in any terms but those of the common law, and this was part of what Sir Edward Coke meant when he instructed the understandably annoyed James I in the nature of "artificial reason." But sometimes the act of translation is possible. Since reading Skinner's *Foundations* I have become increasingly interested in the relationship between a rhetorical and humanist language whose fundamental notion was *virtue* and a scholastic and juristic language whose fundamental notion was *right*. There is a sense in which the two were not intertranslatable; what was meant by virtue was not part of what was meant by right and vice versa, and therefore Francesco Guicciardini, who was a doctor of laws, never used juristic language when writing about the *vivere civile*. It seems to have been Spanish Jesuits who invented the idea that Machiavelli was the author of a doctrine of *ratio status* (about which he says nothing) by translating him into the idiom of natural law, which is founded on the idea of *recta ratio*. Unlike Leo Strauss and Harvey Mansfield in our own day,[11] the Jesuits did not contend that Machiavelli ought to have been talking about natural law, that he had therefore deliberately and of evil intent chosen not to talk about natural law, and that he was therefore talking about natural law most particularly when he was not. Because natural law was a preponderant idiom in the society which both Machiavelli and the Jesuits inhabited, the latter were not wrong in drawing attention to the illocutionary force his writings possessed when read by them; they were on questionable ground only in attributing to him the intention of performing that illocution. Here is an excellent illustration of the transformation of a text by reader translation and of the problems in historical reconstitution to which it may give rise. It was Leo Strauss who propounded something called "the pure and merciless laws of logographic necessity," according to which there were texts that performed all the illocutions that could possibly be read into them and whose authors had intended to perform all of them. This suggests that Strauss was trying to explode the concepts of both translation and history.

The most interesting acts of translation are anachronistic. They are performed by readers who live in times during which the matrices, idioms, and language games have been modified, so that texts that are still current and still acting as the matrices for action are no longer limited to the performance of the illocutions they performed at first publication, and perhaps are no longer capable of performing those illocutions. Because the printed word is rather durable, many texts outlive the modification of their initial contexts, as well as outliving their authors. Some of them acquire the sort of authority that leads individuals living in a series of modified contexts to recur to them, and these become the subjects of what are called traditions of interpretation, which are continuous histories of anachronistic—or, if you prefer, diachronic—translation. It may be that traditions operate according to predictable laws; I once tried to formulate some in an essay called "Time, Institutions and Action."[12] However that may be, we have here a most interesting category of texts surviving in language matrices that modify the actions performed with them but that they continue to modify through their surviving capacity to act in themselves as matrices for action.

Of some of these texts we say that they are classics; that is, that their traditions of interpretation have been prolonged into the present in which we ourselves live. How these classics are selected I will not attempt to discuss, except to say that the persistence of both original writing and textual archaeology ensures that texts newly written or newly recovered may become classics in relatively short time; examples could be given from several disciplines. When a text is being read, responded to, and employed in various kinds of illocution, in

any "present," some of those making use of it will have the concerns
of the historian; they will want to reconstitute the actions of its author
(if any) and its readers at various moments in past time. Others will
want to perform actions in the matrix it provides, which will be actions
performed in the present and which will not entail knowing what
others were doing in the past or—if this were possible—knowing
what one is doing oneself in the same way that one can know what
another was doing by reconstituting his action. The reason why it is
difficult to have historical knowledge of our own actions is that such
knowledge is attained by reconstituting an action in a context designed to render it explicable, and it is very difficult to reconstitute
an action in the moment of performing it for the first time. To be both
playwright and actor is possible during the first run of the play; to
be both playwright and critic is almost impossible (though if Stoppard
did not want to expose himself to critics, he would not publish his
plays). The respondent to a classic text who wants to use it in an
original act of illocution is like the actor; the respondent who wants
to perform the act of reconstituting another's illocution is more like
the critic. Perhaps it is unfortunate that the word "critic" is often used
to define the former, whereas the word "historian" is very justly used
to define the latter.

The former category, when referring to those responding to political texts, commonly embraces political theorists and philosophers;
when referring to those responding to texts of "literature," it embraces
critics of the kind who were once called New Critics. It should be
obvious by now that the actions of philosophers and New Critics are
wholly legitimate, that the actions of historians are wholly legitimate,
and that the two kinds of legitimacy do not negate each other. Yet
historians and nonhistorians frequently quarrel. I think it is unnec-
essary for them to do so, and being a historian myself I naturally
think that historians are blameless (except when stupid) and quarrel
with nonhistorians only when the latter are stupid enough to deny
the legitimacy of what we are doing or think we are denying the
legitimacy of what they are doing. If A wants to employ text Z in
performing act P, and says "Z means P," I know that this is shorthand
for "Z enables me to perform P." I do not say "Z does not mean P";
still less "if Z means P, then Z is wrong." I may say, "Nobody before
A, to my knowledge—and this goes for the author of Z—has ever
used Z to mean P," or I may say, "That is very interesting; to hear
that A finds P in Z suggests that others before A may have used Z
to perform P, since A's action may be historically continuous or dis-
continuous with the actions of others before him." Perhaps it would
help A to know which it was; but it would not help A to perform the

illocution P, only to know what kind of act it was when he performed it. Only if P was the kind of act that entailed making statements about the previous history of actions performed in the matrix Z provides could A's statement about the "meaning" of Z be true or false from the historian's point of view.

The word *meaning* has now taken on more meanings than one. In listening to the discourse of students of political thought, I have found it a good rule of thumb that if someone says, "Hobbes said . . . ," he means, "Thomas Hobbes (1588–1679) said or meant to say . . ." and is speaking as a historian. Whereas if he says, "Hobbes says . . . ," he means, "Hobbes means to me, or enables me to say . . ." and is speaking as a theorist or philosopher. That is how it *should* be, in any case; unfortunately there is a historic present I find it hard to avoid myself. It is also clear that the status of the word "Hobbes" varies from sentence to sentence. To change the scenario a little: in 1976 I attended two conferences marking the bicentennial of the death of Hume, and at each it was evident that for the philosophers present, to say "Hume says" meant using the word "Hume" as little more than a trigger that set in motion various language games they desired to play. They did not care or need to know about the historical David Hume who was born in 1711 and died in 1776 and performed many acts of various kinds between those dates. For the historians present, the word *Hume* was a historical expression denoting the life and actions of that individual, and they used it only to introduce historical statements. The difference between the two usages was so absolute that it caused no confusion, only noncommunication. Things might have been worse if it had been supposed either that the philosophers were talking history, or that the historians were negating the statements of the philosophers. Then there would arise a sort of historical fiction, a history of political thought constructed on nonhistorical grounds and claiming historical truth for nonhistorical reasons. All that the historian has to say to the philosopher, or to the New Critic, is that the latter's statements need not be history now but will be history in a few moments. The Owl of Minerva is never in the present, but its flight will return.

BIBLIOGRAPHY

In addition to works cited in the Notes, the last decades have witnessed a dramatic expansion of literature on the methods of studying the history of political thought. Here follows a list of works especially relevant to the contents of this essay.

Boucher, David. *Texts in Contexts: Revisionist Methods for Studying the History of Ideas.* Dordrecht: Martinus Nijhoff, 1985.

Condren, Conal. *The Status and Appraisal of Classic Texts: An Essay on Political Theory, Its Inheritance, and the History of Ideas.* Princeton: Princeton University Press, 1985.

Dunn, John. *Political Obligation in Its Historical Context: Essays in Political Theory.* Cambridge: Cambridge University Press, 1980.

Gunnell, John G. *Political Theory: Tradition and Interpretation.* Cambridge, Mass.: Winthrop Publishers, 1979.

Hollinger, David A. *In the American Province: Studies in the History and Historiography of Ideas.* Bloomington: Indiana University Press, 1985.

King, Preston, ed. *The History of Ideas: An Introduction to Method.* Totowa, N.J.: Barnes and Noble, 1983.

Pocock, J. G. A. *Politics, Language and Time: Essays on Political Thought and History.* New York: Atheneum, 1971, 1973.

———. *Virtue, Commerce and History: Essays on Political Thought and History, Chiefly in the Eighteenth Century.* Cambridge: Cambridge University Press, 1985.

Rorty, Richard, Schneewind, J. B., and Skinner, Quentin, eds. *Philosophy in History: Essays on the Historiography of Philosophy.* Cambridge: Cambridge University Press, 1984.

3
Politics of Discourses and the Rise of the Aesthetic in Seventeenth-Century England

Michael McKeon

In the eyes of posterity, the secularization of religious categories and values is manifestly an exercise, for good or ill, in demolition and redevelopment. But the secularizers themselves often are more likely to see their sponsorship of the political, the historical, and the material as fully consistent with the continued health of the religious realm. They may conceive of this sponsorship as a defensive demarcation of religion's territory against admittedly alien encroachments, as when Francis Bacon argues the wisdom of giving "to faith that only which is faith's" in order to ensure against "not only a fantastic philosophy but also an heretical religion." Or they may see their work as, on the contrary, the reinforcement of religion by an allied power: Bacon's invidious distinction between "the Idols of the human mind and the Ideas of the divine" throws religion and the new philosophy together in pursuit of the latter, which are "the creator's own stamp upon creation, impressed and defined in matter by true and exquisite lines."[1] What is crucial to the process of secularization, in other words, is certainly not an outright assault upon religion; nor, for that matter, either its alliance with or its opposition to the forces of the secular. The crucial element is the categorial self-consciousness itself, the preoccupation with the fundamental problem of boundaries. Religion exercises its authority by a tacit dominion: to inquire closely into its relationship with other realms is automatically to question its claim to superintend and to suffuse them all.

In the following essay I will approach the "politics of discourse" in seventeenth-century England by asking some questions about its "politics of discourses." What sorts of territorial disputes arise over the proper boundaries of the several spheres of discourse—"religion," "politics," "history," and "literature"? How are these disputes negotiated, and how are the boundaries redrawn over the course of the century? I have begun by describing the secularization process because I think its contradictory character provides, in several respects, a generally instructive model for the way in which the politics of discourses is conducted at this time. There is, first of all, good reason to use the well-documented fortunes of the category "religion" in seventeenth-century England as a guide to the less visible career of "literature," for there are many parallels between them. Like "religion," "literature" undergoes a delimiting scrutiny during this period, so that by the end of the century its boundaries are far more confidently intuited (if by no means known) than at the beginning. Moreover, "literature" also attains its greater specificity both in alliance with and in opposition to the crucial spheres of "politics" and "history." Part of my aim, therefore, will be to pursue some of the more suggestive features of the analogy between the respective developments of "religion" and "literature." But I will also be obliged to observe, in the course of that comparison, some important differences. For although there is an obvious sense in which literature, too, was "secularized" in the seventeenth century, this is not my principal concern. In fact, the very access to an abstract category "literature" is to some degree anachronistic at this time, referring either backward to a broadly inclusive idea of *litterae humaniores* or forward to our modern notion of a sharply defined and autonomous realm of written objects that possess an "aesthetic" character and value.

The seventeenth century is a critical stage in the movement from the former to the latter way of thinking, a movement that is very different from that undergone by "religion." For the increasing and self-conscious preoccupation with the compass of the realm of "religion" in the early modern period signals its desuetude and decline, whereas the specification of "literature" as an autonomous category is a ritual of birth. In fact, the relation of similarity between the two movements at a certain point becomes also a relation of contiguity. Despite the analogy between their respective interactions with the secularizing forces of "politics" and "history," in the end "literature" does not suffer the fate of "religion" because, so far from being "secularized" in a comparable fashion, it becomes itself a powerful engine of secularization. A comfortable commonplace by the nineteenth century, the secularization of religion not only by politics but also by literature—the "replacement" of religious by literary spirituality—has its origin two centuries earlier. The decline of religion therefore is not only coincident with but also a function of the rise of the aesthetic.

I

At the beginning of the seventeenth century, the dominant categories for describing political conflict were by and large religious categories; by the end of the century this was obviously no longer the case. Although the change in terminology was a continuous and long-term process, the outbreak of hostilities in the 1640s no doubt gave it an essential impetus. The happy discovery that religious offenses were responsive to ecclesiastical alterations confirmed both the political dimension of reformation and the fact that a large part of its labor yet remained to be done once the political reform of the church had been accomplished. "It is not the unfrocking of a Priest," said John Milton,

> the unmitring of a Bishop, and the removing him from off the *Presbyterian* shoulders that will make us a happy Nation, no, if other things as great in the Church, and in the rule of life both economicall and politicall be not lookt into and reform'd, we have lookt so long upon the blaze that *Zuinglius* and *Calvin* hath beacon'd up to us, that we are stark blind.[2]

Some of Milton's contemporaries learned to regard sectarian terminology as essentially political in nature, and therefore to see its customary ascendancy as a mystification of more fundamental motives. Writing on the eve of the Restoration, William Sprigge remarked that "men complain much, and seem to have a great sense of the many Factions and Divisions in Religion, as they are pleased to term them; but how inconsiderable are these to the grand National or civil Factions."[3] Decades later, writing in the wake of another revolution, Charles Davenant carried the critique much further, directing it against political terminology itself. Insisting that the principles of the new Whigs were quite the opposite of those of the old, he charged that the bulk of the party now "consists of those who are of any Side where they can best make their Markets."[4] These are increasingly radical affirmations, by disillusioned men, of the determinant priority of political and material "interest." But the relationship between the spheres of "religion" and politico-economic "interest" could be investigated more circumspectly and experimentally than this. The debates on church unity that accompanied the return of the restored Church of England provided one occasion for such inquiry.

A basic argument of those who favored one or another program for the toleration or comprehension of non-Anglican Protestantism was that such policies would serve the interest of England by discouraging political turmoil and encouraging commercial industry. The very title of John Corbet's *The Interest of England in the Matter of Religion . . .* (1661) celebrates the hopeful alliance of politics and religion, and it moved Roger L'Estrange to seek immediate clarification on the content of these categories: "I would fain know what is meant by, *The Matter of Religion,* as it stands here related to Civil Interest?"[5] Those supporting a strict Anglican uniformity were inclined, on the basis of the past twenty years' experience, to dispute the idea that toleration might conduce to public peace. As Richard Perrinchief argued, "*Faction* in the *State* being thus interwoven with *Dissentions* in *Religion,* the Toleration of one sort is the permission of another."[6] Yet the official policy of religious persecution to which this argument pointed could be rationalized by two very different approaches to how the boundaries of "the matter of religion" were most accurately delimited.

On the one hand religious persecution redefined the scope of the religious sphere by subjecting it to a political takeover. In this view the Clarendon Code was an act of conquest that sought to reduce the vast territory of "religion" to the preserve of "private conscience." "Religion" was narrowed to enclose whatever is not politically (which is to say, physically) prohibitable: it is what remains standing once the interwoven vines of "political faction" and "religious dissension" have been jointly uprooted. To some contemporaries, the most attractive solution to the problems of priority raised by religious persecution was first of all definitional. An Anglican reproached a Roman Catholic in the following terms: "We hold it Necessary to maintain the Authority of the King, and the Peace of the Nation. If you call any thing *Religion,* that is contrary to these, must we therefore alter our Laws? or ought you to mend your Religion?"[7] Here the politics of discourses entails the conquest and annexation of one sovereign realm in the name of another, and religion becomes truly the realm of the invisible. On the other hand it is undeniably a "religious" persecution that penal laws enact, and from this perspective the antitolerationists do not so much reduce the territory of religion as silently expand it to include even civil behavior. The tolerationist Peter Pett demystified this position when he observed,

if it be said that a man may think himself bound in Conscience to oppresse people in spiritual things, but not in civil; I answer, most certainly then his Conscience will lead him to put them out of a condition to assert their spiritual liberties so opprest. It is with restraining the freedom of Conscience as the denying a *mare liberum* to neigbouring [*sic*] nations, which any Prince that doth must not trust to prescription of long time, or imaginary lines in the heavens whereby the compasse of his dominion of the Sea may be determined, but to powerfull Fleets.

The power of persecution is inseparably a power of definition. Those who would restrain liberty of conscience

> intend to be judges how far mens civil and spirituall liberties reach, and what are the frontires of both. . . . And 'tis most certain that he who doth impose any thing upon the people under the species of Religion, would not leave them a power to judge whether it be in order to it or no. For if they are the Judges, they will say that any thing in Religion which displeaseth them opposeth their civil liberty, and so nothing at all will therein be enjoyned.[8]

The debates on church unity help to vindicate the idea that the secularizing impulse is signaled most tellingly not by the ostentatious imposition of "politics" on "religion" but by the capacity to engage in the experimental manipulation of these categories and of the boundaries between them. If antitolerationist policies explicitly subject "religion" to "political" rule, the tolerationists, in the very defense of religious freedom as politically expedient, subject it to what is implicitly acknowledged as a more privileged and persuasive standard of "interest": that by which all else is justified. It is from this perspective that the historian of religious toleration in England regards the "political" and "economic" arguments of the Restoration period as essentially foreign to "the theory of religious toleration."[9] In this judgment he echoes the views of those antitolerationists who, like Herbert Thorndike, sensed that there was something wrong with the very premises on which the debate was being conducted: "Men may amuse themselves, with the instance of the *United Provinces;* which, they say, flourish in trade and riches, by maintaining all Religions. But the question is of Religion, not of Trade, nor Riches. If it could be said, that their Religion is improved, with their Trade, the example were considerable."[10] But this rearguard attempt to rescue "religion" from the encroachments of its putative allies was doomed to fail by its equal dependence on an alliance with extraordinary penal legislation. To the degree that political support of the religious establishment ceases to be tacit and customary, it is "religion" that has come to serve "politics" rather than the other way around. The Clarendon Code announces not the hegemony of religion but the fact that it is in crisis.

II

The religious persecution legislated by the Clarendon Code coincides with the "literary" censorship legislated by the Printing Act of 1662 and ferociously enforced by Roger L'Estrange until its lapse at the Exclusion Crisis. Here the quotation marks are obviously indispensable. If the category "religion" has acquired more than a little volatility by 1660, the category "literature," in our sense of the term, does not yet even exist; L'Estrange's target was simply politically offensive matter that appeared in print. Earlier in the century, however, a policy of censorship was enacted that has long been notorious for its specifically "literary" significance as an attack upon "beauty" and "art": the closing of the theaters in 1642. In recent years the Puritan iconoclasm expressed by this policy has effectively been shown to be neither particularly "Puritan" nor particularly significant of a hostility toward "art."[11] Nevertheless it bears a relevance to the politics of discourses in seventeenth-century England. The complex Protestant attitude toward the use of figures is analogous to the complex Calvinist attitude toward the theology of works. The repudiation of the conventional, dangerously externalized, and corruptible mediators of Christian truth and grace is a negative gesture that implies its positive counterpart, the discovery of more immediate and self-authenticating paths to the realm of the spirit. In Protestant soteriology this entails the doctrine of sanctification and holy discipline, which minimizes the mediating process itself by psychologizing and collapsing the distance between the conviction and the attainment of grace. In Protestant rhetoric it involves an implicit reliance on the figurative language of Scripture as the one true sense and "literal" word of God.[12]

The relevance of the Protestant use of rhetorical figures to what I have been calling the politics of discourses lies in its deployment of a mediation that all but lays claim to immediacy. According to commentators, the spiritual signification of a figure is so fully implicated in its facilitating signifier that what appear to be two senses must be conceived as one: "When we proceed from the sign to the thing signified, we bring no new sense, but only bring out into the light what was before concealed in the sign. . . . For although this sense be spiritual, yet it is not a different one, but really literal."[13] The spiritual is almost seamlessly enclosed within the literal. The boundary between the discourse of the "literal" and that of the "spiritual," between the "historical" and the "mystical," is inscribed and obscured in a single movement:

It may be said, that the historie of Abrahams familie here propounded, hath beside his proper and literall sense, a spiritual or mysticall sense. I answer, they are not two senses, but two parts of one full and intire sense. For not onely the bare historie, but also that which is therby signified, is the full sense of the h[oly] G[host].[14]

Of course, William Perkins's language explicitly reflects the typological mode of thought that in its Protestant revaluation was extended to include not only sacred but contemporary and private "history." Dryden's *Absalom and Achitophel* (1681) marks one significant climax in this Protestant revaluation, the point at which the rhetorical function of implicating the "spiritual" within the "literal"—the strategic purpose of ethical legitimation—can be felt to separate from and predominate over its theological function. This is because the formal operation of Dryden's poem insists upon the consequences of the Protestant extension of typology. As soon as the antitype is permitted to occupy a position that is chronologically but not spiritually conclusive, the mechanism of typological fulfillment has become at least potentially divided against itself. In *Absalom and Achitophel* this potential is actualized: the sacred history that is embodied in the Old Testament types of Samuel takes on the signifying and facilitating function of an ethically valorizing historical precedent, bringing "out into the light what was before concealed in the sign" of secular English history. Dryden's poem is acutely sensitive to the political exploitation of typological argument—to its susceptibility to enlistment under any political banner, including that of the king—and for that very reason it is a brilliant example of the early modern shift in the status of typology: from that of an unusually historicizing technique of spiritual ascription to that of an unusually spiritualizing technique of reading history.[15]

Protestant thought sees history, like Bacon's natural "matter," as "impressed and defined" by "the creator's own stamp." The investment of history and nature with unprecedented spiritual authority which occurred under the aegis of reformed religion and the new philosophy of empiricism could be undertaken with piety rather than skepticism because God was understood to have accomplished his most intimate internalization of the spirit within these apparently profane realms of the phenomenal. Yet the great daring of this assumption also revitalized the old and deadly fear of human sufficiency, of mistaking the signifier for the signified, one sphere of discourse for another. The tension is explicitly articulated in the famous poems of Donne, Herbert, and Marvell that meditate in different ways upon their own procedure, but it is implicit elsewhere: for example, in Donne's apprehensive account of astronomical conquests:

> For of Meridians, and Parallels,
> Man hath weav'd out a net, and this net throwne
> Upon the Heavens, and now they are his owne.
> Loth to goe up the hill, or labour thus
> To goe to heaven, we make heaven come to us.[16]

Donne's cautious guide to scriptural exegesis provides a gloss both for the substance of these words on human materialism and for their characteristic formal enticement to be taken at their own rich literality: "The literall sense is always to be preserved; but the literall sense is not alwayes to be discerned: for the literall sense is not alwayes that, which the very Letter and Grammar of the place presents."[17]

Some of Herbert's poems, such as "Redemption" and "The Pilgrimage"(1633), exploit the experience of reading allegorical narrative to express, in the tension between the ongoingness of a literal plot and the stasis of its implicated spiritual referent, the central tension between nature and grace. The discourse of lease and manor, tenant and landlord, ascent and travel fitfully mediates to another, higher discourse—the death of the body and the end of the poem—whose interruption of this one both negates it and is inconceivable without its aid.[18] John Bunyan concludes his own later pilgrimage with this ingenuous warning against mistaking his spiritual narrative for a strictly "historical" discourse:

> *Take heed also, that thou be not extream,*
> *In playing with the out-side of my Dream;*
> *Nor let my figure, or similitude,*
> *Put thee into a laughter or a feud;*
> *Leave this for* Boys *and* Fools; *but as for thee,*
> *Do thou the substance of my matter see.*[19]

The warning is well taken. For the pedagogic triumph of Bunyan's immensely compelling plot is inseparable from the perpetual possibility of its total failure. Its very concreteness threatens to preclude the process of allegorical "spiritualization" altogether and to become both signifier and signified. In such a case the reader is left with a "mediator" so immediate that it stealthily has come to constitute its own mode of discourse and must be relied upon to make truly one sense in and of itself.

The designation of this sort of discourse as "the novel" occurred only in the following century, but the radical experiments of this one helped make the notion of so fully "materialized" and self-sufficient a discourse more acceptable. For Gerrard Winstanley idolatrous worship, the love of the "outward object," is synonymous with "the selfish imagination [that] would be a god still." "Imaginary man" externalizes and imposes his vain desires on the world in the "fourfold power" of ministry, magistracy, judicature, and the "imaginary art" of commerce. Winstanley's response is not to repudiate the imagination but to recapture the literal sense of Scripture figures. If man has literalized his selfish imagination, Christ provides us with images whose materialization will undo this creatural vanity. It is "imaginary invention," for example, that moves man "to enclose parcels of the earth into several divisions, and calls those enclosures proper or peculiar to himself." By this means we project imaginary enclosure into real enslavement. But the Son within "is coming on amain, to break down all your pinfolds and to lay all open to the common; the rough ways he will make smooth, and crooked ways straight; and level mountains and valleys." So the Diggers were really only enacting the one true sense of Scripture in their radical program of social reform.[20] Of course, there are other models for the translation of religious language into radical social action during this period. Millenarian movements, commonly saturated with the mystical discourse of Daniel and Revelation, tended to have a remarkably materialistic notion of what that discourse entailed. Thus the Fifth Monarchy man Thomas Venner was at pains to explain that what he meant by the imminent kingdom of Christ was not "some strange thing" but distributive justice, full employment, the protection of native trades and manufactures; "and whatsoever can be named of a common or publick good, we mean by the Kingdome of Christ."[21]

The seventeenth century marks a critical stage not only in the development of the Protestant problem of mediation but also in the institutional imposition of censorship. Recently Annabel Patterson has argued persuasively that the requirements of political censorship played a central role in conditioning the emergence of the modern idea of "literature." According to this argument, writing under censorship demands a veiled and difficult discourse whose "functional ambiguity" bespeaks an implicit code by which writers may produce meaning both for a censoring authority and for the audience whose meaning that censor would putatively proscribe.[22] In the present context it may be useful to add that the problem of writing under censorship may be seen as a secularization of the problem of mediation. In the early modern discourse of the spirit, the literal or historical level works, as of old, as a parabolic mediation that provides access to the authoritative meaning of divinity; yet it is also invested, problematically but increasingly, with a sufficiency and adequacy of its own. During this same period divine authority is gradually delegated both to the absolutist state and to the creative individual. So in the early modern discourse of censorship, parabolic language works rather to "mediate"—to block by means of an acceptably deceptive decoy—the discredited authority of the state, allowing the creative author the freedom to produce meanings for which no external authority is felt to be required. In this respect the golden age of state censorship in England may be seen as a temporary but crucial factor in helping to liberate the modern notion of "literary creativity" from submission to an overarching authority that, in its more traditional theological guise, was far more difficult to evade. But there are, of course, other factors in this complex modern emergence, and I will now turn my attention to them.

III

The growing autonomy and authority of "politics," "history," and social reform that we can associate with the Protestant and empiricist influence was reinforced by the increasing weight of Aristotle's *Poetics* in English literary culture. The Renaissance rediscovery of Aristotle's seminal distinctions between "poetry" and "history" and between "poetry" and "politics," which made a considerable contribution to the early modern empiricist revolution, was in the first instance rather a consequence of its founding dedication to distinguishing the present from the past.[23] Thereafter the effect of the *Poetics* on the politics of discourses was complicated by two factors. First, although many sixteenth-century commentators accepted and affirmed the general idea of the autonomy of "poetry" and the universality of the truth that it teaches (Sir Philip Sidney among them), many others did not, either misunderstanding these central features of the *Poetics* or constructing taxonomies of the several discourses in which the relative dominance of "politics" and "history" bespeaks as much a Platonic or a Horatian influence.[24] Second, the parallelism between the analogous relationships with which we are dealing is not symmetrical. In the intellectual movements on which I have focused "politics" and "history" are seen gradually to emerge from their subordination to "religion." The effect of the *Poetics*, however, is to free "poetry" and its kind of truth from their presumed subsumption under "politics" and "history."

Despite this asymmetry, during the seventeenth century the two streams were able to inform and to reinforce each other's influence.

This is because in both the Protestant and empiricist movements I have described, "political" or "historical" discourse was understood, with varying degrees of explicitness and conviction as the century progressed, to have been purged of its dangerous profanity by its internalization of the spiritual signified. Such discourse therefore could dovetail with what was its true counterpart in the neo-Aristotelian movement: not "politics" or "history" at all but the liberated discourse of "poetry." Of course, the full "liberation" of poetry was the work not of the seventeenth century but of more recent times. And the eclectic serviceability of these categories can be seen in the way "the father of English literary criticism" is still able to juggle them in different contexts. In *The Indian Emperor* (1667), the neo-Aristotelian Dryden has "neither wholly follow'd the truth of the History, nor altogether left it: . . . it being not the business of a Poet to represent Historical truth, but probability." However, he calls *Annus Mirabilis* (1667) "an Historical Poem" rather than an epic, precisely because it consists of a "broken action, ti'd too severely to the Laws of History." Yet although not "the Inventour" but "only the Historian" of *Absalom and Achitophel*, Dryden is nonetheless pleased to call it "a Poem."[25]

The category "politics" can be discussed in more general terms. It is posterity, and not the Restoration itself, that identified the major literary product of that period as "political poetry," designating with this term a kind of discourse that in its own view approached the condition of paradox.[26] But posterity was right to draw attention to the Restoration's extreme dedication to the "public" or occasional capacity of verse as a divergence from the broad English tradition, in which the occasional is more tacitly accepted as one of the "natural" realms of poetic discourse. And over the longest term (which is posterity's), the meaning of that dedication is not celebration of the convergence of the two discourses but a nagging, neo-Aristotelian suspicion of its incongruity. With increasing aid from Aristotle's categories, "poetry" and "poetic truth" are learning to question their subordination to "politics." As the Clarendon Code announces a crisis in the reign of religion over politics, "political poetry" declares a crisis in the reign of politics over poetry. Five years after the Toleration Act of 1689, the Printing Act was allowed to expire.

My concentration here on the category of "poetry" may have suggested to the reader a third complication in the influence of Aristotle's *Poetics* on the seventeenth-century politics of discourses. What about the discourse of prose narrative? Aristotle's intent, of course, was to formulate a poetics that might include prose, and he criticized the common tendency to define poets as poets "not by reason of the imitative nature of their work, but indiscriminately by reason of the metre they write in."[27] Yet it was overwhelmingly the case that early commentators construed him as having designated verse as in some fashion a necessary condition of poetry. One obvious reason for this is the understanding of "history," quite customary in the Renaissance, as a prose form: the very authority of Aristotle's differentiation of "history" from "poetry" militated against the admission of any prose form as "poetic."[28] So in the crucial instance of prose, the conflation of the Protestant and empiricist sense of "history" and the neo-Aristotelian sense of "poetry" came up against considerable obstacles. This may be reflected in the fact that seventeenth-century prose narrative resists the temporary terminological rapprochement, evident in the poetry of this period, between "historical" and "poetic" modes. Instead it defines itself as "history" or "true history," in resolute opposition to "poetry"—or, to use the term for discredited prose most current among contemporaries, to "romance."

This is not universally so. Attempts to categorize the several discourses of prose narrative in the latter half of the century can be quite bewildering to the modern sensibility, suggestive less of a competitive "politics" of discourses than of an acquiescent capitulation to sheer anarchy. The bookseller John Starkey, for example, published a catalogue of his books in 1672 that is divided into the following six categories: divinity, physic, law, history, poetry and plays, and miscellanies. Under the heading "history" he includes Suetonius, Rabelais, the "Novels" of Quevedo, biographies, travel narratives, and a popular romance.[29] Yet the catalogue of William London, published fifteen years earlier, obligingly separates "History" from "Romances, Poems and Playes."[30] A third bookseller, Francis Kirkman, tends to use the terms "history," "romance," and "novel" interchangeably.[31] Thus the categorial competition between "history" and "romance" did not possess the clarity of open warfare for all contemporaries. Moreover, some writers overcame what I have described as the implicit prohibition against the neo-Aristotelian, poeticized truth of "romance" in prose narrative. This is particularly true in the French romance and among those English writers whom it most influenced.[32]

Yet the great tendency is for prose narrative of this period to claim the status of "true history" in explicit opposition to "romance" and to protest the historicity of its subject matter—to claim that it really happened. The situation is a complicated one. At a time when spiritual truth was increasingly in thrall to the putatively ministrating mediations of historical and empirical truth, the terms of Aristotle's distinction between "poetry" and "history" offered a model for a fully secular species of truth-telling that was not also historicizing and empiricist. But because of the apparently special status of prose, that

distinction also reinforced, at least temporarily, a bifurcated notion
of how to tell the truth in what was increasingly, if obscurely, perceived as the single realm of "literary" discourse. This is complicated
enough. Spiritual ends, however, precisely because of their compromised status, were perhaps the dominant concern of Restoration culture, and they had to be served by whatever discursive means were
available. This confluence of forces resulted in a number of strikingly
unstable literary forms; for example, the apparition narrative. Because
the naive empiricist claim to historicity subserves here the explicit
end of teaching the Christian truths of the spirit, in the apparition
narratives of the Restoration period the politics of discourses discloses
itself with the unarticulated energy of raw contradiction.

The reasoning behind the apparition narratives seems impeccable.
As Richard Baxter explains,

> I found that my Faith of Supernatural Revelation, must be more than a
> *Believing Man,* and that if it had not a firm Foundation, and rooting, even
> *sure Evidence* of *Veracity, Surely Apprehended,* it was not like to do those
> great works that Faith had to do. . . . Apparitions, and other sensible
> manifestations of the certain existence of Spirits of themselves Invisible,
> was a means that might do much with such as are prone to judge by
> Sense.[33]

Even if the aims of rhetoric are those of the discourse of the spirit,
only a materialistic discourse can speak, it would seem, to those who
"judge by sense." So powerful are the secularizing forces of empiricism and skepticism that even those who would resist their erosion
of belief in an invisible and spiritual reality find themselves fighting
on the materialistic territory of the enemy and obliged to employ his
discursive weapons. The best-known apparition narrative of the period, Defoe's *A True Relation Of the Apparition of one Mrs. Veal . . .*
(1706), gives a good idea of the circumstantial and authenticating
detail that is involved in the discourse of the claim to historicity:
names, places, dates, events, eyewitness and "earwitness" testimony,
attentiveness to stylistic "sincerity," denials of special bias, and the
like. There is not a great distance separating this discourse from that
of the novel, but it is equally continuous with the productions of the
recent past: with the rhetorical figures of Donne and Herbert and with
their ambition to mediate a spiritual truth that is intimately and fully
implicated in the literal sense.

IV

The most general aim of the apparition narratives was to demonstrate
that despite the incredulity of modern freethinkers, God still reveals

his being and his will through extraordinary and immediate acts of providence.[34] This aim—the vindication of providence—was shared by an extraordinary range of writings of the period, and it was served by a variety of discursive means that, although related in interesting ways to the claim to historicity, are quite distinct from it. One such means is physico-theology and the philosophical argument from design.[35] Another is the doctrine of poetic justice, which plays an important role not only in the prose fiction but also in the drama of the Restoration period. First prescriptively formulated by Thomas Rymer in 1677, the doctrine was embraced by many participants in the famous debate that was touched off two decades later by Jeremy Collier's *A Short View of the Immorality, and Profaneness of the English Stage* (1698). Recently it has been argued that poetic justice, because "it stood for the mirroring of God's justice in literary form," itself reflects and confirms a widespread belief in providential justice.[36] But it is the contradictory nature of the crisis of faith to evoke not only skepticism but also extreme justifications of what heretofore might have been taken "on faith" and tacitly assumed to be true. It seems to me more likely that the discourse of poetic justice would become important— even crucial—for a culture in which divine justice is felt to be in jeopardy.

The most exhaustive historian of the subject finds evidence for belief in divine providence in seventeenth-century England in a wide variety of cultural institutions and activities, but he also suggests that providential belief is in decline at the end of the century.[37] Yet to observe that people of the Restoration felt the need to improve on providence is not in itself to distinguish them in the least from their predecessors. For most Christians in all periods have allowed themselves to recognize that what is noteworthy about providence is that it *cannot* be relied on to be just—at least not in this world. As Samuel Butler observed, "the world is so vile a thing, that Providence commonly makes Fooles, and Knaves happy, and good men miserable in it, to let us know, there is no great Difference between Happiness and misery here."[38] In the words of Abraham Jenings,

> affliction (if properly such) is an argument of Divine Affection; and they that miss of troubles temporal, may doubt of happiness eternal. . . . And to me there is not a stronger Argument [than earthly injustice] . . . for a general Day of Judgement, and Recompence in a World to come. . . . For if Goodness ought to be rewarded, and Vice punished, as all allow, then there must be a time allotted in which it shall receive this reward.[39]

What is unusual about the Restoration is that it should have elaborated this special method—poetic justice—of compensating for the deficiencies of providential justice, rather than having continued to rely on the traditional and orthodox method of the afterlife. It was during this same period that the reality of Hell and its "vindictive" justice began to be questioned openly and explicitly.[40] In other words, the discourse of poetic justice does not simply countervail the observed shortcomings of providence; it also competes with the chief means by which those shortcomings traditionally have been compensated for, the discourse of the hereafter. This was very clear to Samuel Richardson, at least by the time he was engaged in the defense not of Pamela's rewarded virtue but of Clarissa's more saintly sacrifice:

> And after all, what is the *poetical justice* so much contended for by some, as the generality of writers have managed it, but another sort of dispensation than that with which God, by Revelation, teaches us, He has thought fit to exercise mankind; whom placing here only in a state of probation, he hath so intermingled good and evil, as to necessitate us to look forward for a more equal dispensation of both.[41]

Thus poetic justice operates most profoundly not as a representation of the divine but as a replacement of it. At the same time it is a compensation for the failings of the phenomenal world, for the discourse of "politics" and "history." As Francis Bacon pointed out, "since the successes and issues of actions as related in true history are far from being agreeable to the merits of virtue and vice, Poesy corrects it, exhibiting events and fortunes as according to merit and the law of providence."[42] This is in fact one way of moralizing, and thereby making palatable, Aristotle's idea of the distinguishing universality of "poetic truth." It is with *"historical Justice"* that Rymer contrasted *"poetical Justice."*[43] And long before that Sidney had remarked that it is not in "history" that we see "virtue exalted and vice punished—truly that commendation is particular to poetry, and far off from history."[44]

But the coming autonomy of "poetry"—of "literature"—is most evident and arresting in its capacity to replace not "history" but "religion." The rise of the aesthetic consists in the assumption by "art" of those tasks that traditionally were performed by religious belief and experience. It entails a humanizing of Spirit, an internalization of divine as human creativity. And it is thoroughly indebted to empiricist epistemology, most of all for its insistence that the several spheres of discourse are more fully separable from one another than premodern culture had believed. But the autonomous aesthetic could gain its full ascendancy only when the coarser and more material vestiges of empiricist thought had been ejected by the realm of discourse that in modern thought is designated as the last refuge of transcendent spirit, the discourse of literary and artistic experience. Doctrines of "realism" reformulate the problem of mediation for a world in which spirituality has ceased to represent another realm to which human creatureliness has only difficult and gratuitous access, and has become instead the capacity itself of human creativity. Realism validates literary creation for being not "history" but "history-like," "true" to the only external reality that still makes a difference but also sufficiently apart from it to be true to itself as well.[45] The discourse of realism exists to concede the accountability of art to a prior reality, without seeming to compromise the uniquely modern belief that such reality as it is answerable to already is internalized in art as a demystified species of spirituality.

What the Puritans and their contemporaries opposed was not art or beauty but the willingness to forbear from sanctification and to indulge the illusion of self-sufficiency. When art becomes an end in itself, it becomes "art" as we know it, the self-sufficient signified.[46] But the triumphant discourse of the aesthetic is not, as we have seen, entirely an invention of the early modern period. If to some degree it "replaced" the religious impulse, it received its first formulation long before the Christian spirit itself had any existence. Ernst Kantorowicz has argued that Christian doctrine, "by transferring the political notion of *polis* to the other world and by expanding it at the same time to a *regnum coelorum*, not only faithfully stored and preserved the political ideas of the ancient world, as so often it did, but also prepared new ideas for the time when the secular world began to recover its former peculiar values."[47] There is surely no basis for the notion that the Aristotelian category "poetry" played any part in Christian thought. There is some justice, however, in a view of the *Poetics* as a long-term sanctuary for the secular conception of the creative spirit, faithfully storing and preserving, in the sheer persistence of the text, the ancient discourse of the aesthetic until the secular world was ready to make use of its recovery.

Many years ago Frank Kermode wrote what was the most trenchant of the several critiques leveled at T. S. Eliot's thesis of a seventeenth-century "dissociation of sensibility." Eliot had maintained that the poets of the early part of the century possessed a capacity to express thought and feeling as a unified experience, which the poets of the later part of the century already had lost. Kermode charged that Eliot's thesis was not so much a contribution to seventeenth-century literary history as "an attempt to project upon the history of poetry a modern theory of the image," one dedicated to "defending the poet's distinct and special way of knowing truth." Kermode associated this theory with the antipositivist tradition in aesthetic discourse that extends from the English romantics to the French symbolists and beyond, and he disclosed the tendentious heart of the theory in its positive corollary: the belief that modern poetry, by re-creating the undissociated image as it existed before the seventeenth-century fall into intellection, might be seen to embody the true essence of the poetic.[48]

The brilliance of Kermode's demystification of this theory in its normative and self-serving tendencies should not lead us to reject out of hand its basic account of historical change, which is, after all, separable from those tendencies. True, the account is too particularly and catastrophically trained upon a limited range of poetic practice whose implications can therefore be seen plausibly to point in opposite directions. (Samuel Johnson represented the "metaphysical poets" as an instance less of unified than of dissociated sensibility.)[49] But the very emergence of the romantic discourse of the poet's "special way of knowing truth"—the rise of the aesthetic which still so dominates our modern way of thinking—testifies to the fact that something definitive did occur in the early modern period: not the "dissociation of sensibility" but a complex and deeply consequential episode in the ongoing division and specialization of knowledge. And to recollect the politics of discourses in seventeenth-century England can be useful not in recapturing a spurious golden age before the fall but in relativizing what otherwise may too easily appear to be the "natural" boundaries of our own discursive terrain.

4

Lucy, Countess of Bedford: Images of a Jacobean Courtier and Patroness

Barbara K. Lewalski

Lucy Harington Russell (1581–1627), wife of Edward, third Earl of Bedford, was easily the most important patroness of the Jacobean court, except for Queen Anne herself.[1] As favorite lady-in-waiting to the queen from Anne's accession in 1603 to her death in 1619, the Countess of Bedford influenced the queen's patronage directly and had the ear of the king's ministers and favorites. Accordingly, she was a power to be reckoned with in the disposition of offices, the arrangement of marriages, and the shaping of Jacobean cultural life.[2]

Lady Bedford gained that eminence despite, rather than because of, her husband. The earl was given to extravagant entertainment and display in youth, but in 1601 he was disgraced, heavily fined, and exiled from court for his part in Essex's rebellion (1601). Even after the exile was lifted his apparent preference for country life, his heavy debts, and the partial paralysis and stammer occasioned by a fall from a horse in 1612 kept him from court.[3] Therefore the Countess of Bedford's prominent role as Jacobean courtier and patroness was attributable almost entirely to her own (Harington) family connections and to her considerable talents, brilliance, and style. Hers is a patronage chiefly based on influence rather than financial largess.

Because Lady Bedford's place in the Jacobean court is so largely a self-designed role, I am concerned here with the literary imagery through which that role was created and sustained. In part this is a study of a Jacobean countess' self-fashioning (in Stephen Greenblatt's useful phrase);[4] or, in the fashionable Neoplatonic language of the age, it is a study of the figuring forth of the Countess of Bedford as the "Idea" of a Jacobean female courtier and patron. It is also an inquiry into the effect Lady Bedford had upon the literary scene— most obviously through the poems or other works addressed to her or taking her as subject. Evidence on these matters may be obtained from contemporary comments about her life at court, portraits painted of her, masques in which she danced, numerous literary tributes to or about her, and her own extant letters and one poem—all more or less consciously designed mirrors that reflect her in a variety of images. These images present, in various combinations, the same distinctive qualities: glamor, power, strength of mind, learning, wit, and earnest Calvinism.

I

The known facts of the countess' life can be briefly summarized. Born in 1581 to John Harington of Exton and Anne Kelway at their estate, Coombe Abbey, she grew up in a religious and educated family, with a younger brother John and sister Frances. She was kinswoman to Sir Philip Sidney and the Countess of Pembroke (through her grandmother, Lucy Sidney) and to John Harington of Kelston, poet and translator of Ariosto. In 1594, at age thirteen, she was married to Edward Russell, third Earl of Bedford (then twenty-one), bringing a handsome dowry of £3000 and the estate of Minster Lovell. A lavish life-style at court, extravagant entertainments, the expenses of the Garter ceremonies for the earl, and an encumbered estate kept the Bedfords continually in debt, even before the earl's disastrous association with Essex's rebellion brought him a fine of £20,000 (later reduced to £10,000).[5]

After the Essex debacle the countess undertook to make her own way at court. In a brilliant and lucky coup immediately upon the death of Queen Elizabeth, Lucy and her mother hastened to Edinburgh (as did some other nobles and ladies) to pay their respects to James I and Queen Anne; Lucy was appointed at once to the queen's bedchamber, and Lord and Lady Harington were given charge of the young Princess Elizabeth's education. Thereafter the Countess of Bedford was the recognized favorite among the queen's ladies and also maintained a close friendship with Princess Elizabeth both before and after her marriage to the Elector Palatine in 1613. Lord and Lady Harington accompanied the Electress to Germany, and Lady Harington returned as her chief attendant in 1617; John Harington, Lucy's brother, also became a close friend of the heir apparent, Prince Henry.

The death of her father in 1613 and of her brother John the following year made the countess heir to two-thirds of the Harington estate. But this new eminence only compounded her financial problems since the estate was encumbered by almost £40,000 debt.[6]

From 1608 to 1617, the countess resided chiefly at Twickenham when she was not at court, making that estate a salon of sorts for writers and artists, though not on the scale of the Countess of Pembroke's Wilton. Most of her literary and other clients were occasional guests rather than resident-dependents: her financial situation hardly permitted the latter kind of patronage. Her entourage at Twickenham included, at various times, Sir Henry Goodyere, gentleman of the privy chamber to James and the Earl of Bedford's servant, who acted for her in acquiring the estate; one "Mistress Goodyer" (a daughter or niece of Sir Henry) as young waiting-woman; Jane Meutys, who married Sir William Cornwallis in 1608 and was the countess' closest female friend and correspondent in later life; Bridget, Lady Markham and Cecilia Bulstrode, ladies of the queen's bedchamber and kinswomen of the countess; Carew Gorges, son of the author and translator Sir Arthur Gorges; and Dr. John Burges, the Calvinist minister-physician who attended her during a serious illness in 1612–13 and whose career she subsequently forwarded.[7] Donne visited her at Twickenham on several occasions while he was resident at Mitchem, and so probably did other writers and musicians among her clients— Jonson, Samuel Daniel, John Dowland, John Davies of Hereford, and George Chapman.[8]

On two occasions the countess was desperately ill and close to death: in 1612, a stroke rendered her speechless for a time, and in 1619, a bout with smallpox left her disfigured.[9] Also, 1619 brought the death of her patron Queen Anne and of her mother. After 1617, the countess resided chiefly at Moor Park (granted by the king to the Bedfords in that year), where she laid out the magnificent landscape gardens later praised by Sir William Temple as "the most beautiful and perfect, and altogether the sweetest place, which he had ever seen in England or in foreign countries."[10] But she remained an active courtier and patron until the accession of Charles in 1625, working chiefly through her great friends the Earl of Pembroke (the lord chamberlain) and James, Marquis of Hamilton (steward of the household). The Earl of Bedford died at Moor Park on 3 May 1627 and was buried at Chenies; the countess died in the same month, 27 May 1627, and was buried with her own family at Exton. She had no living children: a son born in 1602 died a month later; a daughter born in 1610 lived only two hours; and there was apparently no issue from other rumored pregnancies.[11]

Early to late, the countess won general respect in her public role as courtier, projecting an image of power, strength of mind, and loyalty to family and friends. The young Lady Anne Clifford records in her diary for 1603 that "my lady of Bedford . . . was then so great a woman with the queen, as that everybody much respected her, she having attended the queen from out of Scotland."[12] In a letter to Lord Harington seeking to put an end to the countess' efforts in 1605 to arrange a marriage between her brother and Robert Cecil's daughter, Cecil paid grudging tribute to the countess' tenacity of purpose:

> I must be thus far bowld with my Lady the Countesse, as to say that if she hathe not more resembled her sex in loving her owne will than she dothe in those other noble and discrett parts of her mynd (wherein she hath so great a portion beyond most of those that I have knowne) she myght have moved you to suspend the sending upp of any particularities at this tyme. . . . Your nobel daughter . . . is made of a better mould to discerne truth and report it than many others in this place, but yet I have not hidd it from herselfe, that I have found her so absolutely fixed uppon a resolution to allow of no reason which she finds not justly concurrent with your satisfaction.[13]

In 1618, one of Sir Dudley Carleton's well-wishers advised him to press his request for a secretaryship through "mylady of Bedford (who is above measure powerfull with both the Marquesses and mylord Chamberlaine)."[14]

Over the years she promoted the cause of the Elector Palatine and the Electress Elizabeth, who were dethroned as King and Queen of Bohemia in 1619 and whose plight became a *cause célèbre* in the struggles of international Protestantism against Rome and Spain. In 1621 she made a hazardous sea voyage to visit Elizabeth in the Hague[15] and frequently wrote news and advice to her—sometimes urgently, as when (through Sir Dudley Carleton) she warned of dangerous rumors to the effect that the queen planned an unauthorized visit to England:

> For Gods sake preache more warning to the Queene whom she uses freedom to, else she will undo herselfe, and make others afrayd how they interest them-selves in her servis, though for my part I will never omitt making good my professions to her as becoms a faithfull and carefull servant.[16]

Elizabeth gratefully acknowledged the countess' continued efforts in the exiles' behalf:

Dear Bedford, I see by your lines that you are still the same to me in your affections as I have ever found you, which I will ever requite with my most constant love, since I have no better meanes to shew my thankfulness. I would that others were of your mind then I hope there woulde be taken a better resolution for us heere then yett there is.[17]

II

As Masquer, Lady Bedford's image was one of splendor, beauty, fantasy, and often of special privilege and power. For the countess as for the monarchs, court masques were a major vehicle for transforming Jacobean social and political realities into idealized images.[18] The makers of masques, of course, had the royal family principally in view, but Lady Bedford's closeness to the queen gave her special status as participant in and arranger of masques. Samuel Daniel acknowledged that she recommended him to the queen to create the Christmas masque of 1604, and she also served as *rector chori* or leader of the masquers in that performance.[19] A letter from Donne to Sir Henry Goodyere in November 1608 associates her closely with the queen in planning the Christmas masque of that year, and John Chamberlain identified her to Carleton as "Lady and Mistress of the Feast" at which Jonson's *Lovers Made Men* was performed.[20] Whether or not any masque roles were specifically imagined or created for her, it is not unreasonable to suppose that she often chose which roles she would portray and through them projected, consciously or unconsciously, a desired image.

In the first of the Jacobean Christmastide or Twelfth Night masques, Daniel's *Vision of Twelve Goddesses* presented on 8 January 1604, the queen and eleven noble ladies were portrayed as classical goddesses offering their characteristic qualities and blessings to grace the new reign. According to Daniel, the queen chose to represent Pallas (signifying Wisdom and Defense), flanked on either side by Juno (Power) and Venus (Love and Amity). The Countess of Bedford portrayed Vesta—not at first glance the most honorific role, and one that placed her in the second rather than the first triad of goddesses in the procession. By Daniel's account of the allegory, Vesta represented Religion, garbed "in a white Mantle, imbrodred with gold-flame," with "a burning Lampe in one hand, and a Booke in the other." As Vesta, or Religion, Lady Bedford's role associated her most closely with the queen, who portrayed Pallas, and with the blessing specified in the masque as the primary support of the realm:

> Whose maine support, holy Religion frame:
> And *Wisdome, Courage, Temperance,* and *Right,*
> Make seeme the Pillars that sustaine the same.[21]

She took a clearly preeminent role among the queen's ladies in the Jonson-Inigo Jones *Masque of Blackness* on 6 January 1605 and in its sequel, *The Masque of Beauty,* on 10 January 1608. In the first, the queen and eleven of her ladies—all garbed alike in azure and silver with rich pearl ornaments—were portrayed as daughters of Niger, having every quality of inner and external beauty except for their black skin. These ladies are led to Britain, whose sun-king's brightness could blanch an Ethiop, and are promised that after observing due rites for a year they will attain full perfection. In the course of his highly critical report on the production, Carleton notes the countess' place of honor:

> At the further end was a great Shell in the form of a Skallop, wherein were four Seats; on the lowest sat the Queen with my Lady *Bedford;* on the rest were placed the ladies *Suffolk, Darby, Rich, Effingham, Ann Herbert, Susan Herbert, Elizabeth Howard, Walsingham,* and *Bevil* [and Wroth]. Their Apparell was rich, but too light and Curtizan-like for such great ones. Instead of Vizzards, their Faces, and Arms up to the Elbows, were painted black . . . *but it became them nothing so well as their red and white, and you cannot imagine a more ugly Sight, then a troop of lean-cheek't Moors.*[22]

Jonson's notes indicate that the queen represented Euphoris (Abundance) and Bedford, Aglaia (Splendor, one of the three Graces); they carried a golden tree laden with fruit as a symbol of their conjoined qualities.

In the sequel (postponed for two years because the intervening Christmastides required wedding masques), the ladies have achieved the perfection of white skins. The cast of masquers is largely but not entirely identical with that of *Blackness,* but the allegorical names are somewhat altered and the role each lady plays is not specified. The queen is obviously Harmonia—enthroned, with golden crown and a dress having some qualities of all the others. Almost certainly the Countess of Bedford again represents Splendor, the only personage to bear the same name as before, and again presented first—"In a robe of *flame* colour, naked brested; her bright hayre loose flowing."[23]

The countess also took part in the Jonson-Inigo Jones wedding masque, *Hymenaei,* celebrating the ill-starred nuptials of the Earl of Essex and Frances Howard. The conceit involved Reason moderating the four affections and four humors, after which eight ladies representing powers of Juno Pronuba came down to confirm the union. Lucy Bedford and the Countess of Rutland portrayed the two most important powers—Cinxia, who defends the unclad Bride, and Telia, who perfects the union at last—but Jonson's note does not specify which was which.[24] Lucy Bedford chose to be painted (by John De Critz) in the gorgeous costume designed for these lady masquers, described by Jonson in great detail:

> The Ladies *attyre* was wholly new, for the invention, and full of glorie; as having in it the most true impression of a *celestiall* figure: the upper part of *white* cloth of silver, wrought with JUNOES *birds* and *fruits*; a loose undergarment, full gather'd, of *carnation*, strip't with *silver*, and parted with a golden *Zone:* beneath that, another flowing garment, of *watchet* cloth of silver, lac'd with gold; through all which, though they were round, and swelling, there yet appeared some touch of their delicate *lineaments*, . . . their haire . . . bound under the circle of a rare and rich *Coronet*, adorn'd with all varietie and choise of jewels; from the top of which, flow'd a transparent *veile*, downe to the ground. . . . Their shooes were *Azure*, and gold, set with Rubies and Diamonds; so were all their garments.[25]

The countess is not portrayed as a masquer in Isaac Oliver's miniature (ca. 1605), but the gauzy veils, richly floral gown, curled hair, and large jewels project much the same aura of fantasy and magnificence.[26]

The next masque in which the countess is known to have danced is the spectacular Jonson-Inigo Jones *Masque of Queenes*, presented on 2 February 1609 at Whitehall. Its argument, according to Jonson, celebrates "honorable, & true Fame, bred out of Virtue." In the antimasque twelve hag antagonists to true fame—Ignorance, Suspicion, Credulity, and so on—are overcome by Heroic Virtue; in the masque Bel-anna, Queen of the Ocean (Queen Anne), and eleven other virtuous queens of antiquity and legend come forth from the House of Fame. Although Jonson states that the particular parts were disposed "rather by *chance*, then *Election*," Lucy Bedford's personation of Penthesilea, queen of the Amazons, is not likely to be accidental. As the most ancient queen, the martial Penthesilea led the procession, figuring forth power linked to virtue, valor, and beauty, as Jonson indicates:

> The most upward in time was Penthesilea. She was Queen of the Amazons. . . . She lived and was present at the war of Troy, on their part against the Greeks, where, as Justin gives her testimony, "among the bravest men great proofs of her valour were conspicuous." She is nowhere mentioned but with the preface of honour and virtue, and is always advanced in the head of the worthiest women. Diodorus Siculus makes her the daughter of Mars. She was honoured in her death to have it the act of Achilles. Of which Propertius sings this triumph to her beauty: "to her

whose bright beauty conquered the conquering hero, when the golden helmet left her brow bare."[27]

Inigo Jones's costume designs depict Penthesilea with elaborately plumed classical helmet, sword, a virtually transparent corselet, and skirts of "deep pink color, deep morray (mulberry), skie color."[28]

During the next decade the countess is mentioned only occasionally in relation to masques and entertainments.[29] Jonson identified her as a (speaking?) character—"Mogibell overbery"—in an undated, unpublished, and now lost pastoral drama, *The May Lord*, which may or may not have been produced.[30] We know that she organized for Lord Hay the feast and the Masque *Lovers Made Men* on 22 February 1617 in honor of the French Ambassador Baron de La Tour, and probably led the ladies in the revels as *rector chori*.[31] The countess may have eschewed the masquer's image deliberately, at least for a time. According to Chamberlain, her serious illness in the winter of 1612 resulted in a conversion of sorts and a changed way of life:

> Mary, she is somwhat reformed in her attire and forbeares painting, which, they say, makes her looke somewhat straungely among so many visards, which together with theyre fisled, powdred haire, makes them looke all alike.[32]

The story may be more complex, however. After 1610, the queen and her ladies were much less prominent as masquers: several masques planned by the queen were "postponed" or canceled, and there is a clear shift to men's masques, tilts, and barriers when Prince Henry came of age to present masques with his attendants. Later the king's male favorites took over that function.[33] In 1619, the queen died, and smallpox ravaged whatever vestiges remained of the countess as personification of Splendor. Chamberlain reported, "the worst is they say the masterpocks hath setled in one of her eyes whereby she is like to lose it." Edward Howard wrote to the same purpose: "The small pocks hath seased on the Lady of Bedford, and so seasoned her all over, that they say she is more full and fowle then could be expected in so thin and barre a body."[34]

III

A very different image of the countess is projected by the dedicatory epistles and verses acknowledging or seeking the countess' patronage—that of learned lady and poet. Although the countess has less claim to learning than Mary Sidney or the Cooke sisters, the consistency of such praise testifies to its credibility on some grounds, as well as to the fact that she wished to be praised in such terms. Although all noble ladies of the period are praised for virtue, beauty, and generosity, the countess is one of the three or four regularly celebrated as fit audience and worthy critic for works of literature and learning, and also as a talented poet.

The tributes indicate that she knew several modern languages (though probably not Latin). Holyband, possibly her tutor for a time, dedicated a language book to the two-year-old Lucy, urging her to learn languages in obedience to her parents' desire.[35] John Florio, sometime member of the Harington household, dedicated his *World of Words* (1598) to the countess, praising her great proficiency in reading, writing, and speaking Italian, French, and Spanish, but especially her concern for the matter conveyed in those languages.[36] Dedicating his translation of Montaigne's *Essays* (1603) to the countess and her mother (among others), Florio noted that he completed it while resident with the Haringtons, and that Lucy read, encouraged, and offered helpful suggestions for the work in progress.[37]

Some tributes associate her with her Sidney relatives. Around 1600, John Harington of Kelston sent three of the Countess of Pembroke's psalms to her, declaring that "none coms more neere hir, then your self in those, now rare, and admirable guifts of the mynde, that clothe Nobilitie with vertue"; he also included some of his own verse meditations and promised more, "as your cleare-sighted judgement shall accept or praise them."[38] In the dedication to his *Divine Meditations*, John Davies of Hereford joined Lucy Bedford with the Countess of Pembroke and Elizabeth, Lady Cary as the three Graces—"at once Darlings as Patronesses, of the Muses" and "Glories of Women"— and commended Lucy particularly for "Wit and Sp'rit, in Beauties Livery."[39] In a similar vein, George Chapman addressed her as "faire Patronesse, and Muse to Learning"[40] in one of the dedicatory sonnets to his *Homer,* and Arthur Gorges's son presented his father's translation of Lucan's *Pharsalia* to her as "an honourable lover and Patronesse of learning and the Muses."[41]

Yet another image appears in dedications by prominent English Calvinists and Puritans. Here the countess is presented as a religious woman of Calvinist leanings, associated through her family and by her own proclivities with Puritan reformist elements in England and with the cause of international Protestantism abroad. These dedications do not offer personal praise, but praise is implicit in the assumption that she will value the worthy and profitable lessons the treatises contain and through her patronage aid their dissemination.

In 1595, William Perkins offered her a meditation on death, reminding her of Solomon's adjuration to "Remember thy Creator in the days of thy youth." In 1608, Thomas Draxe dedicated his treatise on predestination and the final conversion of the Jews to her. In 1614, Richard Stock's funeral sermon for young John Harington urged his mother and sisters to emulate his "worthy graces and practise of godliness." In 1615 the noted translator of Calvin, Clement Cotton, offered a treatise on martyrs to the countess and her mother, and in 1620, he presented Lady Bedford with his translation of Calvin's lectures on Jeremiah. In 1621, John Reading proposed to her a meditation on the uses of both sickness and health—very appropriate in the wake of her bout with smallpox.[42]

Although dedications throughout her life portrayed the countess as a Puritan, that image was especially prominent after her illness in 1612. Chamberlain reported the external signs of a religious conversion, which he ascribed to the ministrations of the Puritan John Burges—who was banished from the court for his pains:

> Mary, she is somwhat reformed in her attire, and forbeares painting. . . . Burges (who is turned phisician) was much about her in her sickness, and did her more good with his spirituall counsaile, then with naturall phisike. . . . The king . . . was so moved that he should dogmatise (as he called yt) in his court, that he commaunded the archbishop to look to yt who . . . injoined him not to practise within ten miles of London.[43]

The countess labored for Burges's reinstatement (which occurred in 1616) and sought his advice on several occasions.[44] Her chaplain, Nicholas Byfield, dedicated a set of sermons to her in 1617, noting that she had already heard many of them "with great attention."[45] In 1620 this sober religious image of the countess at age thirty-eight was captured in a striking portrait attributed to Cornelius Jansen: in a black dress adorned with black jewelry, against a somber black background, she reflects an attitude of pensive meditation with her head reclining on her hand. But some hint of the earlier showy display remains in the gold coronet, the warm ash-blonde hair, the large and elegant lace ruff, cuffs, and handkerchief.[46]

Her recognition as a major patroness and her position at the center of Jacobean culture invites the question of how much she actually influenced the literature of the period. Although she evidently had some shaping influence upon the early development of the court masque through her own activities and her patronage of Daniel and Jonson, she did not directly promote other literary kinds and experiments (as the Countess of Pembroke promoted quantitative verse, classicizing verse drama, prose romance, and religious lyric). The poetry she inspired and invited was almost exclusively poetry of compliment, centered upon herself, her family, and her household. Such poems by her major literary clients—Drayton, Daniel, Jonson, and Donne—are worthy of attention in themselves. Most of them play upon various metaphorical possibilities in the etymology of her name (Lucy, light) in creating literary embodiments for the fascinating images she projected. Also, the fact that she was closest to the best poets of the age—Donne and Jonson—affords some indication of her taste in poetry and praise. At the least she provided a fit audience for and thereby some encouragement to their development of new poetic styles and modes of praise.

She did not long sustain her association with Michael Drayton, the first important poet to proclaim himself her poetic servant—a role he played out in courtly feudal terms. At the death in 1595 of his first patron, Sir Henry Goodyere of Polesworth, Drayton proclaimed himself "bequeathed" by Goodyere to Lucy Bedford. In 1594 he dedicated his legend of *Matilda* to the thirteen-year-old Lucy Harington, identifying her with his heroine, as "being in full measure, adorned with the like excellent gifts, both of bodie and minde." In 1595, a dedicatory sonnet to his epyllion *Endimion and Phoebe* proclaimed the newly married Countess of Bedford the "essence of my cheefest good," alluded to the "sweet golden showers" she has before rained upon him, and implored her to grace his Muse, "Whose faith, whose zeale, whose life, whose all is thine."[47] In 1596, he continued his obsequious posture as her feudal servant and creature, inscribing to her his collected legends of Robert Duke of Normandy, Matilda, and Piers Gavaston:

> If any thought of worth live in mee, that onely hath been nourished by your mild favours and former graces to my unworthy selfe, and the admiration of your more then excellent parts shyning to the world. . . . The Light I have, is borrowed from your beames.[48]

His most sustained poetic praise of the countess occurs in the stanzaic dedication to his historical epic, *Mortimeriados* (1596), in which he apostrophizes her as "Rarest of Ladies, all, of all I have, / Anchor of my poore Tempest-beaten state / . . . My hopes true Goddesse, guider of my fate," and promises to secure her fame by his verses, which themselves are the products of her "great power." He also interrupts his epic twice with invocations to Lucy Bedford as his Muse.[49]

Evidently the countess soon ceased to respond to such approaches. In 1597, Drayton dedicated the first pair of his *Englands Heroical Epistles* to her in very restrained tones, analogous, he said, to the speaker

Rosemond's "modesty" in addressing King Henry II. After this he wrote no new dedications or praises to her or her family, and in 1603, he removed all references to her when he revised *Mortimeriados* as *The Barons Warres*.[50] In 1606, in a revised version of *Idea the Shepheard's Garland*, he created a bitterly satiric portrait of her as Selena, who abandoned the "faithfull Rowland" she once rewarded, to favor the "deceiteful *Cerberon*" (Ben Jonson?):

> What dainty flower yet ever was there found
> whose smell or beauty mighte the sence delight
> wherewith *Eliza* when she lived was crown'd
> in goodly chapplets he for her not dight
>   which became withered soon as ere she ware them
>   So ill agreeing with the brow that bare them.
>
> Let age sit soone and ugly on her brow,
> no sheepheards praises living let her have
> to her last end noe creature pay one vow
> no flower be strew'd on her forgotten grave.
>   And to the last of all devouring tyme
>   nere be her name remembred more in rime.[51]

The collapse of Drayton's high hopes for the countess' patronage probably had something to do with her financial difficulties and something to do with Drayton's own penchant for raising hackles in high places.[52] But the fact that the countess apparently made no effort to further Drayton's career in the Jacobean court also suggests that his Spenserian poetry and his conventional courtly praises in the posture of feudal servant had ceased to interest her.

By contrast, she played a significant role in advancing Samuel Daniel's career with the new court, even though he was much more closely associated with other patrons.[53] She evidently took some part in planning the visit King James made to her family's house in Rutlandshire in April 1603 en route to the coronation: the entertainment was a reading of Samuel Daniel's "Panegyricke Congratulatory," a grave and thoughtful praise of James for the virtues he ought to acquire, consonant with Daniel's already established character as moralist-historian in the *Civil Warres*.[54] Some months later she recommended him to the queen for the Christmas masque of 1604, *The Vision of the 12. Goddesses*. In dedicating the printed text to the countess, Daniel defended it against its many critics, so as to "cleere the reckoning of any imputation that might be layd upon your judgement, for preferring such a one, to her *Maiesty* in this imployment."[55] These early opportunities opened the door to court appointments: in 1604, as licenser to the Children of the Queen's Revels; in 1607, as groom of the queen's bedchamber; and commissions to write other masques and dramas for the court.

The countess' interest in Daniel may have been prompted by the Florio connection (Florio was Daniel's brother-in-law), but she may also (as Puritan) have been attracted to Daniel's high moral seriousness and to the novelty of his weighty, plain style. I suspect she was also greatly pleased by the kind of praise he accorded her in the very fine verse letter published with the *Panegyrick*. In a serious tone intimating true regard, Daniel compliments the countess by taking her as an exemplum through whom important moral lessons may be illustrated. Particularly pleasing, no doubt, was Daniel's recognition of her difficult situation as female courtier and his judicious praise of her in terms of qualities she especially valued—notably the intelligence and learning that enabled her to escape the restrictions of the female role:

> And this faire course of knowledge whereunto
>> Your studies, learned Lady, are addrest,
>> Is th'only certaine way that you can go
> Unto true glory, to tru happiness:
> . . . .
> And no key had you else that was so fit
> T'unlocke that prison of your sex, as this,
>> To let you out of weaknesse, and admit
>> Your powers into the freedome of that blisse
> That sets you there where you may over-see
>> This rowling world, and view it as it is;
> . . . .
> How oft are we forc't on a cloudie hart
>> To set a shining face, and make it cleere;
>> Seeming content to put our selves apart,
> To beare a part of others weakenesses!
>> As if we onely were compos'd by Art,
>> Not Nature, and did all our deeds addresse
> T'opinion, not t'a conscience, what is right:
> . . . .
> And though books, Madam, cannot make this minde
>> Which we must bring apt to be set aright,
>> Yet they do rectifie it in that kinde,
> And touch it so, as that it turnes that way
>> Where judgement lies:
> . . . .
> And therefore in a course that best became
>> The cleerenesse of your heart, and best commends

> Your worthy pow'rs, you run the rightest way
> That is on earth, that can true glory give;
> By which when all consumes, your fame shal live.[56]

Ben Jonson also addressed several poems to the countess, though not as his major patron; that role was filled collectively by members of the Sidney-Pembroke family.[57] Nevertheless, early in his career (1599) Jonson included a passage in his "Epistle" to Sir Philip Sidney's daughter, the Countess of Rutland, acknowledging Lucy Bedford's "timely favors" and his competition for them with another poet (probably Drayton). This passage transforms the mistress and poet-servant convention, countering Drayton's obsequiousness with a tone of respectful praise grounded upon proper self-regard:

> You, and that other starre, that purest light,
> Of all LUCINA'S traine; LUCY the bright,
> Then which, a nobler heaven it selfe knowes not.
> Who, though shee have a better verser got,
> (Or *Poet*, in the court account) then I,
> And who doth me (though I not him) envy,
> Yet, for the timely favours shee hath done,
> To my lesse sanguine *Muse*, wherein she'hath wonne
> My gratefull soule, the subject of her powers,
> I have already us'd some happy houres,
> To her remembrance; which when time shall bring
> To curious light, the notes, I then shall sing,
> Will prove old ORPHEUS act no tale to be:
> For I shall move stocks, stones, no lesse then he.[58]

Those favors evidently involved influence at court, gracefully acknowledged by a gift copy of *Cynthia's Revells* (1601) inscribed to "CYNTHIAS fayrest Nymph." Whether or not she aided Jonson to become the principal maker of masques at James's court and to gain an annual pension, he certainly called upon her good offices when he was jailed with George Chapman in 1605 for satirizing the king in *Eastward Ho*.[59] During the Twickenham years small personal gifts suggest a more familiar relationship: a copy of Donne's satires for the countess, a deer for Jonson. His notorious epigram on Cecilia Bulstrode (#49, "The Court Pucell") provoked the countess' displeasure, but he hastened to make amends with a wholly laudatory epitaph for Bulstrode's death in 1609.[60]

Jonson's poetic portraits of Lucy Bedford often begin with interpretations of her name, as symbol of her wit and intelligence. An ode addressed to her in manuscript apostrophizes her beauty and "illustrate brightness" but especially celebrates "Her wit as quicke, and sprightfull / As fire; and more delightfull," and her "Judgement (adornd with Learning)."[61] The inscription to *Cynthia's Revells* compliments her wit by assuming her appreciation of witty epigram: the book is sent "unto the bright, and amiable / Lucy of Bedford," and directed to claim as reward "a Kisse (if thou canst dare it) / of her white Hand: or she can spare it."[62] Similarly, his deft "Epigram 84" gratefully acknowledges her offer of a deer, while noting wryly that an offer is not yet a gift:

> MADAME, I told you late how I repented,
>   I ask'd a lord a buck, and he denyed me;
> And, ere I could aske you, I was prevented:
>   For your most noble offer had supply'd me.
> Straight went I home; and there most like a *Poet*,
>   I fancied to my selfe, what wine, what wit
> I would have spent: how every *Muse* should know it,
>   And PHOEBUS-selfe should be at eating it.
> O *Madame*, if your grant did thus transferre mee,
>   Make it your gift. See whither that will beare mee.[63]

In two of his finest epigrams, Jonson assays Lady Bedford's mind and character in a tone of utmost judiciousness, thereby creating a literary image at once wonderful and credible. "Epigram 94," sent with Donne's Satires, pays special tribute to her literary taste and moral judgment in requesting a copy of Donne's satires, developing the theme, "Rare poems aske rare friends." It begins and concludes with an apostrophe to her as "Lucy, you brightnesse of our spheare, who are / Life of the *Muses* day, their morning-starre." And it offers as proof of her worth the fact that she can read and enjoy satire (which all sinners hate).[64] Even finer is "Epigram 76," which portrays Jonson's ideal mistress made flesh in Lucy Bedford, and which highlights her learning, her strong mind, and her most unusual freedom to control her own destiny:

> This morning, timely rapt with holy fire,
>   I thought to forme unto my zealous *Muse*,
> What kinde of creature I could most desire,
>   To honor, serve, and love; as *Poets* use.
> I meant to make her faire, and free, and wise,
>   Of greatest bloud, and yet more good then great;
> I meant the day-starre should not brighter rise,
>   Nor lend like influence from his lucent seat.
> I meant shee should be curteous, facile, sweet,

> Hating that solemne vice of greatnesse, pride,
> I meant each softest vertue there should meet,
> Fit in that softer bosome to reside.
> Onely a learned, and a manly soule
> I purpos'd her; that should, with even powers,
> The rock, the spindle, and the sheeres controule
> Of destinie, and spin her owne free houres.
> Such when I meant to faine, and wish'd to see,
> My *Muse* bad, *Bedford* write, and that was shee.[65]

The countess was closer to Donne than to her other literary clients; indeed, for a time he was virtually her laureate. Sometime in 1607 or 1608, when he lived near Twickenham at Michem, Donne was probably introduced into the the countess' circle by his good friend Sir Henry Goodyere. Donne's letters of 1608–1612 report that he dined at Twickenham on several occasions; that the countess stood godmother to his second daughter (who was named for her); that she was prompt and active in supporting him for an office he sought; that he sent her literary works (some of his poetry, a translation she requested, some fashionable French poems from abroad); that she was often generous in relieving his needs; that he paid deathbed visits to Cecilia Bulstrode at Twickenham; and that he exchanged poems with the countess on at least two occasions.[66] During these years he wrote to her several times, addressed six verse letters and two other occasional poems to her; titled his lyric "Twick'nam Garden" after her estate; and wrote elegies for Lady Markham, Cecilia Bulstrode, and (in 1614) her brother John.[67]

At one level theirs was a patron-client relationship, in which Donne received some financial assistance and some support in his constant (and unavailing) quest for secular office.[68] His letters often reveal the anxieties of clientage: his concern about pressing too many letters or verses upon her, his uneasiness about addressing praises to other noble ladies, his worry that he would demean himself in her eyes by publishing some of his poems, his tenuous explanations for his extravagant praise of Elizabeth Drury in the *Anniversaries*.[69] But his letters also show genuine admiration for the countess. He declared to Goodyere in 1609, "I have made her opinion of me the balance by which I weigh myself"; and a little later, "I would write apace to her, whilst it is possible to express that which I yet know of her, for by this growth I see how soon she will be ineffable."[70]

In a letter written probably in 1609, Donne requested some of the countess' poems, complimenting them as excellent exercises on an "ill" subject:

I . . . make a petition for verse, it is for those your Ladyship did me the honour to see in Twicknam garden, except you repent your making; and having mended your judgment by thinking worse, that is, better, because juster, of their subject. They must needs be an excellent exercise of your wit, which speak so well of so ill: I humbly beg them of your Ladyship, with two such promises, as to any other of your compositions were threatenings; that I will not show them, and that I will not believe them; and nothing should be so used that comes from your brain or breast.[71]

Her poems in this vein (courtly love poems? bawdy verse?) are unfortunately not extant. It seems likely, however, that Donne's "Twicknam Garden," an exaggerated Petrarchan lament in which a weeping, sighing speaker bemoans his mistress' cruelty in the "paradise" of the countess' garden, belongs to some such game of poetic exchanges on conventional love themes. And the title and themes of "A Nocturnall upon S. Lucies Day" suggest that this poem may also be for (though clearly not about) the countess.[72]

Donne's verse letters to the countess develop a distinctively Donnean portrait of her agile mind, subtle wit, and exemplary character, although he also praises Elizabeth Drury, the Countess of Huntingdon, Prince Henry, Lord Harington, and some others in similar terms. In his hands the poem of praise undergoes a sea-change, transformed from conventional hyperbolic compliment or quasi-Petrarchan adulation into an audaciously witty but profoundly serious metaphysical inquiry into the bases of human worth.[73] It might fairly be argued that Donne developed his poetics of praise in the poems to the Countess of Bedford, as he addressed her first and most often in this vein. Specifically, he proposes to study, or meditate upon, or contemplate the countess (as image of God) in order to explore through her some general proposition about virtue, religion, death, or sorrow. By addressing such poems to her, Donne projects an image of the countess as able logician, metaphysician, and literary critic, in whom wit and religion are (as they should be) perfectly fused: "nor must wit / Be colleague to religion, but be it."[74]

In the poem, "Reason is our Soules left hand, Faith her right / By these wee reach divinity, that's you," Donne analyzes the conventional Petrarchan topic of the celestial or divine lady with theological precision, appearing (for a while at least) to conflate the Countess of Bedford with God Himself. Donne seeks to reach her first by reason, then by faith; to study her in her "Saints, / Those friends, whom your election glorifies," and then in her deeds; and finally to understand her goodness—which consists chiefly in "learning and religion / And vertue." The apparently outrageous hyperbole finds resolution in his recognition of her as "Gods masterpeece, and so / His Factor for our loves"; that is, God's image and agent to attract mankind to love Him. The final lines urge her attention to the next life, while alluding wittily to his hopes from her in this one: "For so God helpe me, I would not misse you there / For all the good which you can do me here."[75]

Most often Donne's verse epistles make the countess the embodiment or incarnation of virtue. Often they pose and resolve a philosophical question: how can (her) complete virtue exist in, act in, or manifest itself to an essentially wicked court or world? In "You have refin'd mee, and to worthyest things," he defines the countess as the embodiment or essence of both beauty and virtue—her virtue manifesting itself chiefly at court, where that virtue is rare, and her beauty chiefly in the country, where that quality is also rare. The resolution comes with the perception that she embodies the Platonic identity of beauty and virtue:

> If good and lovely were not one, of both
>   You were the transcript, and originall,
> The Elements, the Parent, and the Growth,
>   And every peece of you, is both their All:
> So'intire are all your deeds, and you, that you
>   Must do the same thing still: you cannot two.[76]

In "T'have written then, when you writ," Donne identifies her as the locus of virtue in an otherwise amoral court:

> I have beene told, that vertue'in Courtiers hearts
> Suffers an Ostracisme, and departs.
> Profit, ease, fitnesse, plenty, bid it goe,
> But whither, only knowing you, I know;
> Your (or you) virtue two vast uses serves,
> It ransomes one sex, and one Court preserves.[77]

Inviting her to "meditate" with him on the evils of the world, he asks whether unalloyed virtue can act in a wicked world without taking some tincture of vice, and he concludes that in her it can. A verse letter to her "At New-yeares Tide" (1610) queries how the lowly Donne can praise her worthily (being perfect virtue), but God provides the resolution by exercising her with doubts and trials, so that she becomes comprehensible to weaker mortals. "Honour is so sublime perfection" poses the similar question of how her perfect virtue can be manifested to or praised by the unworthy and finds the answer in her perfect fusion of discretion and virtue, wit and religion, whereby her external behavior fully reveals her inner state. She is both "great and innocent," and he urges her to remain so.

The poems on the occasions of the various deaths in her family develop a similar strategy. The verse epistle, "You that are she and you, that's double shee," sent to her with the elegy on Lady Markham, analyzes the Platonic commonplace on friendship: "they doe / Which build them friendships, become one of two"; it concludes that all Lady Markham's virtues are now contracted in the countess. The elegy itself is an analysis of the extent and limitations of death's power in its constant, perpetual conflict with mankind. It concludes that death has no true power over the souls of the regenerate. Donne's first "Elegie on Mistress Boulstred" magnifies the power of death over all things, but at length concludes that Death is paradoxically defeated by taking the souls of the just who cannot die. His second elegy for Bulstrode analyzes the problem of sorrow in relation to such deaths. The long "Obsequies to the Lord Harrington" is a meditation upon the uses of good men and the world's loss by their death.

The relationship between Donne and the countess cooled somewhat after 1613: Donne looked increasingly to other patrons; the countess' new religious seriousness after her illness seems to have made her more critical of Donne.[78] She raised scruples about his decision to take orders in view of his past life (for which he blamed Dr. Burges). And she was less generous than he expected in helping him to settle his debts before he took orders. Donne elaborated upon his suspicions and his disappointment in a letter to Goodyere, but he recognized the reality of the countess' financial problems:

> Of my Lady Bedford, . . . I would say nothing of her upon record, that should not testify my thankfulness for all her graces. But . . . she had more suspicion of my calling, a better memory of my past life, than I had thought her nobility could have admitted; . . . yet I am afraid they proceed in her rather from some ill impression taken from Dr. Burges, than that they grow in herself. . . . I am almost sorry, that an elegy should have been able to move her to so much compassion heretofore, as to offer to pay my debts; and my greater wants now, and for so good a purpose, as to become disengaged into that profession, being plainly laid open to her, should work no farther but that she sent me £30, which in good faith she excused with that, which is both parts true, that her present debts were burdensome, and that I could not doubt of her inclination, upon all future emergent occasions, to assist me. . . . this diminution in her makes me see, that I must use more friends than I thought I should have needed.[79]

There was, however, no rift: Donne continued to refer to her as "the noblest Countess," and on 7 January 1621, he preached an eloquent sermon before her at Harington House. The text, "Loe, Though he slay me, yet will I trust in him" (Job 13:15), was certainly chosen for its applicability to her own trials in the recent death of her mother and her mistress, the queen.[80]

IV

The countess' self-image, her conception and representation of herself, can be glimpsed in several letters—especially those written from 1613 to 1625 to her good friend Lady Jane Bacon (whom she always addressed as "Dear Cornwallis")[81]—and also in her single extant poem. Her self-portrait conforms in many respects to her clients' images of her. Her writing shows self-reliance; confidence in her own abilities, judgment, and taste; strong religious faith; and real (if unstated) satisfaction with her remarkably independent life, so largely free from a husband's control and the usual confinement to the domestic sphere. The Earl of Bedford is almost never mentioned in her letters, but there are a few wistful allusions to her childless state and some expressions of concern for her mother's safety and health in attending upon the Queen of Bohemia.[82]

It is quite clear that the countess considered herself first of all a courtier, a public person at the center of affairs who wields influence and likes to do so. Indeed, her personal letters show surprisingly few signs of the anxieties and compulsions Greenblatt traces in the "self-fashioning" gestures of contemporary male courtiers—perhaps because she clearly understands and accepts the limits of her role. She often complains to Cornwallis about the strenuous demands of court attendance, but it is clear nevertheless that she relishes those demands:

> I deferred my wrighting to you till I cam into the contry, wheare within 8 days the K[ing] overtooke me; against whos coming, and during his stay att my house, all my tyme and litle witt was so taken up about the busnes of house keepinge as itt made me lay all else aside. Within 3 days after . . . I mett with a peremtory commandement from the Queene to wayte upon her at Woodstocke, which I did, though with so ill health as I had much adoe to get heather to use the helpe of some phisicke.[83]

She writes continually about appointments and arrangements: a preferment to the Elector Palatine for one Will Gombleton; a secretaryship at home for the Dutch ambassador Dudley Carleton; a chaplain for the Queen of Bohemia; a marriage for her niece; an appointment as gentleman usher for a son of Lady Bacon.[84] She also comments from time to time about the course of public affairs—indicating, for example, that God "the only Wyse" has worked a great improvement in Prince Charles after the Spanish marriage fiasco: "I will give you my testimony that the Prince is the most improved man that ever I saw, and that my Lo. of Buckingham recovers much of what he had lost."[85] On occasion she confronts the moral dilemmas of courtiership with some courage, as when she found it important to manifest her indignation by absenting herself from the court after the queen dismissed her friend Lady Roxbrough from service (for failing to consult her about her husband's appointment as Prince Charles's chamberlain): "Of the Queen's court I can say little good, for her resolution to part with Roxbrough still continues. . . . No measuer of favor could often invite me theather, whear ther is no hope of any good to be donne."[86]

She also sees herself as a competent woman of affairs, with sufficient practical intelligence and business acumen to cope with the exigencies of her encumbered estate, debts, and legal problems. After a brief report to Cornwallis in 1614 on her husband's illness she moves quickly to such matters:

> Now I thanke God I can say, that out of a very great and almost hopeles danger My Lord of Bedford hath recovered so much health and strength as we are out of all fear of him, and doe conseave that the violent fever he hath had hath done him some good for his palsy, his speach being better then itt was before he fell sick, though his lamenes be nothing amended. His present state setts me at liberty to follow my terme busnesses, which daylie are multiplied upon me, and make me heavile feel the burden of a broken estate; yett doe I not doubt but by the assistance of Almighty God I shall ear long overcum all those difficulties which at the present contest with me.[87]

To meet some of her debts and expenses, the countess received long-standing personal loans from Lady Cornwallis, for which her letters continually apologize.[88] From the king she sought and received a grant of £2000 a year in 1619 and patents at various times on copper farthings, sea coal, and gold and silver thread; she also took a share in the Burmudas Company.[89] In 1621, she wrote Cornwallis that she was at last getting her affairs in order by arranging to sell Coombe Abbey: "I intend to turn Combe wholly into money, bothe to make myself a free woman from debt, and with the rest of itt to rayse as good an estate for lyfe as I can, having now nonne but myselfe to provide for."[90]

On the personal side, she saw herself as a loyal and devoted friend to a few individuals (men as well as women): Jane Cornwallis and her husband, Nathaniel Bacon; William Herbert, Earl of Pembroke; and James, Marquis of Hamilton. In the exigencies of sickness and death her ready recourse was to seek for herself and offer her friends the consolations of religious faith. Her relations with her dear Cornwallis were especially close, cemented by frequent exchanges of letters and visits, by gifts of hunting dogs to the countess,[91] and by letters of comfort to Cornwallis, who was given to melancholy and apprehension during her pregnancies:

> It is one of my misfortunes, and such a one as I assure you I am very sensible of, to be thus farre from you. . . . You must not consent to sincke under that melancoly . . . which I grieve hartely to heare hath already rought so ill effects upon your health, and so strong aprehencions in your minde, though I trust our good God will with a safe deliverance of a happy bearth restore you.[92]

She writes often about death, analyzing her own grief and that of others with some precision and assessing how religiously it is endured. Writing to Cornwallis after her mother's death in 1619, she compares that loss with one suffered by her friend the Earl of Pembroke:

> What a mother I have lost I need not tell you, that know what she was in herselfe, and to me. Yet God, that sees no affliction to worke sufficiently upon me, hath this last night added another heavie one to my former woe, having taken My Lord Chamberlain's sonne. . . . Now itt is com to the trial I am confident he will show well tempered effects of that religious resolution, and bear with pacience what the Almighty hath donne.[93]

Her report to Cornwallis on the death of the Marquis of Hamilton (steward of the Household) reveals that their friendship was based on both personal regard and political usefulness. In this death she mourns the loss at once of a dear friend and a powerful protector at court:

> I acknowledge that I feele so to the quicke this last affliction God hath pleased to lay upon me as no worldly comfort will ever be able to prevaile against itt, for I have lost the best and worthiest freind that ever breathed, whom I could not love enoffe for what he was to me, nor sufficiently admire for what he was in himselfe and to all the world. . . . But he is, I doubt not, now wheare nothing of felicity is grudged him. . . . [F]or my-selfe I must trewly say I am a maimed body and worse, and so is my Lo. Chamberlain, the last person left of power that I can relie on for the worth

of his affection and friendship to me; and, to speake freely to you, the only honest harted man imployed that I know now left to God and his countrie.[94]

In a more detached vein, her account of Lady Richmond's response to her husband's death, written to "entertaine" Cornwallis in one of her spells of melancholy, reveals a good measure of artistic self-consciousness, an ironic wit, a lively style, and a considerable flair for narrative and psychological analysis:

My La. of Richmond's losse, though it weare such a blow from Heaven as I must confesse I never knew given, will not kille her, of so strandge resisting stue are our hartes made. She was the happiest woman I thinke that lived. . . . She had of glorie and greatnes as much as a subject was capable of, wealth of all kinds in abundance, health and extraordinary beautie even at this adge, and, above all, a noble husband, that was the love of her harte, and doted on her with the same pasion to the last ower of his lyfe that he did the first month of his being in love with her. Out of those loveing armes she rose not two owers before he died, and left him, as she thought, well, only troubled with a litle paine in his head, which made him desirous to sleep a litle longer; . . . I much feared the first violence might have distracted her, but her pasion had so liberal vent as I thinke itt wrought the less inwardly. Her haire, in discharge of a vowe she had formerly made, she cutte off close by the rootes that afternoone, and told us of som other vowes of retirednes she had made if she should be so miserable as to outlive him, which I hope she will as punctually performe. For my part, I confesse I incouradge her to itt, which, som say, hereafter she will love me nothing the better for; but itt is the counsel I should take to myselfe in her case, and therefore I cannot spare to give itt.[95]

The countess also sees herself as a person with highly developed artistic interests and taste. She is passionate about the garden she is laying out at Moor Park, soliciting Nathaniel and Lady Bacon for "som of the little white single rose rootes I saw att Brome," and any other "extraordinary" flowers they may have. At one point she declares herself "so much in love with" her gardens at Moor Park, "as, if I wear so fond of any man, I wear in hard case."[96] Her passion for art collection, and especially for Holbeins, is indicated by her readiness to bid for them (through her friend Lady Bacon), even as the owner is drawing his last breath, and to pay any price:

I was told the last night that your father in law was like to die and that he had som peeses of painting of Holben's; . . . I beseech you entreate

Mr. Bacon, if they will be parted with to any, to lay hold of them afore hand for me . . . for I am a very diligent gatherer of all I can gett of Holben's or any other excellent master's hand; I do not care at what rate I have them for price, but shall thinke itt an extraordinary favor if Mr. Bacon can procure me those, or any others, if he know any such thereabouts, upon any conditions; whos judgement is so extraordinary good as I know nonne can better tell what is worth the having. Som of those I have, I found in obscure places, and gentleman's houses, that, because they wear old, made no reckoning of them; and that makes me thinke itt likely that ther may yett be in divers places many excellent unknown peeses, for which I lay wayghte with all my freinds; and when Mr. Bacon coms to London, he shall see that though I be but a late beginner, I have prety store of choise peeses. Dear Madam . . . be not curious to thinke I may pay too much [for the Holbeins], for I had rather have them then juels.[97]

Her single extant poem indicates that she also saw herself as a poet of sorts—talented enough to produce verses on appropriate occasions and exchange them with her coterie. But like most members of her class, she seems to have regarded poetry as a social grace rather than a serious endeavor, making no effort to save or collect her poems. The poem we have is from a poetic exchange with Donne in 1609, occasioned by the death of Cecilia Bulstrode. It was good enough to be ascribed to Donne himself in the 1635 edition and often thereafter,[98] and it offers a deft response and correction to Donne's first elegy for Bulstrode. His elegy begins by alluding to his Holy Sonnet, "Death be not Proud," and recanting its argument: "Death I recant, and say, unsaid by mee / What ere hath slip'd, that might diminish thee."[99] At great length and with great vividness it describes the whole world as a universe of death, all life devoured by Death and served up to his table. At length, Bulstrode's death is said to be a defeat for Death because she lives now in heaven, but in the context this resolution is not very effective.

The countess' poem, like Donne's, is in heroic couplets, and it begins by quoting (against the author) the first line of Donne's "Death be not Proud." Its argument is that the death of the just (as Bulstrode was) is a summons from God, not from Death. In the spirit of Donne's sonnet, the countess affirms that Death cannot harm the just, that it has power only over the reprobate—defined in Calvinist terms as "people curst before they were." Then, referring obliquely to the scandals about Bulstrode, the countess appeals to the visible evidences of her sanctity at her death. The elegy ends with the consolation expected from the genre—"Weep not"—and its final couplet proposes as an appropriate celebratory hymn for Bulstrode the Pauline text affirming victory over death:

Death be not proud, thy hand gave not this blow,
Sinne was her captive, whence thy power doth flow;
The executioner of wrath thou art,
But to destroy the just is not thy part.
Thy comming, terrour, anguish, griefe denounce;
Her happy state, courage, ease, joy pronounce.
From out the Christall palace of her breast,
The clearer soule was call'd to endlesse rest,
(Not by the thundering voyce, wherewith God threats,
But, as with crowned Saints in heaven he treats,)
And, waited on by Angels, home was brought,
To joy that it through many danagers sought;
The key of mercy gentle did unlocke
The doores 'twixt heaven and it, when life did knock.
   Nor boast, the fairest frame was made thy prey,
Because to mortall eyes it did decay;
A better witnesse than thou art, assures,
That though disolv'd, it yet a space endures;
No dramme thereof shall want or losse sustaine,
When her best soule inhabits it again.
Goe then to people curst before they were,
Their spoyles in Triumph of thy conquest weare.
Glory not thou thy selfe in these hot teares
Which our face, not for hers, but our harme weares,
The mourning livery given by Grace, not thee,
Which wils our soules in these streams washt should be,
And on our hearts, her memories best tombe,
In this her Epitaph doth write thy doome.
Blinde were those eyes, saw not how bright did shine
Through fleshes misty vaile the beames divine.
Deafe were the eares, not charm'd with that sweet sound
Which did i'th spirit-instructed voice abound.
Of flint the conscience, did not yeeld and melt,
At what in her last Act it saw, heard, felt.
   Weep not, nor grudge then, to have lost her sight,
Taught thus, our after stay's but a short night:
But by all soules not by corruption choaked
Let in high rais'd notes that power be invoked.
Calme the rough seas, by which she sayles to rest,
From sorrowes here, to a kingdome ever blest;
And teach this hymne of her with joy, and sing,
The grave no conquest gets, Death hath no sting.[100]

   Given the restrictions upon women in the period, the countess had
scant opportunity to engage her considerable talents and strength of
character toward large accomplishments. But she found some scope

for them within the important social institutions of courtiership and patronage, whose cultural codes allowed noblewomen some access to power and influence. Lucy Bedford enjoyed unusual freedom from patriarchal familial constraints due to the early death of her father and brother (which made her an independent heiress), to the disgrace and incapacity of her husband, and to her childlessness. These circumstances gave her the privileged status of a wealthy, titled widow without in fact being one. In consequence, she was able to a remarkable degree to "spin her owne free houres."

She used them to enhance her position at court and to elicit and create various idealized images of herself in literature and art, making the role of courtier-patroness into something of a cultural myth. The older literary code of Petrarchan adulation is not part of that myth; instead, the patron-client relationship she developed with certain literary figures at least—Ben Jonson and especially Donne—has much the character of coterie friendship and interchange. Nor is there much sign that Lucy Bedford thought of herself—or that others thought of her—as a "weaker vessel," though we have no real access to the psychological strains she may have felt in projecting and sustaining her remarkable public persona. She shows herself, in her various images and reflections, as a figure of power and influence, of splendor and grace; of literary and artistic discrimination, of intelligence and wit; and as a staunch Protestant, a shrewd judge of people and affairs, and a talented writer and poet. The real and the imaginary cannot be disentangled in this portrait, and that is just the point. For it is through such consciously devised literary images that the particular reality of Lucy, Countess of Bedford, is transformed into the myth of the ideal Jacobean courtier-patroness.

5

Macbeth and the Politics of Historiography

David Norbrook

Political analysis of Shakespeare's plays has changed radically in recent years. From the 1920s to the 1960s, critics tended to praise the plays for keeping alive a mature, traditional worldview based on analogies between social and natural hierarchies, against a new, reductive, Puritan or scientific worldview.[1] Today it is precisely the notion of a "natural" order that is called into question, and critics are beginning to concentrate on the inherent contradictions between the attempt to ground a stable social order in nature and the fact that language, the basis of social conventions, is composed of arbitrary and unstable signifiers. The values of previous critical generations are being inverted. The witches in *Macbeth*, previously seen as the embodiments of a transcendent, universal Evil, are now greeted by Terry Eagleton as the real heroines of the play. Alan Sinfield has argued that Shakespeare can be as easily appropriated by the left as by the right, and shows that *Macbeth* can be read from the viewpoint of the democratic theorist George Buchanan rather than as a statement of James I's beliefs.[2]

The new radical criticism has the merit of adopting a broader political perspective, being no longer content simply to endorse the more authoritarian currents of Renaissance thought as absolute truths about human nature. And the alternative readings answer to the fact that the plays appeal to a far wider range of political opinions than do conventional statements of Elizabethan and Jacobean political orthodoxy. But it is difficult to find ways of accounting for the plays' universality without losing sight of their political specificity. Traditional criticism has often celebrated Shakespeare's plays for "transcending" politics in their total impartiality and moving up to a higher level of universal human values; but such readings fail to engage with Shakespeare's politics in that they simply discount the political sphere. The new radical readings insist that all texts are political; but their "appropriations" of Shakespeare's plays can seem too easy. The very plays that a generation ago were acclaimed as bastions of traditional values in a declining world are now seen as radically subverting all values and authority. Then, when this approach seems inadequate, it may be argued that this subversion in fact subtly reinforced the very power structures that were being challenged. Political options, by this analysis, were polarized between total submission to power, authority, and the state on one hand and radical subversion on the other. This polarization was mirrored in the linguistic realm by the opposition between legitimist discourse, which made its univocal signifieds appear natural, and the radical subversion involved in the free play of signifiers. One problem with such polarities is that they effectively reduplicate the stark oppositions presented by absolutist propagandists: either monarchy or anarchy; "take but degree away. . . ." Such a focus fails to do justice to the many Renaissance thinkers who had a conception of political order which involved neither hereditary monarchy nor total anarchy, and a conception of linguistic order which permitted rational communication without reinforcing feudal social relationships.

These more rationalistic and constitutionalist currents of thought were prominent in Renaissance historiography, and hence in many of the texts that formed the bases for Shakespeare's plays. I believe that a fuller inquiry into the ideological connotations of his sources might permit a more concrete analysis of the plays' political concerns. Conventional studies of sources still tend to see them as inert raw material, waiting to be converted into the pure gold of art in the alembic of the creative imagination. During the Renaissance, however, historical writing was heavily politicized; and by the standards of the age the political tendencies of some leading historians were fairly radical. The particular political complexion of Shakespeare's plays can perhaps be determined by analyzing the confrontation between radical sources and the pressures imposed on the public stage by convention and censorship. The result is not bland "impartiality" but a tension, varying from play to play, between sources and dramatic reworking.

I

I have chosen *Macbeth* as an example, and in some respects it is an extreme case. For though it bears the marks of an especially courtly play, written to vindicate the king's public image, it draws on sources whose political vision was in many ways inimical to James's. Some of these sources, it is true, were inaccessible without knowledge of Latin, and to have picked up their constitutional implications would have required a certain amount of intellectual sophistication. Most standard accounts of Shakespeare's sources assume that his scholarly and intellectual equipment were fairly meager, that he would have been content to go to the simplest and least problematic authorities. There is remarkable persistence in the notion that Shakespeare's worldview was essentially that of the average common sense of his age, that he was the antithesis of the learned Ben Jonson. Some recent scholars, however, have reopened the question of Shakespeare's learning; and if he was in fact aware of the political controversies that motivated Scottish historiography, then *Macbeth* must look rather different.[3] It can be seen to represent a fairly drastic revision of the political viewpoint implicit in its sources. I have tried to bring out this fact first by setting out at some length the views of the major Scottish historians and then demonstrating the many ways in which *Macbeth* revises their material.

This procedure has its limitations. I shall be treating the play primarily as a linguistic statement and paying little attention to its dramatic aspects; and the circumstances of performance may considerably affect a text's political implications.[4] Moreover, in concentrating on the political contrasts between *Macbeth* and its sources I run the risk of underestimating the continuities: it could be argued that the very thoroughness with which the play engages with opposing viewpoints ensures that they become inscribed within it as a stubborn subtext. I am certainly concerned to show that the play's position is part of a debate, not an unreflective statement of a received worldview. But in order to reveal the terms of the debate it is necessary to sharpen some of the contrasts. And while acknowledging the possibility of radical subtexts in Shakespeare, it seems worth paying more attention than has been customary to some texts whose radicalism was definitely noticed by contemporaries.

II

Most authorities, having surveyed various possible sources for *Macbeth*, conclude that "Holinshed was the main source of the play."[5] This judgment tells us less than it seems to, however, and it may imply a rather limiting view of Shakespeare's intellectual capacity. For by the 1590s sophisticated intellectuals were already looking down on Holinshed as an old-fashioned historian. The *Chronicles* draw together materials from many different kinds of sources, with discourses ranging from bare chronological reportage to the most sophisticated humanist historiography. The editors made no real attempt to unite these different discourses in order to provide a coherent ideological perspective.[6] Humanists such as Gabriel Harvey were demanding something very different from history: a discipline with a philosophical basis and a literary form of expression, drawing on a bare stock of factual material in order to shape a vision of political conduct and the psychology of those in authority.[7] In the case of the *Chronicle of Scotland*, it could even be argued that the English edition marked a regression from its source material. For the basic source, the history of Scotland published by Hector Boece in 1527, was a pioneering instance of humanist historiography in northern Europe. Boece presented a fairly consistent view of the whole pattern of Scottish history and freely invented lengthy formal orations in order to present the general political issues that underlay the narrative of events. The version printed in Holinshed constantly disrupts Boece's narrative with corrections of factual details by reference to other chronicles, or attacks on his anti-English bias, but does not offer any more generalized historiographical vision. It is true that by the publication of Holinshed's first edition Boece's history was fifty years old and humanist tastes had changed.[8] The fashionable influence now was not Livy, with his florid style and penchant for improbable supernatural portents, but the concise and skeptical Tacitus. But the 1587 edition of Holinshed was in a position to bring the Scottish narrative fully up to date, for in 1582, a history of Scotland had been published which was more in accord with advanced humanist taste: shorn of colorful prodigies and with a heightened emphasis on political debate. The author of this new history, George Buchanan, was probably the best-known British writer in sixteenth-century Europe, renowned as a poet and dramatist. His English admirers, who included Sir Philip Sidney, had eagerly urged him to persevere with his history at moments when he was losing patience with it; and its publication, which was eventually posthumous, was viewed with anticipation throughout Europe.[9] An English translation of his work, one might have expected, would have brought a new luster to the Holinshed compilation.

The editor of the Scottish chronicles in the 1587 edition, Francis Thynne, did indeed draw on Buchanan to correct some points in earlier sections of the chronicle and to bring the narrative up to date beyond the point at which Boece had broken off, but he did so without enthusiasm. The account of Scottish writers which concludes the chronicle describes Buchanan as "greatlie learned, but manie times maliciouslie affected"; Thynne declares that he will not enter into details about what was wrong with Buchanan because this might give offense. He mentions with some satisfaction that another Scottish writer, Adam Blackwood, is working on another history of Scotland to refute Buchanan's. The three references to Buchanan in the index are all disparaging. In a lengthy "digression against Buchanan" Thynne reveals the chief reason for this hostility: "his book is 'now iustlie forbidden in England, and (as I heare) more iustlie in Scotland.' " A discourse that draws on Buchanan breaks off to declare that Buchanan is justly forbidden.[10] Thynne was indeed in an awkward position. Buchanan's history, at least in its final phases, had had a strong polemical purpose: it was written to provide a historical and ideological justification for the Protestant coup d'état that had deposed Mary Stuart in favor of her son James. The work's explicit defense of deposition made it unwelcome to the Elizabethan authorities; publication of the work was banned in England, and James VI, securely established on his throne by the time the work appeared, himself had it called in (initially until corrections were made; but no edition was in fact produced in Scotland after 1582). By 1587, Mary's situation was again controversial in England; Elizabeth had indirectly consented to Mary's execution, and the government for a time lifted the veil of diplomatic tact that had surrounded public references to her and permitted the publication of some strongly anti-Marian propaganda. Thynne was thus encouraged to include some of the most vehement passages of Buchanan's history, though even so some dubious theoretical sections were heavily trimmed and much reference was made also to the pro-Marian writings of Bishop John Leslie. The authorities lost their nerve, however, and some leaves were ordered to be cut from the 1587 edition before it was published—including "a detailed account of the sad ends to which Scottish rulers bearing the name of James had come." The English government's quarrel was with Mary, not with James, and most of Buchanan's indictments of her were allowed to stand, with the important proviso that they be presented as personal attacks on a wicked Popish woman rather than as theoretical expositions of the right to resistance.[11]

"Holinshed," then, is not an inert "source" that Shakespeare had to transmute into poetry: in the Scottish chronicle the discourses of Boece and Buchanan, themselves slightly differing in emphasis, are in continual tension with editorial controls. The writing of Scottish history was no less controversial when Shakespeare was composing *Macbeth*. James was now on the English throne and was anxious to repudiate both Buchanan's general political principles and his attacks on his mother. When he learned early in his reign that the French historian de Thou was planning to base the Scottish section of his history of modern Europe on Buchanan, he urged his representatives in France to put pressure on de Thou to take a more favorable view of Mary, and he instructed the English historian Camden to put the record straight in his history of Elizabeth's reign. Camden certainly had his doubts about Buchanan's veracity but resented this kind of political pressure; his history appeared in 1615 with a dedication not to James but to God, his country, and posterity, on the altar of Truth.[12] Thus the merest common prudence would have made it worth Shakespeare's while, when embarking on a Scottish play, to find out where the sources of political controversy lay. In 1604, the King's Men, trying to counter the wave of anti-Scottish propaganda following the king's accession, had staged a *Tragedy of Gowrie* dramatizing the king's escape from a conspiracy; but this play displeased the authorities, presumably because direct representation on the stage was felt to demean the king's dignity.[13] The utmost tact and circumspection were needed even when paying the king the highest compliments.

There is no reason to suppose, however, that Shakespeare's interest in history was confined to political expediency, given his long succession of historical plays. He probably knew Camden personally through their common friend, Ben Jonson. At the time of the king's accession Jonson and Camden had been staying with the antiquarian Robert Cotton, who obligingly inserted "Bruce" into his name to compliment the king. Cotton had a portrait of Buchanan in his house.[14] Jonson owned a copy of Buchanan's history, presented to him by the Scottish poet William Drummond, who was himself to compose a *History of Scotland* which can be regarded as an antidemocratic "answer to Buchanan."[15] Most scholars acknowledge that Shakespeare may have consulted Buchanan, but they are curiously reluctant to acknowledge that he may have been capable of understanding the ideological issues at stake in the study of history. And yet, as we shall see, Shakespeare chose to set his play in a period that both sides in the controversy over Scottish history agreed was a key turning point, a crucial moment for the destiny of monarchy.

Shakespeare's concerns, it may be objected, were those of a dramatist, not a historian, but during the Renaissance such a firm distinction was difficult to make. Buchanan had drawn on his literary skills to compose fictitious orations in which his historical personages explained their motives. Conversely, his play *Baptistes* explores some of the political ideas to which he had given more explicit expression in the treatise *De iure regni*, of which *Baptistes* can be seen as a "poetical draft."[16] By putting dangerous political views into the mouths of dramatic characters, one could disclaim responsibility for them. Buchanan's English admirers, such as Sidney, could publicly express their admiration for his plays more easily than for his historical and political writings. And they themselves used drama as a medium for commenting on Scottish affairs: John Pickering's *Horestes* (1567) used Greek legend to endorse the Leicester circle's campaign for Mary Stuart's execution.[17] In 1590 the Senecan tragedy *Gorboduc*, which had urged that monarchs should consult Parliament over the issue of succession, was reprinted during a propaganda campaign to have James VI recognized as Elizabeth's heir.[18] Sidney regarded *Gorboduc* and Buchanan's plays as the only good British plays produced in his lifetime. His friend Fulke Greville wrote some politically sensitive plays in the 1590s. Greville was a friend of another Senecan dramatist, Matthew Gwynne, who wrote a slightly defensive dedication of his tragedy about Nero to James I, explaining that his play was fully panegyrical even though it portrayed a tyrant. One of Gwynne's friends compared him to Buchanan. It was Gwynne who wrote the address to James on a visit to Oxford which is often held to have inspired *Macbeth*.[19]

If critics have been reluctant to believe that Shakespeare took a sophisticated political interest in Scottish history, it is perhaps because they have assumed that Scottish affairs looked very marginal from an English viewpoint. Despite the subsequent eclipse of his reputation, however, in his own age Buchanan was a commanding figure on the European intellectual scene. And his first writings in defense of the deposition of Mary had been among the earliest salvoes in the war of ideas that had raged throughout Europe in the latter part of the sixteenth century between advocates of resistance to tyrants and champions of absolute monarchy. The radical tract, *Vindiciae contra tyrannos*, drew on Buchanan's precedents from Scottish history; it appeared with a false Edinburgh imprint, and the author styled himself "Stephanus Junius Brutus, Celta."[20] Buchanan had been educated and spent much of his life in France, and his Latin writings may be considered as belonging to the French as much as the Scottish Renaissance. He had been tutor to Montaigne, who took a keen interest in his writings on Scotland. Sixteenth-century Scotland was in some ways more open to innovative intellectual influences than England.[21]

At its most radical, Renaissance humanism championed a decisive break with traditional modes of political thought: the Augustinian assertion of the primacy of the contemplative over the active life, the feudal insistence of the rigid stratification of social ranks, the justification of monarchical and ecclesiastical legitimacy by appeal to institutional continuity. In England the full reception of the more rationalistic Roman law was impeded by the continuing authority of the tradition-based common law, and political discourse remained strongly influenced by the language of custom and precedent. Relations between monarch and Parliament might become strained but were not fully conceptualized into a clash of opposing principles. The Church of England took care to emphasize its institutional continuity with older religious forms and resisted Puritan demands to make more radical breaks with the past; the English Reformation could be seen as something handed down from above by the monarch. In Scotland, however, the Reformation had involved more of an active struggle against the monarchy and could thus be seen as something made by civic activism; the English apocalyptic myth of the "godly prince" proved harder to establish there. Demands for participation in church government by an elective, Presbyterian system were correspondingly greater. The reforms of the educational system championed by Peter Ramus, resisted by Oxford and Cambridge, were introduced at Scottish universities. Scotland did not have a full equivalent of the English common law, and the language of tradition did not play such an important part in Scottish political discourse. Scottish traditions in any case involved an ambivalent attitude toward the monarchy, combining fierce pride in the antiquity of the royal house with a willingness to take action against individual rulers who stepped out of line. As an English member of Parliament put it in 1605, the Scots "have not suffered above two kings to die in their beds, these 200 years."[22]

The three main Scottish historians of the sixteenth century—John Major, Hector Boece, and George Buchanan—had all studied at the Sorbonne when it was a center of radical political thought, and their histories reveal a common hostility toward absolute monarchy. Major was indeed primarily a theological and political theorist in the "conciliarist" tradition, and he turned to history late in his career in order to illustrate his views. When describing the deposition of John Baliol in favor of Robert the Bruce, he pauses for the observation that "the King holds his right as king of a free people, nor can he grant that right to any one against the will of that people."[23] Major's ideas were grounded in scholastic philosophy rather than in humanism; but the histories of Boece and Buchanan are in a more literary and moralistic vein. Buchanan often cuts out episodes narrated by Boece; sometimes he seems to be differing from Boece simply in order to display his own independence. At all events, his history is often more concise than Boece's and somewhat different in emphasis. But it is possible to paint a composite picture of their interpretation of Scottish history, which differs from earlier chronicles by a much greater interest in constitutional and ideological issues.

Boece's introductory "Description of Scotland" presents the course of Scottish history in a manner familiar to students of Roman and Renaissance republican writers. He idealizes the austere virtues of the Scottish people of old and laments that they have since fallen into decadent and luxurious ways. This decline is reflected in the introduction of new social distinctions and the "vain puffes" of new titles of honor.[24] These titles are introduced by King Malcolm: thus Boece, at the very beginning of his history, signals as a source of historic decline the creation of the earldoms that Shakespeare places prominently in the last speech of his play. Boece goes on to describe the early history of Scotland before these signs of corruption appeared. He proudly declared that he had found a new source that threw much new light on early Scottish history; Major had had to give a perfunctory account of this period. Boece claimed to have discovered an old chronicle, by one "Veremund," which gave much more detailed information than any other source about the early years of the Scottish monarchy, between Fergus I, founder of the dynasty, and Fergus II, who reigned in the fifth century. This chronicle emphasized that from the very beginning of Scottish history the nobility had had the right to depose tyrannical rulers. On his arrival in Scotland Fergus asks the people whether they would prefer to be ruled by one man or by the aristocracy collectively, and the vote is for a monarchy. But it appears that this decision is not a binding one for future occasions, for on Fergus's death the matter is discussed again. Boece reports a debate between those who favored a system of primogeniture and those who preferred a more indirect system of succession to avoid the evils attendant on a minority; if the deceased king's son were under age, the succession should pass to his brother, whose nephew would succeed thereafter.[25] There was some historical foundation for this debate: for many centuries the Scottish monarchy did follow the Celtic system of "tanistry" in which the succession passed down not by direct primogeniture but by alternation between different branches of the royal house. Earlier chroniclers who had noted this fact, such as John of Fordun, had not paid it any particular attention; it was simply a peculiarity in the transfer of authority which had led to a certain amount of confusion and inconvenience and eventually gave way to primogeniture.[26]

In the chronicle of Veremund, however, the old system takes on new ideological significance. The narrative of early Scottish history repeatedly records occasions when rulers became tyrannical and were deposed by the nobility. Kings who had been described in earlier sources as good rulers who died in office were transformed into evil authoritarians who were justly deposed. There can be little doubt that the chronicle of Veremund was in fact a fabrication devised to justify the events of 1488, when a group of noblemen overthrew James III and had him killed.[27] Boece, whose interests were not primarily political, may have been genuinely deceived by the forgery; but by the time Buchanan came to finish his history, the Welsh antiquary Humphrey Lhuyd had published a scathing attack on Veremund's "fictions." Buchanan may have been at least half-convinced by Lhuyd's arguments; but the early kings were too ideologically important to his whole conception of Scottish history for him to sacrifice them, and he retained their stories, though cutting down details apart from what he considered to be the essential factors—the consistent actions of the people in overthrowing bad kings.[28]

This healthy state of affairs is first threatened by the eightieth king since Fergus, King Kenneth III. Kenneth comes to power, in standard Scottish fashion, after his predecessor, Cullen, has been deposed by an assembly of nobles for his tyrannical behavior. By the normal conventions Kenneth should have been succeeded by his nephew, Malcolm Duff, who had been proclaimed Prince of Cumberland. But Kenneth is overcome by what Boece calls "the blind love he bare to his owne issue" and has Malcolm Duff murdered. Kenneth proceeds to change the laws of succession, introducing a system of primogeniture and proclaiming that his son Malcolm will succeed him. Boece puts into Kenneth's mouth a speech in which he argues that the old system instituted after Fergus's death had led to chaos.[29] He succeeds in intimidating the nobility, including Constantine, the rightful successor after Malcolm Duff according to the old law, and the constitutional change is voted through. But Kenneth is haunted by guilt at the selfish pride in his own blood that led him to murder the lawful successor, and he is eventually assassinated by one of Malcolm Duff's relatives. Many noblemen have refused to accept the validity of Kenneth's change in the laws, and there is a protracted civil war between the supporters of Malcolm and those of Constantine, who assumes the throne on the basis of the older laws. Buchanan puts into Constantine's mouth a long oration rejecting the principle of hereditary kingship: "What could be more foolish than to withdraw that, which above every thing else was the most important, from the decision and suffrages of the wise, and commit it to the will of fortune; and to bind themselves to obey a child, forced upon them by the accident of birth?" Kenneth's new law was in fact not a law but "a shackling of public liberty."[30] On Constantine's death, Grim, the nephew of Malcolm Duff, is elected at Scone, but Malcolm rallies his forces and imposes on Grim a compromise settlement: Grim will retain the crown during his lifetime, but thereafter it will pass to Malcolm and his sons by direct primogeniture. On Grim's death, Malcolm assembles the nobility at Scone and makes them swear to observe the laws established by Kenneth. Eventually, however, Malcolm becomes tyrannical, and the nobility, reverting to old traditions, have him put to death.

At this point Buchanan opens a new book of his history with the words, "I have shown in the former book, the keen pertinacity with which Kenneth and his son Malcolm, endeavoured to fix the hereditary succession to the throne; with what felicity will appear in the sequel." We are invited to read the period up to Alexander III— including the stories of Duncan, Macbeth, and Malcolm—as illustrating the relative merits of elective and hereditary kingship. The introduction continues with a further attack on primogeniture, arguing that under such a system we "commit the power over the whole people, to such as have no power over themselves." The new law risked making tyranny perpetual. In any case, the desire to perpetuate one's name is often futile; an attempt to give "that which is weak, fluctuating, and obnoxious to every accident, an eternity, which they neither have themselves, nor can expect to have."[31]

Like many republican writers, Buchanan contrasts the instability and subjection to Fortune that ensue from personal rule with the greater degree of rational choice permitted by an elective system. In the case of King Kenneth, fate punishes dynastic ambition: just as the voice of conscience had warned him, his plans are futile, for his son dies without male heirs. A system that was meant to decrease political instability has led only to civil war. Malcolm does have two daughters, however, and the succession goes to the son of one of them, Duncan. According to the new system, Duncan would expect to be succeeded by his son Malcolm. But there were still noblemen whose allegiance was to the older system according to which Macbeth, son of Malcolm's other daughter, would have had a strong claim. Macbeth is indeed given heart by a prophecy from three "nymphs." Shortly after this, however, Duncan dashes Macbeth's hopes by nominating not Macbeth but Malcolm as Prince of Cumberland. Boece emphasizes Macbeth's political motives: under the "old lawes" he had a "just quarell" to take the throne.[32] He gives greater weight to Macbeth's claims by arguing that Duncan had his faults as a ruler, that his excessive clemency led to increasing disorder; Macbeth, though too cruel, would have kept better order in the realm. Thus his murder of Duncan, which is passed over without much comment by Boece, appears as just one more in a line of depositions, sanctioned by the nobility, of ineffective or tyrannical rulers.

For much of his reign Macbeth is a good ruler; only after ten years does his conscience drive him into tyranny. Buchanan, who is fond of sharper moral contrasts, amplifies Macbeth's guilt and does not justify it with a political motive. It is legitimate for public-spirited groups of noblemen to put a tyrant to death; but Duncan, whatever his defects, is not a tyrant, and Buchanan presents Macbeth as motivated by personal ambition rather than a concern to defend the old laws. The nobility eventually decide to depose him in favor of Malcolm. This is a politically ambiguous act. It could be read as a decisive acceptance of primogeniture; conversely, Malcolm would have had a good claim to succeed Macbeth under the old system. (Boece and Buchanan mention the fact, omitted by Shakespeare, that Macbeth had a son who was killed by Macduff.) Malcolm certainly tries to consolidate the hereditary system, introducing new titles of honor. Boece, as has been seen, condemns these titles, noting that they introduced inequalities between noblemen who had formerly been equal. Buchanan describes the new titles as "barbarous" and links them with the Stuart dynasty by declaring that "thanus" sometimes gave way to "Stuartus." He has already condemned Malcolm II for attempting to introduce new titles—"empty sounds"—observing that before his reign there were no titles save thane, sheriff, and knight.[33] Malcolm III had become a figure of legendary piety in Scottish history, and Boece and Buchanan give broadly favorable accounts of him. Boece mentions, however, that he brought with him from England not only the new titles but also a large number of English courtiers and various courtly luxuries. Boece reports that the nobles begged the king to return to the nation's ancient sobriety. On Boece's account there is a nationalist backlash, and on Malcolm's death the old controversy about the succession breaks out again. His son Duncan claims the throne but is opposed by his brother Donalbain, who champions older traditions of cultural austerity and elective monarchy. Donalbain kills Duncan in battle, and Boece records that most of the people approved of this act.

From this point Boece and Buchanan begin to part company in their interpretation of events. Boece's initial "Description" represented the establishment of hereditary monarchy under Malcolm as the start of a regrettable lapse from earlier austerity. The chronicler Veremund, with his insistence on the people's power to depose tyrants, lived in the reign of Malcolm: Veremund's view of history can thus be seen as expressing the viewpoint of those who dislike Kenneth's new laws. Boece also invented the story of Banquo, ancestor of the Stuart dynasty, and the later part of his narrative, once it is accepted that the new system of succession is irreversible, turns into a more orthodox account of the triumph of the Stuart dynasty. This more courtly viewpoint anticipates the researches of Shakespeare's contemporary, Sir Thomas Craig, who traced the foundation of feudalism in Scotland to the reigns of Kenneth, Malcolm II, Macbeth, and Malcolm III. For Craig, a firm legitimist, the fact that Scotland established feudalism before England is a source of national pride.[34] Buchanan was not so sure, however, that Malcolm III's reign marked a decisive turning point. If he did not insist as much as Boece on the corruption of manners under Malcolm, it was perhaps because he was reluctant to concede that the older traditions had ever been completely abandoned. Again and again in the later sections of his narrative, the nobility shake off the yoke of tyrannous rulers. When dealing with the reign of James IV, he argues that it was quite legitimate to appoint a regent who was not in the direct line of succession because the innovations of Kenneth III had proved to lead to instability and had been discarded.[35] And in the most recent stage of Scottish history, the aftermath of Mary's deposition, Buchanan describes a long statement by the Earl of Morton—which may in reality have been drafted by Buchanan—in which he justified the coup by reference to the Scottish tradition of limited monarchy: the people had given power to the monarchy in the first instance only on strict conditions, and if those conditions were not fulfilled they had every right to depose their rulers.[36]

Buchanan's history of Scotland was, then, effectively an extended political treatise. Its political standpoint is wholly in harmony with the more systematic theory of kingship that Buchanan presented in *De iure regni*, which was probably first drafted in the late 1560s at the same time as the bulk of his work on the history. This work is in a quasi-dramatic form, a dialogue in which the conservative Thomas Maitland puts forward stock arguments in favor of order and degree and is firmly answered by Buchanan. At one stage Maitland claims that although it may be legitimate to depose an elected ruler, the Scottish monarchy is hereditary and hence resistance is never justified. This gives Buchanan a cue for a discourse on Scottish history. Who, he asks, grieved over the death of James III? The estates voted that he had been justly slain. Up to the time of Kenneth III, the sovereignty of the people in creating kings and controlling the succession was clear. Kenneth's new law was introduced either by persuasion or by force. If by force, it would soon have been changed back, for laws introduced by force may be undone by force. If by persuasion, it is inconceivable that the people would have made such a huge concession—for all kings wish to have control over the succession, this being a major prop of their power—had they not demanded some benefits in return, such as new limitations on the royal prerogative. Thus if the monarchs reneged on their part of the agreement, the people would still retain the right to depose them.[37]

At the basis of Buchanan's thought is a critical rationalism that is hostile to all forms of unreasoning submission to traditional institutions and hierarchies. His scorn for tradition, in fact, limits the direct political significance of his history: despising those who justify absolutism by reference to tradition, he is unwilling to ground his own theory of limited monarchy on custom and precedent alone. When Maitland complains in the *De iure regni* that regimes Buchanan attacks as tyrannical are established by custom, Buchanan replies that custom is a tyrant, that we should follow instead the principles of reason.[38] And in the history Morton justifies Mary's deposition by reference not just to Scottish positive laws and tradition but to natural law: the principle of mutual consent between ruler and governed is "not one of these laws which are obnoxious to the change of times, but is one of those statutes which, in the primary constitution of our nature, are stamped upon the heart, are verified by the mutual consent of almost every people, and, like the universe itself, must remain unbroken and eternal." Morton goes on to cite as the best examples of such conformity to the laws of nature the constitutions of ancient Athens, Sparta, and Rome and of modern Venice—all of them, of course, republican.[39]

Buchanan's wariness about historical precedents may reflect his increasing unease about the validity of the chronicles of Veremund; but in any case his interests ultimately lay in what he considered to be general, rational principles rather than in mere precedent. Virtuous action was a matter of transcending corrupt traditions in order to affirm true rationality. Thus whereas for absolutist theorists tyrannicide was the most monstrous of all crimes, infinitely worse than the murder of a commoner, for Buchanan as for many Italian republicans it was veritably a type of virtuous action, a vindication of reason. In trying to introduce primogeniture Kenneth III was subjecting the realm to the vagaries of Fortune; rule by the many, for Buchanan, was much more rational than rule by one fallible individual. Buchanan did make concessions to some of the traditional prejudice against the "many-headed monster" as inherently irrational; but he argued that an elected assembly could escape such limitations and become far more rational than any decisions reached in private by a monarch. Buchanan is entirely vague about just how many of the people should be represented in such an assembly. At one point he speaks of the greater part of the population, but it is not clear whether this is a qualitative or quantitative judgment, referring to the nobility or to the people as a whole.[40] But in his play *Baptistes*, which has much in common with the *De iure regni*, Buchanan repeatedly presents unfavorably those who speak with scorn of the people, in the broadest

sense of the *mobile vulgus;* those he admires are open to arguments
from below, are willing to recognize that men of ability equal to princes
may come from the lower orders. However defined, the people definitely have the right to depose a tyrant. Tyrannicide is therefore a
heroic act, redeeming public rationality from private passion. Buchanan's rationalism makes him wary of introducing theological terms
into his discourse, but he is prepared to argue that tyrannicide may
be inspired by a divine calling:

> God has called poor and almost unknown men from the ranks of the
> common people to execute vengeance on an arrogant and worthless tyrant.
> God, as has been said before, orders evil persons put out of the way; nor
> does he except any rank, or sex, or condition, or person whatsoever; and
> kings have from him no consideration that is denied to beggars.[41]

Buchanan points out that the ancient Greeks provided public rewards
and honors for those who killed tyrants. Renaissance republicans
were reviving the iconography of classical republicanism: Lorenzino
de Medici had marked his assassination of his tyrannical cousin Ales-
sandro by a medal in imitation of Brutus's coin commemorating the
murder of Caesar, with daggers and a cap of liberty on the obverse.[42]
Buchanan used rather similar iconography for a coin he designed
after Mary's deposition. As an emblem of the crown's proper relationship to the people he presented a crown balanced on the point
of a sword, with the motto: "pro me (se mereor) in me" (if I deserve
it the blade will be used in my defense, if not it will be turned against
me).[43]

It is not surprising that King James was still having nightmares
about his old tutor many years after his death. James reacted very
firmly against Buchanan's precepts. He could, of course, gain a certain
amount of prestige from having been educated by this much-admired
humanist, and it became acceptable at his court to admire Buchanan's
poetic skills while lamenting that he had been led astray by dubious
political ideas.[44] James's own treatise, *The True Law of Free Monarchies*
(1598), drastically revised Buchanan's political priorities. A number
of polemicists, including Adam Blackwood and Ninian Winzet, had
already taken issue with Buchanan's reading of Scottish history, contesting the notion that the people had ever had the right to depose
tyrants and arguing that in any case that right had long since been
abrogated by the changes in the succession laws. James briskly dismissed the whole historiographical tradition started by Veremund by
insisting that there had never been an elective element in the Scottish
monarchy, that Fergus and his successors "were the authors & makers

of the lawes, and not the lawes of the Kings." Scotland was a "free Monarchie" in the sense that the ruler could not be bound in any way by a political contract: in theory he had duties to his subjects, but the subjects had no right to enforce them. He rejected the analogies Buchanan had made between the Scottish constitution and that of Venice with its "limited government." Subjects therefore had no right to resist tyrants: they must simply be patient.[45]

Recent historians have argued that James's political practice was cautious and constitutional, but there can be no doubt that his theory represented a radical break with earlier traditions and completely contradicted the assumptions that were present from beginning to end of Buchanan's history.[46] James did not, however, succeed in obliterating the memory of Buchanan's history; it reportedly became "the most widely read book in the covenanting armies," and after the execution of Charles I it was frequently cited by defenders of the regicide. The parliamentarian propagandist John Hall of Durham, urging the Scots to reject monarchy, gave a twenty-page summary of Buchanan in order to make Scottish history appear a grisly black comedy, with monarchs constantly degenerating into tyranny and the people overthrowing them but never learning enough from their history to reject the institution altogether. Another republican turned to early Scottish history to contrast the heroic freedom of the Scots nobility with the present *"emasculated"* state of the aristocracy.[47]

III

Shakespeare's task in writing *Macbeth* was, then, extremely problematic. The most prestigious recent history of his chosen period was under a ban from his royal patron; earlier versions of the story were under attack as either politically suspect or inauthentic. In *The Royal Play of "Macbeth,"* H. N. Paul argued that James must have adopted the royal viewpoint. Such critics as L. C. Knights, Maynard Mack, and Wilbur Sanders, though reluctant to concede that Shakespeare would have descended to political propaganda, present a view of his play that, perhaps unconsciously, echoes the most determined of absolutist theorists. They see the play as presenting an absolute choice between natural, harmonious, monarchical order and an amoral energy that, though exercising an imaginative appeal, ultimately descends to barbarism and savagery.[48] There is little suggestion in such analyses that Renaissance writers might have been concerned with liberty and the rights of the people as well as with order, let alone that killing a king might have been regarded in some circumstances as a virtuous act rather than the quintessence of absolute Evil.

More recently Michael Hawkins has questioned such one-sided readings, calling attention to a number of highly problematic areas.[49] Shakespeare could, had he chosen, have made Banquo a less shadowy and ambiguous figure, and thus made the dynastic compliment more direct. Why does he cooperate with Macbeth even after Duncan's murder? If Macbeth's ambition to found a dynasty is evil, is it so very different from Banquo's "hope" (III.i.10)? Duncan himself is a less unambiguously admirable figure than some critics have assumed. We see him at the opening of the play standing piously by and applauding the bloody deeds he lets Macbeth do for him; and he is no very impressive judge of character. Critics tend to exaggerate his sacramental character: unlike Edward the Confessor, he does not have magical powers. The abruptness with which he switches from rewarding Macbeth to nominating his son Prince of Cumberland—if it is not to be explained in terms of authorial or editorial cuts—seems somewhat clumsy and perhaps allows the audience to sympathize a little with Macbeth's sense of being excluded.[50] If Duncan has to nominate his son, presumably the implication is that he could have nominated someone else, that the system is not one of pure primogeniture. If Macbeth is a usurper who holds "the due of birth" (III.vi.25) from Malcolm, it is difficult to see why the nobility, including Banquo, apparently accept his succession in the first place. But if he is a lawfully anointed sovereign, would James have been pleased by a play representing his overthrow? The legitimists are shown to need the aid of the English, and Scotland is represented as a wild and lawless country. Is the play really an appropriate compliment to a Scottish king? Macduff and Malcolm, the restorers of legitimacy, are slightly ambiguous figures. Macduff abandons his wife at a moment of crisis. Malcolm's sudden shift in act IV, scene iii from self-denunciation to pious self-praise is disconcerting to audiences; and his language is decidedly wooden in comparison with Macbeth's. When he describes Macbeth as

> bloody,
> Luxurious, avaricious, false, deceitful,
> Sudden, malicious, smacking of every sin
> That has a name (IV.iii.57–60)

the audience is likely to feel this indictment as a somewhat external, propagandistic view of a man to whom we have given considerable imaginative sympathy. As Hawkins drily observes, the list includes "vices which Macbeth himself hardly had time, let alone inclination, to commit." Malcolm's concluding speech has a similar aura of stiff, official language: "we shall not spend a large expense of time" is not the most eloquent opening, and the description of Macbeth as a "dead butcher" does not do justice to our experience of the play.

Macbeth is certainly not crude propaganda: it is a tragedy, not a masque. But it may also be misleading to conclude that Shakespeare is not really interested in ideological issues, that his real concerns are pragmatic and that he keeps opposing viewpoints completely open. Hawkins's view is in keeping with a tendency among recent historians of the Jacobean era to minimize the significance of ideological conflicts in that period; but it may be that an understandable desire to avoid anachronism has led them to underestimate the contemporary interest in theoretical issues. It is true that Duncan's Scotland is not, on closer examination, an ideal polity calculated to gratify James's national pride. As long as some credence was given to Veremund, however, it was difficult for a monarch to look back on early Scottish history with complete satisfaction. As has been seen, James tried simply to deny the whole tradition of limited monarchy, but this was harder to do when it came to specific and much-chronicled examples. *Macbeth* is set in a period when the dynasty was at last starting to strengthen royal authority, but the process is seen to be as yet imperfect. Scotland lacks civility; and James did not share Buchanan's enthusiasm for the rugged virtues of the old Highlanders. The opening of the play presents the disorder that was seen in Boece and Buchanan as springing from rejection of the elective system and implies that the real cause is the weakness of the principle of legitimacy. And the strengthening of this principle will require pragmatism as well as piety, cunning tactics in order to procure virtuous long-term ends. James proceeded in his project of strengthening royal authority in precisely this way, and even his theoretical writings acknowledged the need for cunning as well as holiness. Moreover, the Scottish polity in the time of Duncan is incomplete in another way: it is cut off from England. The union of the two nations was one of James's most cherished projects, and his enthusiasm for it cut across merely nationalist sentiments. Shakespeare handles this issue with characteristic tact. English supporters of a Stuart succession had tried to combat hostility toward rule by a foreigner by arguing that many Scottish kings had paid homage to English monarchs, that in this sense Scotland really was already united with England. One of the examples often cited was Malcolm's paying homage to Edward the Confessor. Several plays in Elizabeth's last years—including a lost play about King Malcolm—treated this theme of homage, drawing on Holinshed.[51] Such arguments aroused the fury of many Scottish writers, who attacked Holinshed for falsifying the evidence to suit English nationalism.[52]

Neither Boece nor Buchanan had shown any enthusiasm for the idea of union. Writing for a predominantly English audience at a time when anti-Scottish sentiment was very strong, Shakespeare presents English aid to a Scottish king in a favorable light but does not bring Edward on stage; consequently Malcolm's exact relationship to him remains ambiguous. In a panegyric published in 1605, Sir George Buc presented the alliance between Malcolm and Edward as prefiguring the Union and traced James's ancestry on the English side back to Edward.[53] *Macbeth* looks forward to a future beyond its own epoch. As for the problem of overthrowing an anointed king, the play is set in a period of constitutional uncertainty, and even a firmly promonarchical writer like Bodin was prepared to justify the overthrow of a legitimate ruler who became a tyrant provided that the intervention was supported by a foreign prince.[54]

Many of the anomalies and contradictions in *Macbeth* can be explained not as manifestations of Shakespeare's desire to remain totally neutral but as difficulties inherent in the source material. In Holinshed there is a constant tension between some of the views held by Boece or Buchanan and the editor's controlling voice. This does not mean that the editor is neutral but that he is dependent, as a historian, on sources of which he does not fully approve. Once committed to a historical subject that was perhaps originally selected for its dynastic theme, Shakespeare could not have avoided some of the difficulties without changing well-established facts. What he could do was to remain silent about some problematic areas. As Hawkins points out, Shakespeare omits the long period when, all sources agreed, Macbeth ruled well.[55] By making him lapse into a tyrant immediately on taking office, Shakespeare gives the impression that bad rule follows inevitably from lack of legitimacy. Among the Scottish historians, by contrast, the emphasis is on the almost inevitably corrupting effects of power, so that it is essential for there to be machinery to remove a bad ruler. Shakespeare, however, evades the central issue of the debates over the Scottish monarchy, that of accountability. Hawkins argues that James might have been better pleased by an overt presentation of the ideological debates between different systems and a demonstration that primogeniture was preferable. But James took strong exception when a debate on the relative merits of elective and hereditary monarchy was staged before him on a visit to Cambridge. The very act of laying hereditary rule open to too much rational questioning could be held to undermine its mystique.[56] It is unlikely that many people in the audience would have noticed the vestigial elements of the older system that can be traced in the play; but if Shakespeare had tried to dramatize the issues explicitly, he would have run into difficulties.

This can be illustrated by another Jacobean attempt to transform Macbeth's reign into imaginative literature: the abortive epic *La Stuartide* by the French Calvinist Jean de Schelandre (1611). Schelandre, who was also a dramatist, may have seen a performance of *Macbeth*, but the play had not yet been printed. In any case it is clear that he did his research independently, drawing on Boece and Buchanan rather than Holinshed. He dedicated the poem to Prince Henry, and the hero, Fleance, is taken as a model for the young prince. But there are passages concerning his father Banquo, including a scene in which Macbeth complains to his friend that Duncan's nomination of Malcolm as Prince of Cumberland has done him an injustice: Macbeth has served Duncan much more than Malcolm, whose only virtue is that he happens to be the king's son. In his reply Banquo makes fully explicit the constitutional issues that are left mysterious in the comparable scene in Shakespeare (II.i). Banquo sympathizes with Macbeth and seems to be allying himself with the faction that contested the change in the laws of succession; his voice is that of Buchanan's political rationalism:

> Les vieilles loix ne sont tant abolies
> (Qu'oy qu'on ait fait au siecle[a] precedent)
> Que par merite on n'aille succedant,
> Et que la brigue (estant le peuple arbitre)
> De[b] Constantin le dernier de ce titre
> Ne puisse encor l'emporter vne fois;
> Les royautés doiuent tomber au choix,
> Et n'est raison qu'vn si gros apanage,
> Don personnel, se tourne en heritage . . .
>
> > [a] Kenneth III. fut le premier qui
> > rendit la couronne hereditaire
> >
> > [b] Qui rompit la loy de Kenneth

Such sentiments, however, are not exactly tactful in a poem designed to celebrate the Stuart dynasty and dedicated to James's own son; and Banquo suddenly shifts ground from the rationalistic to the patriarchal:

> L'enfant Malcolme à vous est preferé . . .
> Mais vn bon pere ayme sa geniture,

«Et d'estre pere à vn pere on deffend
«Luy deffendant d'aggrandir son enfant.[57]

Schelandre seems to have felt unable to unite these conflicting elements in his source material with his panegyric purpose; a few pages later Banquo is spirited away by supernatural forces and the poem breaks off.

Shakespeare chooses not to confront the constitutional issue so directly. Insofar as he does retain episodes that indicate older constitutional forms, he shifts the emphasis: where in Boece and Buchanan there is much stress on the active role of the nobility in choosing and deposing their rulers, in *Macbeth* references to elections are normally cast in the passive voice and are assimilated to the workings of Fortune. Macbeth concludes that "Chance"—not the people—may crown him (I.iii.144). The episode in which Duncan nominates Malcolm presents the king as sole source of the title; Duncan adds that he will scatter new "signs of nobleness" on his followers, so that the nobility are seen as reflecting, not creating, the king's glory (I.iv.41). The signs of honor are compared to stars, thus linking the social hierarchy with the natural order: Macbeth has to urge the stars to hide their fires if he is to overthrow Duncan (I.iv.50). Although we are told that the nobility have named Macbeth as Duncan's successor, both nomination and election take place offstage, and again there is no emphasis on the conscious agency of the nobility. Ross and Macduff speak of the nomination in the passive voice: "the sovereignty will fall upon Macbeth. . . . he is already nam'd and gone to Scone / To be invested . . . / may you see things well done there" (II.iv.30–37). Macduff warns that their "old robes" may "sit easier than our new": the recurrent clothing imagery implies that traditionally sanctified "signs of nobleness" have a natural dignity denied to the robes worn or conferred by the usurper. Before long the official line is that Macbeth is an "untitled tyrant" who holds "the due of birth" from Malcolm (IV.iii.104, III.vi.25). This means that the concluding acclamation by the nobility appears as a mere confirmation of an established right, not as a transfer of power.

Shakespeare's play, then, seems to be an attempt to revise the more radical views implicit in its sources, rather than an impartial survey. This does not mean, however, that the play is a direct echo of James's propaganda. There were, after all, different ways of reacting against Buchanan's insistent rationalism. James had chosen the option of building up a systematic alternative theory, but another of Buchanan's old pupils, Montaigne, chose a different course. Feeling that democratic and rationalistic ideas had nourished the passions and rebellions that threatened to eradicate civility in France, Montaigne adopted what Quentin Skinner has called an "almost Burkean form of conservatism," urging awareness of the irredeemably irrational elements in human motivation that seemed to render custom and tradition more important than reason.[58] Montaigne bought a copy of his old teacher's history of Scotland and read with interest both the *De iure regni* and Blackwood's reply. Montaigne took issue with both sides in the debate: "The popular makes the King to be of worse condition than a Carter: and he that extolleth Monarchy, placeth him both in power and soveraignty, many steps above the Gods."[59] But Montaigne's stance of neutrality already committed him to rejecting theories of resistance and hence in some measure to throwing his weight behind those who were strengthening royal authority. Montaigne influenced Shakespeare a great deal, and it may well be that he would have viewed the debate between Buchanan and his adversaries in similar terms. All Shakespeare's political plays are arguably as interested in emotional and unconscious motivations for political action as in rational principles: in Richard II's self-humiliation and Bolingbroke's remorseless but seemingly unconscious movement toward the crown, in the disparity between Brutus's republican ideals and the murkier motivations that are hinted at beneath them. In *Macbeth* a reaction against the rationalism of a Buchanan operates not merely in the outline of the plot but at a deeper level of discourse, in innumerable shifts of linguistic emphasis. This process can be illustrated by consideration of his handling of political action in relation to time, of patriarchal order, and of language and dramatic unity.

Buchanan insisted that public action could overcome the power of Fortune and institute a more rational political order. As Pocock has shown, a revaluation of the ideas of Time and Fortune was central to Renaissance political thought.[60] Political action could lay claim to inherent dignity even though it belonged to the lower order of temporality, the *saeculum*, which Augustine had compared unfavorably to celestial *aeternitas*. In Scotland, especially from the 1590s onward, it was the Presbyterians, admirers of Aristotle's *Politics*, who insisted on the dignity of the particulars of political action, claiming that their nation could "escape fortune's wheel and the politics of coup and countercoup by means of a massive and indeed monumental act of social reorganization"—including the creation of the church. Conservatives like James, by contrast, tended to stress "the timeless order underlying all mutation and transience."[61]

Some monarchical theorists claimed that a royal dynasty could lay claim to a special, intermediate order of temporality between *saeculum* and *aeternitas*, the *aevum*. Frank Kermode has suggested that Macbeth should be seen as presumptuously trying to lay claim to the dignity of the *aevum* for his usurping, illegitimate attempt to found a dynasty. Indeed throughout the play a contrast is established between legitimate and illegitimate orders of time and action.[62] Hawkins argues that the play reveals a characteristically Renaissance concern with the active life, but he does not observe how often action that is merely secular and political is revealed as futile.

Macbeth's frenzied activism is closely connected to his unnatural relationship with time. The captain's speech, which introduces us to Macbeth, presents him as vigorously active, "disdaining Fortune," that "rebels' whore"—an image, perhaps, of Machiavellian virtù, but a somewhat sinister one, presented as simultaneously a passive instrument of violence, as "Valour's minion" carving his way to victory like a butcher. Malcolm's final description of him as a "dead butcher" is not, as some critics have argued, without support elsewhere in the play. This sense of strained overactivity is reinforced when the captain compares Banquo and Macbeth to "cannons overcharg'd with double cracks" which "doubly redoubled strokes upon the foe." This echo of the witches' "double, double, toil and trouble" is the first of many verbal links between Macbeth and the dark sisters. Macbeth's doubleness is a manifestation of both restlessness and duplicity. The witches' prophecy stirs in him an ambition to force events, to cut through due process of time. Though at first he decides that chance may crown him without his stir, he cannot allow himself for long to be subject to fortune. Lady Macbeth shares this desire for liberation from time:

> Thy letters have transported me beyond
> This ignorant present, and I feel now
> The future in the instant. (I.v.56–58)

Doubleness and activism are also associated with Lady Macbeth. She welcomes Duncan with the words:

> . . . . All our service,
> In every point twice done, and then done double,
> Were poor and single business, to contend
> Against those honours deep and broad, wherewith
> Your Majesty loads our house. (I.vi.14–18)

Her "double" ominously rhymes with Duncan's "trouble," stirring memories of the witches. She is speaking here of ceremonial action, of what her husband has described as the loyalty which "in doing it, pays itself": they "do but what they should, by doing everything Safe toward your love and honour" (I.vi.23–27). In fact Macbeth and his wife have no real regard for decorous, ceremonial action; they strip from their acts all traditional ritual meanings.

Macbeth himself has an anguished recognition that he is going against the natural order. His soliloquy before the murder begins by presenting him as motivated by Machiavellian virtù:

> If it were done, when 'tis done, then 'twere well
> It were done quickly: if th' assassination
> Could trammel up the consequence, and catch
> With his surcease success; that but this blow
> Might be the be-all and the end-all—here,
> But here, upon this bank and shoal of time,
> We'd jump the life to come. (I.vii.1–7)

Macbeth goes on to claim that only secular, not eternal, considerations make him hesitate, but already his language is beginning to betray an awareness of the transcendental order he is consciously rejecting. "Success," in the sense of completed action, conjures up the associations with hierarchical succession and legitimacy that Macbeth is trying to suppress; the sibilants explode in his face. It is Lady Macbeth who recalls him to action, seizing on another sense of "doing"—that of sexual performance. When Macbeth says that "I dare do all that may become a man; / Who dares do more, is none," she taunts him for his lack of virility, and he is led to praise her as worthy of bringing forth "men-children": it is she who has the virtù. The conspiring couple thus becomes linked again with the moral and sexual disorder of the witches, who exclaim orgiastically, "I'll do, I'll do, and I'll do." Lady Macbeth strips any moral or supernatural aura from political action, and all that remains is the bare, dehumanized "perform": "What cannot you and I perform upon / Th'unguarded Duncan?" (I.vii.70–71). The hallucinatory dagger that leads Macbeth toward the murder is a stock republican emblem of tyrannicide and the vigilant defense of liberty (consecrated by Buchanan in the coin he designed). There is a heavy irony in Macbeth's comparison of himself to Tarquin, whose rape of Lucretia led to the fall of the Roman monarchy; here, perhaps, we can feel subtextual pressure. The comparison also foregrounds the links between his deed and perverted sexuality. There is a note of despair in his words, "it is done" (II.i.62), for his earlier soliloquy recognized that it was not done when it was done; in its very unceremonious bareness the phrase also evokes the *consummatum est*. His deed is against nature and time: the earth threatens to "take the present horror from the time," and in murdering sleep, he has destroyed the natural rhythm of time. From now on he can survive only by suppressing his deed from his own consciousness: "To know my deed, 'twere best not know myself" (II.ii.72).

Critics have noted that Shakespeare borrowed from Buchanan some of the details of Macbeth's remorse, but not that he inverts the assumptions behind Buchanan's account of Kenneth III's grief, making the disruption, not the establishment, of a hereditary system the source of guilt.[63] His words to Lennox are not entirely insincere: he recognizes that Duncan's murder has destroyed a "Blessed time," has demystified "mortality" until there is nothing "serious" in it. His own coronation is an empty act, "things" that are "well done." Macbeth perceives Banquo's relation to temporality as quite different from his own: "every minute of his being thrusts / Against my near'st of life" (III.i.116–117). The *aevum* of the royal dignity is to become perpetual in his dynasty. Time, like the social order, is hierarchically structured, a stately progress from generation to generation by hereditary right. The witches may try in the short term to disrupt this universal order, but they cannot overrule it. Macbeth's attempts to "make assurance double sure," to make his dissimulating deeds bear fruit, are futile. No longer daring to act directly himself, he enlists as instruments others who are willing to resist fortune (III.i.77, 111); but his vain complaint to Banquo's ghost that "thou canst not say, I did it" rings hollow (III.iv.49). More and more his mind becomes dissociated from his body, his thoughts from his words; he becomes a mere machine for generating deeds:

> Strange things I have in head, that will to hand,
> Which must be acted, ere they may be scann'd (III.iv.138–139).

> Time, thou anticipat'st my dread exploits:
> The flighty purpose never is o'ertook,
> Unless the deed goes with it. From this moment,
> The very firstling of my heart shall be
> The firstlings of my hand. . . .
> This deed I'll do, before this purpose cool. (IV.i.144–149)

Under Macbeth's rule time is fertile only in crime: the grief "of an hour's age doth hiss the speaker; / Each minute teems a new one" (IV.iii.175–176). The more he reduces himself to naked, unceremonious action, the more empty time becomes for him: "recorded time" is no more than a series of empty syllables (V.v.21). His adversary Macduff brings in his severed head with the cry that "the time is free"; and Malcolm announces that his coronation will be performed "in measure, time, and place." It is certainly true that Malcolm and

Macduff have had to act themselves and to resort to doubleness and equivocation. Macduff has been "untimely ripp'd' from his mother's womb" (V.viii.16); the antithesis between "natural" and "unnatural" forces is not absolute. Malcolm may well be a more effective ruler than the saintly Duncan precisely because he will not have to delegate unpleasant military matters so completely to men of war. The fact remains that Malcolm's actions are finally in harmony with a wider principle of legitimacy, and that without that legitimacy, however competent he might be, his rule would be felt to lack something. It was, after all, Caesar, the founder of the imperial dynasty, who gave his name to Macduff's "unnatural" birth.

This emphasis on natural succession is strengthened by the constant analogies between king and father. Buchanan had tended to stress the distinctions between public and private roles: government was a rational activity that required consultation with large numbers of advisers to avoid the ruler's becoming swayed by personal emotions. As he pointed out, the republican hero Lucius Junius Brutus put public duty above patriarchal responsibilities by condemning his own monarchist sons to death.[64] His dislike of irrationality and emotionalism in politics was the main reason for his hostility to rule by women, who seemed to him the quintessence of unreason. To be governed by a woman was to be subject to Fortune, to mere whim and caprice: women, he believed, found it harder than men to distinguish between the public and the private.[65] In the *History* he almost always associates tyranny with lust, with abandonment of the self-control necessary for rational government. James agreed with Buchanan that lust was a distinctive feature of tyrants, but he also gave a more positive emphasis to the ruler's sexuality by stressing the mystical analogies between king and father. In a hereditary monarchy the public and the private, the state and the family were in perfect harmony.

This "patriarchal" tradition of political thought was becoming increasingly influential in the seventeenth century.[66] In *Macbeth* the patriarchal themes are developed. Although Malcolm includes luxuriousness in his list of Macbeth's sins, in fact this point is never developed: Macbeth appears as a ravisher only in the symbolic sense, in comparing himself to Tarquin when about to commit regicide. It is not so much that passion overcomes his reason as that his sexuality becomes displaced from its "natural" patriarchal role. He accuses Malcolm and Donalbain of "parricide" (III.i.31), but his murder of the king is presented as being itself a violation of familial as well as political bonds. Lady Macbeth cannot murder him because he reminds her of her father. And his crime is punished by his inability to become a father himself; his crown is "fruitless," his scepter "barren," and his successor will be "unlineal" (III.i.62). Banquo's ghost later rubs this point in by proudly gesturing at his royal offspring; and his pride in his dynasty is presented as natural and commendable. This emphasis contrasts sharply with Buchanan's constant condemnation of those who confuse public with private concerns. In Buchanan's *History* it is Kenneth who is punished with childlessness for trying to found a more narrowly personal dynasty. Shakespeare invents the scene of the murder of Lady Macduff and her son in order to bring home the "natural" links between the public and the private. Macbeth's rule strikes against the basis of the family. It is appropriate that Macduff, rather than Malcolm, should kill Macbeth: crimes against the family and against the state are avenged in a joint triumph.

Macbeth's disruption of familial order is manifested in his relationship with his wife, whom he allows to usurp the "masculine" role. Shakespeare's apparent inconsistency in making her at one point express a willingness to beat out her baby's brains and describing her elsewhere as childless indicates his concern to emphasize her rejection of the "natural" womanly role. Banquo's description of the exterior of the castle, with the nesting birds' "pendent bed, and procreant cradle" (I.vi.8), contrasts sharply with the unmotherly woman within. The proper female role (in the ideology of the play) is nurturing rather than political action; but Shakespeare does not make such sharp distinctions between male and female roles as does Buchanan. Lady Macbeth's "unnaturalness" manifests itself not only in taking on masculine characteristics herself but also in trying to impose on Macbeth an exaggerated ideal of masculinity as ruthless, dissociated aggression and violence, a Machiavellian virtù devoid of tender emotions. She addresses him as "husband" only after Duncan's murder, but the emotional strains imposed by trying to live out this ideal of public virtù manifest themselves unconsciously. While her conscious mind insists on her goals, her body reveals her remorse first in her faint after the murder and then as she walks in her sleep, recognizing the true end of her cult of amoral activism: "What's done cannot be undone" (V.i.64). The sense of "unnaturalness" in Lady Macbeth's behavior would perhaps have been reinforced in Jacobean productions by the fact that the part would have been played by a boy. The speech in which she calls on the evil spirits to "unsex" her (I.v.41) also contains allusions to the pall and the knife, which were associated with tragic acting. The effect of an "unnatural" sexual charge between Lady Macbeth and her husband may have been heightened by the fact that men who dressed in women's clothes, for whatever reasons, were regarded by many contemporaries as perverting heterosexual identity. The implication is, then, that for a woman to take any kind of political initiative leads to perversion.

On a symbolic plane the many links between Lady Macbeth and the witches reinforce the idea that the inversion of natural sexual roles leads to political disruption. Boece and Buchanan had not emphasized the theme of witchcraft. Boece was vague about the precise identity of the "three in woman's shape" who greeted Macbeth; Buchanan, ever anxious to minimize the mystical and irrational, speaks only of "three women . . . of more than human stature."[67] In the 1590s, however, witchcraft had become a central political issue in Scotland. James believed that a storm that nearly sank his ship on his voyage to bring back his bride from Denmark had been raised by supernatural agency, and unleashed a wave of persecutions.[68] In act I, scene iii Shakespeare draws particular attention to the witches' powers over sailors and the sea; the third witch threatens to drain a sailor "dry as hay"—that is, to drain him of his semen.[69] In a hereditary monarchy, of course, a threat to the monarch's sexual potency was also a threat to the continued stability of the realm. More generally, witches could be seen as special enemies of monarchs because they claimed for themselves the kind of divine, quasimagical authority that absolute monarchs were trying to concentrate in their own hands. Witches were doubly heinous in claiming any kind of active power for the weaker sex. It is not surprising, then, that Bodin, a major theorist of monarchical authority and one opposed in principle to rule by women, should have written against witches. James's eagerness in taking up the campaign against witches reflects his general concern to be in the vanguard of European monarchical theory, which implied, by the 1590s, a heightened insistence on the dignity of monarchy. In Scotland, it is true, hostility toward witchcraft was not specifically a monarchist view: justification for persecutions could be found in the apocalyptic interpretation of Scripture which was becoming increasingly influential among the Presbyterians and which James himself, up to a point, supported.[70] Shakespeare chooses, however, to lay the emphasis on the witches' challenge to authority in the sexual hierarchy of the family, and hence by extension to authority in the state, though he gives the added twist that the witches themselves know that even to try to gain complete autonomy from monarchical power is futile— that the Stuart succession is preordained.

A similar concern with "natural" legitimacy informs the play's presentation of language. It is a commonplace that humanists believed the health of language and the health of society to be intimately connected, and that they insisted that both should be governed by rules of decorum.[71] Such generalities obscure some significant differences of emphasis, however. Buchanan was one of those humanists who looked back nostalgically to the early days of the Roman republic as a period of linguistic as well as political purity, before social and literary forms became corrupted by imperial decadence. He viewed Scottish history in somewhat similar terms: he admired the austerity of the old Highland culture and viewed with disfavor the introduction of "barbarous" titles of honor that accompanied the consolidation of feudalism in Scotland. His history differs in emphasis from Boece's in that just as he denied that even after Malcolm's accession the principles of primogeniture ever became firmly established, so he denied that the new names and titles introduced in Malcolm's reign marked a permanent break in Scottish cultural traditions. Boece opens his discussion of Malcolm's reign with a long list of family names first adopted at this time; Buchanan argues that many of the names were much later innovations, stresses the continuing vitality of Gaelic, and claims that the title of "thane," far from having been abolished, still survives in some areas, along with the elective system for clan chiefs.[72] Buchanan's linguistic primitivism did not lead him to advocate the revival of Gaelic, but his notion of decorum was a fairly austere one, requiring "a fusion of the fiercely independent spirit characteristic of the highlands" with "a refinement of the ancient virtue by the introduction of a more sophisticated civic-mindedness." His rationalism marked his linguistic as well as political views: just as local political traditions must be overlaid by general rational principles, so language must free itself of the accidents of courtly fashion and represent ideas as clearly as possible. Williamson has noted that the Scottish Presbyterians' critique of traditional religious forms often entailed a "deepened classicism," a "linguistic radicalism" or "nominalism" that was extremely skeptical of any attempt to assert a natural relationship between traditional linguistic forms and general truths.[73]

In the later sixteenth century, however, there were important countercurrents to such ideas. Courtly aestheticians such as Castiglione and, in England, Puttenham were urging that linguistic forms be made more sensitive to social distinctions. Rejecting a nominalistic dualism of sign and thing signified, they insisted on an extremely elaborate hierarchy of signifiers. Such views were consistent with a more conservative attitude toward religious forms; and indeed the most extensive Elizabethan discussion of decorum was provided by Richard Hooker, defender of the Church of England against the Puritans.

Hooker insisted that we must respect traditional signs—sacraments, images, vestments, titles—whether or not they have a completely scriptural justification. These signs might not be, as the Catholic idolatrously maintained, "natural" signs that magically contained what they signified; but one must not fall into the opposite dualistic error of making them mere "naked signs" completely separable from what they communicated. Communication, in both religion and society, was a matter of body as well as soul, of signifier as well as signified; the maintenance of traditional hierarchical distinctions in society depended on a general reverence for decorum. "Weigh these things in themselves, titles, gestures, presents, other the like external signs wherein honour doth consist, and they are matters of no great moment. Howbeit, take them away, let them cease to be required, and they are not things of small importance, which that surcease were likely to draw after it."[74]

In Hooker's view, the Puritans were cutting through this hierarchical decorum, finding all signs purely arbitrary, "signifying nothing"; and Shakespeare's *Macbeth* is presented as reductive in a comparable way. The play's concern with titles and linguistic and social decorum is established in the second scene, whose heightened, quasi-epic diction constantly draws attention to linguistic performances. (A secondary function may have been to give a sense of geographical remoteness without resorting to Scottish words and accents, which were regularly used by satirists to raise a laugh.[75]) The captain emphasizes that Macbeth well deserves the name of "brave" and is complimented himself for his fine speech.The process of stripping the Thane of Cawdor of his title and transferring it to Macbeth is the central action of the first few scenes. A chain of imagery often noted by critics links titles and compliments with ceremonial clothes. The careful observation of rules of decorum means that linguistic exchanges are not merely communications of information but communions that link individual speech with collective language. Duncan responds to Macbeth's compliments by declaring that "in his commendations I am fed; / It is a banquet" (I.iv.55–56). Macbeth himself acknowledges that after Duncan's murder "the wine of life is drawn" (II.iii.93), that "life's feast" has been disrupted (II.ii.39). Under his reign "bloody knives" disrupt "feasts and banquets" (III.vi.35). Macbeth's crime against Duncan is intensified by the fact that he is the king's host, and his first great setback comes when Banquo's ghost, with ironic courtesy, attends the hypocritical banquet and Lady Macbeth has to remind him with a nervous pun that "the sauce to meat is ceremony; / Meeting were bare without it" (III.iv.35–36). These links between meet language and courtly conspicuous consumption form a strong contrast with the disapproval of excessive feasting so often found in Boece and Buchanan. When Macbeth denounces the English as "epicures" (V.iii.8), he is speaking with the voice of anticourtly humanism, a voice that the play discredits.

Macbeth and his wife disrupt the linguistic hierarchy. The reductiveness that makes them turn all social action into a naked "deed" is also a linguistic reductiveness: every proposition for them becomes a simple clause around the word "do." When they do use more ornate language, it is with stiffness that reveals it as unnatural: Lady Macbeth tries to stifle Macbeth's conscience by making him look at the grooms as no more than "pictures" (II.ii.53); Macbeth gilds them with blood and later speaks of Duncan's silver skin as laced with golden blood (II.iii.110). In the end such external glosses on his naked deeds fade away, as fast as the gloss of the erroneous "golden opinions" he has worn, and life becomes no more than a series of empty syllables, with ceremonial language reduced to "mouth-honour, breath" (V.iii.27).

Language can take its revenge on the individuals who rebel against its rules. After the regicide Macbeth finds himself unable to say "Amen": he cannot make the signs do his bidding; they resist him, so that there is force in Macduff's claim that the regicide cannot even be named (II.iii.63). He refuses to spell out the nature of the deed to Lady Macbeth because "the repetition, in a woman's ear, / Would murther as it fell" (II.iii.83–84); and indeed she faints soon afterward. Whether or not this faint is genuine, before long the moral truths she has tried to repress from her conscious mind reappear in the obsessive repetitions of the sleepwalking scene. No conscious agency can "raze out the written troubles of the brain" (V.iii.42). The witches, in a sense, function as the unconscious of the play; and even their disorderly language points to an ultimate order. Phrases such as "fair is foul, and foul is fair" disrupt strict logic, but they are nevertheless highly patterned; in trying to turn orthodox values upside down the witches nevertheless testify to the need for order. They deceive Macbeth not by lying but by telling the truth; they are "imperfect speakers" (I.iii.70) not so much in the moral sense as in the sense that their utterances are incomplete, and such imperfection necessarily implies the possibility of perfection, which is part of a wider order. Macbeth's attempt to be "perfect" without such an order (III.iv.20) is futile.

Shakespeare's treatment of the witches' language is strikingly different from the more orthodox strategy of Jonson's *Masque of Queens*, played by the King's Men in 1609. Jonson's witches are malicious slanderers, the natural enemies of the poets who transmit good fame; interestingly, their leader also adopts anticourtly rhetoric, claiming, in the manner of Buchanan, that "soft peace" corrupts "natiue manners." But the very sight of the House of Fame, presided over by Queen Anne, is enough to put the witches to flight.[76] Shakespeare subtly reworks masque conventions in order to redouble the compliment: it is the witches themselves, the forces of the antimasque, who call up the main masque, a masque in honor not of the usurper but of the truly legitimate line. Only after this vision do they pay the conventional (but in this context ironic) tribute to Macbeth, the "great King" (IV.i.131). Their vision is prophetic only: in the present of the play Scotland lacks an authoritative ruler, the most complete image of legitimate language is provided by the description of Edward the Confessor, who cures the King's Evil by hanging a "golden stamp" around the sufferer's neck, "put on with holy prayers." The "gift of prophecy" that goes with royal authority transforms the artificial sign into a natural one; language becomes sacrament. This gift is hereditary.

Language is used ceremoniously in Duncan's Scotland too, but pre-Stuart Scotland is as yet politically imperfect, and there are some indications that this imperfection is reflected linguistically. Harry Berger has noted that there is a sense of strain behind the compliments exchanged in the early scenes.[77] Duncan's first address to Macbeth (I.iv.14–21) is so effusive that it might have been more appropriately addressed by a subject to a king; and yet he breaks off his praises to nominate Malcolm, an act that galls Macbeth and undermines the sense of obligation his words might have created. At the end of the scene, however, Duncan calls Macbeth a "peerless kinsman," as if he were the king's equal. There is an odd confusion of identities in Ross's announcement to Macbeth that the king's "wonders and his praises do contend, / Which should be thine, or his": the news of Macbeth's success "silenc'd" him (I.iii.92–93). Angus interrupts Ross, almost as if he feels that the praise is going too far; but Ross goes on to hail Macbeth as Thane of Cawdor, almost as if he were conferring the title himself, not just announcing Duncan's intention of conferring it. All this praise lavished on Macbeth seems defensive, as if Duncan and the courtiers are afraid of his military power and need to buy him off linguistically. There may also be an element of aggression in their praises. Ross rather oddly compares the compliments paid to Macbeth to a thick shower of hailstones; thick, congealing substances tend to be associated with evil (I.iii.97, compare I.v.43, 50 and III.ii.50), and the word "hail" echoes the hail of "All hails" with which the witches have just greeted Macbeth, intercepting the message Ross was bearing from the king. Duncan has told Ross to greet Macbeth with Cawdor's "former title," having just termed him a "most disloyal traitor." This kind of immediate transferral of title would probably have seemed a miscalculation to the original audience.

Laws of decorum insisted that in honoring a nobleman one must also honor his name. The intimate interrelation between the title and its bearer easily developed in the popular mind into the notion re-

ported by Camden, that the title was a natural sign naturally linked
to the nobleman, "as though the names and natures of men were
suitable, and fatall necessitie concurred heerin with voluntary motion,
in giving the name." Camden condemns such superstitions, but he
does argue that there is a reciprocal relationship between name and
bearer: a noble name can stimulate its bearer to great deeds.[78] Conversely, when the country's leading nobleman, the Duke of Norfolk,
rebelled under Elizabeth's reign, his title was destroyed along with
the individual. In Scotland, it appears, the relationship between title
and individual is more casual. Thaneships are not directly hereditary,
and Buchanan insists in his *History* that the custom of giving noble
families names derived from their lands—a custom that established
a natural relationship between name and reality—had not yet begun
in the reign of Malcolm.[79] Rather than inspiring natural reverence,
titles here seem to stir up artificial competitiveness. When greeted by
the witches with his new titles, Macbeth declares, "By Sinel's death
I know I am thane of Glamis" (I.iii.71). This somewhat cold acknowledgment of filial ties emphasizes that one can gain a title only by
another's death. The title "Thane of Cawdor" echoes like a refrain
through act I, scene iii, being spoken nine times, and there is a steadily
accumulating confusion of identities. When Ross greets him with the
title, Macbeth protests, as he had done to the witches, that "the Thane
of Cawdor lives," and Angus corrects him: "Who was the Thane, lives
yet" (I.iii.108–109). But when Macbeth says that the witches "gave
the Thane of Cawdor to me," the metonymy carries the suggestion
that the rebel's personality too has been transferred. Within a few
lines he declares that "I am Thane of Cawdor" (line 133); but at the
opening of the next scene Duncan asks whether execution has been
done on Cawdor.

Even before Macbeth directly disrupts the political order, then,
there are some hints that prefeudal Scotland is not entirely a harmonious "organic community." And the further the split between sign
and meaning is pushed by Macbeth's usurpation, the harder it becomes even for the forces of legitimacy to retain a pure and harmonious relationship between external speech and inner conviction. All
ceremony involves an element of trust, a willingness to respect the
public role even if its bearer may be imperfect; the hope is that the
honor paid to the role will have a psychological effect on the individual. Macbeth has corrupted public language to such an extent,
however, that much trust would simply be self-defeating. When Malcolm complains that Macbeth's "sole name blisters our tongues"
(IV.iii.12), he is indicating the depth of the crisis: nobody can speak

well in this corrupt body politic. After Duncan's murder, Malcolm and Fleance had to hold their tongues (II.iii.118). As the Lord has said, they cannot "do faithful homage, and receive free honours" (III.vi.36). Malcolm has to forgo the normal courtesies and inquire suspiciously about Macduff's motives, pleading, in terms that reflect the depth of the crisis,

> Let not my jealousies be your dishonours,
> But mine own safeties: you may be rightly just,
> Whatever I shall think. (IV.iii.29–31)

In order to establish Macduff's trustworthiness, Malcolm has to dishonor himself, completely dissociating his words from his inner nature by acting the part of the tyrant. Paradoxically, it is only by modeling himself on Macbeth's own strategies of dissimulation (IV.iii.117–119) that he can prove Macduff's virtue: if any degree of sincerity showed through in his speech, Macduff might be forewarned and would himself be able to dissimulate. Understandably, this linguistic crisis reduces Macduff to silence (line 137), and there is an interlude in which the doctor's description of a truly legitimate king brings out by contrast the chaos of Macbeth's Scotland. When Ross appears, he too begins to equivocate, fearing that to tell the truth about the fate of Macduff's wife and son would make his "ears despise my tongue for ever" (line 201). Malcolm, however, insists that Macduff should utter his grief, should make it a public act of mourning; a purely silent, private grief is unhealthy (lines 209–210). But in Macbeth's Scotland, an unnatural realm where trees can speak (III.ii.127), dissimulation is still necessary, and the forces of legitimacy must adopt the disguise of branches. Before legitimate peace can be restored, the virtuous forces must use violence: Macduff must not sheathe his sword while it is "undeeded" (V.vii.20). When he confronts Macbeth he declares,

> I have no words;
> My voice is in my sword. (V.viii.6–7)

The tyrannicide's dagger is redeemed by speaking with the voice of legitimacy. This final fulfillment of the witches' prophecies resolves their ambiguities, reveals the providential meaning behind their "double sense" (V.viii.20). Macduff is able to proclaim an end to dissimulation, a decisive move from hidden, private meanings to a triumphantly public language:

> I see thee compass'd with thy kingdom's pearl,
> That speak my salutation in their minds;
> Whose voices I desire aloud with mine,
> Hail, King of Scotland! (V.ix.22–25)

Malcolm's accession is not just a restoration but the foundation of a new and more stable order: the image of deceptively moving trees gives way to a truly organic unity in which the seeds of time are finally ripening and Malcolm's deeds are "planted . . . with the time" (V.ix.31).

Macbeth, then, establishes a norm of social and linguistic decorum that is considerably less austere than Buchanan's. The difference extends to the play's own dramatic decorum. Had Buchanan written a play on Macbeth—or had Milton carried out his early plan for such a play—the result would probably have been a drama of rational debate, with the merits and demerits of the opposing theories of succession being much debated and the supernatural element played down. Many Renaissance humanists were somewhat suspicious of the popular theater of their day, complaining that it appealed to the emotions rather than to the intellect. Always fresh in their minds was the idea that the Roman emperors had used spectacle to distract the people from their loss of liberty; theatrical metaphors in their writings often had negative connotations. They preferred a highly intellectual drama dependent on complex verbal ironies rather than spectacular incidents.[80] Their admiration for Greek and Roman tragedy was heightened by political considerations. Buchanan was a great admirer of Euripides and translated into Latin two of his tragedies, whose skeptical and ironic character appealed to humanists of a critical political temper. He was Milton's favorite dramatist, and a sixteenth-century editor singled out as an instance of Euripides' political wisdom a passage in praise of democracy which Milton placed at the head of *Areopagitica*. (It must be said, however, that one of Buchanan's Euripides translations also won the favor of Queen Elizabeth—possibly because of its theme of female sacrifice.)[81] The plays of Seneca, while politically ambivalent, offered criticisms of absolute rulers and affirmations of natural equality beneath the external façades of courtly roles. Buchanan appended the celebrated second chorus from the *Thyestes* to the *De iure regni* in order to illustrate his constitutionalist moral; the Presbyterian leader Andrew Melville inscribed in his copy an epigram claiming that if the matter were put to the popular vote, Seneca would be preferred to Nero, possibly alluding to the relative popularity of Buchanan and James among his party.[82] Buchanan's own plays follow Seneca in making a strong opposition between the beauty and harmony of the natural world and the artificial inequities of a corrupt society. The prophetic individualist who is the hero of *Baptistes* is accused by his enemies of having overthrown order and degree *(sustulit/rerum universa et ordinum discrimina)*, of threatening to cheapen the dignity of the royal title. The play fully endorses the Baptist's willingness to risk conservative accusations of democratic "popularity."[83]

Critics have often noted that *Macbeth* is, for Shakespeare, a particularly "Senecan" tragedy, the shortest of the major Jacobean tragedies, with no subplot and a rigorous dramatic economy. His adoption of this Buchananesque mode in a tragedy on a Scottish theme suggests the possibility of a certain "anxiety of influence": Buchanan's prestige was much higher then than it is today. Certainly Shakespeare not only imitated but also revised the Senecan mode.[84] One characteristic of Seneca and his Renaissance imitators is the listing of parts of the body in order to convey emotion.[85] Shakespeare too uses this device, but he gives it a slightly different emphasis. In Seneca the emphasis is on the need for rational control of a passionate body. Macbeth and his wife, however, are not so much overrun by unruly passions as forcing their bodies to carry through their calculating political stratagems. And their bodies resist this rebellion against natural order, as if the principles of monarchy and hierarchy were too deeply implanted in the body to be overcome. Macbeth's "hangman's hands" (II.ii.27) seem to warn the grooms even in their sleep, and Macbeth fears that they may pluck out his own eyes, as if judging his crime (II.ii.57; cf. Matthew 18.9). Lady Macbeth has to call on the spirits to transform her body, to unsex her. Inga-Stina Ewbank points to the contrast between Shakespeare's heroine and Seneca's Medea: Medea "finds her heroic self *through* evil," whereas Lady Macbeth, "unwomanized, becomes 'fiend-like' and hence less than a woman." Shakespeare is far more confident than Seneca, or Buchanan, that woman is "naturally" submissive and obedient. Ewbank further points out that Boece describes Scotswomen in early times as bathing themselves in blood to raise their spirits before going into battle; such conduct is not compatible with the symbolic order of Shakespeare's play.[86] Lady Macbeth's womanly body eventually asserts itself over her unnatural mind, in the gesture of compulsively washing her hands while sleepwalking. In the end, the disruption between soul and body destroys her and she takes her life "by self and violent hands" (V.ix.3). The doctor comments that her illness "more needs . . . the divine than the physician" (V.i.71).

If any physic could cure her, it would be the power of Edward the Confessor's hands, whose magic potency is the symbol of correct relationships within the body politic and body natural. Buchanan had compared the king's function to the doctor's in a secular, rationalistic spirit, emphasizing that kingship was simply an art that had to be learned, and James had taken strong exception to this analogy as too low and "mechanical."[87] Shakespeare does present Malcolm as "the med'cine of the sickly weal" (V.ii.27); but Edward's blessing has sanctified the medicine. Shakespeare's emphasis on the role of the body as well as the mind in influencing political decisions implies the need for a dramatic form less cerebral and more physical than Buchanan's neoclassicism permitted. There is a characteristic difference of emphasis in the two writers' handling of the Birnam Wood legend. Buchanan firmly declares that the legend of the moving trees is mere fable, "more adapted for theatrical representation, or Milesian romance, than history." His own drama, in any case, no more allowed for such fables than his historical discourse. He goes on to give a rationalizing explanation: the soldiers were so confident of victory that they put green boughs in their helmets, the imagery of an army marching home in triumph, not going to war, and Macbeth was so unnerved by this confidence that he fled.[88] Shakespeare, however, works the tree legend into a whole network of allusions to organic political order. Thus his play ends on a note of the restoration of harmony between natural and social orders, which is alien to Senecan tragedy.

The differences between Buchanan and Shakespeare as dramatists extend to their conceptions of dramatic unity; and these too, arguably, reflect their ideals of political unity. The traditional metaphor of the body politic, though open to different interpretations, implied some kind of mystical cohesion between the different levels of the social hierarchy. The more rationalistic humanist thinkers tended to prefer more abstract and artificial models of political unity. Rejecting charges that the old elective system led to disorder and disunity, Buchanan replied that in fact it preserved unity but at a more abstract level than the traditional metaphors allowed. The contention of rival armies did not necessarily lead to bloodshed, for the contests were effectively ritualized; but the existence of such safety valves for dissent sacrificed short-term harmony to much greater long-term stability: the Scottish dynasty had endured much longer than the royal houses of England, France, or Italy. Buchanan's disciple, David Hume, took issue with those who defended hierarchy in the Church by appealing to the order of nature, drawing analogies with bees and other natural creatures. By nature, he declared, all were free, and all social orders were artificial.[89] The Presbyterian notion of the Church as unified according to an abstract "platform," a rational, scripturally grounded Discipline rather than by traditional hierarchies, could be extended, as it was by Milton, to artistic form. His notion of decorum implies conformity to universal principles rather than to social convention. Milton may have translated Buchanan's *Baptistes*, and the two men certainly had comparable conceptions of dramatic unity.[90]

By such standards Shakespeare's plays must appear disorganized: they lack the clear divisions between tragedy and comedy and between different stages of the action demanded by neoclassical theory. Nor does Shakespeare provide the rigorous reflection of social divisions in diction demanded by the more courtly neoclassical theorists. The diction ranges from the elaborately latinate to the colloquial, and Lady Macbeth will use a "low" word such as "blanket." Consequently, critics in the late seventeenth and earlier eighteenth centuries found it difficult to see any unity in his plays. The unity often operates at a more subliminal level, notably in the dense and elaborate patterns of imagery. This phenomenon is by now so familiar that it is taken for granted, but it is still worth pointing out that he develops such image patterns far beyond other classical and Renaissance dramatists. The effect is that the social order, like the play, seems to be bound together not just by some abstract plan but also by a host of intricate only semiconscious symbolic interactions. Lady Macbeth's language is socially differentiated from the porter's, and yet corruption in the one is reflected in the other. The comic elements reinforce the sense of social decorum on a deeper level.[91]

IV

An extended comparison between *Macbeth* and some sixteenth-century humanists would seem to call into question Shakespeare's alleged independence from political ideology. It becomes easier to see why Shakespeare appealed so strongly as a source of political wisdom, of an ideal of "organic unity" in art and society, to literary theorists of the Romantic epoch such as the Schlegels, Adam Müller, and Coleridge. As Marilyn Butler has pointed out, these writers were concerned with social as well as literary issues and were anxious to combat the rationalism of contemporary radical thought in the aftermath of the French Revolution; Shakespeare's position had affinities with their own.[92] There were articulate republicans in France and barricades in the streets of Paris in the 1590s as well as 1790s; Shakespeare's patron, the Earl of Southampton, was alleged to have imbibed republican ideas when living in Paris.[93] The analogy extends to the character of these different generations' revisions of radical ideas. Müller, while idealizing a traditional, hierarchical order, accepted that a certain accommodation with new social forces was inevitable in order to avoid the worse danger of revolution, and he became a theorist of the new capitalist science of political economy. Coleridge contrasted the English legacy of moderate, traditionalist politics with the French extremes of rigid absolutism and Jacobinism. If Shakespeare's plays revise certain radical currents of thought, they do so in a subtle, oblique, carefully weighed manner, rather than through violent reaction.

The result is that the plays retain elements of the attitudes they are rejecting. As a regicide who was condemned equally by Buchanan and by conservatives, and yet had half-buried associations with constitutionalist traditions, Macbeth was a figure bound to evoke ambivalent responses from a Renaissance humanist. If the audience can sympathize with Macbeth even though he outrages the play's moral order, it may be because vestiges remain of a worldview in which regicide could be a noble rather than an evil act. Shakespeare may have come under pressure from his royal patron to substitute a mystical and legitimist version of Scottish history for the rationalist and constitutionalist viewpoint of the old tutor who haunted his nightmares,[94] but it is impossible to exorcise a ghost without first summoning forth its presence.

ACKNOWLEDGMENT

Research on this article was facilitated by an English-Speaking Union Fellowship at the Folger Shakespeare Library. For help and comments I am grateful to Boyd Berry, Patricia Duncker, Donna Hamilton, Sally Mapstone, Annabel Patterson, and Alan Sinfield. It also seems appropriate to acknowledge here a longer-standing debt to my school and university teachers in Aberdeen.

6

Cavalier Critic? The Ethics and Politics of Thomas Carew's Poetry

Kevin Sharpe

Historians have argued that in the early seventeenth century there was a developing cultural rift as well as mounting political polarization. The contemporary labels "court" and "country," we are told, delineated distinct and antagonistic cultures and styles that presaged the division into Royalists and Roundheads in the English civil war.[1] In *The Causes of the English Revolution* Lawrence Stone proclaimed, "By the early seventeenth century England was experiencing all the tensions created by the development within a single society of two distinct cultures, cultures that were reflected in ideals, religion, art, literature, and theatre, dress, deportment and way of life."[2] In *The English Civil War* Robert Ashton concurred, identifying the emergence of a distinct court culture that was "exclusive, aristocratic and authoritarian."[3]

Literary scholars have tended to agree. In his essay, "Two Cultures? Court and Country under Charles I," Peter Thomas wrote of "two warring cultures" emerging in the 1630s as an Elizabethan national culture fragmented into parts. One was a Caroline court, which "seemed to speak for narrow snobbery and effete indulgence."[4] Most recently, Graham Parry has attributed to the cultural interests of Charles I the most sinister political intents. When criticism of or obstacles to royal policies presented themselves, Parry argued, Charles I regarded it as the function of culture to dispel them: to present an ideal image that might mold a more tractable reality or that might at least divert men from consideration of that reality. So in the cult of

Neoplatonism, Parry maintained, Charles "saw an admirable means
of projecting a royal image in a way that distracted attention from the
political aspects of his kingship." In culture, as in politics, it was the
"grateful, uncritical mind" that was favored by the court of Charles
I.[5] Accordingly, the man of free spirit, independent judgment, and
truly creative genius could find no home there. Milton was to become
the literary antagonist of the Caroline regime.[6]

Such an interpretation of the cultural and political history of early
Stuart England is enshrined in the idea of "Cavalier" literature. When
we think of Caroline dramatists or "Cavalier Poets," we think of a
group of courtiers, flamboyant and gay, engaged only with the concerns of the courtly *précieux*, with love and the chase, irresponsibly
insensitive to the moral questions and political problems of their age;
or worse, uncritical servants and sycophants of an autocratic king
who maintained them principally for their flattery.[7] Cavalier drama
as characterized by Alfred Harbage was a fawning spectacle devoted
only to the foolishly sentimental and romantic concerns of an exclusive
coterie.[8] And, in the words of George Parfitt, "Cavalier poetry shows
a narrowing of range of reference and interest, becoming courtly in
a sense which suggests a decisive split between "court" and "country"
and a consequent concentration upon few areas of emotional experience."[9] Where Jonson and Donne aired problems and criticisms within
a world still united by common values, the Cavalier playwrights and
poets of the 1630s, it is said, sang the swansong of an exclusive and
authoritarian caste doomed to be defeated.[10]

Thomas Carew may stand as a test of any such characterization of
Cavalier poetry and Caroline court culture.[11] For Carew was in the
most exact sense a courtier: a gentleman extraordinary of the Privy
Chamber and sewer in ordinary to the king, he attended personally
upon the monarch in the royal privy lodgings.[12] Carew's place, diet,
and livery freed him from the necessity of earning a living and might
have qualified him to be one of those courtly gentlemen who, in
Pope's phrase, "wrote with ease." He epitomized the amateur court
poet. Moreover, Carew was evidently close to Charles I. In the words
of Clarendon, "He was very much esteemed by the most eminent
Persons in the Court, and well looked upon by the King himself."[13]
Charles singled him out for office and advanced him over a rival
Scottish candidate.[14] To damn him still further, Carew was also the
author of a masque, allegedly that most courtly and sycophantic of
modes, indeed, of what may claim to be the most brilliant court
masque of the early Stuart period—a masque in which (at least at
one level) the apotheosis of the monarch was taken to its greatest
height.[15] Carew may be taken, then, to represent the court: during

the 1640s he was regarded by the Puritans as the emblem of its frivolity, immorality, and illegitimacy.[16]

Carew's biography, however, does not read like that of a model Caroline courtier. For Charles I's court reflected the new monarch's personal style, which was in marked contrast to the bawdy revelry of the Jacobean court: Charles I issued orders that prescribed decorum, morality, and chastity. As a young man Carew had led a profligate life and contracted syphilis.[17] Throughout his life he was best known to his contemporaries for his erotic verse, especially "A Rapture," and as a libertine—a reputation to which he himself alluded in his masque.[18] To describe Carew as a courtier, then, is accurately to define his official position at the Caroline court, but it is not to illuminate his personal style; and it should not substitute for an examination of his values and beliefs. Carew is usually studied as one of the "Cavalier Poets." But to call him a Cavalier is to be guilty of anachronism, for Carew died in 1640, two years before civil war divided the realm into these rival camps.

It is my purpose in this essay to repatriate Carew in the decades of early Stuart England *before* the civil war. This is the England of Renaissance humanism: a commonweal of values in which virtue and politics, morality and poetry were believed to be inseparable. The leading citizen of that commonweal was Ben Jonson, whose own art— be it verse epistle, epitaph, comedy of humors, or masque—emerged from deeply held ethical premises and was written for both private instruction and public counsel. Carew, I wish to argue, was a "son of Ben," not only as a legatee of Jonson's style but, more important, as the heir of Jonsonian morality.

I

Since the 1640s many have depicted Carew as an exponent of unrestrained eroticism. Others have described him as a spokesman for the graceful elegance of Caroline England. That both positions have been powerfully argued may lead us to conclude that there were contradictions and tensions in Carew's verse and life—between explicit language and artful poise, between hedonism and self-control. It is these tensions that I wish to examine futher. For through these ambiguities we may see Carew as a poet exploring both personal dilemmas and some of the most important social and political issues of his age, not disengaging from them. More generally, by such a study of Carew, by an emphasis upon the moral weight behind the lightness of touch, I hope to suggest that in order to understand

"Cavalier poetry," we need to appreciate the bequest of Jonson's ethical beliefs and concerns: the governance of human nature; the relationship of virtue and politics; the role of the artist in the commonweal. For once we relocate Carew and other Caroline poets and playwrights in pre-civil war England, we may begin to see serious consideration of such questions rather than retreat from them, a preoccupation with common rather than exclusive or partisan concerns, doubts and questions rather than self-congratulation, criticism of courtiers and king as well as compliment. We may begin to see a serious political vision and personal morality.[19]

In the sphere of personal morality, it might be thought that Thomas Carew had little to tell anyone. Known as a libertine in his own age, he has been chiefly remembered since then for "A Rapture," one of the most erotically explicit poems in the language. Such an observation alone should cause us to reconsider any accusation of flattery, for Carew's eroticism seems out of place in a court devoted to the cult of Platonic love—a cult to which his poetry appears at times to be an irritated reaction: "Let fooles thy mystique formes adore, / I'le know thee in thy mortall state."[20] But to know Carew's poems only in their mortal state would be to misunderstand them—or to hear only one of the voices through which the poet spoke on love and morality.[21] For there is an ambiguity about love and passion both between various poems and within them. The first thirty or forty lines of "To A.L. Perswasions to Love," for example, read as the conventional rhetoric of seduction: as an incitement to a young girl to indulge the pleasures of the flesh before time robs her of her beauty. All the seducer's persuasive tricks and tropes are there: the pleasure that the maiden will herself enjoy; the responsibility to use Nature's stock of beauty with liberality; the point that lesser lights shine when the greater are hid under a bushel.[22] These tropes are standard, but we note that it is precisely such persuasive eloquence that forms the subject of Carew's "Good Counsel to a young Maid," in which, conscious of the seductive powers of (his own?) verse, he warns his pupil,

> Netts, of passions finest thred,
> Snaring Poems, will be spred,
> All, to catch thy maiden-head.[23]

The young woman is warned to be on her guard, for the rhetoric of seduction is not to be confused with the reality of love. She must resist the powerful anguished overtures of the seducer's eloquence lest consent bring her shame.[24] Chastity, the maid is told in this poem,

is central to her honor, and only honorable love should be allowed
to conquer it. And this, for all the seductive opening lines, is also the
point of "To A.L. Perswasions to Love." For, as we read on, it becomes
clear that here the poet-lover offers not merely the sexual gratification
of the moment but love for life. And like the young maid, A.L. is
advised to select only such a suitor:

> Cull out amongst the multitude
> Of lovers, that seeke to intrude
> Into your favour, one that may
> Love for an age, not for a day;
> One that will quench your youthfull fires,
> And feed in age your hot desires.[25]

The conjunction that opens the last line lends its force to the whole
verse. The poem becomes not simply an act of seduction but advice
to use the gift of youthful beauty in order to purchase that life-long
love which might legitimize the indulgence of sexual passion without
loss of honor.

Love involves physical passion, but mere lust is not the same as
love. In another poem Carew tells his mistress of "The difference /
Twixt heat of soule and sence."[26] And he debates the difference between them in one of four songs that he wrote for a court entertainment:

> Quest. By what power was Love confinde
>   To one object? who can binde,
>   Or fixe a limit to the free-borne minde?[27]

The question evokes the arguments of fashionable Platonic lovers as
expressed, for example, by Queen Atossa in Cartwright's *The Royal
Slave*.[28] The answer, however, dismisses the implication of the question; before a court audience Carew denies the veiled polygamy in
Platonic love:[29]

> An. Nature; for as bodyes may
>   Move at once but in one way,
>   So nor can mindes to more than one love stray.[30]

Unlike mere lust, Carew asserts, love is faithful. Unlike mere lust, it
is also timeless. It is "Eternitie of love protested" in Carew's song, as
in "To A.L. . . . .":

> True love can never change his seat,
> Nor did he ever love, that could retreat.[31]

Honorable, faithful, and eternal love, love both physical *and* spiritual—such an interpretation of Carew's position seems to be at odds with our traditional reading of his most famous erotic ode. For in "A Rapture" these qualities are scorned. Honor is "but a Masquer"; the "nobler" lovers refute it and act oblivious of reputation.[32] The poem is usually read as an incitement to sexual license, and it is easy to see why. At one level the poem reads as a playful but sophisticated act of seduction, in which the poet seeks to answer all his mistress' and society's objections to the free vent of sexual passion. To read the poem as *only* frank hedonism or as a mere *jeu d'esprit*, however, is to oversimplify it. For the context of Carew's sexual freedom is not society but an Elyzium where "All things are lawfull."[33] Sexual license here is not at odds with social order. Carew writes of a world apart from society, a paradise, a land of innocence free of sin where men do not know the names "of husband, wife, lust, modest, chaste, or shame."[34] In this Elyzium men live virtuously by acting according to their natural instincts. Here what society has labeled sinful bears no such taint. In this Elyzian ground Carew playfully sees Aretine's works, handbooks of sensuality, become "divine" lectures of love and Daphne surrender to Apollo.[35] Here where "Beautie and Nature, banish all offence," the social labels of moral and immoral, honorable and dishonorable, have no place.[36] This is Carew's own rapture: an Elyzium in which the tensions between man's natural instinct and social order and morality are resolved. "A Rapture" is, we might say, a laboratory in which Carew creates an ideal condition so that he may better explore an actual problem.[37]

In Elyzium "All things are lawfull—that may delight / Nature, or unrestrained Appetite."[38] From this location honor is seen to be only a social attribute—one at times at odds with religion and values natural to man. Where honor dictates that men kill "religion bids from blood-shed flye"; in Elyzium he enjoys "steadfast peace."[39] Society, necessarily perhaps, erects codes that restrain men's natural instincts and so creates tensions between natural and social behavior. Carew envisions a paradise in which man's innocence removes the need for restraint and dispels such contradictions. "A Rapture" is located in and hankers for that world of natural innocence, a world, as "The Second Rapture" describes it, "of lust and lovers"—for in innocence they are one.[40] Carew's quest for a reconciliation of sexual passion and virtue may be behind "The Second Rapture" as well. For all the frank eroticism of the imagined sexual union with a young girl, the imagery is religious and the maiden remains chaste. Lynn Sadler has observed that the poem plays on the biblical story of the virgin presented to David "that my lord the King may get heat."[41] The maiden may "renew the age" by a reunion, a reconciliation of "lust" and "blisse" that man enjoyed before the fall tainted him with sin.[42] From this perfect state man had fallen. Though he knew all too well that man was a creature of appetite, Carew seems to have believed in man's potential for virtue. It may be, then, that Carew's hope for himself and mankind lay not in mere obedience to the social dictates of honor and reputation but in striving to live by the natural innocence of man's perfect state.

In society, it would seem, Carew at times suggests that the best reconciliation of love and passion, appetite and order, was found in marriage. The subject of his poem "On the Marriage of T.K. and C.C. the morning stormie" is the resolution of tensions. Carew depicts marriage as a calm in a world of tempests. Marriage puts an end to the unruly winds and waters, the sighs and tears of unrequited love; it brings peace to the soul. And marriage unites lovers in a physical union now that they are joined by holy sacrament to each other. When the priest unites the bride and groom,

> From the misterious holy touch such charmes
> Will flow, as shall unlock her wreathed armes,
> And open a free passage to that fruit
> Which thou hast toyl'd for with a long pursuit.[43]

In society, outside matrimony, it had been forbidden fruit; within marriage it is the fruit of the garden of innocence to which, by partaking of it, the couple return. Marriage, that is, returns them to innocence. It removes them, like the Elyzium of "A Rapture," from the values and language of a fallen society. So the bride's exclamations of sexual pleasure become "pleasing shreekes"; the "fight of love" is become peace; "Tis mercy not to pitty" the virgin for her blood spilt.[44] Their natural love expressed in marriage reconciles contradictions rendering chaste what was impure, honorable what was shameful, moral what was immoral. Marriage, because it orders man's passions, enables him to partake of sensual pleasure without being debased by it.[45] It unites in harmony and orders the potentially contradictory and unruly aspects of his own nature. If, as Sadler points out, Carew writes with the most frank and free eroticism about married love, it is because in marriage pleasure is reconciled to virtue.[46]

Such an interpretation of Carew's verse and the morality of his poetry might seem to detach the poetry from the poet—a man who, we recall, was brought close to death by a life of license and by syphilis. On the contrary, I suggest that a strong personal sense of the ungoverned anarchy of his own appetite and passion, some internal quest for order and regulation, dominated Carew's life as well as his poetry. Evidently he contemplated marriage: there were rumors in 1624–25 that he might wed the rich widow of Sir George Smith.[47] At a time when his fortunes were at a low ebb, economic motives might well have been to the fore. But Carew's correspondence with Sir John Suckling concerning his marriage plans supports the suggestion of the poet's search for regulation in his life as well as his art.[48] Suckling attempted to dissuade his friend from matrimony. With more than a hint of irony—induced, no doubt, by the prospect of the pox-ridden Carew taking the marriage vows—Suckling ribaldly urged him to consider that fruit trees multiplied only when transplanted. "Do but make love to another," he counseled, and the "homely meal" of marriage would soon pale before the varied dainty dishes available to the lover's palate.[49] Carew, significantly, remained adamant in his reply. Love, he agreed with Suckling, was natural, but "if *love* be *natural*," he added, "to *marry* is the best *Recipe* for living honest."[50] For marriage he defined as the expression of love that was fixed and immutable; and, as we have seen, Carew maintained that there was no other love. "*Love* changed often doth nothing; nay 'tis nothing: for *love* and *change* are incompatible."[51] In marriage alone love seeded, bore fruit, and multiplied. Carew responded to Suckling in his friend's own coin: the tone of his answer is jocular, bawdy, and coarse. To us, perhaps, Carew's argument for sexual fidelity is couched in less than appropriate language: "one steed shall serve your turn as well as twenty more."[52] But, as often was the case with Carew, the language and tone should not be simply equated with the meaning. As he told Suckling, " 'Tis not the want of love . . . if every day afford not *new-language*, and *new waies* of expressing affection."[53] Carew's coarse language, like his erotic verse, also makes a point: it is itself a frank acknowledgment of those physical, animal urges that marriage accommodates and to which marriage may give vent. The sensual and the physical are as significant in Carew's reply as in Suckling's letter. Carew's final conclusion, however, is not the same: "I know what marriage is and know you know it not." For Carew believed that in condemning marriage, Suckling denied what was natural, in the sense of that which might restore man to his higher nature, the original innocence of his uncorrupted nature. In the words of the *Book of Common Prayer* marriage was "instituted of God in paradise in the time of man's innocency" and "ordained for a remedy against sin."[54]

Marriage for Carew was the literal as well as metaphorical expression of the poet's "attempt to impose a civilized order upon the desperate chaos of man's inner realities."[55] It accommodated the physical and spiritual in man, natural instinct and social order. Once we see that there is more to Carew than the libertinism of "A Rapture," we may also begin to appreciate that there was more to his love lyrics than the celebration of court love games played by the *precieux*. We may come to see that while he worked within the conventions of Petrarchan love poetry, Carew reemployed, adapted, and even subverted them as he brought to them the concerns and problems of his age. Through a poetry of beauty, love, and nature, we may see, Carew did not retreat from contemporary issues and problems; rather, he examined not only amorous but also social and political relationships.

II

The celebration of beauty is a *raison d'être* of the love poem. The equation of a lover's physical attributes with the features of the natural or celestial spheres was conventional in the poetry of the Renaissance. Carew's delightful love song "Aske me no more" places him firmly within the convention. Even in this poem, however, apparently sung simply in the key of celebration, the refrain transcends the mere flattery of a mistress. The lady's beauty is not compared to roses; it becomes the very essence or idea of roses and so captures the essence of nature itself.[56] In "The Comparison" Carew makes his departure from the conventions of the love poem clear:

> Dearest thy tresses are not threads of gold,
> Thy eyes of Diamonds, nor doe I hold
> Thy lips for Rubies: . . . [57]

For Carew beauty does not reside in his mistress' fair hair (though "threads of lawne"), her coral lips, her "teeth of pearle," or even in her wit (though "pure and quicke").[58] The poet loves her "for all," and it is "the complement" of each part to the other rather than the compliment of a suitor that gives that poem its title.[59] Beauty expresses the harmony of nature in the universe, not merely its earthly manifestations in a mistress. And so "The Comparison" is that of the maiden with the purest essence of nature: her lips are "Nector," her breath frankincense; her cleavage is a "Paradise." Celia is a "faire Goddesse" to be worshipped: the goddess Nature herself.[60]

As Nature's legate, Beauty influences men with all the might of nature's sway. The beauty of nature leads men necessarily to love:

"Love flow from Beautie as th' effect."[61] It has a magic that enchants
men so that the greatest beauty most attracts. Such a power needs to
be exercised with responsibility. Those endowed with nature's gifts
must acknowledge it—"Confesse thy beauty"—and attune their behavior to their outward appearance: "tis fit thou thine owne valew
know."[62] The beautiful, those endowed with the quintessence of nature, must lead the life of the beautiful—that is, the virtuous life. For
beauty's authority is legitimate only when founded upon virtue. In
his "Epitaph on the Lady S.," Carew offers an encomium on the union
of beauty and virtue to her:

> Whose native colours, and purest lustre, lent
> Her eye, cheek, lip, a dazling ornament:
> Whose rare and hidden vertues, did expresse
> Her inward beauties, and minds fairer dresse.[63]

Such a fusion of outer beauty and inner virtue represented and restored the divine image in which men were molded before the fall of
nature. Like the first man and woman, however, not all endowed
with such beauty lived according to their divine image. The mistress
of Carew's "The Comparison," for instance, is a "faire Goddesse"
only in outward appearance. "The Comparison," it becomes clear, is
not only or primarily between the woman's beauty and the hues and
features of nature; it is a comparison—or, rather, an unfavorable but
forceful contrast—between a divine appearance and a personality that
failed to live up to it. The mistress is not praised but chided:

> Faire Goddesse, since thy feature makes thee one,
> Yet be not such for these respects alone;
> But as you are divine in outward view
> So be within as faire, as good, as true.[64]

The powerful commandment of the last line emphasizes the didac-
ticism of Carew's love poetry. Here, as elsewhere, Carew adopts the
conventions of the poetry of compliment but, as Jonson, employs
them with an independent and radical force. He instructs rather than
flatters. And while appearing to describe the charms of a mistress he
posits a view of beauty that implies a morality.

Beauty is depicted as vulnerable to the ravages of time, and Carew's
treatment of this theme has encouraged us to read his verse in conventional *carpe diem* terms, hedonistically urging men and women to
seize the pleasures of the hour. Does not "A Rapture" open with a

line redolent with the hot impatience of sexual passion: "I will enjoy thee now my Celia, come"? Does not "Perswasions to Enjoy" warn Carew's Celia of the pressing need to "reape our joyes / E're time such goodly fruit destroyes"?[65] We must recollect, however, that "To A. L. . . ." concludes not in advice to seize the moment but rather an exhortation to secure the long term, to lay the foundation of eternal love rather than to indulge immediate sexual urges. And this may offer us insight into Carew's more serious preoccupation. In the battle against time, the eternal enemy of mankind and the special preoccupation of the Renaissance consciousness, Carew's weapon is love. Love is shown to transcend the externals of beauty and so to be free of that decay natural to physical substance. Carew's Cleon reassures his fearful mistress: "Though beautie fade, my faith lasts ever."[66] For Cleon dotes not only on Celia's "snow white skin" but on her "purer mind," and that is incorruptible.[67] When the two exchange their tokens of a love so founded, they know that they have won the victory over time: "Thus we are both redeemed from time."[68] And the poet, by celebrating their love—any true love—may redeem others. The publicization of love by the poet may lead others to transcend time, as Celia acknowledges:

> . . . CE. And I
> Shall live in thy immortall rime,
> Untill the Muses dye.[69]

Cleon and Celia, like the shepherd and the nymph in another poem of the same title, are speakers in "A Pastorall Dialogue."[70] It is not only a dialogue between them but a conversation among Time, Love, and, as the title suggests, Nature. Nature, though it expresses the passage of time in the seasons, is yet eternity itself. Men conquer time then when they accord and act with nature. By returning to a virtuous life lived in accordance with innocent nature, Carew is arguing, man may triumph over his enemy, Time.[71]

Man, Carew suggests, returns to nature through love. In Carew's poetry metaphors drawn from nature (a commonplace of Renaissance love poetry) are employed with unusual freshness and vigor to articulate a real and philosophical rather than an allegorical or metaphorical relationship between nature and love. Love's language and tactics, in Carew's verse, are the voices and movements of nature. The mistress whose heart lies in "The Torrid, or the frozen Zone" is unwarmed by the beams of love.[72] The bold lover, however, is a sun whose powerful rays cannot be resisted by the most unyielding of nature's flowers:

> Marke how the bashfull morne, in vaine
> Courts the amorous Marigold,
> With sighing blasts, and weeping raine;
> Yet she refuses to unfold.
> But when the Planet of the day,
> Approacheth with his powerfull ray,
> Then she spreads, then she receives
> His warmer beams into her virgin leaves.
> So shalt thou thrive in love, fond Boy.[73]

That "So" transcends simile. Nature *is* a lover and love is natural. In the Elyzium of "A Rapture" nature provides the lovers' bed and pillows from her stock of flowers and down.[74] The woman's body is itself a garden through which the lover wanders partaking of the "warme firme Apple, tipt with corall berry" and "the vale of Lillies."[75] "A Rapture" expresses an ideal state in which nature and love are one, pure and innocent. In society, nature no less than love has become corrupted and disordered. Passion and lust manifest the chaos of a wild, unruly nature. Carew has told us, however, that perfect, faithful, timeless love may restore men to innocence. So, we may see, that as perfect nature instructs lovers, the right love may reciprocally rule and reorder the chaos of fallen nature. The beauty of Carew's mistress, singing, "Stills the loude wind; and makes the wilde / Incensed Bore, and Panther milde."[76] Or, as the ode "To the Queen" makes clear, the "great Commandresse," who orders love and tames lust, also disciplines nature. Her example of love

> . . . shewes us the path
> Of Modestie, and constant faith,
> Which makes the rude Male satisfied
> With one faire Female by his side.[77]

The power of love's example subdues even the "wilde Satyr." Ultimately love's law will rule the flood and "free" man through the "deepe divinitie" of love from the fall.[78]

The love that may regulate nature must be the model of order, drawn from nature's first perfection. Love expresses the peace, order, and eternity of nature. Mutability and infidelity are not the attributes of love but of its opposite, lust, which is (the word is often used) "wilde," the behavior of man cast into the wilderness because he fell slave to appetite.[79] Legitimate love, by contrast, manifests "calme desires" and displays "milde aspects."[80] It distills the harmony of nature, uniting body and soul, the physical and spiritual, appetite and order. Such a love, we have seen, Carew believed to be best found in marriage. Marriage may now be understood not only to calm the tempests of man's personal turmoil; as we shall argue, it might also restore the harmony and order of nature and so effect the redemption and reformation of society and the commonweal.

It is this universal ethical vision—the restoration of the state of perfect nature and reformation of society—that is the subject of two of Carew's poems usually described as "country house poems":[81] "To Saxham" and "To my friend G.N. from Wrest." At one level these poems, like "To Penshurst," are undoubtedly charming celebrations of the pleasures Carew enjoyed at the country seat of two friends and patrons, Sir John Crofts and Henry de Grey, Earl of Kent.[82] Like "To Penshurst," however, there is more to them than that. Like Jonson's, Carew's poems transcend their particular circumstances; they are representations of an idealized nature that was central to Carew's ethics and social attitudes.

"To . . . G.N. from Wrest"opens with a contrast between the "temperate ayre" of Wrest and the "raging stormes" of the "cold nights out by the bankes of Tweed."[83] Carew has just returned from the king's campaign against the Scots and the discomforts of the royal camp near Berwick-upon-Tweed.[84] He has also returned to a garden of peace from a wilderness that threatened disorder.[85] Wrest is described as a haven of nature, of an idealized, perfected nature: the garden is pregnant with Nature's seed and fertile with her fruits. It is a world free of social artifice; there are no compounds or "forraigne gums" but "pure and uncompounded beauties" expressing all the gifts of a fecund, ordered, and uncorrupted nature.[86] Where by the Tweed there were "bleake Mountains," "fierce tempests," "everlasting winter," Wrest caresses its guest with "balmie dew," "odours sweete" and "with the warme Suns quickning heate."[87] Wrest symbolizes the harmony of perfect nature. And so in Carew's hands it becomes, like nature itself, a model of behavior. Everything at Wrest follows nature's dictates and is good. The virtues of natural activity are found within the house as well as its fruits outside. Wrest offers the warm hospitality of "cheerfull flames"to all strangers; its ornaments are "living men."[88] Hierarchy is respected here because it, too, is natural: "Some . . . spun of a finer thred" are fed with daintier fare, but there is plenty for all, and all live together there in harmony.[89] A natural hierarchy does not preclude the natural community of men. At Wrest nature is not merely represented in images, in statues or marbles of gods. And Carew wishes us to appreciate that the natural imagery of his poem is more than poetic conceit or "gay Embellishment.">[90] Wrest *is* a portrait of perfected nature. Ceres and Bacchus do not stand as stone figures in niches there, nor are they useless decorations for Carew's poem:

> We offer not in Emblemes to the eyes,
> But to the taste those usefull Deities.
> Wee presse the juycie God, and quaffe his blood,
> And grinde the Yellow Goddesse into food.[91]

Those who "presse the juycie God" are not only making wine; they are extracting nature's essence. And it is this that Carew wishes to distill through his poem. His readers are being urged not to live with the images of nature (or with a poetry concerned with them) but to return to nature itself.

Grey's house, of course, was built by man's art, but in it we find the gifts and attributes of nature. Outside in the garden, in the world of nature, "we decline not, all the worke of Art." In the garden the lake and winding stream represent man's capacity to order Nature's wilderness and to perfect her, as in the house Nature perfects man's art and society. Wrest "directs" the "course" of nature and so enjoys "fertile waters," fecundity, and fruit.[92] Religious imagery pervades the poem, suggesting a garden paradise. Nature, we are told, doth "blesse / this Mansion." Here all men "freely sit / At the Lords Table."[93] In this garden of innocence, as in "A Rapture," erotic love, once again innocent, has full rein: "*Vertumnus* sits, and courts / His ruddie-cheek'd *Pomona*" on the bank.[94] To this "blest Place" Carew has come, perhaps from his own personal wilderness as well as the raging storms of the Scottish border. "Thus," he announces to his friend G.N., "I enjoy myselfe."[95] The simple half-line has an unusually quiet force. Carew does enjoy *himself*; that is, he finds himself in this perfect state of nature and so finds calm. By contrast, his friend, hunting, strives against nature and so toils (the word is Carew's own) in the wilderness.[96] Wrest beckons all men who strive in the wilderness to return to the garden of innocence.

Saxham too is an idealization of nature. Where outside the house the inclement season bore little fruit, "thou hadst daintyes, as the skie / Had only been thy Volarie." Once again the language is religious: Nature's sweets "blesse" Saxham; animals come thither "as to the Arke."[97] At Saxham there is no striving in the wilderness, for here animals freely offer themselves as sacrifice on this altar of Nature:

> The willing Oxe, of himselfe came
> Home to the slaughter, with the Lambe,

> And every beast did thither bring
> Himselfe, to be an offering.[98]

Even the elements paid "tribute to thy fire." Here is a paradise again, eternal, outside time. At Saxham it is "endlesse day." The shrine of Nature welcomes every "weary Pilgrim" come to worship. Its "chearfulle beames send forth their light," beckoning all who travel in darkness.[99] He who saw the light might, like the lamb, "bring Himselfe" and so find, by worshipping at Nature's shrine, that "inward happinesse" he seeks.

"To my friend G.N. from Wrest" and "To Saxham" are usually studied as country house poems. In this context one critic has dwelt upon Carew's "mutations" of the Jonsonian mode, pointing to the relative isolation of Saxham compared with Jonson's "Penshurst" and to a sense of the Crofts' house as a retreat. So far I would not dissent. To M. McGuire, however, Saxham thus becomes a "cavalier justification of the country house as a private stronghold, within which aristocratic comforts and powers can be preserved against the rising tide of opposition."[100] Such an interpretation reveals extraordinary ignorance of the historical circumstances and, I would suggest, a misunderstanding of Carew's poetry and values. It is not clear who in the 1620s or 1630s was "rising" in opposition to aristocratic comforts and powers: ideological challenge to aristocratic privilege was virtually nonexistent. Although Saxham and Wrest are undoubtedly portrayed as retreats, they are not socially exclusive. Both households, it is stressed, open their doors and offer unlimited hospitality to the poor and strangers as well as those of "finer thred":

> Thou hast no Porter at the doore
> T'examine, or keep back the poore;
> Nor locks, nor bolts; thy gates have bin
> Made onely to let strangers in.[101]

Nature does not, as McGuire would argue, support only aristocratic society. It offers its fruits to all societies that live in accordance with its dictates. Saxham and Wrest are models of how men in society might return to nature: they are in some ways poetic parables. They offer the pattern of a peaceful, ordered, hierarchical, yet communal life that might bring men closer to the perfection of that first ideal commonweal: the kingdom of nature and love.[102]

III

In Saxham and Wrest we may begin to see, then, that nature and love are the bases of Carew's attitudes toward politics as well as ethics.

This should not surprise us. For all Carew's poetry was public poetry, even (perhaps especially) that love poetry that we delineate as the most private.[103] The interrelation of love and politics pervades Carew's language and metaphors. Carew's lover may be now subject, now monarch, but his relationship with his mistress is most often expressed in political terms. The lover acknowledges his duty to a mistress who commands him to return her letters: "so powerful is your sway / As if you bid me die I must obey."[104] Her letters have been merely her ambassadors, which now return to their "Soveraigne," leaving the lover's "vassall heart," "ever hon'ring her," as a "true Servant and subject to her selfe."[105] In "A deposition from Love," by contrast, the lover is a conquering prince rather than a servant, waging a war against "your rebell sex" in order to take the citadel of his mistress' heart. The victory, however, is short-lived and Carew's abandoned lover

> . . . he that is cast downe
> From enjoy'd beautie, feels a woe,
> Onely deposed Kings can know.[106]

This is the language of politics employed not merely as metaphor but as the discourse of a common world of lovers and kings, a world that does not rigidly distinguish what we would call the private and public domain. As Carew himself put it, "Service in prose, is oft call'd love in verse."[107] The relationships of men and women are described in political language because they are public and political relationships. No less, by corollary, political relationships may be examined through the language of love. Charles I and Henrietta Maria expressed their political ideals and values through the language of Platonic love, representing through their marriage the regulation of passion by higher understanding, the rule of the soul over the senses.[108] In his love poetry, then, Carew employed and articulated a discourse that was intrinsically political in Renaissance England and a language through which, in the 1630s, the monarch directly expressed his political values. The poetry of love and nature, therefore, should not be read as mere amorous banter or as Carew's retreat from political problems and realities, but as the discourse through which he examined political relationships and, in the guise of a lover, offered counsel and complaint to king, court, and commonwealth.

Carew is usually depicted as one of the court lackeys whose poetry celebrates uncritically the virtues and values of the Caroline court.[109] Once we have appreciated his attitudes toward nature and ethics, however, we may come to see that Carew's verse was independent and critical of the court. Let us consider the poem "To the King at his entrance into Saxham," written by Carew to be delivered to James I by John Crofts.[110] Saxham, as we have seen, enshrines the virtues and gifts of nature. And here, as the king enters the house, his host welcomes him to country hospitality: the fruits and beasts of the local countryside rather than the "rarities" or "dainties" (compare the "foraigne gums" of Wrest) "that come from farre" but that are found, of course, at court.[111] At Saxham along with simple fare the king is offered plain entertainment, a country dance, and with it the plain language of loyalty, love, and "pure hearts." Here Crofts and his family are devoted to their country and to nature as well as to their monarch; they pay their "pious rites" to "our household Gods" as well as to their king.[112] Their tone is loyal and loving but not flattering or sycophantic. For the king himself is also expected to adjust to their world—to bring the mercy, "not the greatnesse" of his majesty and to appreciate their endeavors.[113] In Saxham, as at Wrest, the king may find the greatness of the state of nature, which may enhance and direct even his rule. Both implicitly and explicitly the richness and honesty of their world is contrasted with the superficiality and deception of the court. Wrest, for instance, boasts no outward finery but offers sincere hospitality:

> No Dorique, nor Corinthian Pillars grace
> With Imagery this structures naked face,
> The Lord and Lady of this place delight
> Rather to be in act, then seeme in sight.[114]

At Wrest, we recall, Bacchus and Ceres are not merely represented in statuary; at Saxham there is no porter to exclude the poor. Pillars, porters, and statues, "Emblemes to the eye," "outward gay Embellishment"; the images evoke the Caroline court, its paintings and marbles, and perhaps the images that they in turn portrayed.[115] They also suggest a society that would seem what it is not, an unnatural society beside Saxham and Wrest where "we presse the juycie God."

Criticism of the insincerities of the court is made more explicit in other poems. Carew's "Obsequies to the lady ANNE HAY" opens with the powerful shock of a death that has changed the normal course of all behavior: "I saw the sleeke / And polisht Courtier, channell his fresh cheeke / With reall teares."[116] Sincerity beneath the polish is evidently exceptional at court, where everything is unreal, a veneer that covers a less attractive fabric. From such a world the most honest men were inclined to withdraw. The Earl of Anglesey (Carew reminded his widowed countess), a man of exemplary virtues, rather than compromise his credit "chose not in the active streame to swim" but "retir'd from the tumultuous noyse / Of Court, and suitors presse."[117] Living apart from the court, and only by so doing, Anglesey enjoyed "Freedome, and mirth, himselfe, his time, and friends"; "all his actions had the noble end / T'advance desert."[118] At court, by contrast, there was only dependence and hollow laughter, rivals rather than friends. At court a man must deny himself and his nature for falsehood and deception. And at court, Carew indicates, noble ends and desert find little place.

In early Stuart England the court was still expected to prescribe models for behavior and values to be emulated.[119] But Carew contrasts the values of the court with those of the virtuous life. The court is supposedly concerned with honor and reputation. Honor to Carew, however, is "but a Masquer" that deludes "baser subjects" but is disdained by "the nobler train."[120] This appears to be paradoxical, but Carew's point is that honor as traditionally understood is a mere appearance—a concern with reputation in society rather than with true virtue, irrespective of public estimation. And society and reputation, he makes clear, may often be at odds with the truth:

> . . . malice can on vestals throw
> Disgrace, and fame fixe high repute
> On the close shamelesse Prostitute.[121]

When morality is so overturned, all order is subverted. True virtue lies not in potentially false reputation but in personal integrity, in a return to that innocence of man's first (and presocial) existence:

> Vaine Honour! thou art but disguise,
> A cheating voyce, a jugling art,
> No judge of vertue, whose pure eyes
> Court her own Image in the heart.

Carew's lines come from a chorus he wrote to the court performance of a play.[122] And that powerful "Court" of the last line may be intended to reinforce the point: virtue courts her own image in the heart, but the image of the court, honor, is but a disguise for the "jugling art" practiced there. The court continues to boast and advocate a virtuous code of conduct, but in reality courtly values have become detached from virtue and so the court has lost its claim to prescribe morality.

During the 1630s, as we know, the courtly code of honor and the ethical and political values of the court were expressed through the idea of Platonic love. As the court gossip James Howell described it,

Platonic love was "a love abstracted from . . . sensual Appetite"; it consisted "in contemplations and ideas of the Mind, not in any carnal fruition."[123] Some critics have dismissed its importance for Caroline poetry,[124] but there can be little doubt that Carew recognized the importance of Platonic love for courtly values and addressed some of his verse directly to the subject. Some poems appear to be a critical response to it. Carew himself, as we have seen, writes of a spiritual love that transcends the merely physical, and his language at times suggests the influence of Neoplatonism. In "A Pastoral Dialogue" Cleon dotes not on Celia's pure white skin "but on thy purer mind."[125] But Carew showed little sympathy for the courtly cult of Platonic love or for its ethical and political implications. In his poetry the spiritual relationship never supplants or negates the physical. Nor can the one be divorced from the other. In the famous "Disdaine Returned" ("He that loves a Rosie cheeke . . . ") Carew loves not with the spirit or body alone: he seeks in his mistress both "a smooth and steadfast mind" *and* "lovely cheekes, or lips, or eyes."[126] The union of body and spirit is the ultimate expression of love and of human nature, beside which all else is second best. So Carew's lines to his mistress "in absence" describing their closeness while apart emerge in the end as a device to pass the time before they may come together again in flesh as well as in spirit:

> Wee'le cheat the lag, and lingring houres,
> Making our bitter absence sweet,
> Till soules, and bodyes both, may meet.[127]

That "both" unites them all—soul to soul, body to body, and, perhaps most significantly, body to soul. Here and there are suggestions that in accordance with Neoplatonic ideas, Carew believed in a progress of perception from the world of sense and material to the sphere of spirit and knowledge.[128] Whether or not this is the case, physical love in the poetry does elevate men and women to a spiritual union. Spirit and sense feed each other, and love is the union of body and soul both within the lover and between the lover and his mistress. Carew's position, then, may be described as Neoplatonic, but his emphasis is quite different from the Platonic love of the court and court masques in which the world of spirit and idea *transcends* the physical universe as masque dispels antimasque.

It is noteworthy that Carew's "Separation of Lovers" was one of four songs, all on the subject of love and honor, that he wrote for "an entertainment of the King and Queene" evidently in 1633.[129] It may be that the songs were intended as a commentary upon, and to some extent a criticism of, the cult of Platonic love that had just taken the court by storm in the production of Walter Montagu's *The Shepherds' Paradise*.[130] It is almost inconceivable that Carew would not have seen the play, and Rhodes Dunlap has drawn attention to the close echoes in lines 9–12 of "To My Mistresse in Absence" of the speech by Melidoro, Montagu's Platonic lover.[131] Beyond that we cannot be sure, but what is clear is Carew's awareness of Platonic love and his reaction to the cult:

> Let fooles thy mystique formes adore,
> I'le know thee in thy mortall state.[132]

It would appear that for Carew courtly Platonism was an abstraction that denied the senses and thereby negated what Carew lamented the absence of in "A Divine Mistris"—the "humanitie" of man, his nature.[133] If so, we may understand how he might have regarded it as an affront to his beliefs. The criticism, however, goes farther, because Platonic love was the metaphor through which the court articulated a political philosophy as well as an ethical code.[134] Carew may well have been more optimistic than Charles I about the capacities of men, the king's subjects, to regulate themselves and so may have been less attracted to an ethical and political system that enshrined the king as the soul of the commonwealth, ruling over creatures of appetite. Carew's rejection of courtly Platonism amounted, as we shall see, to a challenge to the political ideology of the court, to a critique of the court's vision of the commonweal, of the monarchy, and of the relationship between the king and his people.

The description of the commonweal as the "body politic," with the king the head and his subjects the members, is a commonplace Renaissance image. In Carew's poetry, however, the idea of the "body" takes on literal as well as metaphoric reality. The king and people Carew presents with freshness as literally conjoined so that sensations in one part of the body rapidly affect the other. When sickness befalls the monarch,

> Entring his royall limbes that is our head,
> Through us his mystique limbs the paine is spread,
> That man that doth not feele his part, hath none
> In any part of his dominion.[135]

The language of feeling and pain imparts a physicality that transcends metaphor. The king and his people are one body physically as well as theoretically united, just as Carew's lovers are joined in body as well as soul. And it is just such a love, physical as well as spiritual, of the people for the king that afflicts them with his pain:

> This griefe is felt at Court, where it doth move
> Through every joynt, like the true soule of love.[136]

Such a grief "shewes a good King is sicke, and good men mourne."[137] The repetition of the epithet underlines the fact that Carew as often is prescribing an ideal relationship while describing an actual one. The best relationship between a *good* ruler and *good* subjects is like the perfect union of true lovers: it is a physical togetherness as well as spiritual; it unites ruler and ruled, virtue and government. And so sickness, which threatens the good monarch, is a "Tyrant" ruling by arbitrary will that king who has governed in conjunction and love with his people.[138] It is "the minister of death," the most arbitrary of all rulers who knows no regimen but merciless conquest.[139] The union of king and subjects, and mutual love between them, Carew is saying, is essential to the health—indeed, the very life—of the body politic. And the good king of this ideal polity is not only God's lieutenant on earth but is possessed too, as was Carew's ideal mistress, of "humanitie"; he is the "Darling of the Gods and men."[140]

To Carew, kings are not gods who may decree what is virtuous and what is vicious. They too live in and are of a society that has fallen from virtue and so may themselves be susceptible to the corruptions of fallen nature. Absolute authority is beyond them. Carew tells his mistress who commands the return of her letters that although a monarch, she too must account for her actions and heed his wishes:

> If she refuse, warne her to come before
> The God of love, whom thus I will implore.[141]

Monarchs, Carew informs a lady resembling his mistress, may establish by their own authority values in their own kingdom, but there remains an absolute morality, a universal virtue to which they too are subject. The poet explores the idea, with unconventional implications, through the disarmingly familiar metaphor of the coin that bears the king's stamp:

> To Lead, or Brasse, or some such bad
> Metall, a Princes stamp may adde
> That valew, which it never had.
>
> But to the pure refined Ore,
> The stamp of Kings imparts no more
> Worth, then the mettall held before.

>   Only the Image gives the rate
>   To Subjects; in a forraine State
>   'Tis priz'd as much for its owne waight.[142]

A debased coinage was regarded in early Stuart England as the currency of an ailing kingdom. Here, of course, it is a kingdom falling from virtue and, incidentally, one in which outward values have become detached from intrinsic (metallic) value. Thus, Carew argues, a good king is he who comes closest to intrinsic worth, to nature, and stamps its values with his image, so that society takes by his authority nature itself as its currency. The good ruler's responsibility is to return society to those inherent, natural values of its first pure refined condition—that of man before society (and its sham concern with reputation) in the garden of innocence. A vision of nature, we may see, is central to Carew's political as well as ethical system. The function of government he still perceives as the rule of virtue: politics and morality are not divorced; government and love are not distinct. Rulers, like lovers, ought to renounce the empty considerations of honor and reputation by which princes, like all men, were evaluated in a fallen world. They were to take their standards of government from uncorrupted nature, to exemplify nature's first innocence in their persons, and to codify nature's dictates as the maxims of their rule.

We have suggested in discussing Carew's ethics that men and women rediscover their nature through a pure and eternal love, a love sealed in society by the physical and spiritual union of marriage. I would like to suggest that for Carew it is through the marriage of ruler and ruled, of the king and his people, perhaps in Parliament, that the commonweal too comes nearest to the kingdom of virtue. Carew's lovers, as we have seen, are political beings—sometimes monarch, sometimes subject. The lover is unfulfilled, however, in either role if, in the one case, his sovereign mistress spurns his "vassall heart" or when, as a conquering prince, his power does not secure him her love.[143] Whether ruler or subject, man as lover is complete and fulfilled only when love is spiritual and physical, mutual and reciprocated. So a king who conquers but rules without love is no king at all: He is, as "A deposition From Love" makes clear, "deposed."[144] And so in the commonweal as in the polity of love (for the two are really one) true kingship depends upon reciprocal love. Monarchy is the marriage of ruler and ruled that conjoins authority and love and so leads society, as it does man, to the virtue of nature.

The place of love and marriage in Carew's political thought may be understood most clearly from his poem "Upon my Lord Chiefe Justice his election of my lady A.W. for his Mistresse."[145] Law and love are here betrothed. In consequence the "government Tyrannicall" (compare the "tyrant Mistresse" of "An Elegie on the La: Pen") of "Vsurping Beauties" is to be brought under the rule of law.[146] Marriage controls the passions by governing them. Law and government in their turn, however, are to lie "In Love's soft lap" exchanging rigor and coercion for love and union:

> Harke how the sterne Law breathes
> Forth amorous sighs, and now prepares
> No fetters, but of silken wreathes,
> ....Love hath fi'lde
> His native roughnesse, Justice is growne milde.[147]

The marriage improves both potentially arbitrary love and overrigorous law. In their union "The golden Age returnes"—that is, an age in which outward appearances and inner virtues become one ("the fayre shall all be kind"); in which love is reciprocal ("who loves shall be belov'd"); in which men find their true and perfect nature (only the "froward mind" is "To a deformed shape . . . confin'd").[148] This is Carew's state of nature and perfect commonweal; it is the ideal vision of his politics of love: heavenly justice has now come to earth, as Astraea returns to rule.[149]

Carew's poem, however, is addressed to a specific person and has too a more particular application. The chief justice of the verse is Sir John Finch, who became Lord Chief Justice of the Court of Common Pleas on 16 October 1634. Finch was close to the court and a vigorous upholder of the royal prerogative; in 1637, he was the leading spokesman for the crown in the Ship Money case.[150] Finch, then, stands not only for justice in the abstract or in general but for royal justice and the exercise of royal justice during the years of the personal rule of Charles I. Finch's mistress, "my Lady A.W.," is Anne Wentworth, niece to Sir John Crofts, whose country home, Saxham, Carew regarded as a haven of nature and virtue. In Saxham there is no crime because men cannot steal what is given freely: "And as for thieves, thy bountie's such / They cannot steale, thou giv'st too much."[151] The rigor of justice has no place in this perfect society, as there is no sin in "A Rapture." Even in society, Carew tells us, men are not mere wild beasts to be tamed by "dreadfull Rods" of "sterne law" but have the potential for virtue in their nature.[152] And so in society and in the polity men should be ordered by love as well as authority so that they might rediscover their own higher nature and achieve that self-regulation that is the best government of all. If marriage regulates the sexual passions without denying man's sensual appetite, so in gov-

ernment the marriage of love and justice may order society without
denying the humanity and inherent good of man. There is more than
a hint of criticism in the poem—that justice needs to be softened and
government should woo with "silken wreathes," not "fetters."[153] The
reference to Astraea "new enthron'd" could not but have evoked
memories of a Queen Elizabeth under whose rule love had softened
the harshness of government.[154] Carew's "Upon my Lord Chiefe Justice . . . " argues for in general what it celebrates in particular: a union
of love and justice as the best form of government.

Charles I, as we have seen, communicated his vision of the best
government through his marriage represented as a Platonic union of
souls. Significantly the royal marriage is the central subject of the
poetry that Carew addressed to both the king and queen, but Carew's
depiction of that marriage is very different from the king's. Love and
government are intertwined in a verse that wishes for the monarch
as "A New-Yeares gift" the physical joys and fertile fruits of marriage:

> Season his cares by day with nights
> Crown'd with all conjugall delights,
> May the choyce beauties that enflame
> His Royall brest be still the same,
> And he still thinke them such, since more
> Thou canst not give from Natures store.
> Then as a Father let him be
> With numerous issue blest, and see
> The faire and God-like off-spring growne
> From budding starres to Suns full blowne.

In this important extract many of the strands in Carew's ethical and
political thought are interwoven. Love ameliorates the cares of government. The king retains his right to the title through a love that is
pure and constant, yet physical as well as spiritual. Such a love, such
a marriage is indeed "from Nature's store." In this physical and spiritual union the king not only lives and rules virtuously, he seeds and
sires virtue as his offspring, giving birth to "God-like" children—that
is, children made like the first man in God's image, "Suns" who, as
nature's light, may rescue a fallen world from darkness. The perfect
ruler is become the true lover. And in fashioning his government by
his marriage the king may secure "loyall hearts" and "conjugal de-
lights" with his subjects. *This* marriage—between the king and his
people—would see "One great continued festivall" of joy, that golden
age of love and justice united.[155] It is the prescription of this perfect
polity that is Carew's "New-Yeares gift. To the King."

It is, as it were, the other side of the government-love equation that Carew addresses to the queen. If the good ruler is, in Charles's case, the right lover, then here the true lover may have the best claim to rule. The queen, who exemplifies love, is a "great Commandresse" who has ordered the unbridled excesses of "wilde lust." Her government flows directly from her love by example rather than coercion. She teaches men that love is constant and fruitful, and as a result of her influence disordered nature itself submits to her government willingly. The "rude male" becomes satisfied with one partner; the very Satyr is "reconciled" to order.[156] The queen in Carew's poem, however, is not the Platonic lover of the masques. Like the "numerous issue" of "God-like off-spring" wished for the king, the queen's example and love is fertile: a "pregnant fire," which will engender virtue and order throughout the natural world. In both poems Carew's message is the same: true love is the government of nature, and the only true government is that which is founded on a love both physical and spiritual.

Carew's position on love and the politics of love, then, is very different from the tone and stance of the courtly Platonic love cult. The subject and images of Carew's love poetry are more physical; his language is more explicitly erotic than the abstractions of courtly Platonism. But we should not conclude from this that his poetry is less serious or less political. Language and tone reinforce Carew's argument. For Carew believes strongly in the potential for virtue in man's nature and so advocates not the transcendence or *denial* of the potentially wild manifestations of nature but that *marriage* of the senses and the spirit, or the reason, in which alone man may fulfill his nature. Accordingly, Carew sees right government not as the suppression of man's anarchic natural appetite by abstract authority ruling by coercion. Rather, he prescribes as the purpose of government that reordering of men's nature so as to restore them to the purer condition of their original state of nature in which no government was necessary. Such a regimen must be founded upon love. And in the commonweal as well as in the world of ethics (the distinction would have meant much less to him than to us) Carew advocates marriage—here the union of the ruler and the ruled in love and virtue—as the mean between the anarchy of unordered appetites and the sterility of an authority that, in suppressing the sensuality of man, denied his nature and nature itself.[157]

Marriage, we recall, Carew described as a condition of peace in a polity of love beset by the tempests of tears and sighs of wild or unsatisfied passion.[158] Love—illicit, unrequited, or lust—is often depicted in Carew's poetry in Petrarchan martial imagery as a struggle or battle. In returning his letters to the mistress who now spurned him, Carew recalled in defeat his "former fights, 'gainst fiercer foes, then shee / Did at our first incounter seeme to bee."[159] "A deposition from Love" compares the conquest of a mistress to a siege; it is "Truce in Love entreated" by he who has in his heart "No voyd place for another Dart."[160] Constant and mutual love, by contrast, secures, as Carew describes it in "A Rapture," "steadfast peace" where "no rude sounds shake us with sudden starts," that "Halcion calmnesse" of the Elyzium in which the poem is located.[161] It may be, then, that it is *this* peace and calmness—that of a paradise located outside time and history—that Carew wished for society and the commonweal as well as for individual men in prescribing a politics of marriage as the best mode of government.

In this context we may begin to understand Carew's most difficult and most obviously political poem, "In answer of an Elegiacall Letter upon the death of the King of Sweden from Aurelian Townshend . . . ."[162] During his personal rule Charles I, it is often said, was dedicated to a policy of peace in order to avoid resummoning Parliament. Cavalier poetry celebrating the "halcyon" days of the 1630s is accordingly read as uncritical idealization of the king's ignoble and enforced withdrawal from European affairs—as, once again, the sycophantic celebration of a royal policy that was not for the good of the realm. Carew's poem is usually regarded as the classic example of this flattery of Caroline foreign policy, and it is not difficult to see why.[163] At one level Carew's poem exemplifies that retreat from European engagement that characterized Charles I's foreign policy and alienated some of his subjects. In reply to Townshend's exhortations "inviting me to write" on the death of Gustavus Adolphus, Carew counsels his friend:

> But let us that in myrtle bowers sit
> Under secure shades, use the benefit
> Of peace and plenty, which the blessed hand
> Of our good King gives this obdurate Land.[164]

The poet's place, Carew argues, is to celebrate this peace rather than to dwell upon the ravages of a European war from which England is fortunately free. Townshend's own court masque, *Tempe Restored*, is held up as a more fitting subject for his muse.[165] And yet for all his disclaimer, the subject does concern Carew—for one of his longest poems of 104 lines! There is a suggestion of irony too—or at least of some divorce between words and meaning—in the poem. The forcefulness of "Bellow for freedome" is a noise that must awake the reader as Townshend's "shrill accents" sounded an alarm to Carew's "drowsie eyes."[166] Gustavus Adolphus forces himself upon the stage of Carew's poem as a figure "mightie," "victorious," "majesticke."[167] Carew's obvious praise for the King of Sweden appears inexplicably at odds with his advice to Townshend about the appropriate subjects of his art. There is a tension within the poem that may reflect Carew's own ambivalent attitude toward royal foreign policy. The discrepancy may also be understood otherwise, for Gustavus is presented as a figure beyond poetry:

> His actions were too mighty to be rais'd
> Higher by verse, let him in prose be prays'd,
> In modest faithfull story, which his deedes
> Shall turne to Poems: . . .[168]

He is, for Carew, a figure *outside* poetry. Gustavus represents the flux and change, victories and defeat, of action in the world—a world of noise, of time and events, of death, of fate, of history. It is this world rather than Gustavus Adolphus that Carew rejects as a subject for his muse:

> Let us to supreame providence commit
> The fate of Monarchs, which first thought it fit
> To rend the Empire from the *Austrian* graspe,
> And next from *Swedens* . . .[169]

Carew does not reject Gustavus Adolphus specifically. He wishes to distance his verse from chronicle, from the relation of events, the rise and fall of states.[170] He does so because poetry, as Sidney had claimed, may express higher truths than history. Carew's poetry "of Love and Beautie" has a more sublime purpose and engagement than with the flux of European power politics: it is concerned with reformation, the restoration of a golden age of innocence beside the calm of which the battles of Germany seem but a noise in time. So halfway through his "answer" Carew commends to his friend Townshend's own poetry of love and nature as a more fitting subject for his muse. For Townshend's "past'rall pipe" and "Angel-shapes" in his masque for the queen "brought us from above / A patterne of their owne celestiall love."[171] Townshend's masque had risen above the world of events: its "ravishing sounds" did "dispense / Knowledge and pleasure, to the soule, and sense."[172] Townshend had instructed in that pure love that might lift men and monarchs beyond the noise of time and events to the calm of an earlier condition of innocence. All man's strivings in the world could secure no more. The "*Halcyon* days"

Carew celebrates is that 'Halcyon calmnesse' of the lovers in the Elizium of "A Rapture."[173] It is far from clear whether Carew believed that those days had come to England during the 1630s: he acknowledges that England is not the land of perfect peace and harmony but an "obdurate" country, resistant to reformation. But we may be sure that for Carew the securing of such a condition was the purpose of poetry. If Carew believed that the restoration of uncorrupted nature might be attained by the poetry of love, then we may more clearly understand his disclaimer that the noise of strife and battle (the antithesis of love) "concernes not us."[174]

If we are to argue that Carew's poetry expounded ethical and political beliefs, if we are to suggest that Carew believed in the power of poetry to effect important change, then we must withdraw Carew from Pope's company of gentlemen who wrote with ease. It is right that we do so, for too many since Pope have been led to assume that because Carew was a courtier, because his lines often read with effortless simplicity, he did not take his poetry seriously or have anything serious to say. His contemporaries, however, did not make the same mistake. Suckling, for example, rejected (probably with tongue in cheek) Carew's claims to the crown of the wits because

> His Muse was hard bound, and th'issue of's brain
> Was seldom brought forth but with trouble and pain.[175]

Carew himself acknowledged his painstaking industry in a less scatological metaphor, spurning what he called the "unkneaded dowebak't prose" or ballad rhymes of his contemporaries. Carew worked at his poetry and admired others who labored to refine their verse.[176] "Thy labour'd workes," he assured Ben Jonson, "shall live, when Time devoures / Th'abortive off-spring of their hastie houres."[177] Such labor did not always guarantee appreciation. Poets, Carew reminded his mentor, wrote not for their reputation in a "dull age" but for "after dayes," "immortall Bayes" that placed them, as it did their poetry, beyond reputation and time. Jonson, unlike the rhymesters, struck "soules" into his verse and so wrote not for an age but for all time.[178]

Carew took his own poetry seriously because he appreciated and made claims for the importance—indeed, the power—of poetry. The claim to poetic power is conventional, but Carew asserts it with particular force to remind the lover of his authority. And given the political freighting of love poetry, this was also to argue, in the 1630s, for the power of poetry in the commonweal. When the poet speaks— often through the lover—in Carew's lines, he asserts the power of his art. Though she spurns him, Celia is forcefully reminded of the poet's power in the aptly titled "Ingratefull beauty threatned":

> Know Celia, (since thou art so proud,)
> 'Twas I that gave thee thy renowne:
> Thou hadst, in the forgotten crowd
> Of common beauties, liv'd unknowne,
> Had not my verse exhal'd thy name,
> And with it, ympt the wings of fame.[179]

Celia's "killing power" is the gift of the poet—and the poet may as easily take it away. The power to create and to "uncreate" remains in the poet's hands.

Herein lay the power of poetry: the power of creation and immortality. The poet's power to create and to immortalize derived from a treasury of which he was the sole beneficiary—the treasury of nature. Carew offers to a mistress in return for her favors "Rich Nature's store, (which is the Poet's Treasure)."[180] The only true poetry was that which distributed nature's wealth in order to give life. So Jonson's poems were "births," as Donne "kindled first by thy Promethean breath."[181] Poetry alone offered images of virtue that could effect reformation. To Carew nature's perfection could not be represented in pictorial images. "Canst thou," he challenges in "To the Painter," ". . . tell how / To paint a vertue?" The answer is already clear: "your Artifice hath mist." But nature can be faithfully represented through love:

> Yet your Art cannot equalize
> This *Picture* in her lovers eyes,
> His eyes the pencills are which limbe
> Her truly, as her's coppy him,
> His heart the Tablet which alone,
> Is for that porctraite the tru'st stone.
> If you would a truer see,
> Marke it in their posteritie.[182]

Love is perfect nature's expression. And so the poet who writes of love does what the painter cannot: he distributes nature's treasure— virtue—in order to renew his age.

The inculcation of virtue through a poetry of love and nature was Carew's contribution to his age. But the inculcation of virtue in this age was also the business of government. We have seen how Carew's lover is depicted in political language. No less the poet, nature's lover, is presented as a monarch. Jonson, for example, is advised to dispel any concern about criticism of his verse, because his less good is judged by the standards of his best: "the quarrel lyes / Within thine own virge."[183] The virge is the boundary of the royal domain: poetry is Jonson's court and he, its monarch. The parallel is succinctly made in Carew's famous epitaph on Donne:

> Here lies a King, that rul'd as hee thought fit
> The universall Monarchy of wit.[184]

Carew defines wit in "A Fancy" as the didactic content of art.[185] The monarch of wit, then, was a king indeed, leading men to knowledge and establishing rules of behavior. For Carew the purpose of government was to make each man his own ruler by restoring him to the innocence of his first nature. Poets shared with kings this responsibility and power. Carew's purpose then could not have been loftier or his claim for the power of poetry greater. Studying Carew's poetry, we have come a long way from the stance of frivolity and flattery that allegedly characterized the Cavaliers:

> . . . cause you underneath may find
> A sence that can enforme the mind;
> Divine, or moral rules impart
> Or Raptures of Poetick Art.[186]

7

Andrew Marvell, Oliver Cromwell, and the Horatian Ode

Blair Worden

An Horatian *Ode upon* Cromwel's *Return from* Ireland

The forward Youth that would appear
Must now forsake his *Muses* dear,
   Nor in the Shadows sing
   His Numbers languishing.
'Tis time to leave the Books in dust,
And oyl th' unused Armours rust:
   Removing from the Wall
   The Corslet of the Hall.
So restless *Cromwel* could not cease
In the inglorious Arts of Peace,   10
   But through adventrous War
   Urged his active Star.
And, like the three-fork'd Lightning, first
Breaking the Clouds where it was nurst,
   Did thorough his own Side
   His fiery way divide.
For 'tis all one to Courage high
The Emulous or Enemy;
   And with such to inclose
   Is more then to oppose.   20
Then burning through the Air he went,
And Pallaces and Temples rent:
   And *Cæsars* head at last
   Did through his Laurels blast.
'Tis Madness to resist or blame

The force of angry Heavens flame:
  And, if we would speak true,
  Much to the Man is due.
Who, from his private Gardens, where
He liv'd reserved and austere,   30
  As if his highest plot
  To plant the Bergamot,
Could by industrious Valour climbe
To ruine the great Work of Time,
  And cast the Kingdome old
  Into another Mold.
Though Justice against Fate complain,
And plead the antient Rights in vain:
  But those do hold or break
  As Men are strong or weak.   40
Nature that hateth emptiness,
Allows of penetration less:
  And therefore must make room
  Where greater Spirits come.
What field of all the Civil Wars,
Where his were not the deepest Scars?
  And *Hampton* shows what part
  He had of wiser Art.
Where, twining subtile fears with hope,
He wove a Net of such a scope,   50
  That *Charles* himself might chase
  To *Caresbrooks* narrow case.
That thence the *Royal Actor* born
The *Tragick Scaffold* might adorn:
  While round the armed Bands
  Did clap their bloody hands.
He nothing common did or mean
Upon that memorable Scene:
  But with his keener Eye
  The Axes edge did try: 60
Nor call'd the *Gods* with vulgar spight
To vindicate his helpless Right,
  But bow'd his comely Head,
  Down as upon a Bed.
This was that memorable Hour
Which first assur'd the forced Pow'r
  So when they did design
  The *Capitols* first Line,
A bleeding Head where they begun,
Did fright the Architects to run;   70

And yet in that the *State*
Foresaw it's happy Fate.
And now the *Irish* are asham'd
To see themselves in one Year tam'd:
    So much one Man can do,
    That does both act and know.
They can affirm his Praises best,
And have, though overcome, confest
    How good he is, how just,
    And fit for highest Trust: 80
Nor yet grown stiffer with Command,
But still in the *Republick's* hand:
    How fit he is to sway
    That can so well obey.
He to the *Commons Feet* presents
A *Kingdome*, for his first years rents:
    And, what he may, forbears
    His Fame to make it theirs:
And has his Sword and Spoyls ungirt,
To lay them at the *Publick's* skirt.   90
    So when the Falcon high
    Falls heavy from the Sky,
She, having kill'd, no more does search,
But on the next green Bow to pearch;
    Where, when he first does lure,
    The Falckner has her sure.
What may not then our *Isle* presume
While Victory his Crest does plume!
    What may not others fear
    If thus he crown each Year!   100
A *Cæsar* he ere long to *Gaul*,
To Italy an *Hannibal*,
    And to all States not free
    Shall *Clymacterick* be.
The *Pict* no shelter now shall find
Within his party-colour'd Mind;
    But from this Valour sad
    Shrink underneath the Plad:
Happy if in the tufted brake
The *English Hunter* him mistake;   110
    Nor lay his Hounds in near
    The *Caledonian* Deer.
But thou the Wars and Fortunes Son
March indefatigably on;
    And for the last effect

Still keep thy Sword erect:
Besides the force it has to fright
The Spirits of the shady Night,
The same *Arts* that did *gain*
A *Pow'r* must it *maintain*.[1]

I

Andrew Marvell's "An *Horatian* Ode upon *Cromwel's* Return from *Ireland*" is the most private of public poems. It may be a solitary meditation; it may be written, after Horace, for a "forward youth" whose identity is now unknown to us; but it scarcely seems addressed to the public audience of Marvell's tribute to Cromwell in "The First Anniversary." We enter an imaginative landscape beyond politics, outside the movement of history, where the figures of the ode appear stilled as upon some ancient vase: restless Cromwell, the bowing royal actor, the clapping soldiers, the running architects, the confessing Irish, the hunted Pict. Yet the poem's transcendence of events need not be taken for detachment from them, or its privacy for retreat. I want to suggest that the celebrated poise and urbanity of the poem have been created out of an urgent preoccupation with current political debate. Marvell has given timelessness to a desperate and portentous moment in his country's history, the arrival of Oliver Cromwell in England in the summer of 1650. Language has been immortalized too: the language of ephemeral tracts and newspapers, which is near enough to the surface of the poem to suggest a younger Marvell as close to the world of political journalism as the Restoration M.P. and Whig pamphleteer were to be; a Marvell around whose head there ran the phrases of the arguments that presented Englishmen with such grave choices during that dismal year.

In 1650, Marvell was twenty-nine. To simplify, he was a Royalist before that year, and a Cromwellian and then a Whig after it. Marvell, as always, resists such simplification. He is a man, as his correspondence and pamphlets testify, who can inhabit a range of voices, each of them authentic at the moment of delivery. His public poems are occasional poems, responsible only to their occasions. To describe as Royalist the political poems that survive from the late 1640s is to risk forgetting the sympathies that traversed party lines, and to court the danger of mistaking Cavalier nostalgia or personal loyalty for commitment to a political cause for which Marvell, who spent the years of the first civil war on the Continent, never fought. The hatred of the regicide that is unmistakable in the two political poems of 1650—

the Horatian Ode and "Tom May's Death"—is foreshadowed only in a poem that cannot be attributed to Marvell with perfect confidence, the bitter elegy proposing revenge for the death in battle of the Royalist Francis Lord Villiers in 1648. Some readers find the poems of 1649 to the Royalist poet Richard Lovelace and on the death of that forward youth of a Royalist house, Henry Lord Hastings, to be Cavalier only in a looser sense.[2] Even so, 1650 marks a divide. After that year Marvell's public poems all support the Roundhead cause. There is the poem early in 1651 to Oliver St. John, Cromwell's cousin and intimate friend. "The First Anniversary," written in the winter of 1654–55, and the elegy on Cromwell in 1658, unambiguously favor the Cromwellian regime.

Like Horace, Marvell becomes a lesser poet once he has accepted the new order. Did he observe the resemblance? Horace, the republican soldier of Philippi, came to terms with the rule of Augustus Caesar. The political odes of Horace that are most admired, those of the first three books, convey the losses as well as the gains of that painful transition. Marvell's Horatian Ode does something similar. Marvell would doubtless have been glad by the mid-1650s to hear his relationship with Cromwell compared to that of Horace with Augustus. The ode of 1650 tells us about Marvell's Horatian transition. It may even have assisted it.

II

The opening lines of the Horatian Ode, as is well known, refer to those early passages of Lucan's *Pharsalia* which relate Julius Caesar's decision to cross the Rubicon and the chill dread of the inhabitants of Ariminum as he camped before the town. The allusion has been more often explained than felt. We need to understand why Cromwell's return across the Irish Sea could seem as critical an event in England's history as Caesar's crossing of the Rubicon had been in Rome's, and why at that moment an Englishman might feel an affinity with the people of Ariminum.

Oliver Cromwell was the leading personality of the regime that emerged after the execution of Charles I in 1649. To the surprise of his contemporaries, his preeminence received no formal recognition. He was second-in-command of the army, but the army was the servant of the purged House of Commons, the Rump, of which he was one among many equal members, and which was to hold power until he forcibly dissolved it in 1653. In the summer of 1649, aged fifty, he led an expedition to Ireland, where the alliance of Royalist and Catholic forces threatened the infant republic. The massacres of Drogheda and Wexford in the autumn added to his long and, as it seemed to his friends and foes alike, divinely appointed sequence of military triumphs. In May 1650, just before his return to England, he successfully concluded the protracted siege of Clonmel, not now one of his best-known victories but known well enough to contemporaries to earn a proud place in Marvell's elegy on Cromwell in 1649.

Before his departure for Ireland in 1649, Cromwell had somehow held the regime together, by reconciling moderate with radical M.P.s and by persuading Parliament and the army to suspend their many differences. In the winter of 1649–50, when the government's fortunes reached a low ebb, his guidance was sorely missed. Royalist plots and Presbyterian propaganda threatened national security. Even if the Royalist resistance could be overcome, there was the potentially still greater threat of an invasion from Scotland, led by Charles II. The republic's attempts to broaden the base of its support had backfired; taxation was soaring; and it proved difficult to raise and finance the recruits anxiously needed to revive the county militias and to strengthen the new model army both in England and in Ireland. Politicians and pamphleteers lamented the divisions within the Puritan cause. M.P.s alternated between panic and despair. One of them committed suicide on the first anniversary of the king's execution, 30 January 1650; another died the following month after depression about the regicide; a third found himself "full of melancholy and apprehensions of death"; Lord General Fairfax was said to be "melancholy mad"; and the army officers wondered whether God had turned against them. Sir Henry Vane, one of the leaders of the republic, admitted in April 1650 that his colleagues

> were now in a far worse state than ever yet they had been; that all the world was and would be their enemies; that their own army and General [Fairfax] were not to be trusted; that the whole kingdom would rise and cut their throats upon the first occasion; and that they knew not any place to go unto to be safe.[3]

Well might Marvell write of England's new rulers, in lines 69–70 of the ode,

> A bleeding Head where they begun,
> Did fright the Architects to run. . . .

Royalists derived what cheer they could from the republic's difficulties, but their morale was no higher. Bitterly divided, embarrassed by their dependence on foreign aid, they could win no more enthusiasm in England than could the government. The mood was no happier across the broad spectrum of opinion committed to neither cause. In the political literature and the private correspondence of 1650 there can be detected a pervasive sense of political and moral dislocation. Regicide seemed to have been both a divine punishment for national sins and an act of constitutional rape, so traumatic that no one before Marvell could write adequately about it. A rash of millenarian speculation in the pamphlet literature reflected a yearning for an apocalyptic solution, beyond the exhausted resources of human responsibility and choice.

In the first five months of 1650 the absent Cromwell held the public imagination, where he had acquired an elemental force. Royalist satire paid tribute to his public stature by portraying him as a demon, a monster with a huge, copper, swathelike nose. He was feared and hated, but respected too. He seemed what Clarendon would later call him: "a brave, bad man." On 4 March 1650 the underground newspaper *The Royal Diurnal* acknowledged of Cromwell's Irish exploits: "Noll yet goes on without fear of the strength or combination of enemies about him. Brave desperate rebel! And in an ill cause too! Were his cause just or honest, I profess I should love him." Such ambivalence is worth recalling when we assess Marvell's presentation of Cromwell in the Horatian Ode. So may be the experience of another poet whose loyalties during the Interregnum have proved hard to chart: Abraham Cowley, a Royalist who submitted to the Protectorate in 1656 and who would remember of Cromwell that "sometimes I was filled with horror and detestation of his actions, and sometimes I inclined a little to reverence and admiration of his courage, conduct and success."[4]

The Royalists of early 1650 claimed to be certain of Cromwell's intentions. He would swiftly return to England, replace Fairfax as Lord General, turn out Parliament, and either become king or install John Bradshaw, the president of the Council of State, as a puppet monarch.[5] Yet Cromwell remained in Ireland. Why? As the months passed, the question became a mystery. On 8 January the Commons "desired" him "to come over and give his attendance here in Parliament." State palaces and gardens were awarded him on 25 February, in anticipation of his arrival. On 19 March, still without an answer to its earlier request, the Commons asked "to know your resolution, and when we may expect you." Puzzled Royalist propagandists improvised explanations: Cromwell was ill; Cromwell was dead; Cromwell was trapped by the Irish army. Parliament dispatched a more urgent message on 27 March; there were two further letters in April, when a ship was sent to collect him; an "express" followed on 4 May; and on 10 May the Commons resolved to inform him "that the House still continues in its resolution of having him over; that he is therefore to have his affairs in order that he may repair hither." It was in response to this last instruction that he finally returned at the end of May.[6]

An obvious solution to the puzzle is the politically innocent one that Cromwell believed himself to be needed in Ireland, where a winter of sickness and death had weakened the army's morale. While Parliament longed for his safe return, he waited with equal anxiety for fresh supplies of men and money with which to finish the surprisingly tenacious Irish resistance. Yet that explanation may not be complete. There may have been a political motive as well, although if so it will have lain not in Cromwell's ambition but in the lack of it. Always hesitant before major political decisions, he tended especially to delay those that would elevate him. Whatever the tone of lines 81–95 of the Horatian Ode, which dwell on Cromwell's subservience to Parliament, they tell the truth. He had not "grown stiffer with Command," and he was "still in the *Republick's* hand." He always liked to think of himself as a servant rather than a master in politics, and he encouraged the army to do the same.[7] Even his enemies acknowledged, although they were unable to comprehend, his strenuous attempt in the summer of 1650 to persuade Fairfax to keep his command. Yet as the pressure for his return to England increased, he must have known that the crisis born of Fairfax's disaffection and of the Scottish threat would elevate his position. It would have been in character to postpone the grasping of the nettle.

Had Marvell sensed Cromwell's reticence? If so, he was unusually perceptive. An unambitious Cromwell accorded with few people's suppositions. When he accepted command of the Irish expedition in 1649 Cromwell felt it necessary to counter the notion that he was prompted by "private respects."[8] At the beginning of February 1650, the M.P. Lord Lisle, noting Cromwell's failure to answer Parliament's invitation to return, had "some doubt of his coming, his interest, I believe, being in many respects to stay there."[9] Bulstrode Whitelocke, another M.P., noted in his memoirs for April 1650 that by his Irish successes Cromwell "got a great interest, not only in the officers of the army, both here and there, but likewise in the Parliament and Council of State, with their whole party."[10] It would not have seemed cynical to suppose that by remaining at the head of his victorious forces Cromwell was biding his time before crossing his Rubicon. At the time of his subsequent reentry into England, in August 1651, when he allowed the Scots to move south and followed them with his own army, members of the Council of State "raged and uttered sad discontents against Cromwell, and suspicions of his fidelity."[11]

The suspicions of his fidelity in 1650 were heightened by the publication of a disingenuous letter of 2 April in which he explained to the Speaker his continued absence. That document, with its recurrent use of the words "obey" and "obedience," gives an edge of irony to (and could lie behind) Marvell's observation that Cromwell "can so well obey" (line 84). At first, wrote Cromwell, he had learned of Parliament's resolutions only through "private intimations." He had awaited a formal letter, "which was to be the rule of my *obedience* . . . it being not fit for me to prophesy whether the letter would be an absolute command, or having limitations with a liberty left by the Parliament to me, to consider in what way to yield my *obedience*." Thinking that the Commons might have changed its mind now that the spring campaign in Ireland was under way,

> I did humbly conceive it much consisting with my duty, humbly to beg a positive signification what your will is; professing (as before the Lord) that I am most ready to *obey* your commands herein with all alacrity; rejoicing only to be about that work which I am called to by those God hath set over me, which I acknowledge you to be; and fearing only in *obeying* you, to *disobey* you.[12]

Marvell's Cromwell is "fit to sway" and "fit for highest Trust." Since "So much one Man can do," what role will be left for the disordered factions of Parliament now that he has returned to England? Can we expect that the Cromwell who has crossed the Rubicon, and who in the concluding couplet of the ode is to maintain power by the military arts that have gained it, will be content to remain a submissive "Falcon" (line 91) throughout the Scottish and the continental campaigns which the later part of the poem foresees? The Cromwell of the ode (unlike the Cromwell of the later poems) may not seem to be a particularly Horatian (or at least not a particularly Augustan) figure. Burning through the air, rending palaces and temples, he has something of the demonic Cromwell painted by Royalist newswriters. With his "wiser Art," "twining subtle fears with hope," and with his "Courage high," we might take him for the Royalists' brave bad man—until we learn in line 79 that he is "good." The same line calls him "just"—even though in line 37 justice has vainly protested against the fate that has advanced him. What do we make of these seeming contradictions? Is line 79 ("How good he is, how just") an informed assessment? Is it ironical? Is it wishful thinking? Is it praise of the kind legitimized by the panegyric, which exhorts to the virtues it describes? Perhaps we should not, perhaps we could not close the door Marvell has left open. The poem's ambiguity about Cromwell's constitutional intentions is apposite to the tense uncertainty that greeted his return to England. Fear and hope, twined by Cromwell in the poem, were inseparable in the public expectation of him.

He landed at Bristol on 28 May. Volleys of gunfire saluted him, as they were often to do in the days that followed. Accompanied by "some few gentlemen and officers of the army," he reached Windsor on 31 May, where he was met by

> many persons of eminence, Members of Parliament, and of the Council of State, and chief officers of the army; after much time spent in expressing civil respects one to another, and in congratulating his welcome thither, they had some discourse on the affairs of Ireland, and of the prosperous success wherewith it hath pleased God to crown his happy undertakings.[13]

So reported the government press, which stressed the "modesty" of Cromwell's demeanor and his desire to be spared excessive "pomp" on his entry into the capital the following day. His reception, on 1 June, was nevertheless heroic. It was the greatest public event in London at least since Cromwell's return from the suppression of the Levellers a year earlier, and perhaps since the execution of the king. After a large gathering of M.P.s and officers had welcomed him on Hounslow Heath, he passed through Hyde Park to arrive at Westminster, "accompanied by many more lords, and most of the Members of Parliament and the Council of State, the officers of the army, and many hundred well-affected gentlemen and citizens." On 2 June he had a private conversation with Fairfax, an interview distinguished, the official press nervously asserted, by "remarkable expressions of love and courtesy," "sufficient to check the false tongues." The same day brought a delegation to Cromwell from the mayor and aldermen of London, who acknowledged "God's mercy in carrying his Excellency through so many difficulties in Ireland and bringing him victoriously hither, etc. Unto which his Lordship made a modest reply, returning the praise and glory to God alone." On 4 June, when the Commons gave Cromwell "the hearty thanks of this House for his great good service," the Speaker delivered "an eloquent oration, setting forth the providence of God in those great and strange works, which God hath wrought by him, as the instrument."[14]

The events of the week that followed Cromwell's landing on 28 May are the occasion of the Horatian Ode. We cannot be certain when

Marvell wrote the poem (or know whether he ever revised it), but the evidence we shall consider suggests that, at the least, the work had taken shape in his mind within a short time of Cromwell's reception in London—perhaps within a matter of days. Admittedly it was not known in early June that Cromwell would replace Fairfax and lead the military campaign that is foretold near the end of the poem, but both developments had been long and confidently predicted in the press. Both, in any case, came about quickly. Cromwell succeeded as lord general in late June and led the army into Scotland in July. The expedition was to produce the seemingly miraculous victory at Dunbar in September and to end a year later in the Scottish invasion and defeat at Worcester.

Cromwell's move across the Scottish border in July 1650 was regarded and presented by the government as the only alternative to an incursion by the barbarous Scots, whose presence in England during the civil wars had fortified the traditional hatred of them. As early as March 1649 Cromwell, wondering whether to lead the forces to Ireland, had understood that campaigns against England's neighbors might unite the country against Charles II:

> The quarrel is brought to that state, that we can hardly return unto that tyranny that formerly we were under . . . but we must at the same time be subject to the kingdom of Scotland or the kingdom of Ireland, for the bringing in of the King. Now that should awaken all Englishmen, who perhaps are willing enough he should have come in upon an accommodation [with his English opponents], but not that he must come from Ireland or Scotland.[15]

Cromwell's argument is vindicated by the concluding, almost messianic section of the Horatian Ode, a poem that appears to enjoy its mockery of both Irishmen and Scotsmen. Marvell, like Horace, is a national poet, looking to a great leader who, through foreign conquest, will rescue a land torn by civil war and restore harmony to its troubled inhabitants. During the Protectorate, when he wrote nationalist (or jingoist) war poetry against the Dutch and the Spanish, his love of Cromwell would belong to his love of country.

So a patriotic task might await the forward youth, who, at a time when the government is stepping up its recruitment drive, must lay down his pen for the sword. Some months earlier the government newspaper, *A Brief Relation*, in a rare editorial comment, had suggested that peaceable pursuits were appropriate only to peaceful times, and had urged "such whose genius leads them to the sword, and who desire instruction in the art military" to read a forthcoming book by the London militia captain Richard Elton, *The Complete Body of the Art Military.* There Elton addressed himself to "the apt and forward soldier" and to "the young soldier." The forward youth of Marvell's poem was not alone in being offered Cromwell as a model: a government publication describing Cromwell's reception at Windsor on 31 May hoped that readers would "imitate" the "valour" he had shown in Ireland;[16] and on 5 July a new government newspaper, *Perfect Passages,* reported from Lancashire that

> a regiment is raising in these parts for his Excellency the Lord General [Cromwell], and many young men of quality are seeking that employment, desiring to do something worthy of their births . . . for where there is discourse of war, it is a shame for a gentleman to say that he hath read it only, [not] that he saw it.

It sounds as if Marvell's forward youth, taking down rusty armor in the hall, likewise has a birth of which to prove worthy.[17]

III

Although Marvell's treatment of Cromwell's constitutional intentions raises a live issue of the summer of 1650, the vision of the poem is hardly a constitutional one. By 1650 the constitution was dead. It had been put to the sword in the winter of 1648–49 by Pride's Purge and the regicide. Like Hobbes, whose *Leviathan* appeared in 1651, Marvell has moved beyond arguments about legality:

> Though Justice against Fate complain,
> And plead the ancient Rights in vain:
> But those do hold or break
> As Men are strong or weak.

The lines say what page after page of government propaganda in 1650 tried to say. John Wallace is right to set the Horatian Ode (as Quentin Skinner sets *Leviathan*) against the controversy that convulsed the country after the government's decision, at the start of the year, to impose an "engagement" of loyalty on the nation.[18] Opponents of the regime faced a stark problem of conscience. If they remained loyal to the defeated cause, they would lose their political and legal rights. Government apologists adopted a Hobbesian argument that obliged subjects to give allegiance to any government that afforded protection. De facto theories of obedience may seem vulnerable or amoral to men who study them during times of constitutional security; in periods of breakdown they can acquire a pressing logic.

The Horatian Ode gives poetic life to the public mood fostered by the engagement controversy. We do not know whether Marvell was required to take the engagement, but the prospect must have confronted him, and he will have been aware of the bitter divisions that the test brought to his native Hull, that contentious garrison town.[19] No lettered Englishman could have escaped the engagement controversy. Of the pamphlets that supported the government's position, one of the most eloquent was Marchamont Nedham's *The Case of the Commonwealth of England Stated*, published in May 1650, the month of Cromwell's return from Ireland. "The power of the sword," Nedham asserts, "is, and ever hath been, the foundation of all titles to government." E. E. Duncan-Jones has noted a series of striking verbal resemblances between the pamphlet and the Horatian Ode.[20] The careers of Nedham and Marvell, both "particular friends" of John Milton,[21] have suggestive parallels. Before 1650, while Marvell wrote poems about Royalists, Nedham wrote Royalist tracts. But Nedham (a year Marvell's senior) was also a poet of sorts. The volume of elegies that marked the death of Henry Lord Hastings in the summer of 1649, *Lachrymae Musarum*, "The Tears of the Muses," carried an appendix of poems that appear to have been submitted after the book had reached the printer. The first of these poems is Marvell's. The second is by "M.N.," almost certainly Marchamont Nedham.[22] The possibility of collaboration is heightened if we set Marvell's lines

> Therefore the *Democratick* Stars did rise,
> And all that worth from hence did *Ostracise*

beside Nedham's couplet (later appropriated by Dryden)

> It is decreed, we must be drained (I see)
> Down to the dregs of a Democracie.

To Nedham, who did not hesitate to take the engagement, the winter of 1649–50 presented what a less acrobatic conscience might have found a more searching test. Imprisoned for his Royalist activities, he was offered release and employment if he would turn his nimble pen to the government's use. Having duly produced *The Case of the Commonwealth* in May, he became in June the first editor of the weekly republican journal, *Mercurius Politicus*.

Where Nedham can alter allegiance without pain, even with relish, the Marvell of the Horatian Ode is a man of troubled and divided loyalties. Even so, we may profit from a comparison between the ode and the early issues of Nedham's *Mercurius Politicus*. The first number, published on 13 June, although appearing too late for Cromwell's return to be news, included a full account of it and remarked that Royalists should "stoop with reverence at the name of that victorious commander Cromwell," whose

> most famous victories in Ireland, being added to the garland of his English victories, have crowned him in the opinion of all the world, for one of the wisest and most accomplished leaders, amongst the present and past generations. . . . It is the wonder of our neighbour nations, that so much should be done in so little time.

On 25 July, Nedham's readers learned that Cromwell was "as restless in his own sphere" (compare "So restless *Cromwel* could not cease") "as the great intelligencers are in theirs" (compare "Urged his active Star"). Cromwell would defeat the Scots "because it is the privilege of this General, consigned from Heaven, to conquer wherever he goes" (cf. "'Tis Madness to resist or blame / The force of angry Heavens flame").

The proximity of the ode to propaganda becomes striking in the nationalist conclusion to the poem. That propaganda drew on literary and mythological inheritances which likewise surface in that part of the ode. Despite the government's difficulties at home, the might of its army and navy had raised England's standing abroad. Lines 67–70 of the ode

> So when they did design,
> The *Capitols* first Line,
>   A bleeding head where they begun,
>   Did fright the Architects to run

point to Livy's tale of the prophecy that Rome would be "the chief castle of the empire and the capital place of the whole world," and so seem to allude to the notion, which developed in the early 1650s, that republican England would become—in Milton's words—"another Rome in the West."[23] Marvell's Cromwell will clear the path to empire by defeating the Scots and then moving into Europe to level its monarchies:

> A *Caesar* he ere long to *Gaul*,
> To *Italy* an *Hannibal*,
>   And to all States not free
>   Shall *Clymacterick* be.

This vision, which called on an ancient prophetic tradition, also belonged to a tradition of Protestant imperialism by which ancient prophecy had been appropriated: a tradition that had led Sir Philip Sidney (according to Fulke Greville) to believe that if only Europe's Protestants had been able to persuade their rulers to send a united force south, "the passage . . . over the Alps would have been . . . more easy than Hannibal's was." Sidney had urged men to remember

> the state of Italy; which excellent temper of spirits, earth and air, having long been smothered, and mowed down by the differing tyrannies of Spain and Rome, shall we not be confident they would, upon the approaching of these [Protestant] armies, both bestir up those benumbed sovereignties, which only bear the name of free princes, to affect their own manumissions, and help to chase away those . . . oppressing garrisons . . . ?[24]

In the seventeenth century the same idea was taken up both by republicans and by Puritans with apocalyptic hopes. The republicans were particularly concerned with the liberation of Florence from the tyranny of the Medici. Sir Philip Sidney's great-nephew Algeron Sidney, a member of the Rump and an active proponent of its aggressive foreign policy in the early 1650s, would write later of Tuscany and its neighbors: "Nothing is more certain than that those miserable nations abhor the tyrannies they are under"; "many would resist, but cannot; and if they were not mastered by a power that is much too great for them, they would soon free themselves."[25] Marchamont Nedham, writing in *Mercurius Politicus* for 8 January 1652, lamented the extinction of "the Free-State of Florence" ("And to all States not free") but noted that "after so long a time, the old freedom is still fresh in memory, and would show itself again upon a favourable occasion." Puritan hopes of liberating Europe from the Papacy were strengthened by the epidemic of revolutions in Europe in the 1640s. Christopher Hill observes that

> John Spittlehouse in 1650 warned Rome to 'beware of Nol Cromwell's army, lest Hugh Peter [the Cromwellian chaplain] come to preach in Peter's chair.' In the same year Arise Evans had a vision in which he went through France to Rome, where 'a voice came to me saying, So far as thou art come, so far shall Cromwell come.'[26]

It was in 1650 too that the Puritan minister Ralph Josselin began to look forward to "our actings in France," which would usher in the destruction of Rome and Antichrist.[27]

Late in April 1650 Royalist newspapers began to hint at the scenario to which the Horatian Ode alludes. "Must Cromwell to France?" asked one of them. "Is this your way to peace, to make all nations our enemies?" Another's sarcasm dubbed Cromwell "the great conqueror of the world, who when he hath conquered Ireland, must go to conquer France, and so the world over."[28] In May, Nedham's *The Case of the Commonwealth Stated* observed:

> If it be considered how the worm works in many parts of Europe to cast off the regal yoke, especially in France, Scotland, Ireland, and other places, it must needs be as much madness to strive against the stream for the upholding of a power cast down by the Almighty as it was for the old sons of earth to heap up mountains against Heaven.[29]

Again,

> Tis Madness to resist or blame
> The force of angry Heavens flame.

France, which was already engaged in an unofficial piracy war with England, was regularly portrayed by government journals as a battleground between a tyrannous government and the freedom-loving rebels of Bordeaux. Events in France, claimed *Mercurius Politicus* on 4 July, were symptoms of "an age for kings to run the wild goosechase."[30] If Gaul was given warnings by the press, so was Italy. On 20 June *Mercurius Politicus* prophesied that "if things go on as they begin, in Great Britain, Ireland, and France, the Pope himself may in a short time be put to live upon shifts, as well as his faction." In July the government published a document that had been sent by Charles II to Pope Innocent X, and in which the exiled king, seeking papal support, had claimed that England's rulers were "openly asserting . . . that they will invade France, and after that run through Germany, Italy, and all Europe, throwing down kings and monarchs."[31] Cromwell's role in this program was indicated on 3 October by *Mercurius Politicus*, which urged that "this brave Scipio, my Lord General Cromwell, after he hath wholly subdued Ireland and Scotland to the Commonwealth of England, ought to do the like elsewhere, that so our domineering and insolent neighbours may be brought under."

IV

If the moral universe of the poem can be called Hobbesian, can it also be termed Machiavellian? Do Machiavellian ideas, like the Hobbesian ideas of the engagement controversy, figure in the approach of Marvell—that "notable English-Italo Machiavillain"—to the political dilemmas of 1650? J. A. Mazzeo, in an essay published in 1960, thought that Marvell's Cromwell was a Machiavellian prince.[32] His argument, inspired but underdocumented, was coldly received. Perhaps it looks less implausible now that the work of Felix Raab, John Pocock, and others has illuminated the extent and vitality of Machiavelli's influence on the political thought of early modern England, an influence broadened after the first published English translations of *The Discourses* (1636) and *The Prince* (1640).[33] It may look still less implausible now that we have learned how many writers of the late sixteenth and seventeenth centuries drew on Machiavelli for poetic as well as prosaic purposes.[34] Machiavelli's is rarely an easy influence to measure. What looks at first like Machiavellianism may reflect the broader influence of the classical literature of which Machiavelli was but one modern interpreter; or it may be a mere commonplace. We must approach the question whether the ode is Machiavellian tentatively. Even if we cannot find an unequivocal answer, the search for one may help to illuminate the mental context of the poem.

During the Puritan Revolution, the period when Machiavelli's influence in England was at its peak, Machiavelli's prince became the archetype summoned by writers seeking to catch the greatness and meteoric rise of Cromwell, who from 1647, when he reached the forefront of the public mind, was often described in the Machiavellian terms of what Raab called "the hero/villain."[35] Hero/villains were scarcely new in literature, and if Marvell's Cromwell is a hero/villain, then we might be content to see him, with Patrick Cruttwell, as a descendant of Tamburlaine or Macbeth.[36] But he may have been something else too.

Marchamont Nedham, who made extensive use of Machiavelli in *The Case of the Commonwealth* in May 1650, thought of Cromwell as a Machiavellian prince. In the first issue of *Mercurius Politicus* (13 June 1650) he wrote of Cromwell's return from Ireland: "for my part, if we take a view of his actions from first to last, I may (without flattery) proclaim him to be the only *Novus Princeps* that ever I met with in all the confines of history." "*Novus Princeps*" points clearly to Machiavelli, who at the start of *The Prince* distinguishes two kinds of ruler: the hereditary prince, whose task is relatively easy and about whom he has little to say, and the new prince (*"il nuovo principe"*), who reaches power by a coup or by conquest, and whom Machiavelli's book is designed to educate. If the association of Marvell (who knew Italian) with Nedham encourages us to look at Machiavelli, so does his friendship with two other writers. The first is Milton. Not much is known of Milton's reading in 1650, but his commonplace book shows that he was steeped in Machiavelli in 1651–52, and his poem to Sir Henry Vane in 1652 drew directly on Machiavelli.[37] The second is James Harrington, whose *Oceana*, published in 1656 but apparently conceived in the aftermath of the regicide, was to adapt Machiavelli's thought to English experience. Aubrey calls Harrington an "intimate friend" of Marvell, a description given weight by Aubrey's own close acquaintance with Harrington. Like Marvell, Harrington was a youthful poet who turned to prose in later years. Grief-stricken by the execution of Charles I, whom he had personally served and come to love, Harrington sought through his writing to understand and come ·to terms with it.[38] The result was *Oceana*, which placed the personal tragedy of the regicide in an impersonal and inevitable historical process. Is there not, in the Horatian Ode, a similar grief, and a similar struggle for acceptance, likewise resolved by a determinist conclusion? Certainly there is a resemblance between the nationalist conclusion to the ode and the apocalyptic hopes of foreign conquest and liberation announced in *Oceana*.[39]

Harrington was the most profound exponent of Machiavelli's ideas in seventeenth-century England. Another distinguished tribute to Machiavelli's influence is the *History* of Clarendon (whom Marvell is unlikely to have known). Clarendon had no difficulty in reconciling his appreciation of Machiavelli with the conventional morality and the concern for constitutional propriety that run through Clarendon's career and writing, as they run through the later life and prose of Marvell. "From beginning to end," Raab fairly claimed, "Cromwell is to Clarendon the embodiment of Machiavelli's de facto ruler, the Borgia figure."[40] We cannot miss, in Clarendon's condemnation of Cromwell, his awed and (in both senses) admiring grasp of Cromwell's historical stature. Clarendon writes in retrospect of a Cromwell long dead: Marvell's Cromwell has the world—and his country—at his feet; but between the two figures, both of them cunning, ambitious, and valiant, there are resemblances that may indicate a common influence. Machiavelli's frequent reminders that his successful princes had emerged *"di privado"* or *"di privada fortuna"* could lie behind the similarity between the Marvellian Cromwell

> Who, from his private Gardens, where
> He liv'd reserved and austere, . . .
> Could by industrious Valour climbe

and Clarendon's brave bad man, "who from a private birth could raise himself to such a height," and whose "strict and unsociable

humour" attracted "reserved natures."[41] Marvell's "industrious valour" sounds distinctly Machiavellian. "Industry" and "valour" are the
words given by the 1640 translation of *The Prince* for the qualities of
industria and *virtù*, which are prominent and closely associated in the
classical thought interpreted by Machiavelli and which are among the
qualities he most often observes in the successful prince. "Industry,"
which can mean applied skill as well as hard work, is a feature of
Clarendon's Cromwell as well. Like Machiavelli's Agathocles and Borgia, both Cromwells have *"l'animo grande"*: Clarendon's has the "courage" of a "great spirit," Marvell's the "Courage high" of a "greater
Spirit." Machiavelli's prince is also *un prudente;* and Marvell's recognition of Cromwell's "wiser art," placed as it is (in lines 47–48) directly
after a tribute to his feats in battle, and attributed as it is to a man
who "does both act and know," might suggest Machiavelli's observation, which was often recalled during the Puritan Revolution, that
the successful prince must be both a lion and a fox.[42] On its own, a
lion is stupid and ineffectual: with leonine strength must be combined
foxlike cunning. And to Cromwell's courage, industry, and wisdom
Marvell adds another essential quality of the new prince: the appetite
for *gloria* conspicuous in a man who

> could not cease
> In the inglorious Arts of Peace.

Is there a deeper debt to Machiavelli in the poem, to be explained
by a similarity in the circumstances in which Machiavelli and Marvell
wrote? Both men explore the relationship between great men and the
times. For Machiavelli, "the one who adapts himself to the times
prospers"; "it behoves oneself to adapt oneself to the times if one
wants to enjoy good fortune"; men's fortune "depends upon whether
their behaviour is in conformity with the times."[43] We need not propose that a poet preoccupied by time, a subject not on the periphery
of either literary tradition or human experience, must have derived
his interest from Machiavelli. Yet the sense of time that pervades
Marvell's poetry, as a force that either masters or is mastered, brings
him close to Machiavelli's teaching.[44] Marvell measures Cromwell's
greatness against the times in "The First Anniversary." There Cromwell defies "Fore-shortend Time," applying "new Stopps" to "various
Time"; "'Tis he the force of scatter'd Time contracts," while "heavy
Monarchs" tell "an useless time"; "Cromwell alone with greater Vigour runs," as "flowing Time" closes over the heads of lesser mortals.
Is the same theme present in Marvell's earlier political verse? In the
opening of the Lovelace poem of 1649, with its premise that "Our

times are much degenerate from those" chosen by Lovelace's "Fortune," there may be an allusion to the Machiavellian concept of corruption. The opening lines of the Horatian Ode recall Machiavelli's challenge to the prince: the challenge to seize the *occasione* that enables him, through his *virtù*, to tackle *fortuna*. Thus the *occasione* is established (the forward youth must *now* forsake his muses; tis *time* to leave the books in dust) before the *virtù* of Cromwell is introduced: Cromwell, "the Wars and Fortunes Son," who is "To ruine the great Work of Time." It may or may not be pertinent that Machiavelli, who thought *fortuna* arbitrary in her favors, saw her as a friend of young men *(amica de' giovani).*[45] A youth who mastered her would, in Machiavelli's scheme of things, have had to be forward indeed.

The *Prince* and the ode are both written amid national calamity. The crisis for the Royalist Marvell in republican England is similar to that which confronted the republican Machiavelli in Renaissance Florence. Marvell wrote in a postwar wasteland: Machiavelli saw Italy "leaderless, lawless, crushed, despoiled, overrun, lifeless," facing "great changes and variations, beyond human imaginings." Recovery was conceivable only through a single person, *"un redentore."*[46] In *The Discourses* Machiavelli acknowledged that "If in a state which is on the decline . . . a renaissance is ever to be brought about, it will be by the *virtù* of some one person who is then living, not by the *virtù* of the public as a whole."[47]

> So much one Man can do,
> That does both act and know.

There is a similar view in Harrington's *Oceana*, where Cromwell becomes the temporary dictator with power to renew the republic. Is there, then, a merely accidental parallel between the patriotic conclusion of the ode and the concluding chapter of *The Prince*, where Machiavelli addresses his own, Medician *Novus Princeps?* Like Marvell and Horace, Machiavelli had painfully to adjust his political hopes. Marvell and Machiavelli alike want to rescue their country from northern barbarians. Machiavelli "cannot imagine there ever was a time more propitious than the present" for "recognising a new prince": "Italy is waiting to heal her wounds to put an end to the sacking in Lombardy. . . . See how Italy beseeches God to send someone to save her from these barbarous cruelties and outrages; see how eager and willing the country is to follow a banner if only someone will raise it."[48] In the England of 1650 Cromwell, the new prince, the man for the times, will raise a banner, and the forward youth will be eager to follow him.

In the grim mood of 1650 the features of Machiavelli's teaching which may have seemed most obviously pertinent to current events were those closest to Hobbes: the Italian's unyielding subordination of means to ends and of personality and feeling to public necessity; his puritanical dislike of emotional waste; his realization that political solutions depend upon men's willingness to recognize ambition and dissimulation for the political forces they have always been and will always be. This is the Machiavelli of *The Prince* rather than the Machiavelli who celebrates republican civic virtue and republican political participation in *The Discourses*. Yet the two Machiavellis cannot be so easily separated. *The Discourses*, after all, find a role for the prince. There Machiavelli reminds us "what a good man may do, how much good he may occasion, and what great advantages he can bring to his country . . . thanks to his goodness and virtue."[49] Again,

> So much one Man can do,
> That does both act and know . . .
> How good he is, how just,
> And fit for highest Trust . . .

The forward youth of the opening lines is following the course that in Machiavelli's terms makes him a true republican citizen: he is choosing to take up arms on his country's behalf. In the spirited, even cheerful tone of those lines there lies a reminder of that element in seventeenth-century classical and Machiavellian thought which is attracted by the political animation of republics and which favorably compares that animation to the sloth and immobility of monarchies. When Marvell instructs the forward youth to renounce the "Numbers languishing" which he sings in the shadows, we need not take him to be making a peculiarly republican point. Yet it is remarkable how often seventeenth-century writers associated monarchical rule with languor. Francis Bacon (no republican, though a student of Machiavelli) commiserated with "the case of kings; who being at the highest, want matter of desire, which makes their minds more languishing; and have many representations of perils and shadows, which makes their minds the less clear." Algernon Sidney twice observed that when Rome lost its republican liberty, it "fell into a languishing condition." The Marquis of Halifax associated bad monarchy with a "languishing people." At the end of the century Walter Moyle scorned the "slothful measures" that had been designed to make the "mighty genius" of republican Rome "languish in obscurity," while Moyle's fellow republican John Toland, editing Harrington, compared the "languishing" condition of monarchies with the "flourishing" state of republics.[50]

The side of Marvell which was susceptible to republican vocabulary (a susceptibility that does not necessarily make of him a doctrinaire republican) is visible in "The First Anniversary," where he compares the "heavy monarchs" of Europe, who have "slow and brittle" projects, with the vigorous Cromwell, who can "rig a navy while we dress us late." Cromwell

> seems a King by long succession born,
> And yet the same to be a King does scorn.

Here Marvell is again close to Harrington, who observed in *Oceana*, "There are kings in Europe to whom a king of Oceana would be but a pretty companion. But the Prince of the Commonwealth is the terror and the judge of them all."[51] Marvell is also close to Nedham, who, explaining in *Mercurius Politicus* on 11 July 1650 "how sweet the air of a commonwealth is beyond that of a monarchy," claimed that it was "much better to breathe freely and be lively" as a follower of the republic than to "pine, and fret and fume" as a royalist "till wit, soul and all be drowned in ale and melancholy."

> The forward Youth that would appear
> Must now forsake his *Muses* dear,
>   Nor in the shadows sing
>   His Numbers languishing.

Wherever the Marvell of the ode took the future to belong, we are left to doubt whether he can have supposed it to lie with the torpor of hereditary monarchy.

V

Some readers of the ode take a different view of Marvell's feelings about the monarchy that the Rump had abolished in 1649. To them the ode is a Royalist poem, perhaps written to be circulated privately among Royalists, who would have detected in its ironies its secret anti-Cromwellianism. The Cromwell who so craftily engineered the regicide, who staged the memorable scene in which the "armed bands / Did clap their bloody hands," who justified the killing with vulgar and spiteful appeals to providence: such a man could never be trusted to remain a servile falcon, safe in the republic's hand. It is Charles I, doing nothing common or mean, who displays integrity and earns loyalty. So if the forward youth is to fight, he must fight for the Royalist cause.

Although that view seems to me too simple, it is instructive to observe how much contextual support can be adduced for it. For if not a Royalist poem, the ode has roots in keen and bitter Royalist feeling. There are a suggestive number of resemblances between it and other poems written in hatred of the republic, two of them published in 1652.[52] Again, the line "Though Justice against Fate complain" might be read as a mockery of the whole thrust of that propaganda which justified the "engagement" of loyalty, and as a condemnation of a regime that had justified the regicide with such pamphlets as John Goodwin's *Right and Might Well Met*; we might compare Marvell's lines with the sarcastic (and less accomplished) verse of the Royalist Alexander Brome, in a poem that was circulated privately:

> That side is always right that's strong
> And that that's beaten always wrong;
> And he that thinks it is not so
> Unless he's sure to beat them too
> Is but a fool to oppose 'em.[53]

Equally, Marvell's line about the "happy Fate" of the republic (line 71) could be read as an ironic allusion to the invocations of "fatal necessity" by the propagandists of the new regime.[54] And there remains "Tom May's Death," likely to have been written much later in the year than the ode, with its unambiguous denouncement of *"Brutus* and *Cassius* the Peoples cheats," and its equally unambiguous announcement about the "Numbers" which the poet must "sing":

> When the Sword glitters ore the Judges head,
> And fear has Coward Churchmen silenced,
> Then is the Poets time, 'tis then he drawes,
> And single fights forsaken Vertues cause.
> He, when the wheel of Empire, whirleth back,
> And though the World's disjointed Axel crack,
> Sings still of ancient Rights and better Times,
> Seeks wretched good, arraigns successful Crimes.

The ode is close to Royalist prose as well as to Royalist poetry. A pamphlet published in January 1650, *Philo Regis. The Right Picture of King Oliver*, compresses Cromwell's career in the late 1640s in a manner notably similar to that of the ode (lines 50–55). Ironically acknowledging Oliver's "good qualities innumerable," it begins its account of his "mischief out of Machiavelli" with Cromwell's "base betrayal" of "His late Majesty (of blessed memory) into the Isle of Wight," and then moves swiftly to the regicide.[55] In 1650, Royalist pamphleteers described England's governors as "new architectors" who ambitiously strove to "climb," and who had created "a new mould of government" (cf. lines 33, 35–36, 70).[56] There are particularly suggestive correspondences between the ode and Royalist propaganda which appeared in the week after Cromwell had disembarked on his return from Ireland. At this time Royalists, like the government, were eagerly seeking to raise recruits, and to that purpose were publishing declarations, newspapers, and doggerel. There they urged their supporters to take up arms, mockingly predicted the defeat of Cromwell, and prophesied glorious and imminent vengeance on the Roundhead cause.[57] On 3 June the Royalist newspaper *Mercurius Elencticus* opened its commentary by describing the oppressed Royalist as an "afflicted and languishing soul" for whom "how slowly runs the current of swift-footed time"; he is to cheer himself by singing a ditty that begins, "Musing on my restless bed" and that envisages the triumph of the Cavaliers over the regicides. The ditty imagines the response of M.P.s to an invasion by Charles II, "Whereat they all grew sad / And some run raging mad" (cf. "Did fright the Architects to run").[58]

On 31 May 1650, the day before Cromwell's entry into London, there appeared *Traytors Deciphered*, a major effort of Royalist propaganda, published by the Royalist printer Samuel Browne. It offered a belated and lengthy reply to the official declaration of March 1649 in which Parliament had explained "the settling of the present government in the way of a Free State." The term "Free State" was in the air in May 1650, when the title page of Nedham's *The Case of the Commonwealth Stated* proclaimed "the excellency of a Free State above a Kingly Government." Is there irony in the presence of the phrase in the poem ("And to all States not free")? Royalists had long seen in the phrase a hideous illustration of the logic of Puritan rule, under which words came to say the opposite of what they meant. The retreat of civilization before the march of jargon, famously derided by Cleveland, had been hinted at by Marvell's glance at "Word-peckers" in his poem to Lovelace in 1649 (line 17–20). *Traytors Deciphered*, likewise alive to the relationship between semantic and moral confusion, repeatedly condemns the use of the term "Free State" by the rulers of an "Unfree State."

Many passages of *Traytors Deciphered* bring the Horatian Ode to mind. There is the warning, in the concluding section of the pamphlet, that unless England's rulers are resisted, they "may carry the flame abroad to set all Europe on fire."[59] In both works, too, the execution of the king is theater: the royal actor of the ode is clapped upon a memorable scene; *Traytors Deciphered*, which, like the ode, presents submission as the only dignified course to have been open to the condemned king, says that "there was never so dismal a spectacle . . . as this theatre of theirs."[60] Royalists often used theatrical metaphors to recall the death of a monarch who had performed in masques, and who had later been executed before the Banqueting House.[61] But there seems to be a more distinctive parallel between Marvell's lines

> Nor call'd the Gods with vulgar spight
> To vindicate his helpless Right

and the peroration of *Traytors Deciphered*, which, inciting royalists to "revenge" for the "parricide" of the king, proclaims that "men neglect their own honour . . . that omit any endeavour towards such a work, being the vindication of majesty from vulgar contempt." For "it is the principal duty of all men, that live in civil society, to vindicate the right of their government, to restore such, to whom they owe subjection, and expel usurpers."[62] Does Marvell's poem consciously allude to *Traytors Deciphered*? In his prophecy of Cromwell's exploits in Scotland and on the Continent there may lie another allusion. A knowing Royalist reader might have looked back to 15 May 1649, when the Royalist newspaper *Mercurius Pragmaticus* (perhaps in Cleveland's hands) had predicted that Cromwell would be driven by Leveller mutineers across the Scottish Border

> into the barren wilderness of blue bonnets, where he shall with his nose cut a passage through the highlanders, as Hannibal did through the Alps, but when he is got beyond Edinburgh he may chance to meet a Scipio, and then he is an undone man, and will be lost in a Scotch bog.[63]

The idea surfaced again in *Mercurius Pragmaticus* on 28 May 1650, the day of Cromwell's return from Ireland, when the newspaper, mocking the regicides' ambition to "climb so high," warned them of the challenge awaiting them from "the Scotch bonnets . . . 'tis a blue business I'll promise you." So is Marvell foretelling trouble for Cromwell in the "tufted brake" (line 109)? In the summer of 1650 it was easier to expect Cromwell to display greatness in Scotland than to predict his success there. Had Dunbar gone the other way, as by the rules it should have done, Charles II might well have proved a Scipio. "An Hannibal to Italy," would do everything but win. Nedham's *The Case*

of the Commonwealth Stated remarked that "the hand of heaven" had
been against Hannibal, a statement that could give an ironic twist to

> 'Tis Madness to resist or blame
> The force of angry Heavens flame.[64]

So the Royalist reading of the poem may have more evidence to
support it than its exponents have realized. The objection to that
reading is not a contextual but a literary one. The Royalist interpretation alerts us to the sharpness of individual lines, but deprives the
ode of momentum and of any intelligible sequence of thought, not
to say of its gravity and depth. What is described as irony is mere
sarcasm, and becomes as flat as the lines of Alexander Brome that
have been quoted. Nothing reverberates. For all we know the ode
may have begun life as a Royalist poem. Certainly its proximity to
Royalist propaganda suggests a poet with Royalist contacts and Royalist feelings. But however strong those feelings, the ode has taken
on a larger life in the writing.

The poem does not merely resist a straightforward Royalist reading.
It resists any partisan reading. The more one struggles with the elusiveness of the ode, the more that elusiveness appears to be at its
heart. Around the poem there are shadows: the shadows of song
three lines from the beginning, the shades of night three lines from
the end. We should respect them. They are deepened by the metrical
arrangement of the poem, whose shorter couplets soften and question
the longer ones with which they alternate, so that the reader moves
back and forth between a boldly drawn center and a faint periphery.[65]
If we fix a boundary to the ode's meaning, the shadows steal across
it. Is the ode pro-Cromwellian or anti-Cromwellian? It is both, and it
is neither, and yet we know not. A man who will not take sides in
politics is an incomplete man. A man who takes sides in politics
becomes a foolish man. This Marvell knows, as we can deduce from
his later correspondence, for which there have been too few kind
words.

It is not merely that there is ambiguity in the poem. There is layer
upon layer of it. We read the poem through and think we follow its
meaning. Then we try to parse it. When we reach line 4 we do not
know whether "languishing" belongs to "the forward Youth" or to
"His Numbers." That is only the start of our troubles. Everett finds
seven "grammatical uncertainties" in lines 15 to 24 alone, all carrying
uncertainties of meaning or sentiment.[66] If Marvell is choosing his
words carefully—and who would charge his poetry with careless-
ness?—he must be choosing them very carefully indeed. The ode is

difficult enough to remind us that Marvell is a metaphysical poet and to recall Anthony Bacon on Tacitus: "*Difficilia quae pulchra;* the second reading will please thee more than the first, and the third more than the second."[67] The Renaissance assumption, strong in the metaphysicals, that good poetry will be accessible only to the tutored mind was sharpened by the democratization of the press in the 1640s and by the barbarities of civil war polemic. As Marvell tells Lovelace,

> Our wits have drawne th'infection of our times . . .
> The Ayre's already tainted with the swarms
> Of Insects which against you rise in arms.
> Word-peckers, Paper-rats, Book-scorpions,
> Of wit corrupted, the unfashion'd Sons.

It seemed that Renaissance culture could survive only if poetry was arcane. (We might recall T. S. Eliot's statement, in the wake of war and the shadow of democracy, that "it appears likely that poetry in our civilisation, as it exists at present, must be *difficult*." The quotation is from Eliot's essay, "The Metaphysical Poets," which appeared in 1921, the year of Eliot's momentous essay on Marvell.[68]) When we uncover the ode's opening allusion to Lucan—or when, now, it has to be uncovered for us, which is not quite the privileged experience that the lines invite—we know that we shall have to work hard.

Not least, we shall have to work at the ironies. They yield most when we explore them not in search of a partisan allegiance on the poet's part but with a willingness to accept the poem's openness and to recognize in it a victory over the narrowing partisanship of most civil war literature.[69] Time and again the ode discloses a beautifully worked and exactly pitched ambivalence, which leads us beyond clear-cut interpretation into the doubtful territory of myth and imagination. The ambivalences are like perfectly formed coins, each with identical heads on its opposing faces, each eluding our reach as it spins into the shadows. In the baseness of the alloy—of pamphlet prose—there lies evidence of alchemy.

Seventeenth-century irony worked within conventions of political poetry that are not ours. An imaginative distance separates us from the civilization that, in the two generations before Marvell, had produced the Horatian aspirations of Ben Jonson and had glorified its leaders in the court masque. Despite its privacy, the Horatian Ode adopts the conventions of panegyric, as Marvell's later Cromwell poems do. Like the apotheosis in baroque painting, the panegyric transcends historical limits of time and place. So, for example, Marvell can rhetorically ask,

> What Field of all the Civil Wars,
> Where his were not the deepest Scars?

The literal answer, as overzealous hunters of irony observe, is "All of them"; but the literal answer is not the point.[70]

The force of convention may likewise help us to understand Marvell's seemingly perplexing decision, from line 77, to place praise of Cromwell in the mouth of the Irish. In panegyrics it is not uncommon to allot applause to a defeated enemy. The Irish introduce the encomium of Cromwell, but they fade from it, so that we cannot be sure at what point the poet resumes his own voice. Even if we set aside the question of convention, the irony of these lines may be less keen than we might suppose. Drogheda and Wexford, which have troubled the English memory, seem to have disturbed few consciences at the time. In July 1650 the government published a prediction that the Irish leaders "shall be made to think shame of themselves" ("And now the Irish are asham'd").[71] On 31 October *Mercurius Politicus* printed a document penned by inhabitants of Limerick which acknowledged of Cromwell's victories that "such a winter's success in war, by so inconsiderable a party, against so considerable an enemy, was never read or heard of. Alexander the Great, or Julius Caesar, or William the Conqueror never had the like success." Bitterly warring nations will often give dignity to the battles between them by recognizing the military and human qualities displayed by the other side. On 30 May 1650, when Cromwell was on his way from Bristol to Windsor, Bulstrode Whitelocke copied from a government source a report from the English forces that they had "found in Clonmel the stoutest enemy that ever was found by the army in Ireland, and that there was never a storm of so long a continuance, and so gallantly defended, neither in England nor Ireland." Englishmen could well have told themselves that the Irish entertained comparable sentiments about their conquerors, whose military prowess Whitelocke had proudly recorded a little earlier.[72]

Yet while we can explain the invocation of the Irish without an ironical reading, we cannot explain it away. We remain surprised to hear them talking like men who know they deserve what has come to them. A question mark remains and keeps the poem open. The question mark becomes larger when we come upon the Royalist newspaper *The Man in the Moon* for 5 June 1650, which prints the government-inspired tribute to the Irishmen defeated at Clonmel recorded by Whitelocke. The newspaper accuses the government of giving a prejudiced account of the outcome of the battle, and links by association the strength of the Irish resistance with the size of the levies that are being raised to confront Cromwell in Scotland. Of the government-inspired tribute, the newspaper reports that the regicides "confess thus much themselves, that they found in Clonmel the stoutest enemy that ever was found": an observation of which Marvell's statement that the Irish "have, though overcome, confest" (line 78) might seem an ironic inversion. That issue of *The Man in the Moon* had opened its prefatory doggerel with the event to which the title of Marvell's poem refers:

> And art returned (Great Noll) again,
> And left Ireland behind?
> Nay then I see god Nose must reign,
> And Tom-ass [Fairfax] come behind.

Cromwell's ambitions are doomed, however:

> Yet all won't serve; blood cries aloud,
> Grim vengeance is at hand,
> From north to west riseth a cloud.
> That threateneth all the land.
> In vain 'twill be for to resist
> When Jove hath once decreed.
> He will strike home with iron fist,
> And make proud rebels bleed.

So "the time is come" (cf. " 'Tis time to leave the Books in dust") of Royalist victory: "the Scots are advancing in the north, the royal party in the west; strangers are beginning to back these." Trial and execution await Cromwell and the other leading murderers of Charles I. The newspaper mocks Tom May's *History* and mocks, too, the government's appointment of "Keepers of our Liberties"—a phrase that gave Royalists as much derisive pleasure as the republic's use of the term "Free State." Cromwell, we learn, "is designed for Scotland. . . . Yet the Scots are very active in raising new levies" and are forming a huge army. The Horatian Ode may not be a Royalist poem, but an eager Royalist could have read it as one.

So the passage given to the Irish in the poem defies a partisan reading on either side. It might be suggested that our difficulty with it arises not because of Marvell's subtlety but because the twentieth century is ill-equipped to weigh his allusions. But would a careful reader among Marvell's contemporaries have found the passages where irony has been detected easier? Would he have been less perplexed than we are by the comparison of Cromwell with Hannibal, at once a great general and a defeated one?[73] There are equally ambivalent comparisons in the same part of the poem with two other figures: Julius Caesar (line 101) and "the *English Hunter*" (line 110). I take the latter to be Nimrod, the mighty hunter and the archetypal usurper and tyrant; the Royalist press had called Cromwell "proud Nimrod in Ireland."[74] Yet Nimrod, like Caesar, was used by government as well as by Royalist apologists. Writers who favored the imposition of the engagement frequently cited Caesar and Nimrod as usurping tyrants to whom obedience was due by right of conquest, whatever the "means or craft" by which they "did obtain" their power (cf. lines 119–20).[75] The row of antique Cromwells—Caesar, Hannibal, Nimrod—could not be more finely balanced.[76] In the same way the ode's frequent parallels with the writings of Marvell's friend Marchamont Nedham can all be taken both ways—and perhaps can therefore be taken neither way. The difference between the two men appears to be that Marvell feels both Royalist affection, and the force of Cromwellian claims to allegiance, more gravely than ever Nedham did.

We may wonder that a poem born of such perplexity achieves such poise. If we wonder too that a work of such timelessness can contain beneath its surface so many relics of contemporary political argument, then we may need to think again about the relationship between political and literary activity in the seventeenth century. Yet need we leave Marvell on a fence? He may have a problem of torn loyalties, but is it a problem that the Horatian Ode leaves unresolved?

In "Tom May's Death" the defiant poet "Sings still of ancient Rights"; in the ode the "antient Rights" are pleaded "in vain."[77] When Marvell apparently echoes in the ode the claim of the Royalist pamphlet *Traytors Deciphered* to "vindicate the right" of the Stuart dynasty, he tells us that the "Right" of Charles I is "helpless," a statement that seems to undermine the passage to which it alludes. Of course, it is the cause of a dead king that is "helpless": in 1650 the cause of Charles II might not be doomed. Yet Marvell does not seem to be interested in Charles II. When the poem looks at the royal cause, it looks backward. The forward movement of the ode is provided by Cromwell, whether or not we like him. The choice that is present in the poem is not only between the royal actor and the greater spirit but between the past and the future. It is a choice that involves not sympathy (although sympathy may make it harder) but a recognition of the truths taught by Machiavelli and by Hobbes. I shall suggest in the concluding part of this essay that if Marvell—or at least, an important part of Marvell—thinks that the royal cause is "helpless," that is not (or not only) because of any calculations he might have made about the military prospects of 1650. It is because the execution of Charles I seemed to him the end not merely of a king but of an age. The forward youth grasps the point. Being young, and wanting to appear, he looks ahead.

VI

What will Andrew Marvell do with his life? There is much in his poetry about the right and wrong ways to self-fulfillment. Possibly in reading the opening lines of the ode we should recall that Marvell is "near thirty years of age," the age when, as Clarendon says of Edmund Waller, "other men used to give over writing verses"; the age, perhaps, at which a seventeenth-century writer decides whether his poetry is vocational or merely amateur.[78] He is reaching another age too: the age marked by Marvell's friend Harrington, who in his scheme for the organization of the commonwealth of Oceana equated "the youth" with "the military," "all such as are above eighteen and under thirty being accounted youth."[79] Does Marvell regret his absence abroad during the civil war? Do the opening lines of the ode encourage us to think of him, as John Carey invites us to see the young Milton, wearing a sword and wondering whether to be sage or hero?[80] Marvell gives so little away. Sometimes his feelings break through: in his youthful susceptibility to Jesuit persuasion; in his anger at the regicide; in the sense of honor that leads him, as a Restoration M.P., into quarrels with fellow M.P.s that are violent even by seventeenth-century standards; in the uncontrollable affection for his birthplace that warms the formal surface of his letters to the Corporation of Hull. He knows the value of repression, however. Living in troubled times, being "naturally . . . inclined to keep my thoughts private,"[81] he learns to watch his tongue—and, Aubrey tells us, to be careful whom he drinks with. Serving the art of the possible, identifying the boundaries within which he can achieve and move, the Restoration M.P. advocates "moderation" and decides that "truth for the most part lies in the middle." We should shun "the extremities," for extremism is evidence of emotional imbalance, just as "'Tis pride that makes a rebel."[82] He teaches himself the rules of a world that "will not go the faster for our driving," where "all things . . . happen in their best and proper time, without any need of our officiousness," and where "a good cause signifies little unless it be well defended. A man may starve at the feast of a good conscience."[83] ("But those do hold or break . . . ") Yet in his conscience, what he fairly calls his "incorrupt mind and clear conscience,"[84] lies the part of himself to which he holds most firmly.

What will always elude him is a sense of wholeness. There are pain and destruction in the gayest of his poems. He tries to shut out the world, and translates Seneca on the consolations of retreat. In the garden his mind finds "happiness" in withdrawal, in "Annihilating all that's made." His time spent in "busy companies of men," he decides, has been "mistaken." Yet "delicious solitude" carries its own burdens, from which he seeks refuge after 1660 in "diversion, business and activity."[85] Perhaps, as a Restoration poet, he loses himself, even his genius, in them. He would like to separate the public from the private world. But the rows of flowers outside Appleton House become ranks of soldiers; in an intimate letter of condolence his thoughts move abruptly to the fall of Clarendon;[86] and there is always the mower, leveling England as he levels the grass. So it is not surprising that critics find sustained political allegories in the lyric poems and that their readings, although they never quite work, often seem to have something in them. Yet Marvell, however uneasy he is either in solitude or in company, proves a tough and courageous politician. A shrewd appraiser of political hysterics, he will keep his head while others are losing theirs. In the 1670s he will risk his life for Parliament and religion, and laugh at the peril he runs.

Alone of the Cavalier poets of the 1640s, Marvell looks the future in the face. A world has been lost: the world will go on. Civilization, like nature, "hateth emptiness," and if our driving cannot make the world go faster, no more can we slow it down. Poised between past and future, framing a historic present moment, the Horatian Ode records, as nothing else written during the Puritan Revolution does, the fundamental shift in English civilization that, when every reservation has been made, the middle of the seventeenth century brought about. As Miss Everett remarks, "the death of the King was also in some sense the end of ritual, of myth—it was the last Reformation, the final breaking of an icon."[87] It was the end of Renaissance culture too. On one side of the civil wars lie metaphysical and Cavalier poetry, the alliance of thought and imagination, the apparent harmony of power and "antient Rights." On the other side lie the reaction of reason against inspiration, the heroic couplet, the utilitarian prose of the Royal Society, Hobbesian politics.[88] As so often in history, it is the poet who divines the transition: what place will the future hold for the muses? There is Restoration satire, but before the mature Dryden there is not much Restoration poetry. There is Milton's poetry, but Milton proves the rule: an "internal *émigré*,"[89] he is still living in the Puritan Revolution. We do not know whether there is poetry from Marvell that is worthy of him, because we do not know when his lyric poems were written; but even if, as some now think, they were composed after 1660, they remain poetry of retreat.

"Our Civill Wars have lost the Civick crowne." Marvell, who tells this to Lovelace, knows the cost as well as anyone. When he condemns Tom May he summons the shade of Ben Jonson, for it is the "candid age" of Jonson and the sons of Ben that May's Roundhead cause has broken up. Cultural loss and political loss are inseparable.[90] Before the revolution there is the "sweet *Militia*": after it there is the standing army, Marvell's bugbear of the 1670s. In 1660, in his first surviving letter to the Corporation of Hull, when he has yet to master the impersonal style, he gives himself away, albeit to readers who can be expected to agree with him: "I cannot but remember, though then a child, those blessed days when the youth of your own town were trained for the militia, and did methought bear their arms better than any soldiers that I have ever seen there since."[91] Stanzas 41 to 43 of "Upon Appleton House" set the "sweet *Militia*" in a prewar Eden, where "The Gardiner had the Souldiers place." It is a world irrecoverably lost.

> But War all this doth overgrow:
> We Ord'nance Plant and Powder sow.

By 1650 Cromwell has planted his ordnance deep. Where is a Cavalier poet to go? He can write heartbroken elegies on Charles I, the passive martyr, the Christ figure, born to suffer.[92] He can yearn for the Arcadian innocence, the "halcyon days" as they now seemed to have been, of the personal rule. He can refurbish the chivalric values of Beaumont and Fletcher. The Royalist bookseller Humphrey Moseley will publish his work, but it will be forgettable and forgotten. The back of Caroline culture may have been strong or it may have been weak, but it is broken now. Are the "Numbers languishing" in line 4 of the ode the Cavalier poems of defeat? If so, we can see Marvell's point. Line 2 could offer a more particular allusion. Marvell, the Cavalier poet, gives notice that he is forsaking the Cavalier muses. It was in line 2 of the Lovelace poem that he had addressed Lovelace's "sweet Muse."[93] The volume of elegies to Hastings had been called *Lachrymae Musarum*. Now Marvell has dried and cleared his eyes.

If we resist the suggestion of so local a reference, a general point may remain. Marvell settles his accounts with the royal cause, very honorably. Literature has done nothing finer for Charles I than "*He* nothing common did or mean." The poet's keen feelings on the defeated king's behalf are controlled and deepened by the irony with which he protects his independence of voice. But the future belongs to Cromwell, who has razed Cavalier culture, and after Cromwell to the forward youth, who will inherit the world Cromwell will have built. The shape of that world is as yet dark and doubtful. To Marvell, Cromwell is still a force rather than a person, an idea rather than a program. But whatever he is, he is inescapable; and the forward youth, if he follows him, will "make his Destiny his Choice." The decision is grave; yet his spirits sound high enough. Reading the poem through once more, we think that Marvell has declared a commitment after all. Then we see the shadows closing in.

8

Milton and the Histories

Earl Miner

Truth therefore is required, as the foundation of history, to inform us; disposition and perspicuity, as the manner to inform us plainly. One is the being, the other the well-being of it.
—Dryden, *The Life of Plutarch*

What is all knowledge too but recorded experience, and a product of history; of which, therefore, reasoning and belief, no less than action and passion, are essential materials?
—Carlyle, *Signs of the Times*

It takes a great deal of history to produce a little literature.
—Henry James, *The Life of Nathaniel Hawthorne*

THE HISTORIES

Why not "Milton and history"? It certainly sounds better. Yet it should not take much effort to explain that "history" in the singular is a vexed term, and one need not be a nominalist or lexicographer to think so. Three or more senses of "history" and their mutants are commonly appealed to under one label and so confuse distinct concepts. The first major concept of history is the subject of a historian's inquiry, primal history—the course of events or of flux in time and place—in the "real world." The second concept is that of the work of a historian, an account of those presumed events. That might be Ralegh's *History of the World* or Bacon's *History of Henry VII*. And it might be Shakespeare's *Life & Death of Richard the Third* or Samuel Daniel's *Civil Wars between the Two Houses of Lancaster and York* (ottava rima subsequently deserted for prose). The third concept is that of accounts of the second kind of history, as in a history of Chinese dynastic histories or a literary history of English historical poems.

The three concepts are not distinct. We know the primal history only by making history in the second sense. Every history in the

181

second sense that we know of is also a history in the third sense. Except for autobiographical history or accounts by witnesses, there is no *prisca historia*, no first and unsullied account of events in our modern conceptions, although Milton and his contemporaries no doubt would have assigned such priority to the Bible. On the other hand, it is evident that without a belief in history of the first kind— actual events in time and place—the other two make no sense. It seems unlikely that many people currently consider that a history as written record provides for the immediate presence of history as event, or even an open window onto the event. The historian's history is all too obviously a construct of the human mind, a construct, more- over, far more dependent on other, prior historical accounts than on primal history. Without the presumption of primal history, however, the other kinds could not exist.

These distinctions and dependencies have led some people to a kind of historical nominalism in recent years. In fact a general distrust of history in the second sense has been expressed, and writings about it (in the third sense) have sometimes come near to dismissing any faith in the historian's scope beyond the creation of some fictional or artistic house of cards, or to the even more radical presumption that history writing is as lost in meaningless textuality as all else written. The neo-Marxists have been among the principal objectors to this nominalism and sheer textuality.[1] Someone, like myself, less pas- sionately devoted to either extreme must make these distinctions— which is to say, raise skeptical questions. I must also wonder where, if history in the first sense is not to be presumed, textuality and the nominalist can logically exist. At any rate, I can only presume that the world exists as we know it, with whatever distortion or error, or else there would not be a possibility for us to exist. This very simple and highly qualified "realism" provides the possibility even for solip- sism itself. The so-called synchronic or spatial form conceptions of reality likewise depend on a prior assumption of the diachronic or sequential, if only (but not only) because the synchronic historian's account can only follow in time the matters accounted for.

MILTON AND OTHERS

These doubts and distinctions did not matter much to Milton and those just before and after him. To the extent that we might desire a simply historical account of Milton's ideas about history, it may seem superfluous (and unhistorical) to dwell on what we think today. As we have seen, however, a simple historical account is highly problematic, and it is difficult to argue with any consistency that one of us is able to present Milton's views in terms outside our own conception of them. There is another issue of even greater import: Milton's seeming claim to be presenting historical *truth* or historical veracity in his poetry. The gap between his claim and our problems is considerable. Because his claim and our problems are at once related and distinct, we may first try to establish our understanding of what he thought history to be. Before turning to his work, we should inquire (*historia* means inquiry at its root) what those just before and after him seem to have thought.

Near the beginning of his *Advancement of Learning*, Bacon identifies as the two objects of study "the book of God's word" and "the book of God's works" (the Creation, *res naturae*, modern "reality").[2] His concern was largely with the latter, and although not published until 1622, seventeen years after the *Advancement*, his *Historia Naturalis* was believed to have been written around 1603. In addition to this *Natural History* and the history of Henry VII, Bacon wrote a fictional history in his *New Atlantis* and, by allegoresis, discovered a scientific or natural history in the fables dealt with in his *Wisdom of the Ancients*. Within nine years after the death of Milton, Dryden distinguished kinds of history more as we know them. In his *Life of Plutarch*, he divided history into "these three species: *commentaries* or *annals; history* properly so called; and *biographia*."[3] He goes on to distinguish the three kinds, beginning with annals:

> Commentaries or annals are (as I may so call them) naked history; or the plain relation of matter of fact, according to the succession of time, divested of all other ornaments. The springs and motives of actions are not here sought, unless they offer themselves, and are open to every man's discernment. . . . [He praises Caesar especially, adding Tacitus for his *Annals.*] Nay, even the prince of Greek historians, Thucydides, may almost be adopted into the number. For tho' he instructs everywhere by sentences [*sententiae*], tho' he gives the causes of actions, the counsels of both parties, and makes orations where they are necessary; it is certain that he first designed his work as a commentary, every year writing down, like an unconcerned spectator as he was, the particular occurrences of the time, in the order as they happened, and his eighth book is wholly written in the way of annals; though, outliving the war, he inserted in his others those ornaments which render his work the most complete and most instructive [of the kind] now extant.[4]

The realist bent is very obvious. So is that of Hobbes, in a very different tone in the "Review, and Conclusion" to his *Leviathan:*

> Lastly, though I reverence those men of ancient time, that have either
> written truth perspicuously, or set us in a better way to find it out ourselves;
> yet to the antiquity itself I think nothing due. For if we will reverence the
> age, the present is the oldest.[5]

Like Milton and Dryden, Hobbes held that historical truth was in
principle ascertainable, however much one might have to work to
obtain it.

Immediately after the passage on annals, Dryden turns to his second species of history:

> History, properly so called, may be described by the addition of those
> parts which are not required to annals: and therefore there is little to be
> said concerning it: only that the dignity and gravity of style is here nec-
> essary. That the guesses of secret causes inducing to the actions be drawn
> at least from the most probable circumstances, not perverted by the ma-
> lignity of the author to sinister interpretations (of which Tacitus is accused),
> but candidly laid down, and left to the judgment of the reader. That
> nothing of concernment be omitted, but things of trivial moment are still
> [always] to be neglected, as debasing the majesty of the work. That neither
> partiality or prejudice appear, but that truth everywhere be sacred.[6]

Again, with whatever problems, Dryden clearly assumes that the
historian's office and capacity is the presentation of *truth*.

The *raison d'être* of Dryden's account, biography, may be omitted
as not a central Miltonic concern, apart from panegyrics and satire in
his prose writing. Rather, we should consider what conceptions of
narrative were available to Milton, since it is evident that history, or
storia ("story") was conceived in narrative terms. In lieu of seventeenth-century pronouncements, we must turn to the Roman rhetoricians, who, after all, provided us with the very word *narratio*. Quintilian and others distinguished three kinds. First was *fabula*, "which
is not merely not true but has little resemblance to the truth"; we shall
be seeing what Milton makes of that. Second was *argumentum*,
"which, though not true, has yet a certain verisimilitude." Finally,
there was *historia*, "exposition of actual fact."[7] It will be apparent that
truth is the element common to history and to rhetorical conceptions
of narrative. The assumption is not merely that of philosophical realism but of a person's ability to find out and present what is true.

With Goldsmith, Milton is one of the few English poets who wrote
a history, *The History of Britain*. He began with the very dim past and
proceeded to the Norman Conquest. His first book is one lengthy
account of warnings of unreliability, and its first pronouncement is
that "the beginning of Nations, those excepted of whom sacred Books

have spok'n, is to this day unknown."[8] He explicitly dates ascertainable British history from the incursion of Julius Caesar, treating accounts of earlier times as "a modern Fable."[9] "Fable" is a recurrent word. He justifies his dallying with the fabulous with undisguised distrust but for a most interesting reason: "I have therfore determin'd to bestow the telling over ev'n of these reputed Tales; be it for nothing else but in favour of our English Poets, and Rhetoricians, who by thir Art will know, how to use them judiciously."[10]

Given Quintilian's distinctions, Milton's thoughts of benefits for the poet and rhetorician are probably consistent with his own plans for an Arthuriad. He begins his second book, however, in another spirit:

> I am now to write of what befell the *Britans* from *fifty and three years before the Birth of our Saviour* [the modern date is 55 B.C.], when first the *Romans* came in, till the decay and ceasing of that Empire; a story [*storia*, history] of much truth, and for the first hundred years and somwhat more, collected without much labour.[11]

The *History* thereafter offers an account of various rises succeeded each in turn by a "decay and ceasing" explained on largely moral grounds involving political and religious falling offs, down to the Norman Conquest, with two curious emphases. One is on Christmas events in the last book, the sixth.[12] The other curiosity is one appreciated in terms of Milton's poetic career, with its growing insistence that his poetry dealt not with fables or tales but with historical truth.

On one hand, then, we have the assumption in which Milton shared that the first or primal history was knowable in principle and susceptible to presentation as truth, a matter far more troubled in our modern understanding. This may therefore be termed our problem. On the other hand, there is also Milton's assumption in this earlier and later work that history and truth constitute the domain of prose. If there is one element common to the two problems, it is the insistent presence of Milton himself, a divinely inspired narrator. As he pointedly says after the exordium in the first book of *The History of Britain* and, as in his poetry, "imploring divine assistance," "*I now begin.*"[13]

As is well known, Milton's references to himself in his prose are frequent, and a couple of his works (e.g., *Pro Se Defensio*) are devoted almost entirely to the task of defending himself from charges leveled by others. But he is never loathe to bring himself into seemingly any context, and the more prominent—as at the beginning or end—the better. In the prefatory matter of the second book of *The Reason of Church-Government*, Milton presents his famous account of the kinds of epic (and other writing) that he has mulled over.[14] And at the end of *A Second Defence of the English People,* he praises (with no lack of advice and warning) Cromwell, Fairfax, Fleetwood, and others, as well as his fellow English. The last paragraph (if Milton ever writes paragraphs) begins, "As for me. . . ."[15] These intrusions by the historical narrator serve different ends, no doubt including self-advertisement and self-justification. But we must not forget that personal testimony, or ethical proof, was regarded as a major rhetorical technique.

Intrusions by the historical narrator also have an *effect* that is characteristic of numerous works by Milton, whether in prose or verse, early or late. The intrusion introduces a new subject of temporal-historical experience. Many of these intrusions represent one of the oldest techniques in narrative—digression—but Milton is so given to what might be called schemes or layering of subjects and time orders that they amount to a habit of thought. Habits are symptoms of the satisfaction of needs, and we must therefore seek to assess what needs Milton served by these intrusions, digressions, schemes, or layerings.

The opening of the second part of *The Reason of Church-Government* deals with the burden of knowledge and the sorry reception gained by one who offers it, as with an Old Testament prophet, with St. John the Divine, or with Tiresias in *Oedipus the King.* He knows that engaging in controversy will bring him trouble, but "the enforcement of conscience only" has led him to it.[16] If he sought applause, he would have written of other subjects,[17] and not in prose, where he has the use of his "left hand" alone.[18] What he would do with his right is then described (beginning with talk of his education and travels) as being in "that Epick Form," "those Dramatick constitutions," or "those magnifick Odes and Hymns" that are exemplified by the ancients and the Bible.[19] He goes on to justify these arts, urging the government to step in to further and control them, then offering "to covnant with any knowing reader" that after a few years of his controversial writing he will turn to literature,[20] however distasteful the earlier task may be.[21]

Milton clearly needs to justify his writing historical controversy—or, rather, to justify his not writing great literature. He also needs to satisfy himself (and perhaps the reader as well) that there are subjects less distasteful than the acrimonious controversy employed in his day. These needs, with others that might be mentioned, make up one category: that of personal necessity, desire. It is this category that is involved at the end of the *Second Defence.* "As for me," he writes, "I have not borne arms for liberty merely on my own doorstep." And in parallel syntax and with the same verb, he says, "I have borne witness, I might almost say I have erected a monument that will not soon pass away, to those deeds that were illustrious, that were almost beyond any praise."[22] Then in a well-known passage he compares himself with "the epic poet," taking pride "to have celebrated at least one heroic achievement of my countrymen."[23] Here is a transformation of a kind that he had not envisaged in *The Reason of Church-Government*. He has been able to make a *prose* national epic from controversial historical writing. Although his sense of triumph would not last long, its demise seems to have set him on what he knew he was obligated to do all along: write an epic poem that would be the pride of his country.

In addition to these immediate personal satisfactions, Milton also intruded for the less personal ends of clarifying one historical order by another. When his *History of Britain* was first published, he omitted from book 3 a digression comparing fifth-century Britain with his own time and vice versa. In 1647–48, various factions in the state were maneuvering—king, parliament, and the army, as well as other groups headed by them. At this time, however, Milton was thoroughly disillusioned with the Parliament dominated by Presbyterians and with the Westminster Assembly.[24] The effect of the historical parallel is to warn the people of his own age, and that Milton felt a need to do so tells us how alarmed he was. If there is any doubt on this score, we need only recall that books 4 to 8 of *Paradise Lost* function similarly as a gigantic digression establishing a thorough warning to Adam not to sin. The word "history" does not appear in Milton's poetry, but "Hystorian" does once, and it comes, appropriately enough, at the beginning of Book 8, when Raphael has finished his narration of the past. Adam asks,

> What thanks sufficient, or what recompence
> Equal have I to render thee, Divine
> Hystorian, who thus largely hast allayd
> The thirst I have of knowledge?[25]

SIMILAR ISSUES IN
THE EARLIER POEMS

By the beginning of book 8 of *Paradise Lost*, Adam has gained knowledge from Raphael, the "Divine / Hystorian"—knowledge of the War in Heaven and of the Creation. These are matters postulated to be true. If unfallen, archangels do not lie. And Adam will shortly add a presumably equally true account of his own hitherto brief life, much as Milton was given to personal accounts in his prose. Before moving to the late and greatest poems, however, it will be useful to examine his earlier works for symptoms of the same handling of historical orders and of temporalities in digression or layerings. In the opening stanza of *On the Morning of Christ's Nativity,* Milton addresses his "Heav'nly Muse" (line 15) to urge that she (or it) inspire him to compose a poem for the birth of the Christ child. Then comes a curious conflation or layering of temporal orders:

> See how from far upon the Eastern rode
> The Star-led Wisards haste with odours sweet,
> O run, prevent [anticipate] them with thy humble ode,
> And lay it lowly at his blessed feet;
> Have thou the honour first, thy Lord to greet,
>   And joyn thy voice unto the Angel Quire,
> From out his secret Altar toucht with hallow'd fire.[26]

Here the temporal situation of the first Christmas, with thoughts of Epiphany, somehow is intruded on by Milton's Christmas of 1629: in that year, when he attained his majority, he anticipated the coming of the Magi some 1,629 years before. In fact, this extraordinary conception of time is reflected in a dazzling shift in verb tenses in the opening stanzas and on into "The Hymn."[27] In a fashion more readily felt than explained, Milton achieves by this shifting what we have seen, in one way or another, to have been his great need as a writer: magnificence, in its literal and general senses. The second stanza shows something of this:

> That glorious form, that Light unsufferable,
> And that far-beaming blaze of Majesty,
> Wherwith he wont at Heav'ns high Councel-Table,
> To sit the midst of Trinal Unity,
> He laid aside; and here with us to be,
>   Forsook the Courts of everlasting Day
> And chose with us a darksom House of mortal clay.

It is the mystery of the Incarnation, God become man, a paradox poised by Milton's conflation of his own year and that of Christ's birth.

The second and fourth stanzas also foretell Milton's ordering of the "Hymn" as well. The second moves from Heaven to earth, from majesty to the human condition. The fourth moves the human worshipper to the scene in Bethlehem. The "Hymn" will combine features of both. Insofar as its tenses are concerned, the "Hymn" is in two sections, the first running from stanzas 1 to 17 (lines 1–164), and the second from stanza 18 to the last, 27 (lines 165–244). In terms of musical key, the key tense of the former part is the past: "It was the Winter wilde," Milton begins. By going from past to present and back again (making the most of participles for transitions), Milton agitates and magnifies his subject. In the latter section we have the narrative present tense, which we enter with a push: "And then at last our bliss / Full and perfet is" (165–166). A future tense is the obvious one to expect, but Milton gives us as present the heroic deeds of the mighty babe: binding the Dragon, quelling oracles, and so forth. It is as if the narrator is a historian present to see and relate these things, as the introductory stanzas had hinted. Like all other of Milton's greatest poems, this one ends with astonishing quiet, combining the drop at the end of the second introductory stanza and the intensity of the end of the fourth.

> But see the Virgin blest,
> Hath laid her Babe to rest,
>   Time is our tedious Song should here have ending:
> Heav'ns youngest teemed Star,
> Hath fixt her polisht Car,
>   Her sleeping Lord with Handmaid Lamp attending:
> And all about the Courtly Stable,
> Bright-harnest Angels sit in order serviceable. (237–244)

"But see": we readers have also been transported to Bethlehem. And if that is not paradoxical enough, we see a "Virgin" laying her "Babe" to rest as angels "sit" in bright armor ready for duty in a "Courtly Stable," which is an oxymoron, of course, but of a kind like all these paradoxes, promoting magnificence while yet allowing for a peaceful ending.

In *Comus, Lycidas,* and *Epitaphium Damonis,* Milton's doubling takes not the form of digression or paradox but of multiple schemes offered more or less simultaneously and with deliberate crossover. Of these poems *Comus* is the most difficult in many ways, partly because it is not clear that Milton has things the way he wanted them. One scheme that the critics seldom mention (as perhaps beneath their dignity) does, however, show up in performance: the threat to children lost in the dark woods and anxious to get home. Another scheme is that of the supernatural, in which a Neoplatonic middle spirit (the Attendant Spirit) coexists with Comus, son of Bacchus and Circe, with Echo who lives by the Meander. There are also that figure from British lore, Sabrina, and at the end the Neoplatonic celestial Venus, Cupid, and

Psyche. This second scheme is the one that has exercised the critics and, in my belief, is the best example of Milton's trying what works with such ease elsewhere and what fails here. We are left with issues that we do not need: Why classical, British, and spiritual in one plot scheme? Why cannot the lady get from her chair, when chastity is supposed to confer freedom? Is disguise good (the Attendant Spirit) or bad (Comus)?

The rest of the masque works so much better and provides a third scheme, that of the Bridgewater family. As the Spirit says in his opening speech,

> And all this tract that fronts the falling Sun
> A noble Peer of mickle trust, and power
> Has in his charge, with temper'd awe to guide
> An old, and haughty Nation proud in Arms:
> Where his fair off-spring nurs't in Princely lore,
> Are coming to attend their Fathers state,
> And new-entrusted Scepter, but their way
> Lies through the perplex't paths of this drear Wood,
> The nodding horror of whose shady brows
> Threatens the forlorn and wandring Passinger. (30–39)

The main virtue of the second scheme is its spooky investment of the action with danger, because the Bridgewaters' own children, who are acting the parts of the Lady and the two brothers, must be at once themselves and other. The second scheme makes them other by Neoplatonic distancing so that we can feel a sense of danger that could hardly be raised in an audience knowing that the children were only pretending to be lost on their father's lawn or in his hall (depending on interpretation of the acting). Once that otherwise messy second scheme achieves the separation, Milton can find a way to merge the first and third at the end. In the true masque tradition, "*The Scene changes, presenting* Ludlow *Town and the Presidents Castle*" (956 S.D.). The antemasque over, the masque begins. Milton has greatly shortened the Jonsonian proportion for the second part. The Spirit advances with the Lady and her two brothers, tells the dancing shepherds in a song to go to the back, and in the next song presents the children to their parents.

> Noble Lord, and Lady bright,
> I have brought ye new delight,
> Here behold so goodly grown
> Three fair branches of your own,
> Heav'n hath timely tri'd their youth,

> Their faith, their patience, and their truth.
> And sent them here through hard assays
> With a crown of deathless Praise,
>   To triumph in victorious dance
> O're sensual Folly, and Intemperance.[28]

Dances follow, cease, and *"the Spirit Epiloguizes"* (974, S.D.) on classical and Neoplatonic lore that has little connection to what precedes—at least until the last lines, when the Spirit finally begins to give up his loquacity and ends with praise of virtue.

In presenting the children—estranged by threat and that jumble of mythological or supernatural entities—to their parents, we observe that the dark woods have been brought to the human world ideal with "bright" order: "Three fair branches of your own." This marvelous interplay between the first and the third scheme is Milton at his best, reminding us of what happens in *The Morning of Christ's Nativity* and in the intrusions by the historical narrator of the prose. It is a pity the masque could not end there, but Milton apparently knew that even with an addition, he was cutting back the main masque to a very small part.

Lycidas and *Epitaphium Damonis* are wholly successful in their ordonnance of multiple schemes. Although the one is a truly great work and the other simply a fine one, they complement each other. The *Damon* is more pastoral in formal terms. Its refrain, "Go home unfed, my lambs" ("Ite domum impasti . . . agni") reads seventeen times, a kind of poetic ritual probably without parallel in Milton's poetry.[29] In this and other respects the pastoral scheme, the pagan pretense, is far more insistent than in *Lycidas*. Yet no doubt because of that greater pastoralism, Milton feels free to introduce other contemporaries (line 137) and real places by name (lines 126–128). Above all he is free to introduce himself. (There is nothing like a foreign language, even one understood as well as Milton did Latin, for expressing personal, intimate matters.) The references to himself typically come at the beginning of a section just after the refrain, but in fact they may appear anywhere, as the very moving "Remember me, as you take your way to the stars" ("nostri memor ibis ad astra"—line 123). And in lines 162–171 he writes of his epic plans in a tone not very different from the digressions in his prose writing.

Damon both resembles and differs from *Lycidas* in Milton's ordering. It is like the earlier poem in its transcendent vision of the dead friend at the marriage feast of the lamb (198–219). It differs, however, in that *Lycidas* begins and ends with the poet's talk of himself, whereas in *Damon* he begins and ends with talk of Damon. It also differs in the relatively simple distinction between its pastoral scheme and its personal one. One might say that in *Damon* the layered schemes come closer to an allegorical relation than in any of Milton's other major poems. Yet even here there are those passages on real places and people (other than the much intrusive speaker) remarked on previously.

Lycidas has none of the confusions of *Comus*, but it is so complex as to balk our memory that it is fewer than two hundred lines long.[30] Here the layered schemes of most importance to the development are those involving the poet and Lycidas, as in *Damon*, but in different terms. The schemes involve the poet's problems writing the poem at all (1–5 and later passages), finding a solution to a series of pressing problems (five stated or implicit questions) bearing on both Lycidas and the poet, and the pastoral. *"And,"* as the addition to the headnote for the "1645" *Poems* puts it, *"by occasion foretells the ruine of our corrupted Clergie then in their height,"* the occasion often termed "the digression" (lines 108–131). The "Digression" in *The History of Britain* was so labeled, not called an occasional passage, because there fifth- and seventeenth-century Britain are paralleled. In *Lycidas* the climactic "two-handed engine" that has spilled so much ink is no less, or more, a matter contemporary with Milton than the death of Edward King and Milton's problems as a poet.

There are also the matters of the pastoral and the ordering of the poem. The pastoral is no single thing.[31] It is easy to see that a "pastor" is a shepherd in the pastoral scheme, a poet in the personal, and a minister in the religious-historical-biblical. This last illustrates the fusion of the poem. Any "pastor" in the poem may be a priest (except Milton himself), and the corrupt clergy are (bad) shepherds also, and Jesus is the Good Shepherd by implication (line 173). In fact, the pastoral scheme is at once the most multivalent, or unstable, of them all. Unlike the usage in *Damon*, that of Milton in *Lycidas* involves no rigid separation of pastoral from other schemes but constant equivalency and, as it were, dissolution of the figure into what is figured.

The two pastoral elegies raise problems obscured by *Comus* and the prose works. In what I have termed layering or schemes, the effect resembles that in the earlier works of alien elements of a systematic kind being combined in various ways. Combination is a matter of relation (or breakdown if inconsistent, as I believe to be partly the case with *Comus*). Whether relation or breakdown, the major problem lies in accounting for the kind of coherence (or incoherence). To put it another way, we have a difficult problem deciding whether the layering or multiple schemes offer us a species of allegory.

INTERPRETING AS A MEANS TO TRUTH

In more than one sense the issue is a matter of interpretation. We have seen that Milton's best art cannot do without those effects that I have termed layering and schemes (so as not to beg the crucial question of allegory). Probably not many people would treat the prosopopoeia of the episode when Satan meets Sin and death as anything other than allegory (*Paradise Lost*, 2.648–870), with the key passage being taken as the account of the birth of Sin, or the psychology of sin (lines 747–802). Yet the critics seem less ready to consider allegorical the later prosopopoeia of the parallel encounter by Satan with Chaos and night (lines 890–1009). In what follows I shall argue that Milton's sense of interpretation is "literal" in the vexed Renaissance Protestant sense, and that although he assumed typology, analogy, and perhaps allegory, he essentially held to a single final sense that may be termed historical in a secular sense and a matter of faith inspired by the Holy Spirit in a religious sense.

Because the evidence from his poetry and historical writing is the matter in question, the only interpretation available is provided by his *Christian Doctrine*.[32] The matter is extremely complex, but a few quotations will assist us. One principle, *"scriptura sola,"* is addressed to the basis of faith:

> The rule and canon of faith, therefore, is scripture alone: Psal. xix. 10: *the judgments of Jehovah are truth itself.* In controversies there is no arbitrator except scripture, or rather, each man is his own arbitrator, so long as he follows scripture and the Spirit of God.[33]

"Truth itself": Here is an issue to which we shall need to return. The truth involves Scripture (which may come down in corrupt form) and the illumination by the Holy Spirit:

> We have, particularly under the gospel, a double scripture. There is the external scripture of the written word and the internal scripture of the Holy Spirit which he, according to God's promise, has engraved upon the hearts of believers.[34]

"Scripture alone" therefore means what is written as it is interpreted by the engraving of the Holy Spirit on devout hearts. In one sense this places the burden on the individual. In another it frees the justified individual, who has the assistance of the Spirit and of Christ: "Every believer is entitled to interpret the scriptures; and by that I mean interpret them for himself. He has the spirit, who guides truth, and he has the mind of Christ."[35] In typical Protestant fashion, Milton argues for a single sense of Scripture—as opposed to the three, four, or more multiple senses of Catholic interpretation:

> Each passage of scripture has only a single sense, though in the Old Testament this sense is often a combination of the historical and the typological, take Hosea xi. 1, for example, compared with Matt. ii. 15: *I have called my son out of Egypt.* This can be read correctly in two senses, as a reference both to the people of Israel and to Christ in his infancy.[36]

Yet what if the layerings or schemes should seem to fuse, intermingle, or lose their distinct, nonliteral status as "truth"? Milton had something to say about this crucial matter for our concerns:

> Then again, my opponents allege an analogy between baptism and circumcision, which was performed during infancy: Col. ii. 11: *in whom you are circumcised with a circumcision which is not made by any hand. You put off the body of the sins of the flesh through the circumcision of Christ: buried with him through baptism.* But to begin with there is after all no analogy between being *circumcised* and being *buried with him*—no analogy, that is, except that which exists between all sacraments, in spite of their different modes of signification. Secondly, who would claim that things which are analogous must correspond to each other in every respect? Women were able to go without circumcision quite safely, but they cannot go without baptism, either because it is a more perfect sign or because it represents a more perfect thing.[37]

For our purposes, in which we have been seeing from Milton's prose and early poems, the crucial point is the affirmation implied by Milton's question, "who would claim that things which are analogous must correspond to each other in every respect?" The digressions and intrusions (or the layerings and schemes) we have been considering need not wholly agree or be consistent in kind. Yet the "combination" of senses yields "only a single sense" if one interprets Scripture rightly, with the assistance of the Holy Spirit. This effort, with that assistance, brings one to "truth." In other words, Milton posited a standard for inspired writing in which all conduces to a historical or similar truth.

By this standard of interpretation the complexities of the time schemes of the prose works with their intrusions by the historical narrator, or of the poems we have considered with their layerings and schemes, may involve analogies that need not "correspond to each other in every respect" and that may also involve "two senses" that are yet "only a single sense." It is not my concern to prove these matters, beyond holding that Milton interpreted Scripture and, by "analogy," his own writings in prose or verse in the same terms. Is this not what we have been seeing? The digressions so labeled in *The History of Britain* and in *Lycidas* are not adventitious fictions, an author's toys, but are of a historical value consistent with the "single sense" of the whole work: the "digression" in *Lycidas* seems the poem's most historical passage today. The same holds with his intrusions into *The Reason of Church-Government* and the *Second Defence*. I argue that the same holds for his poems. The test and, I believe, the proof of this thesis can be found in Milton's mature poems.

THE EVIDENCE OF
MILTON'S MATURE POETRY

It will be easier to bypass *Paradise Lost* for the moment and to consider the works of his last volume by recalling that the digressions of *The History of Britain* and of *Lycidas* produce the most obviously historical matter, of Milton's own time, for which he had closer access to the primal history as event than he did for early Britain or the pastoral world. *Samson Agonistes* has no digressions in a proper sense because it is a "dramatic poem" rather than a narrative.[38] The nearest to digressive layerings in *Samson Agonistes* are those parts of the work that do not employ direct engagement between Samson and another character. All the choral odes are of this kind, but so is Samson's first speech about himself (lines 1–114, 176–177), and so also (perhaps) the dialogue with the Chorus (180–292); certainly Manoa's dialogue with the Chorus (1445–1540), the Messenger's narration (1541–1659), and Manoa's last speech (1708–1744). In fact, the nonagonistic, nonconfrontational parts of the work are surprisingly numerous, and they frame the successive agons of Samson's encounters with his father, Dalila, Harapha, and the Philistine Publick Officer.

The nonagonistic parts of *Samson Agonistes* have more than one effect. Although least dramatic, they are in many ways the most moving and most affective because in them Samson, Manoa, and the Chorus speak about their feelings and comment on the meanings of issues as they understand them. With the affective, personal emphasis goes another, however, and that is historical. Because the work is meant to be read rather than performed, the *mise en scène* becomes these passages setting forth the personal and larger historical conditions of life in the time of the Judges, or what has transpired "off stage." If one looks with care at Dryden's remarks about history, one will see that a contemporary of Milton could easily have ranged the passages under consideration within a definition of narrative, and as statements assured in truth value. *Samson Agonistes* is termed "A Dramatic Poem" on its title page, is written in verse bespeaking care, and has other such symptoms of rising above quotidian historical prose.

Much the same holds true with *Paradise Regained*. Instead of successive encounters between Samson and others in agons, we have at center a close counterpart—confrontations between Satan and Jesus. Once again there are numerous passages, especially toward the beginning, that do not fit into the agonistic pattern. After the epic preliminaries (1.1–17) there is an account of the baptism of Jesus (18–32), followed by Satan's reaction and his consistory (33–125), and the council in Heaven closing with a hymn (126–181). There follows a soliloquy by Jesus with some introduction and conclusion by the narrator (182–310). Then the encounters of the two principals begin, more or less continuing (with various passages by the narrator) to the end of the first book (502). The second begins with further nonagonistic material, the thoughts of "the new-baptiz'd" (1.1–57), which is followed by a soliloquy by Mary (58–108). There is a brief return by the narrator to Jesus (109–114), followed by Satan's second consistory (115–240), after which the rest of the second book is agonistic (to 486). Such confrontation between the mighty opposites marks all of the third book and most of the fourth (through 561). Then the narrator indulges in the longest stretch of verse in the style of *Paradise Lost* (562–580). The angels prepare a banquet and sing anthems of praise (581–635). The last four lines of the poem offer a transition from the angelic host to the "private" return of Jesus "Home to his Mothers house" (636–639).

Paradise Regained greatly resembles *Samson Agonistes* (an argument for the traditional late dating) in that it also consists of agonistic passages between two principals and other passages of differing nature. The brief epic differs from the "dramatic poem," however, in that its agons are themselves taken to be historical. They have, after all, the securest relation to the gospel account, and they deal with matters historical by any consideration: for example, the situation of Rome at the time of Jesus. In this respect the entirety of *Paradise Regained* is more historical to Milton than is *Samson Agonistes*. For if the agonistic books 3 and 4 are historical in a sense not true of comparable portions of *Samson Agonistes*, the nonagonistic portions of the brief epic serve the same function as do their counterparts in *Samson Agonistes*: affectively and historically. The problem of the historicity of Satan's consistories and of the heavenly council can be deferred.

Satan's concern with who this baptized Son is, Milton's attention to the Son's and Mary's soliloquies, along with the ruminations of the "new baptiz'd" and the quiet ending, work to establish the historical setting of the work. The allusions to the Romans do not go beyond the reign of Tiberius (A.D. 14–37) and indeed set that reign as the historical time of the action. The date is wholly accurate, given Jesus at thirty.[39] This stress, and the unusual emphasis on Mary for a radical Protestant at the time, suggest that Milton is considering, and Satan is tempting, Jesus in his historical or human role.[40] Nothing could make this emphasis on the human, historical figure clearer than the last line and a half: "hee unobserv'd / Home to his Mothers house private return'd" (4.638–639). Presumably God and the angels observed, but the emphasis is so much on the historical scene that their view is omitted.

It is somewhat surprising to discover that the apparent by-passages or notional additions have a historical function (among others). Yet that was true in *The History of Britain* and in *Lycidas*, and it is true in the very like passages (given the differing genres) of *Samson Agonistes* and *Paradise Regained*. It is hard to emphasize enough the unusual nature of this. The *Odyssey* seems so much more subjective than the *Iliad* simply by two devices, both of which have their counterparts in Milton: the splitting of spheres of mental awareness (dwelling on Telemachus for so long) and overlaying with another historical order (Odysseus's relation of his experience to the Phaeacians). I believe that we shall find this true of *Paradise Lost* as well.

Leaving out such things as infernal and heavenly councils, authorial intrusions and passages of description, there are two lengthy passages in *Paradise Lost* that abate the fundamental action of the poem. These are books 4 through 8, which hold off the Fall, and book 11 and much of 12, which intermits the account of the "Fruit" of the Fall, expulsion from Eden. In short, nearly half the poem is intrusive on these gross grounds, not to mention other passages, such as those intrusions and councils mentioned earlier. The books referred to are particularly historical (to Milton's view) in the sense of presenting Adam and Eve, or Raphael, with such events as the War in Heaven, Creation, and Adam's first recollections. And the last two books give a history of what is to come. It is likely to seem far more tolerable to attach the label of "history" to Michael's account of future events than it is to designate Raphael's accounts as history. But by analogy with what we have been seeing and if one can "trust" an archangel, we have history. This and the related question of whether the poem is postulated to be true command a certain amount of interest.

Whether we trust a "Divine / Hystorian" like Raphael or Michael is no single issue. If we decide that *Paradise Lost* is wholly fictional and that they are reliable narrators (things to which most readers would assent), then we trust their versions of history on terms that we would not allow for our version of what Dryden terms "history, properly so called." Again, if we are considering Milton's understanding and claims, it is one thing, and if we are considering our understanding, it is quite another.[41] As primal history in occurrent flux, the events of books 5 and 6 seem out of court. How could Milton pretend to know what happened in the War in Heaven, including speeches by the bad angels and moments of exchange between God and the Son? Books 7, 8, 11, and 12 have at least the Genesis accounts of Creation and history to confirm them. (Milton's "future" in books 11 and 12 amount to specifics only from Genesis and then a leap forward to the last days and beyond.) Books 5 and 6, however, are not even supported by those encrustations of tradition that Milton regarded as papist credulity. Raphael's famous speech on accommodation (5.563–576) has a function quite other, especially in its conclusion, than that usually attributed to it, although the usual explanation also holds. It may be, as Raphael says, that he must liken "spiritual to corporal forms" (line 573) for Adam to understand. The doctrine works the opposite way for the reader, however, amounting to a plea that Raphael's account be taken as a lesser version of what is greater and is true history.

This is not history by any contemporary standard that I know of. If, for the sake of argument, Milton thought it was, how are we to find our way, how to avoid "Vain wisdom all, and false Philosophie" as in Belial's seminar (2.565)? In what follows my aim is to begin indirectly in these matters and then to leap forward over a number of issues to consider the truth status Milton might have conceived for his work. For if his "story" is true, then the "story" deserves ranking as *storia*, history.

THE TRUTH CLAIMS OF
MILTON'S POETRY

To return to points made earlier, the approximately half of *Paradise Lost* in question is set forth as history by Raphael and Michael. These settings forth do resemble the digressions or by-passages of *The History of Britain*, *Lycidas*, *Samson Agonistes*, and *Paradise Regained*, along with the personal entries, the autobiographical matters in the prose works. Except for the discordant elements that I discover in *Comus*, these interruptions (to give them a general name) have the surprising general effect of clarifying rather than simply making more subjective, as is the result of similar passages in the *Odyssey*. In the latter case Milton's long passages in *Paradise Lost* resemble more the interruptions in the *Aeneid*, whether of Aeneas' recounting of his past to Dido or Anchises' account, in the underworld, of the future history of Rome, or of lesser passages. Whether or not we grant the Virgilian interruptions historical status, it is clear that that is their status for Milton in his greatest work. It is also clear that however more complex they make the narrative line of his finest writing, they nonetheless miraculously make things clearer, and even in a genuine sense—of result—simpler. In this lies the major miracle of Milton's genius, second only to his achievement of grandeur.

Paradise Lost is written like the other works in prose and verse in another respect. Milton distinguishes between rival versions, as also between truth and falsehood, although we may have troubles with the latter issue. The opening of *The History of Britain* deserves renewed attention: "The beginning of Nations, those excepted of whom sacred Books have spok'n, is to this day unknown."[42] In positive terms the origins of nations treated in the Bible are known. Again, "That which we have of oldest seeming [apparently of the settling of Britain], hath by the greater part of judicious Antiquaries bin long rejected for a modern Fable."[43] And immediately following,

> Nevertheless there being others besides the first suppos'd Author, men not unread, nor unlerned in Antiquitie, who admitt that [on the settling of Britain?] for approved story [established history], which the former explode for fiction, and seeing that oft-times relations heertofore accounted fabulous have bin after found in them many footsteps, and reliques of something true, as what we read in Poets of the Flood [e.g., Ovid, *Metamorphoses*, 1, "proved" out of the Noah story], and Giants little beleev'd, till undoubted witnesses taught us, that all was not fain'd [Genesis 6:4: "There were giants in the earth in those days"]; I have therfore determin'd to bestow the telling over ev'n of these reputed Tales; be it for nothing else but in favour of our English Poets, and Rhetoricians, who by thir Art will know, how to use them judiciously.[44]

Sorting that out is a labor of truth not unlike that of Psyche in one of Milton's fables of truth-seeking in *Areopagitica* (2.514). By the time he came to write *Paradise Lost*, however, Milton had come to distrust those mere tales and fables, to the extent of dropping his plans for an Arthuriad in favor of what "sacred Books have spok'n."

Milton's masterpiece is extraordinarily strewn with negatives and adversatives for any epic, much less one that aims as steadily as his at grandeur. The only poem of his time that outreaches him in that respect is Butler's *Hudibras*, and in a genuine sense there can be no appreciation of the contrary geniuses of their powers without full knowledge of both. Butler would have appreciated the induction to book 9 (if he read it), with its rejection of "fabl'd Knights" (line 30). And we can see from that "fabl'd" and the whole passage how far Milton has moved from the riddling quotation just given at length from *The History of Britain*. Milton is sleepless in *Paradise Lost* over the need "to compare small things with great" or "to compare great things with small," "compare" always meaning rejection of the insufficient. And, like Butler, he is a master of the dissimile and dismissal: "thus they relate, / Erring" (1.746–747); or at large, "Not that faire field / Of *Enna* . . . nor that sweet Grove / Of *Daphne* . . . nor that *Nyseian* Ile . . . Nor where *Abassin* Kings thir issue Guard . . . but wide remote / From this *Assyrian* Garden" (4.268–385). These and many other examples accumulate to show that Milton was rejecting false accounts in favor of a true one.

As is well known, at the beginning of *Paradise Lost* Milton states his argument and invokes the "Heav'nly Muse" (line 6) so "That to the highth of this great Argument / I may assert Eternal Providence, / And justifie the wayes of God to men" (24–26). "Argument," "assert," and "justifie" are the business of orators, or perhaps those "English Poets, and Rhetoricians" mentioned as possible users of the fables and tales in book 1 of *The History of Britain*. The office of these writers appears to remain the same, but a new claim is made for their truth—or, rather, for the truth available to Milton's narrator. That narrator of *Paradise Lost* claims inspiration from the same spirit who inspired Moses to write the Pentateuch (1.6–10). The counterpart passage in *Paradise Regained* is seldom mentioned and therefore deserves full quotation here:

> Thou Spirit who ledst this glorious Eremite
> Into the Desert, his Victorious Field
> Against the Spiritual Foe, and broughtst him thence
> By proof the undoubted Son of God, inspire,
> As thou art wont, my prompted Song else mute,
> And bear through highth or depth of natures bounds
> With prosperous wing full summ'd to tell of deeds
> Above Heroic, though in secret done,
> And unrecorded left through many an Age,
> Worthy t' have not remain'd so long unsung. (1.8–17)

Years ago William Haller showed that the encounter with Satan in Eden or in the wilderness where Jesus confronts him were the Puritan models of heroic Christian life.[45] Milton was by no means alone in finding in the story of the temptations in the wilderness the true history of Christian wayfaring, although he did so with many embellishments that seem out of place in current historical writing.

The issue of Milton's treatment of the histories in his writing is, then, a Psyche's labor involving sorting out standards that we recognize from those that were on Milton's mind. In those terms, however, we can only exercise historical imagination in dealing with what Milton may have thought but that we cannot accept. As we have seen, the Protestant "literal" sense of Scripture was wider than what "literal" means in modern historical writing, but the issue is one that gets to the complex relations among concepts we designate as fact, fiction, history, and truth, and there are reasons for believing that our own assumptions are not immune to alteration. The difficulty of the matter is seldom recognized or, in our time, is likely to be dissolved into a "textuality" that obscures more than it clarifies. In his life of Waller, Samuel Johnson labored these matters in passages too neglected. At one moment he remarks, "Poets, indeed, profess fiction; but the legitimate end of fiction is the conveyance of truth."[46] In a later passage he deals with Waller's divine poems. The crucial passage begins, "Let no pious ear be offended if I advance, in opposition to many authorities, that poetical devotion cannot often please." After giving many reasons, he concludes, "The ideas of Christian theology are too simple for eloquence, *too sacred for fiction*, and too majestic for ornament: to recommend them by tropes and figures is to magnify by a concave mirror the sideral hemisphere."[47] That the end of fiction is truth is not a proposition with which everyone would agree. Yet to hold at the same time that some truths are above fictional treatment seems inconsistent, unless we privilege them as Johnson did, which seems equally unlikely today.

It is certainly telling that Johnson's account of *Paradise Lost* in his life of Milton does not repeat the strictures against treating the sacred that he sets forth in discussing Waller. I do not pretend to understand all of Johnson's remarks beyond saying what I have just said, but the balance is clear, as a succession of quotations will show.

> Poetry is the art of uniting pleasure with truth by calling imagination to the help of reason. . . . History must supply the writer with the rudiments of narration. . . . Morality must teach him the exact bounds, and different shades, of vice and virtue. . . . To put these materials to poetical use, is required an imagination capable of painting nature and realising fiction. . . .
>
> Of the *probable* and the *marvelous*, two parts of a vulgar epic poem which immerge the critic in deep consideration, the *Paradise Lost* requires little

to be said. It contains the history of a miracle, of Creation and Redemption; it displays the power and the mercy of the Supreme Being; the probable therefore is marvelous, and the marvelous is probable. The substance of the narrative is truth; and as truth allows no choice, it is, like necessity, superior to rule. . . .

Milton's delight was to sport in the wide ranges of possibility; reality was a scene too narrow for his mind. He sent his faculties out upon discovery into worlds where only imagination can travel, and delighted to form new modes of existence, and furnish sentiment and action to superior beings, to trace the counsels of hell, or accompany the choirs of heaven. . . .

Known truths, however, may take a different appearance [from the "good and evil of eternity"], and be conveyed to the mind by a new train of intermediate images. This Milton has undertaken, and performed with a pregnancy and vigour of mind peculiar to himself. Whoever considers the few radical [basic] positions which the Scriptures afforded him, will wonder by what energetic operation he expanded them, and ramified them to such much variety, restrained by religious reverence from licentiousness of fiction.[48]

In his way Johnson raises in these passages the various issues being considered here, not so much in a version of the histories as in terms of fiction and truth. To have formulated the issues, or problems, so well marks Johnson's greatness as a critic. But it cannot be said that he has solved the issues he raises.

The same issues were raised by Marvell in that riddling or "misdoubting" poem he wrote for the second edition of *Paradise Lost*. The opening lines set forth our issues and questions:

> When I beheld the Poet blind, yet bold,
> In slender Book his vast Design unfold,
> *Messiah* crown'd, Gods reconcil'd Decree,
> Rebelling Angels, the Forbidden Tree,
> Heav'n, Hell, Earth, Chaos, All; the Argument
> Held me a while misdoubting his Intent,
> That he would ruine (for I saw him strong)
> The sacred Truths to Fable and Old Song. (1–8)

Marvell has not finished his "misdoubting" with these lines, but they fairly encompass our issues and Johnson's. If any simple conclusion can be reached from Marvell, it is that Milton answered the doubts. Milton treats "All," including much that, as Michael says, leads Adam's "mortal sight to faile" (12.9)—as does ours in the issues posed by Milton's work, along with Marvell's and Johnson's, at least as long as we pose the issues in the terms so far given.

Yet in their ways Marvell and Johnson respond to *Paradise Lost* in ways implicitly, sometimes explicitly, denying distinctions between the factual and historical, the fictional, and the true. Such dissolution seems to be precisely what Milton intended in claiming divine inspiration for an epic at once true and fictional, historical and imaginary. Milton clearly entitled *Paradise Lost* "A Poem." Equally clearly he entered the most extraordinary truth claims (if so often hedged), and his interruptions only made the claims stronger, whether those be the entries of Raphael and Michael or the intrusions of his narrator.

The truth claims in Milton's greatest works are obviously radical ones and, equally obviously, are made for *poems*. We are not accustomed to the combination and are required to adjust our understanding as best we are able. If anything, our ability has decreased since Marvell and Johnson, and for some current critics the zero point has been reached. When we reach such an extreme of bafflement, we have few choices. We may negate what Milton offers for the histories and for truth. Or we may accept our bafflement as the conditions of the situation. Both positions are tenable. We may also seek an alternative to our definitions of literature and its bounds. To those who seek the third way, East Asian concepts offer a way of understanding, of reconciliation. In China, Korea, and Japan there was a lively and enduring sense that what the Chinese termed *wen* and the Japanese *bun* was less restricted than our conception of literature (the usual translation of those words). It included history as well as lyric, and that practice of history is, as many have said, the counterpart of Western epic. To accept this altered or enlarged concept of literature (or at least the East Asian terms and what they signify), we have to expand the bounds of what we mean by "literature" beyond what is traditional in the West and this side of "textuality" by a wide margin. But no other concept of literature accords so well with Milton's claims in his poetry or with the struggles of Marvell's and Johnson's attempts to deal with truth and fiction in Milton. And no other concept explains so well his successive poetic versions of the histories.

9

The Politics of *Paradise Lost*

Mary Ann Radzinowicz

One received opinion concerning *Paradise Lost* tells us that when Milton's political hopes for his nation were dealt the fatal blow of the Restoration, he withdrew into regions of the mind where he could find other-worldly solace and mingled no more with politics. Of this view Coleridge gave the romantic account:

> In [Milton's] mind itself there were purity and piety absolute; an imagination to which neither the past nor the present were interesting, except as far as they called forth and enlivened the great ideal in which and for which he lived; a keen love of truth, which, after many weary pursuits, found a harbour in a sublime listening to the still voice in his own spirit, and as keen a love of his country, which, after a disappointment still more depressive, expanded and soared into a love of man as a probationer of immortality. . . . He was, as every truly great poet has ever been, a good man, but finding it impossible to realize his own aspirations, either in religion, or politics, or society, he gave up his heart to the living spirit and light within him, and avenged himself on the world by enriching it with this record of his own transcendent ideal.[1]

Offered with varying degrees of approbation depending on the critic, that picture of the epic poet abandoning politics for religion, to endow the world with a sublime rather than a politically or historically critical vision, remains current. It is the view made official or marmorealized for this generation in *A Milton Encyclopedia*, for example, in which Michael Fixler writes, "The Restoration guaranteed a political amnesty to all but the worst offenders against the Stuarts, and Milton was one of those who narrowly escaped proscription. Thereafter he was prudently silent, except for an allusion to tyrants in *Paradise Lost* that caused a small flutter."[2]

204

A contrary position argues that *Paradise Lost* participates in Milton's persistent concern with politics but reveals the unrepentant radical wrestling hard to bring his libertarian views into accord with his theology. This stand also received its standard formulation by a romantic, William Blake. Blake located the ideological content of the epic in the struggle between Satan and God, a struggle he said was internalized and unresolved in the poet: "[Milton] wrote in fetters when he wrote of Angels of God, and at liberty when of Devils & Hell because he was . . . of the Devils party without knowing it."[3] Its continuing currency can be seen in Jackie DiSalvo's examination of Milton's "revolutionary contradictions." By her reading, Milton, "spokesman for a new elite as well as the scourge of an old one," deposits in Satan's "democratic, antipatriarchal, irreligious views" his own pre-Restoration republicanism. The resulting "contradictory allegiances of his poem and . . . repressive implications of his ideology" reveal the "double-edged" nature of the poem.[4]

If one might characterize the first position as *Paradise Lost* read without reference to history, the second position reads *Paradise Lost* by historical hindsight or second sight, to find encrypted in Milton's poem political positions predictive of our own. It is not so much that Milton is seen to be a source of some aspects of the thought of our times; rather, it is that he is their prophetic prototype. For Herman Rapaport, for example, Milton becomes the forerunner of the brutalized, dehumanized modern state.[5]

Both these judgments—of politics abandoned and of politics encrypted—draw force from undoubted features of the poem. Its subject is biblical—the Fall of Man—and like the Bible's, its declared object is the justification of God's ways. Both justify God by blaming man's choices for his fall and by registering the salvation of believers. That being so, it can seem either that Milton's eye is on the end of time and he does not care about interim human arrangements or that his faith in the people is too diminished to support politics. Second, its normative language is at once ethical, religious, and political and is just as much the property of devils and fallen men as of angels or inspired men. Hence it can seem either that Milton represents his own earlier positions taken over by bad creatures for bad ends, or repudiated by weak men tempted, or even that he conceals his own political hopes in the good rebellion of the Fallen Angel or the just power of the angelic few.

This essay will offer a different picture of the poem than either the picture of political disengagement or of political encryption. I will argue that in line with Milton's humanistic understanding of the nature and function of heroic poetry, *Paradise Lost* has a public role to play in the poet's own day. Milton responds to the expectation of a "fit audience" for epic poetry that it will "imbreed and cherish in a great people the seeds of vertu, and publick civility."[6] His poem is paideutic. In fitting himself for the writing of heroic poetry, he cautioned himself "not [to presume] to sing high praises of heroick men, or famous Cities, unless he have in himselfe the experience and the practice of all which is praise-worthy."[7] Accordingly he made himself both teacher and public servant before subsuming those vocations in the calling of heroic poet. *Paradise Lost* constitutes a course in political education, and political education serves in Milton's epic the purposes that a political program might play in another kind of work. Accordingly the essay will examine the problems of subject and language— taking up Milton's conception of biblical authority, his radicalization of the story of the Fall, and his ways of using fallen language—as these matters become the very themes in the poem's political education, the problems set by the poet-political teacher in the way a Socratic educator sets problems, the occasions for debate, and instances for correction.[8]

Paradise Lost, then, is directed on the political level "to make the people fittest to chuse, and the chosen fittest to govern."[9] Consequently I will deal with Milton's political ideas as an overt subject in the poem. The overt political thought itself presents a sufficient challenge for interpretation without resort to remoter levels of signification, where dwells the politics of criticism rather than the politics of discourse. The political concepts addressed in *Paradise Lost* are the three dominant ideas of continuous concern to Milton: freedom, order, and degree; their interrelationship; their appropriate protection; and their development through changing institutions in the course of history. Milton's method is not that of the propagandist for this or that institution or program; his method is that of the teacher. The text he sets before his readers is a biblical text, and with the political implications of choosing such a text we may begin.

THE POLITICS OF THE BIBLICAL SUBJECT

Several times as a young writer of prose Milton set himself to prove that a political or legal arrangement—divorce, for example, or the Presbyterian form of church government—which he desired in the 1640s had been especially recommended or urged in Scripture centuries earlier. That is not the method of argument in political matters the heroic poet adopted in *Paradise Lost*. He does not search Scripture seeking precedents, freely interpreting the text in order to find them.

He reads Scripture seeking its rational interpretation. Satisfied that he has rightly judged the significance of this or that occasion, his interpretation does not become the precedent to which current affairs are made conformable; rather, the free use of reason in an act of interpretation becomes the precedent, the mode by which current affairs are judged.

One paradigmatic example may illustrate Milton's political way with the Bible. His procedure is to offer a course in political education through biblical texts set to be interpreted. The persistently corrective effect of reading Scripture is the lesson he now provides, in contradistinction to that youthful practice of arguing that his own positions are supported by decisive precedents. In the prose work closest in time to *Paradise Lost, The Readie and Easie Way . . .* , written in the consciousness of the defeat of the Good Old Cause, Milton holds that "To make the people fittest to chuse, and the chosen fittest to govern" is

> to mend our corrupt and faulty *education*, to teach the people faith not without vertue, temperance, modestie, sobrietie, parsimonie, justice; not to admire wealth or honour; to hate turbulence and ambition; *to place everyone his privat welfare and happiness in the public peace, libertie and safetie.*

The first and last points enjoin his readers not to rest in the insight they already have and not to identify the public welfare with their own private moral well-being. It was not for that exclusive purity of conscience that Milton thought God covenanted with mankind. As teaching the triad of political ideas of freedom, order, and degree is half the point in Milton's Bible course, the other half is teaching the politics of historical covenant and progressive revelation.

The paradigm of Milton's Bible-based political education is Solomon's advice, "Go to the ant." In *The Readie and Easie Way to Establish A Free Commonwealth* (second edition) Milton writes,

> And what madness is it, for them who might manage nobly thir own affairs themselves, sluggishly and weakly to devolve all on a single person; and more like boyes under age then men, to commit all to his patronage and disposal, who neither can performe what he undertakes, and yet for undertaking it, though royally paid, will not be thir servant, but thir lord? how unmanly must it needs be, to count such a one the breath of our nostrils, to hang all our felicitie on him, all our safetie, our well-being, for which if we were aught els but sluggards or babies, we need depend on none but God and our own counsels, our own active vertue and industrie; *Go to the Ant, thou sluggard, saith Solomon; consider her waies, and be wise; which having no prince, ruler, or lord, provides her meat in the summer, and*

gathers her good in the harvest, which evidently shews us, that they who think the nation undon without a king, though they look grave or haughtie, have not so much true spirit and understanding in them as a pismire; neither are these diligent creatures hence concluded to live in lawless anarchie, or that commended, but are set the examples to imprudent and ungovernd men, of frugal and self-governing democratie or Common-wealth; safer and more thriving in the joint providence and counsel of many industrious equals, then under the single domination of one im-perious Lord.[10]

The text from Proverbs is interpreted as supporting Milton's desired commonwealth by an argument from nature, not from scriptural law or revelation. Solomon becomes a good moral naturalist in Milton's hands, not one of God's secretaries.

When the same instance occurs in *Paradise Lost,* the ant enters unaccompanied by Solomon, having just been created with all its political evidency before Solomon's reign:

> . . . First crept
> The Parsimonious Emmet, provident
> Of future, in small room large heart enclos'd,
> Pattern of just equalitie perhaps
> Hereafter, join'd in her popular Tribes
> Of Commonaltie. (7.484–489)

Here the ant predicts both the natural argument and Solomon's way of making it. In both cases made through the "Minims of Nature," the argument from Scripture (Solomon) is really an argument from nature (the ant); in the second case history (the "Hereafter") shows men gaining illumination. God covenants with mankind to protract history so that such increases in understanding may take place.

So it is with all Milton's political instances involving scriptural scenarios in *Paradise Lost.* In them Scripture is history and not au-thority; no interpretation is coercive; no public policy comes with God's fiat behind it to overrule freedom. Furthermore, as in matters of faith the Bible provides progressive revelation, so in matters of civil policy, if rightly read, it records illuminating changes. Even the nega-tive instances of Hell are rendered cautionary by their unreasoned quality and not merely as the vile precedents of evildoers. Sometimes, after all, the fallen angels do well in civil matters:

> O shame to men! Devil with Devil damn'd
> Firm concord holds, men onely disagree
> Of Creatures rational, though under hope
> Of heavenly Grace: and God proclaiming peace,

> Yet live in hatred, enmitie, and strife
> Among themselves, and levie cruel warres,
> Wasting the Earth, each other to destroy:
> As if (which might induce us to accord)
> Man had not hellish foes anow besides,
> That day and night for his destruction waite. (2.496–505)

As the paradigm of the ants predicted, all the biblical kingdoms of Heaven, Hell, and earth are shown in *Paradise Lost* as scenes in a historical or realistic fiction. They permit lessons to be taught about liberty, order, and degree. They are not given as scriptural precedents, offering a divine model, cautioning against a diabolical model, or correcting a human model. When God is shown as King of Heaven in the epic, Milton's principal biblical sources are Ezekiel and Daniel,[11] but his most prominent source is Arthurian romance—Spenser, not Scripture. What Milton utterly repudiated as unfit for "higher argument" ("tinsel trappings," "gorgious knights") he briefly uses to suggest God's glory; but God's heavenly enthronement offers no model for a human state. One scene may stand for all Milton's depictions of kingship in Heaven, that in book 5, in which Raphael opens the education of Adam by describing God's appointment of the Son. On a flaming "holy Hill" sit God and the Son: the "Empyreal Host / Of Angels" are "by Imperial summons call'd" together. They arrive in "orders bright" organized under ensigns, standards, and gonfalons that "Streame in the Aire, and for distinction serve / Of Hierarchies, of Orders, and Degrees" (5.588–591), and they wheel in concentric circles around God's throne. He addresses them proclaiming His Son His heir—or, rather, His kingly vicegerent, since inheritance cannot be at issue where monarch and subject are all immortal. The words of institution Milton writes for God stress the initiation of a peculiar political state:

> This day I have begot whom I declare
> My onely Son, and on this holy Hill
> Him have anointed, whom ye now behold
> At my right hand; your Head I him appoint;
> And by my Self have sworn to him shall bow
> All knees in Heav'n, and shall confess him Lord:
> Under his great Vice-gerent Reign abide
> United as one individual Soule
> For ever happie. (5.603–611)

Here on the heels of a feudal picture of Heaven, Milton installs a vicegerent Son. He rejects the Son's hereditary right for a much more political reason than the theological question of the Father's unique unbegottenness, however. He rejects it in order to instate the Son as Son on the grounds of merit; and, as we shall see, he insists on vicegerency rather than kingly inheritance in order to wash out the political inference that kingship on earth mysteriously resembles or is sanctioned by kingship in Heaven. The Son's merit was the grounds God recognized in book 3 when the offer to die for mankind was made:

> [Thou] hast been found
> By Merit more then Birthright Son of God,
> Found worthiest to be so by being Good,
> Farr more then Great or High. (3.308–311)

The appointment in terms of merit creates a fraternity or a united community that God's imperial decree publishes. The angels are "for ever happy" to be led and united by the best created being, whom the angel Abdiel calls "one of our numbers." It is impossible to argue that this concept of merited "sonship" is a necessary part of the subordinationism so familiar to theology, or that its grounds in God's desire to augment the quantum of freedom and fraternity in the universe is a necessary aspect of that perfectly unheretical doctrine, let alone that either proposition is particularly biblical. Milton enthrones God in a scene from medieval romance made quasi-biblical. He enthrones the Son in a meritocracy of which the natural political result is a loosening of God's empire and a strengthening of ties among creatures. And finally, although he attributes this arrangement to God's calculated relinquishment of power, not to His tightening of it, the arrangement is held to be valuable for its reasonableness (it promotes unity and happiness), not for its divine binding.

A similar delegation of imperial power occurs when God transfers his military arm to the Son:

> To manifest thee worthiest to be Heir
> Of all things, to be Heir and to be King
> By Sacred Unction, thy deserved right. (6.707–709)

Judicial power is equally delegated for explicit reasons of the Son's suitability. After man's fall God speaks again:

> But whom send I to judge them? whom but thee
> Vicegerent Son, to thee I have transferr'd
> All Judgement, whether in Heav'n, or Earth, or Hell.
> Easie it may be seen that I intend
> Mercie collegue with Justice, sending thee

> Mans Friend, his Mediator, his design'd
> Both Ransom and Redeemer voluntarie,
> And destin'd Man himself to judge Man fall'n. (10.55–62)

The kingship of Heaven is so far from presenting a model of absolutism or of the divine right of earthly kings that what one is to learn is the politics of delegated power and the sharing of power not through hereditary but through meritocratic claims. Indeed, Milton's interpretation of God as king comes down to relieving God of the burden of exercising personal power.[12]

Milton's meritocracy endorses hierarchy or degree. That has given it a bad name with those who have not noticed the class structure in their own political arrangements and have gone on to ask questions about the roots of the class structure. What is distinctive about Milton's hierarchy, however—its individualistic, voluntaristic, and meritocratic basis—is equally what makes his concept of covenant distinctively nonbiblical or, as Milton would prefer no doubt, Gospel rather than Old Testament. Covenant in the Old Testament is entirely an external arrangement made by God according to His will, unmerited by human beings, unproposed by the human will, and tribal as often as individual. Milton's sense of gospel covenant or Christian liberty is a different matter. With respect to religious institutions, it produces a fraternity of voluntary Protestants, all equally priests: "Obviously," he writes, "if religious matters were not under our control, or to some extent within our power and choice, God could not enter into a covenant with us, and we could not keep it, let alone swear to keep it."[13] Christian liberty also produces the possibility of sustained political evolution throughout history, the element in which progressive, independent, and free civil covenants are made. Of human covenants, or social and political contracts, Milton is sure that they must be entered into voluntarily, that they bind only as they reasonably fulfill the conditions for which they were made, and that they tend to failures related to man's fall, although the protraction of human history was intended in the divine covenant for their perfecting.

Satan, of course, as we shall see, is one of the sharpest critics of God's first devolution of power in appointing the Son vicegerent. Through the diabolical interpretation of Heaven's civility, Milton makes a number of points about the language of politics in his own day. But what of Satan's own political example? Whatever Satan has to say of God's tyranny and however beautifully Milton conducts that argument to secure political paideia, Satan's actual example is of a frozen meritocracy or tyranny. Like an Alexander or a Tamburlaine, a hero of power, Lucifer leads his own troops into battle. Once seated in Hell on his "Throne of Royal State" made by Mammon more magnificent than "Babilon, / . . . or great Alcairo," he too is "by merit rais'd / To [his] bad eminence." His reign is condemned for its exploitive imperialism (as bad as anything the Turks can parallel) and its rapacity (likened to that of the ubiquitous spice merchants in an irony condemning both). Milton's biblical authority for Satan's bad kingship is Revelation 2.13: "I know where . . . Satan's throne is," but his sultanizing of Satan's tyrannic kingship as well as his echo of Spenser's presentation of Lucifera in the court scene indicates the contemporary associations with Romish pomp, illegal capital formation, and unconstitutional usurpation Milton wishes to promote.[14] (With respect to fiscal morality, from the Lady's hopes in *Comus* for just distribution, through the advice to Fairfax on the subject of sequestration that "Public Faith [be] cleard from the shamefull brand / Of Public Fraud," to Milton's scornful rejection of the economic argument for monarchy in *A Readie and Easie Way* . . .—"lest tradesmen should mutiny for want of trade"—the poet has shown himself to be uneasy about business amorality. He takes the same jaundiced view of exploitiveness in *Paradise Lost* and lodges a criticized commercialism in Mammon's procedures.) As we shall see, Milton entrusts the general political reasoning against Lucifer's claim to uphold freedom in heroic defiance of God's tyranny to Abdiel.

The first presentation of purely earthly kingship in *Paradise Lost* is a sort of divine pleasantry involving Adam's suzerainty over the animal kingdom. When the animals pass before Adam to receive their names, Milton's model is a coronation ceremony:

> . . . each Bird and Beast behold
> After thir kindes; I bring them to receave
> From thee thir Names, and pay thee fealtie
> With low subjection; (8.342–345)

God pretends to see in the animals' inferiority to Adam grounds for their subjection to man and man's pleasure in lording it over them: "They . . . reason not contemptibly; with these / Find pastime, and bear rule; thy Realm is large." Milton uses the occasion, however, to demonstrate the incommensurability of God and man, not of beasts and man, and to do so in a way that once and for all negates any claim that man does well to imitate God's ways, political or other, for he cannot. Adam explains:

> Thou in thy secresie although alone,
> Best with thyself accompanied, seek'st not

> Social communication, yet so pleas'd
> Canst raise thy Creature to what highth thou wilt
> Of Union or Communion, deifi'd;
> I by conversing cannot these erect. (8.427–432)

What Adam can do to increase "social communication" is to multiply his own kind through "wedded Love . . . / Founded in Reason, Loyal, Just and Pure, Relations dear." The scene ends with God's approval of Adam's wish for a mate. Even here the political emphasis is on the establishment of wise institutions after a session of educative reasoning.

Historical kingship as recorded in the Bible, Milton treats in the last two books of *Paradise Lost*, commencing with Nimrod's tyranny that wickedly ends the pure, brotherly, simple historical commonwealth of Noah's stock "dwelling / Long time in peace by Families and Tribes" in "fair equalitie, fraternal state." Adam is shocked by Nimrod's usurpation of authority. He expostulates,

> O execrable Son so to aspire
> Above his Brethren, to himself assuming
> Authoritie usurpt, from God not giv'n;
> He gave us onely over Beast, Fish, Fowl
> Dominion absolute; that right we hold
> By his donation; but Man over men
> He made not Lord; such title to himself
> Reserving, human left from human free. (12.64–71)

Milton's interpretation of Nimrod as a figure of the tyrant follows traditional Christian exegesis. Hughes cites Josephus, St. Gregory, Dante, and Sir John Fortescue, who treat Nimrod as "foiled empire builder"; Fowler adds St. Jerome and St. Basil.[15] But to detest tyranny and to argue republicanism are not the same. And Adam's republicanism is Milton's addition. Clearly human beings left free from other human beings acquire monarch or lord only unwisely.

Michael specifically bends scriptural material toward the presentation of historical lessons of a significantly meritocratic and republican cast. When he praises Adam's condemnation of Nimrod, he makes the point that the burden of upholding liberty falls on man and that political liberty is a matter of individual responsibility. Then he adds,

> Yet sometimes Nations will decline so low
> From vertue, which is reason, that no wrong,
> But Justice, and some fatal curse annext

> Deprives them of thir outward libertie
> Thir inward lost . . . (12.97–101)

Those words commence another stage of God's covenant. Although they fall on the ear with bleakness, sharply critical of Milton's own day and predictive of other eras of mindless polity, they do not result in a disengagement from politics or a flight into simple private paradises within.

Michael's instructions were to "intermix / [God's] Cov'nant in the womans seed renewd." He interprets "renewd" not as once renewed but as renewed down the course of changing history to a foreknown and beneficent conclusion. The politics of the Bible is a politics of the fulfillment of historical if not a national destiny. When a single nation is found incapable of political reason, Michael predicts, then God devises another form of election—maybe not the particular election of single just men, the types of the faithful in the Old Testament dispensation, but a general election of the nation of one such faithful man, from which the education of all tribes and nations will commence. God neither dissolves society (as in Noah) nor gathers Him a tiny few by sporadic raptures to Heaven (as in Elijah). He arranges for the kind of discipline in life that produces an educated meritocracy. His original plan for unfallen man posited a progressively rational meritocracy, in which man's place in the cosmos was not fixed but was to be "improv'd by tract of time" so that at the end of his training he might "at choice / [In earthly] or in Heav'nly Paradises dwell." When Michael educates Adam into Christ's "recuring" of his fall, he educates him into the providential design that will go forward to its historical fulfillment antinationalistically.

This familiar ground has regularly been made to bear the significance of other-worldliness and an interest on Milton's part exclusively in the moral probity of each individual under a rigid single sense of scriptural authority. I have been arguing, rather, that it bears the significance of a continued interest on his part in politics, whose program is "to make the people fittest to chuse, and the chosen fittest to govern" where Scripture is a datum for interpretation and not a set of given precedents. That Milton is indifferent to a more prescriptive political program than education is suggested by the curtness and irony in Michael's treatments of the modern state—"a long succession," "part good, part bad, of bad the longer scrowle." But the very insistence on the progressive movement toward a covenanted historical destiny underlines the element of political education in the poem. Even when he portrays apocalypse, Michael leaves the Earth its centrality. He gives to man's world the standing it enjoyed in

Raphael's moral propaideutics. After the period of darkening in which it goes on "under its own weight groaning," the world is "ripe for dissolution." Then the Saviour returns as judge and earth's monarch, to receive his brothers into bliss,

> Whether in Heav'n or Earth, for then the Earth
> Shall all be Paradise, far happier place
> Then this of *Eden*, and far happier daies. (12.463–465)

A paradise within may be nobler and attract the soul more, but it is not all that Milton thought the rational interpretation of Scripture might teach mankind about how and where to live. He might, after all, inherit

> New Heav'ns, new Earth, Ages of endless date
> Founded in righteousness and peace and love,
> To bring forth fruits Joy and eternal Bliss. (12.549–551)

THE LANGUAGE OF POLITICS
AND THE RADICAL MYTH OF THE FALL

Paradise Lost depicts the course of political evolution, then, and not the values of the Puritan Revolution, as Milton argues in favor of the principles of liberty, order, and degree. To read the politics of the poem demands that we interpret a language common to religion and politics that in Milton's day was appropriated by sectarian and secularist, by conservative and radical. In the controversial prose written nearest in time to *Paradise Lost* and when the collapse of the commonwealth was certain or nearly so, Milton drew on a single vocabulary for matters of both politics and religion to write "against two the most prevailing usurpers over mankinde, superstition and tyrannie" to effect "the liberation of all human life from slavery."[16] He made no linguistic distinction between the spheres of spirit and state. Thus in *A Treatise of Civil Power in Ecclesiastical Causes,* he opens a phrase with the words "a free, elective and rational . . ." to complete it with the word "worship"; in *The Readie and Easie Way* . . . not worship but government attracts the same words, "free," "voluntary," and "rational."[17] In that tract he tells us he is speaking still "the language of that which is not call'd amiss the good old Cause."[18] It is not the case that in writing prose in that language Milton used plain perspicuous terms that differentiated between civil and religious matters, whereas in writing poetry he did not. It is the case, however, that he was well aware that the same terms can signify opposed positions, whatever the medium used. In the end Milton took advantage of poetry's linguistic self-consciousness in proffering his post-Restoration politics in that medium.

That the language of the "good old Cause" can be common property of men of opposed persuasions Milton knew and often said. He referred to that linguistic ambiguity both when he wrote with scholarly skepticism in *De doctrina Christiana*—"if there be anything like a universal meaning for language"—and when he delivered in Sonnet XI, "I did but prompt the age to quit their cloggs," a punning, ironic rebuke to the "detractors of certain treatises," the divorce tracts, and *Areopagitica*. There he turned against his Presbyterian opponents the very phrase they used to attack him, that his divorce proposal was a "meer authorizing of licence," by identifying their "bawle for freedom" with their demand for the licensing of books: "License they mean when they cry liberty."[19] He made a like point about linguistic appropriation through Nimrod, the political tyrant in *Paradise Lost*,

> [Who] from Rebellion shall derive his name,
> Though of Rebellion others he accuse. (12.36–37);

a like point about the sloganeering of language in *Samson Agonistes* when he referred to

> . . . that sore battel when so many dy'd
> Without Reprieve adjudg'd to death,
> For want of well pronouncing Shibboleth. (287–289)

and a like point about ambiguity through the Devil's advocacy when Satan claims in *Paradise Regained* that the title "The Son of God" "bears no single sense" (4.516). In *Paradise Lost* partly because language is ambiguous and important normative words are so susceptible to appropriations, Milton invoked the heavenly Muse Uranie, "by that name / If rightly thou art call'd, . . . / The meaning, not the Name I call" (7.1–2, 5).

To *Paradise Lost* conceived as political text, Milton brought two strategies to stabilize and dramatize his meaning. First he embodied in the poem a radicalization of the story of the Fall; whatever key terms might slip or suffer outright theft the tale itself would record to reinforce his meaning. As we shall see, he radicalized the scriptural story by rationally interpreting several features found in Genesis. He lodged freedom to choose not only in prelapsarian but also in fallen man as the law of his being; he defined Adam's and our humanity as consisting of reason and choice; he identified trial and changed choices as the source of purification for the fallen. Second, he made his course of political education actually turn on the correction of false usages; increasing linguistic sophistication would protect his readers from the misinformation he thought made right choice so difficult. Milton had earlier offered a similarly political account of the fall of Adam and Eve in *Areopagitica* by arguing the hereditability of Adam's freedom for Adam's sons, to demonstrate that the Fall proves the law of liberty to be the very law of God's universe, whatever, at this or that historical juncture, men may take to be their law. In *Paradise Lost* by making Satan's rebellion an antecedent myth of the Fall, repeated in postlapsarian falls (specifically Nimrod's), Milton further radicalizes the story. He extends the Fall into a sequence of falls that, far from necessitating man's fate, reaffirms religious and political liberty. Satan's rebellion is political as well as spiritual, no mere subplot but part of a repeated pattern, a design in which failure itself enforces the doctrine of free choice. So too Nimrod's fall instances the repeated pattern. Every fall involves the misuse of language, resolved only with its correction. And finally, as fall and renewed freedom in religion create the condition for progressive revelation, so by the interconnectedness of political and religious language that same pattern endorses continuous change and development in politics.

Perhaps the simplest way to indicate how the Genesis story was radicalized by the Puritans in general and by Milton in *Areopagitica* in particular is to contrast it with the myth of another garden state implying human choice and perfectability: the myth of Utopia, a myth to which Milton was clearly attracted when he wrote *The Readie and Easie Way. . . .* Both myths carry the emblem of cognate icons: Eden, a tree wrapped about by the serpent reaching for the apple; Utopia, Hermes' winged or twig-tipped staff enwrapped by two serpents. Each icon—the symbol of man's fall and the image of his scientific power—stands for a vision of man and of change. The Genesis story had its parallel in the *Corpus Hermeticum* translated by Ficino in 1471 and disseminated in sixteen editions before 1500. (That work taught that man was made in the image of God and given dominion over the creatures, had divine creativity within himself as brother to the creating Demiurge, took on mortal body by his own choice in an act involving no fall, in his bodily human form retained his creativity, and could therefore as man reacquire his knowledge of nature to use it for good. He could, that is, make scientific utopias.) Respecting change and permanence, the Paradise myth offers a narrative demonstration that things were not always the way they are now; they have been changed by the Fall from their first estate. If changed from what they were, they may be changed again. As Robert Burton put it, "Ye have been otherwise, you may and shall be again."[20] The first change was a horror, a trans*gression* or stepping over the boundary of Eden, of nature and its law. The narrative suggests, however, that change as transgression may become change as trans*cendence*, a change back up and into the circle of God's stability. That version of the fall is a thoroughly conservative myth: "Turn back, o man, forsake thy foolish ways." To radicalize it is to argue that Adam's freedom as well as his punishment are inherited by all his sons: man set on his feet once more by grace and led by his God has only to find in America or make in England a new sacred place and there reform what has been ill-done. If the utopian myth seems more radical in that it does not dub change "transgression," it was not so construed in Milton's country and day. The impulse to make utopias was regularly construed in the English Renaissance as suggesting paternalistic and ritualized social arrangements for stability and permanency. Bacon's *New Atlantis* is a typical case.[21] It is not that utopias cannot render radical political states, for of course they often have. But in Milton's day utopia seldom was, whereas the Genesis myth not only could be but repeatedly was, made to argue social and political reform.

Clearly either myth can make change tolerable and impermanence temporary. *The Readie and Easie Way . . .* , Milton's version of utopia, clearly argues, notwithstanding its courageous republicanism, for a "perpetual Senat" so that the nation "firmly constituted to perpetuitie" may live "forever in a firm and free Commonwealth."[22] While repeatedly drawing biblical analogies to the sinful servitude the people will choose if they restore the Stuart monarchy, Milton does not refer to the Fall at all. But *The Readie and Easie Way . . .* is scarcely a revolutionary document; revolution once over, there will be no more revolution. Certainly Milton never repudiated a free commonwealth as a political ideal for his nation, but among all political corrections in *Paradise Lost* is one self-correction, a correction of the very concept of a permanent and changeless political utopia and an acknowledgment that political wisdom is founded through time and experience by stages of choice. Here is how Milton has Michael describe to Adam the lawgiver Moses leading the Chosen People out of bondage into the "wilde Desert":

> *Moses* once more his potent Rod extends
> Over the Sea; the Sea his Rod obeys;
> On thir imbattelled ranks the Waves return,
> And overwhelm thir Warr: the Race elect
> Safe towards *Canaan* from the shoar advance

> Through the wilde Desert, not the readiest way,
> Least entring on the *Canaanite* allarmd
> Warr terrifie them inexpert, and feare
> Return them back to *Egypt*, choosing rather
> Inglorious life with servitude; for life
> To noble and ignoble is more sweet
> Untraind in Armes, where rashness leads not on.
> This also shall they gain by thir delay
> In the wide Wilderness, there they shall found
> Thir government, and thir great Senate choose
> Through the twelve Tribes, to rule by Laws ordained. (12.211–226)

Here Milton directly recalls the attempt of his own "Readie . . . way" to forestall the rush of the English people back to monarchy in the Restoration, a move he had there likened to the Chosen People's "chusing them a captain back for Egypt."[23] He concedes that the choice of something "*not* the readiest way" led to the "gain" of that very government he so wished for his own people, the "great Senate . . . to rule by Laws ordaind," and by implication he suggests that the patience he regards as the highest kind of fortitude has great political value.

Milton does, however, refer in the *Readie and Easie Way* . . . to Nimrod and his analogue, the tower-builder in Luke, to speculate on how the restoration of monarchy will be received in the rest of the modern political world:

> [W]hat will they at best say of us and of the whole English name, but scoffingly as of that foolish builder, mentioned by our Saviour, who began to build a tower, and was not able to finish it. Where is this goodly tower of a Commonwealth, which the English boasted they would build to over-shaddow kings, and be another *Rome* in the west? The foundation indeed they laid gallantly; but fell into a wors confusion, not of tongues but of factions, than those at the tower of Babel; and have left no memorial of thir work behinde them remaining, but the common laughter of Europ.[24]

Through the reference to Nimrod Milton draws a double historical parallel between Scripture and his own times, not in proof that God requires the English to preserve their commonwealth but that any reasonable man can see how bad statecraft is like bad architecture and the foolish builders of either are worthy of being mocked.[25]

Although *The Readie and the Easie Way* . . . is unrevolutionary in conserving the commonwealth by planning for its frozen permanence, Milton nevertheless makes clear his conviction that kingship implies idolatry, that monarchy implies an apostasy from the rule of free

reason, and that his detestations "tyranny and superstition" are Si-
amese twins. The autocrat is shown there "to pageant himself up and
down in progress among the perpetual bowings and cringings of an
abject people, on either side deifying and adoring him for nothing
don that can deserve it."[26] Religion and politics face the same danger:
idolatry. Idolatry is enslavement whether its agent be potentate or
prelate. Idolatry of ruler is tyranny; of priest, superstition.

More commonly in Milton's hands Genesis provides the radical
myth as Utopia the conservative. Thus two well-known passages in
Areopagitica offer a political reading of the Fall:

> Many there be that complain of divin Providence for suffering *Adam* to
> transgresse, foolish tongues! when God gave him reason, he gave him
> freedom to choose, for reason is but choosing; he had bin else a meer
> artificial *Adam*, such an *Adam* as he is in the motions. We our selves esteem
> not of that obedience, or love, or gift, which is of force: God therefore left
> him free, set before him a provoking object, even almost in his eyes; herein
> consisted his merit, herein the right of his reward, the praise of his ab-
> stinence. Wherefore did he creat passions within us, pleasures round about
> us, but that these rightly tempered are the very ingredients of vertu?

And again,

> It was from out the rinde of one apple tasted, that the knowledge of good
> and evil as two twins cleaving together leapt forth into the World. And
> perhaps this is that doom which *Adam* fell into of knowing good and evill,
> that is to say of knowing good by evil. As therefore the state of man now
> is; what wisdom can there be to choose, what continence to forbeare
> without the knowledge of evill? . . . Assuredly we bring not innocence
> into the world, we bring impurity much rather: that which purifies us is
> triall, and triall is by what is contrary.[27]

As I have suggested, Milton renders the Fall useful for political education (1) by lodging freedom in both prelapsarian and fallen man
as the law of his being, (2) by identifying choice through reason as
constitutive of humanity, and (3) by converting trial, struggle, or
change itself into the source of purification. Given the figure of Adam
in rational choice as the model of the properly human, both religious
and political implications for individual free choice naturally follow.
Only uncoerced faith is true religion, so that "if [a man] beleeve things
only because his Pastor sayes so, or the Assembly so determins . . .
though his belief be true, yet the very truth he holds becomes his
heresie."[28] Autocracy in church or state idolatrously diverts to a human being honor rightly God's alone.

Milton further radicalizes that radicalized myth of the Fall in *Paradise Lost* by charting a sequence of falls, commencing with the rebellion of Satan and his angelic peers. In the course of that fall Lucifer, debating with Milton's spokesman Abdiel, shows clearly that he has read Milton's prose tracts. He opens his oration, which will urge rebellion against God's tyranny:

> Thrones, Dominations, Princedoms, Vertues, Powers,
> If these magnific titles yet remain
> Not meerly titular, since by Decree
> Another now hath to himself ingross't
> All Power, and us eclipst under the name
> Of King anointed . . . (5.772–777)

His contempt for *decree* seems only a slight misapplication of *The Reason of Church Government*: "In the publishing of human lawes . . . to set them barely forth to the people without reason or Preface like a physicall prescript, or only with threatening, as it were a lordly command, in the judgement of *Plato* was thought to be done neither generously nor wisely." His contempt for the *name* of kingship is no misreading at all of *Eikonoklastes*: "the gaudy name of Majesty . . . a name then which there needs no more among the blockish vulgar, to make it wise, admired, and excellent, nay to set it next the Bible, though otherwise containing little els but the common grounds of tyranny and popery."[29] Although Lucifer is familiar with the lines of Miltonic argument, he is not honest. It is, of course, not true that the Father's words implied angelic eclipse of flaunted tyrannous kingship; as we have seen, He proclaimed with precise emphasis "My onely Son . . . anointed," "your Head appoint," "Under his great Vicegerent Reign abide United." Nor does the reader come to the scene unprepared to read its meaning differently, since back in book 3 the offer of the Son to die for man had concluded with a parallel appointment:

> . . . Be thou in *Adams* room
> The Head of all mankind, though *Adams* Son.
> As in him perish all men, so in thee
> As from a second root shall be restor'd,
> As many as are restor'd, without thee none. . . .
> Nor shalt thou by descending to assume
> Mans Nature, less'n or degrade thine owne.
> Because thou hast . . . been found
> By Merit more then Birthright Son of God,
> Found worthiest to be so by being Good,

Farr more then Great or High; because in thee
Love hath abounded more then Glory abounds,
Therefore thy Humiliation shall exalt
With thee thy Manhood also to this Throne . . . (3.285–314)

Lucifer's refusal to pay "Knee tribute . . . prostration vile, / Too much
to one but double how endur'd" prompts him, however, to attempt
the regicide he defended when it had failed in book 1:

. . . But he who reigns
Monarch in Heav'n, till then as one secure
Sat on his Throne, upheld by old repute,
Consent or custome, and his Regal State
Put forth at full, but still his strength conceal'd,
Which tempted our attempt, and wrought our fall. (1.637–642)

His scorn of the authority merely of "old repute . . . or custome"
usurps Milton's very language in the antiprelatical tracts.[30] In the
conclave in Hell the language of Mammon, who calls Heaven a "state
of splendid vassalage," of Satan, who speaks of the "Tyranny of
Heaven," of Beelzebub, who names God "our Conqueror . . . Of
force . . . Almightie," echoing Satan's "whom Thunder hath made
greater"—all that language is preempted from Milton's own words
"In libertys defense," where the English people are praised variously
for resisting vassalage, tyranny, and insolent conquest.[31]

Again speaking "with calumnious art of counterfeited truth" in the
debate with his peers leading to their rebellion, Satan takes a position
on the compatibility of freedom and degree endorsed by Milton himself elsewhere:

. . . Orders and Degrees
Jarr not with liberty, but well consist.
Who can in reason then or right assume
Monarchie over such as live by right
His equals, if in power and splendor less,
In Freedome equal? or can introduce
Law and Edict on us, who without law
Erre not, much less for this to be our Lord,
And look for adoration to th' abuse
Of those Imperial Titles which assert
Our being ordain'd to govern, not to serve? (5.792–803)

Milton repeatedly made the point that "Degrees / Jarr not with liberty." He would appoint the noblest, worthiest, and most prudent to

determine state affairs in his commonwealth, their degree to conform to their merit: "For nature gives the wisest dominion over those less wise, not a wicked man dominion over the good or a fool over wise. Whoever takes away their dominion from such as those behaves altogether in conformity with nature."[32] His model of an ideal state is a class structure with unfixed status for every individual and plenty of room to rise "improv'd by tract of time." Milton's own words likewise endorse Lucifer's outrage at monarchy over such as live by right as king's equals: "a people which has the choice never gives up title to its own power fully and absolutely to its king, and by nature it cannot; the grant is only for the sake of the welfare and freedom of the people, and when the king has failed to secure those the people is taken to have made no grant. . . . A tyrant is he who regarding neither Law nor the common good, reigns only for himself and his faction."[33]

Notwithstanding Milton's apparent endorsement of Lucifer in these echoes, the answer Lucifer receives from Abdiel wrests the language of revolution back from him and reattaches it to a properly political narrative of the Fall. Abdiel's answer comes in two speeches: one in which he objects to Lucifer's claim to speak *contra tyrannum*, and one in which he later defies him on the battlefield on the first day of the War in Heaven. The simplest answer is the second—meeting Lucifer's taunt that the obedient angels, "the minstrelsy of Heaven" he calls them, "through sloth had rather serve." There Abdiel corrects Lucifer's definition of servitude by reanalyzing the relation between degree and liberty:

> Unjustly thou deprav'st it with the name
> Of *Servitude* to serve whom God ordains,
> Or Nature; God and Nature bid the same,
> When he who rules is worthiest, and excells
> Them whom he governs. This is servitude,
> To serve th' unwise, or him who hath rebelld
> Against his worthier, as thine now serve thee,
> Thy self not free, but to thy self enthrall'd. (6.174–181)

That definition of servitude recovers the normative word to stress (1) the rational basis of free government—that merit, not power, secures a just government; (2) the nonarbitrary functioning of providence—that God and Nature are in accord and divine decrees do not by fiat violate reason; (3) the irrationality of tyranny—that its subjects serve their moral inferior; and (4) the self-enslavement of the tyrant to his passions of ambition and pride.

Abdiel's earlier answer to Lucifer takes up Lucifer's pretense to supreme intelligence, to have penetrated beneath God's exaltation of the Son to its arbitrary absolutistic basis. This more complex response is similarly a redefinition, returning the language of the "good old Cause" to its right significance. Abdiel calls Lucifer's usage "impious obloquy." He concedes it "unjust / That equal over equals Monarch reign" but contests Lucifer's appropriation of the word "equal" to claim identical status with the "begotten Son, by whom / As by his Word the mighty Father made / All things"—even Lucifer himself— "and all the Spirits of Heav'n / By him created in thir bright degrees, / Crownd them with Glory, and to thir Glory nam'd / Thrones, Dominations, Princedoms, Vertues, Powers." But Abdiel does more than disallow equality between creator and creature; defining equality, he uncovers or discovers God's political design in exalting the Son: to create not a static meritocracy in Heaven with fixed status for its members under unvarying law but an evolving, organic, unified totality. Of God's motive Abdiel claims experience his teacher:

> . . . by experience taught we know how good,
> And of our good, and of our dignitie
> How provident he is, how farr from thought
> To make us less, bent rather to exalt
> Our happie state under one Head more neer
> United. (5.826–831)

The model of government God institutes by this means is a collective ideal, a concept Abdiel refines when he adds that the angelic powers are not only united under the Son but exalted together with him:

> . . . nor by his Reign obscur'd,
> But more illustrious made, since he the Head
> One of our numbers thus reduc't becomes,
> His Laws our Laws, all honour to him done
> Returns our own. (5.841–845)

Abdiel's intuition of the organic collective ideal is based on several details Raphael has used in his account of the Son's appointment: that the audience when God spoke included all the "Hierarchs in order bright" standing "in Orbes of circuit inexpressible"; that the occasion was "a day, as other solemn dayes": spent in "mystical dance . . . mazes intricate / Eccentric, intervolv'd, yet regular"; and that the formula of appointment was "abide / United as one individual Soule." Those details, interestingly enough, Milton brought together to make a rather different point in *The Reason of Church Government.* There he presented the angelic orders and their disciplined yet spontaneous heavenly dance as metaphors for human felicity and fulfillment in change and variety:

> Yea, the Angels themselves . . . are distinguisht and quaterniond into their celestiall Princedomes, or Satrapies, according as God himselfe hath writ his imperiall decrees through the great provinces of heav'n. . . .[I]t is not to be conceived that these eternall effluences of sanctity and love in the glorified Saints should . . . be confin'd and cloy'd with repetition of that which is prescrib'd, but that our happiness may orbe it self into a thousand vagrancies of glory and delight, with a kind of eccentricall equation be as it were an invariable Planet of joy and felicity.[34]

Abdiel intuitively discovers Milton's long-standing conviction, then, that variation and progress toward augmented community make an ideal state. Against such a state Satan rebels, considering any change in law necessarily an imposition of *ukase*, not an evolution. This is not to suggest that Milton endorses Abdiel's politics of divine benevolent dictatorship as a model for the human state, for of course he does not, as I have shown. Rather, it is to show in the political sphere a force at work like the force of progressive revelation in the religious sphere. For Milton, God facilitates such evolution by way of His contingent decrees: "In fact God made his decrees conditional . . . for the very purpose of allowing free causes to put into effect that freedom which he himself gave them."[35]

A good deal of emphasis has been given to Milton's individualism, and rightly given, by students of his political thought, but Milton himself uses the word "individual" to signify aggregation, not segregation, to mean non-dividual as in the phrase "united as one individual Soule." Nor does the persistent praise of the "one just man" exclude a collective ideal in his view. The "one just man" preserves the possibility of growth for the community. Quite as often as the word "one" affirms value in *Paradise Lost*, it measures incompleteness and is opposed by the normative word of perfection, "all." When Raphael outlines God's original design for mankind by reference to the organic model of biological growth, for example, "all" is his word for initial perfection and "all" his word for collective evolution to higher perfection: "O Adam, *one* Almightie is, from whom / *All* things proceed, and up to him return"; "*one* first matter *all*"; "differing but in degree, of kind the *same*"; "Your bodies may at last turn *all* to spirit, / Improv'd by tract of time."[36] It is against such community that Satan rebels for the self-aggrandizement possible in competition. His fall therefore compounds apostasy and tyranny: he usurps the language of freedom to servile cause, hypothesizes a fixed state under himself, and seeks not freedom for his followers but their idolatry. To him new law is the mark of absolutism; to Milton new law may be the mark of absolutism, but likewise it may be the mark of progressive revelation and increased freedom. The use of the language of liberty by the self-idolizing Satan is corrected by Abdiel, for whom God—not Satan—extends true choice.

To finish with Satan, one might note the fallen angels' use of angelic titles across the poem, a little internal political drama Milton weaves for us. Beelzebub is fearful enough of the loss of glorious entitlement to propose a new style for them all: "these Titles now / Must we renounce, and changing stile be call'd / Princes of Hell?" (2.312–313). Satan himself doubts "if these magnific Titles yet remain / Not meerly titular" (5.772–773) to commence the discussion of rebellion. His final use is a triumphant announcement of self-entitlement:

> Thrones, Dominations, Princedoms, Vertues, Powers,
> For in possession such, not onely of right,
> I call ye and declare ye now. (10.460–462)

The titles no longer describe essential inner being and no longer have the authority of God who created and "to thir Glory nam'd" (5. 839) them. In Satan's use they inscribe a breach between "possession" and "right"; they have become relative and ambiguous words. Moreover, Satan claims implicitly that words mean what Satan says they mean— "*I call* ye and *declare* ye."

Linguistic relativism in the interest of his own tyranny similarly marks Nimrod's rebellion and fall (12.6–79). That fall is another in the sequence of falls, which sequentiality makes political lessons out of the stages of the myth. The episode incorporates Adam's shocked censure of "Authoritie usurpt, from God not given," and Adam's understanding is the argument for his sons to read Milton's poem as, among other things, an education for voters. Nimrod emerges after the sons of Noah, "this second sours of men," have dwelt "long time in peace by Families and Tribes under paternal rule." He is presented as the archetype of a rebel in a composite political and linguistic overreaching "affecting to subdue / Rational Libertie." He first enthralls the "outward libertie" of men by force, then claims "second soverantie" "in despite of Heav'n." Noah's sons governed themselves with "regard to what is just and right," guided not by written law but by the law of nature to spend their days "in joy unblamed." Then arose Nimrod, "of proud ambitious heart . . . not content / With fair equality, fraternal state," who shattered the concord of men on earth and brought about a condition very like Hobbes's "state of nature," not Milton's rational state of nature. Nimrod will "arrogate Dominion undeserved / Over his brethren, and quite dispossess / Concord and law of Nature from the Earth." Declaring himself free from the constraints of fraternity and "Hunting . . . / With Warr and hostile snare such as refuse / Subjection to his Empire tyrannous," he is "styl'd" "a mightie Hunter" "And from Rebellion shall derive his name / Though of Rebellion others he accuse." Then in his "ambition to tyrannize" he and his crew build the tower of Babel "to get themselves a name, least far disperst / In foraign Lands thir memory be lost, / Regardless whether good or evil fame." Like Hobbes again, Nimrod believes that he can make names mean what he wills them to mean: if he stands on a high tower, he is high; if men call him great, he is great. The kind of rebuke he gets from God exactly answers his assault on "Rational Libertie"; God "sets upon thir Tongues a various Spirit to rase / Quite out thir Native Language." The Hobbesian linguistic takeover where terms have meaning only relative to their users results in plurality of tongues. The plurality of tongues thus marks the rupture of coherent truth as it emerges from the Creator and the fracturing of every man's fraternal access to it. (It might be noted in passing that both Hobbes's *Leviathan* and the tower display the marks not only of absolutism and linguistic relativity but also of utopianism, by their claims to fixedness and perpetuity.)

Adam's judgment is Milton's; Nimrod committed both tyranny and apostasy:

> . . . Man over men
> He made not Lord; such title to himself
> Reserving, human left from human free.
> But the Usurper his encroachment proud
> Stayes not on Man; to God his Tower intends
> Siege and defiance. (12.69–74)

Yet as usual Michael extends Adam's reaction in his comment, and Milton converts one more fall into a pattern of radical political paideia. The fall of language into confusion affects men's ability to live in political fraternity. Inner liberty, the reasonable capacity to learn and communicate truth, is the essential precondition for political liberty. Only free men can be brothers; self-enslaved men either struggle for dominion or slackly yield to it:

> . . . Yet know withall,
> Since thy original lapse, true Libertie
> Is lost, which alwayes with right Reason dwells
> Twinn'd, and from her hath no dividual being: (12.82–85)

Michael then draws for Adam an internal model of the external political model he has shown him:

> Reason in man obscur'd, or not obey'd,
> Immediately inordinate desires
> And upstart Passions catch the Government
> From Reason, and to servitude reduce
> Man till then free. (12.86–90)

The deprivation of outer freedom is the inevitable result of the surrender of inner freedom: "Tyrannie must be / Though to the Tyrant thereby no excuse." Justice "deprives men of thir outward libertie, Thir inward lost"; and Michael concludes in tragic vein, "Thus will the latter, as the former World / Still tend from bad to worse."

As the fall of Satan is used to imply a collective ideal of organic change in opposition to his claim that liberty is nothing but the space in which the self competes for self-aggrandizement, so the fall of Nimrod and its consequences in linguistic relativity are used to imply a contrary ideal to his political vision of the imperial tribe of powerful conquerors led by the mightiest of all. What succeeds is a man capable of self-sacrifice and a nation of his lineage "in whom *All* Nations shall be blest." Hence Michael's narrative concludes not with the heroic struggle Adam expects between the usurper tyrant Satan and the greater man but with a "cure" of men to be achieved "Not by destroying Satan, but his works / In [Adam] and in [his] seed." The final lesson of the Fall pattern or sequence is a Christian revolutionary lesson, not a fixed program for political or religious action. Troubles ensue, Michael predicts, even after the Son's atonement. Once again the deeds of the coercers of conscience are described by Milton as linguistic usurpations. Wolves shall succeed for teachers:

> Then shall they seek to avail themselves of names,
> Places and titles, and with these to joine
> Secular power . . . to themselves appropriating
> The Spirit of God, promisd alike and giv'n
> To all Beleevers; and from that pretense,
> Spiritual Lawes by carnal power shall force
> On every conscience. (12.515–521)

If we read the Fall as a sequential pattern, the poem offers scope for heroic virtue by disclaiming the triumph of one sufficient heroic virtue. The pattern enacts a series of radical correctives, affirming each time a movement to renewed choices in stages of enlightenment. Every fall is accompanied by the proposal of one coercive fixed meaning and concludes with the falsity of the claim made clear in the illumination of alternative meaning. Satan poses as liberator, but a contrary vision of organic change as liberation emerges in the free collective fulfillment suggested by Abdiel. Satan triumphs in a supposed permanent conquest of mankind and delivers to Sin and Death an apparently absolute rule:

> . . . on the Earth
> Dominion exercise and in the Aire,
> Chiefly on Man, sole Lord of all declar'd,
> Him first make sure your thrall, and lastly kill. (10.399–402)

To his followers he promises the same kingdom in perpetuity: "What remains, ye Gods, / But up and enter now into full bliss." Adam's fall, however, shows man inheriting liberty as well as fallenness and so "once more on eev'n ground against his mortal foe." Nimrod's fall is Michael's chance to preach the radical politics of self-conquest as the means to eliminate tyranny and to show the absurd falsity of the heroics of linguistic and political usurpation. The expulsion scene goes so far as to correct the very word "fall" into the "great deliverance . . . to come . . . on all Mankind." The openness of the epic's conclusion, with the world all before Adam and Eve, offers to Milton's own time the resumption of the challenge to read correctly the easily abused linguistic sign. Adam is not promised utopia, shown fixity, or taught monocausality, for Milton has successfully resisted the temptation himself to appropriate "the language of that which is not called amiss the good old Cause" for a utopian program.

10

Lines of Authority: Politics and Literary Culture in the Restoration

Steven N. Zwicker

The "art of governing by parties" is conventional wisdom in the study of eighteenth-century politics, and we have been long and carefully tutored in its central themes: the fortunes of Whig and Tory ministries; the Church in danger; opposition rhetoric during Walpole's reign; placemen and corruption.[1] And for those who have sought to understand the character and dominance of politics in eighteenth-century literature, arguments from party and patronage have been especially important.[2] In the past decade the role of party in the political culture that emerged just after the Glorious Revolution has been reexamined. J. H. Plumb's *Growth of Political Stability* provided the crucial arguments, modifying Walcott's Namierite thesis and setting the broad terms in which subsequent historians would trace the sinuous complexity of party politics and ideology for the 1690s.[3] But the years between the Restoration of Charles II and the Glorious Revolution have not been so carefully charted.[4] We know less of the complex and fluid structure of politics in these years than we do of the "rage of party" in the 1690s; and, in turn, we have been hesitant to identify as political and examine in political terms the literary assertions of cultural authority in these years, even in addressing major literary texts or in studying such figures as Marvell, Milton, and Dryden, whose fortunes were bound to politics and whose careers were shaped by the concerns of rhetorical legitimacy and authority.[5]

The contrast between Restoration and eighteenth-century political cultures derives, then, from the very coherence of political party in the eighteenth century and the political pluralism of the Restoration. The story is more complex, however, for the Restoration did not begin with an open acknowledgment of pluralism; it began, in fact, with strenuous efforts to deny faction and dissent. Widespread and nearly uniform assertions of political moderation were made in the early years of the Restoration in an effort to cover deep civic and religious divisions. Standards of nostalgic political value were raised in order to assert stability and commonality in the face of nervous political pluralism. On the surface of Restoration politics we find an almost Jacobean ideal of unitary politics; beneath lay faction and interest, competing and contradictory claims to civic and spiritual authority, a profound diversity of beliefs, interests, and allegiances. In such a contradictory, at points inchoate, political world such issues as literary opposition, literary patronage, and literary canon have been especially difficult to formulate. The interplay of party and literary culture in the Restoration had not hardened into system, and political patronage of literary production had not acquired the determined character in the Restoration that it would assume in the first decades of the next century.[6] Our neglect of the polemical and the politicized in Restoration literature not only reflects the complex and various character of Restoration culture but also reflects the character of our own literary and political histories of that age.

In the writing of political history, the Restoration has been, until recent years, the great wasteland that divides the brilliant work done on early Stuart politics from the study of eighteenth-century history and society. The fate of Restoration literature in our literary histories is similar, although it has proved rather more difficult for literary historians to ignore the age crossed and spanned by the careers of Marvell, Milton, and Dryden. Yet the failure to appreciate how political was the quest for cultural authority among these writers is more than wariness in the face of speculative political history. It derives as well from a more general resistance among literary historians to the politicization of the literary. Even in this most embattled of literary cultures—and perhaps because it is so very embattled, because the literature is so entangled with or contaminated by politics—the literary has seemed to need special defense. We are still asked to cling to the idea that what is most literary in Restoration literature is that which is least political or that which can be elevated above the political.[7] And yet the more closely we examine the circumstances of literary writing, the more fully we sense its political underpinnings and the intricacy of ties between literature and politics in this age. Even if we aim to elevate the literary above the political in this culture, we cannot fully appreciate what is literary without understanding the polemicized nature of literary language, literary subject, and literary authority.

Of course, in some ways the polemical circumstances of Restoration literature are so obvious that they have been difficult to ignore. The fact that Marvell was Member of Parliament for Hull,[8] that Milton was the great and godly Puritan,[9] that Dryden repeatedly drew pen for party are so obvious that they simply may no longer excite curiosity. But they are also facts with complex and troubling consequences, and I suspect that they have passed into the realm of the obvious and unremarkable because they are difficult to use. Milton belonged to the godly party, but his massive reconciliation of classical with Christian culture was not a primary aim of the English Puritans; indeed, it might seem a program more befitting the Neoplatonic masquers of the Caroline court than the godly man struggling to sustain spiritual probity in the court of the gentiles. Nor is the baroque structure of *Paradise Lost* so obvious an analogue for that most Puritan of literary forms, the diary of spiritual life. Nor is the verbal texture of *Paradise Lost*—than which no poem is more insistently learned, no syntax more carefully baffled and defensive—so obvious an expression of Puritan stylistics.[10] These contradictions have not been fully resolved in the critical literature, and such terms as "Christian humanism" can blur both the devotional and the political character of Milton's writing. The relation of *Paradise Lost* to the polemical circumstances of the first years of the Restoration—the debasement and sense of exile suffered by the author of *Eikonoklastes* and *The Readie and Easie Way*—has not been fully considered in reading the claims to cultural omnipotence in *Paradise Lost*. And Marvell's political circumstance after the Restoration, his parliamentary career and his role as opposition controversialist, has been used to discount his contribution to Restoration satire.[11]

These facts provide, of course, a perspective from which to approach the problem of rhetorical legitimation in the first efforts to formulate a country or opposition poetic in the 1660s.[12] The series of *Advice* poems are the initial steps in the formulation of that rhetoric, and the poems need to be read not in competition with Marvell's lyrics and pastorals but, rather, in light of opposition politics, of the emergence of court and country stances and tropes. And what of Dryden's pen for party? The issue is again obvious and paradoxical. That the laureate was a polemicist is a fact that both Dryden and his modern apologists admit to brush aside. The poet himself claims discomfort with the fact of political patronage; he urges elevation above party in the reading of his poems. And yet no poet was received in a more harshly polemicized way than John Dryden. We need to reconcile that reception with those of the poet's own gestures that aimed to elevate poetry above the demands of politics, to claim for poetry the privilege of high culture at a time when no political group exercised exclusive control over the instruments of that culture. By addressing such issues we come closer to an understanding of both the character of Restoration writing and the political culture in which these literary careers were conducted.

I

To suggest that division and faction dominated Restoration politics is hardly to argue a novel thesis. Division and faction characterize political history in these years as they do in the history of every decade of the seventeenth century. Nothing demonstrates the power of factional rift in national politics more sharply than the civil wars. Party history in the seventeenth century is often traced to the decade that led to those wars, to Laud's list "wherein the Names of Ecclesiastical Persons were written under the letters O and P; O standing for Orthodox; and P for Puritan."[13] In the 1640s a number of themes were laid down that would have continued meaning through this century, emerging after the Restoration under such rubrics as court and country, Whig and Tory. Laud's emphasis on hierarchy and obedience, his insistent linking of church and crown, his stress on concord within and reverence to the visible church are important components of the Tory program in the later seventeenth century. The Puritan emphasis on private spiritual authority, the efforts to link property and Protestantism, the critique of popery and ceremony are prominent issues in the translation of godly politics into Whig ideology.[14] There is, moreover, a stylistics inherent in the two early positions. A glance at preaching styles, even at the typography and layout of Puritan and Anglican sermons, will suggest the distance between Puritan and Anglican style. But the translation of those terms into party styles of the later seventeenth century is more difficult to effect than it might at first seem: Milton, for example, emerges as master of the literary baroque, and Dryden prides himself on the art of the "legislative" style. Yet the ideological, ceremonial, and stylistic distinctions that we might draw out for the 1640s and the climax of that struggle for supremacy in the civil wars do not represent a clash of party ideologies. The civil wars were rather a failure to acknowledge the competing interests that party would finally come to legitimate at the close of the century.[15] "Cavalier" and "Round-head," "Puritan" and "papist"—these and a host of other names were instruments of abuse rather than acts of political analysis or self-definition. The sea change that political organization undergoes over the course of this century is the accommodation of dissent and opposition to a system of national politics and the emergence of court interests as part of a spectrum of party activity. The civil war years and the restoration of Stuart monarchy were followed first by an effort to deny the politics of opposition; but eventually a system of political management and accommodation began to emerge. The crucial difference between the factionalism that grew into civil war and the division of interests that came to define themselves as Whigs and Tories late in the seventeenth century is political legitimacy. And this legitimacy accrued to party as both court and opposition politicians came to separate themselves from religious issues and religious passions.

The ties of dissenting religion to dissent in politics, of Anglican hierarchy to king and court, are complex and various during the Restoration,[16] but neither the Exclusion Crisis nor the Glorious Revolution is an example of godly politics after the manner of the 1640s. The legacy of that decade in the rhetoric of Restoration politics is powerful: the interconnections between religion and politics are not to be underestimated in strength or number; but the disengagement of politics from religion over the course of this century, the cooling of those passions that drove religious fervor into godly politics, is a fact in this history which allowed the clearing of sufficient rhetorical space in civic life for party to emerge from the shadow of religion. It is no accident that Locke composed his second Exclusion Crisis treatise in a language so wholly devoid of religious rhetoric;[17] and although Exclusionists had special reasons to dissociate themselves from devotional fervor, to raise high the banner of right reason over their political programs, both court and country understood the meaning and danger of providing political issues with religious or devotional subtexts. The concerted efforts of Charles II to achieve toleration for his dissenting subjects may have been motivated partly by clandestine desires to soften political circumstances for his Roman Catholic subjects, but he understood as well the political efficiency of separating religious conscience from political obedience. While he did not aim to legitimate dissent in politics, the broadly concerted efforts to clear space between politics and religion in the later seventeenth century had the effect of allowing the growth of legitimate party politics.

Of course, the Restoration did not begin with a blithe acknowledgment of party politics; that was slow in coming, and it is an instructive fact that parliamentary electioneering did not fully emerge until after the Glorious Revolution.[18] After the civil wars and protectorate government there was widespread desire to forgo division, to believe once again in that powerful fiction of unitary politics, a fiction under which even the civil wars had, after all, been conducted. And this fiction persisted well into the Restoration. But the tremendous rents in the fabric of unitary politics—"Seames of wounds, dishonest to the sight"[19]—could not long be hidden from view. King and Parliament moved against names and distinctions,[20] and the memory of civil war acted as a brake on the movement of such names into swords.[21] But, paradoxically, that memory also created an appreciation of the necessity for accommodating and legitimating political differences as court and country polarities and then Whig and Tory parties began to define themselves across a range of political topics and through a spectrum of styles and cultural manners. Faction had been anathema in the first half of the century, but in the last decades party was understood as not wholly antithetical to the conduct of politics. "Puritan" and "papist," both devotional epithets, were terms of abuse; "court" and "country," "Whig" and "Tory," were neither devotional nor wholly abusive in contemporary politics. "Whig" and "Tory" had begun as insults, but they lost much of their abusive edge by the end of the century;[22] and even in the Exclusion Crisis, when they emerge in force, we can see that there is an analytical aspect to the categories.

A narrative of political history in the Restoration would begin by documenting the interests of Royalist partisans returning after the Restoration;[23] it would index the issues raised by the Clarendon Code in the settlement of the Restoration Church;[24] and it would chart a course through the powerful charges of corruption and mismanagement that riddled the conduct of the English naval forces during the Dutch wars. The climax to this story in the reign of Charles II would, of course, be the Popish Plot and Exclusion. Here the management of parliamentary maneuvers is openly conducted by parties, and the rhetorical lists are entered by hired guns. Here at last is the conduct of political battle under the open aegis of party. Although the crisis ended with the resounding defeat of Exclusion, the seeming destruction of Whig insurrection, and the triumph of the court in whose name the Tory revenge would now be conducted,[25] it is a defining feature of party politics that defeat is not extirpation, that warfare is political and verbal turmoil rather than military violence. It is tempting to produce a formula that makes inverse relations between the decline of physical violence and the rise of invective; but even if such a generality will not hold, the temper of verbal abuse in the Restoration must in some ways be related both to the fortunes of the censorship laws and to a political climate in which the implications of language seem less portentous than in the late 1630s and 1640s. The resilience of party politics is to be found in the ability of parties to reassemble, to cling to threads of continuity in opposition, even in defeat and temporary exile. For defeat is not the final triumph of godly over wicked forces, and the paradigm of Armageddon is outdated by the time of Exclusion. It is a rhetoric notably absent from the deliberations of the Convention Parliament in 1688–89.

Of course, the Tory triumph of 1682 followed by the accession of James II in 1685 would have seemed to spell the utter doom of dissent in politics, and indeed the quiescence of radical dissent in politics of the later seventeenth century is notable.[26] James II attempted to manipulate the machinery of parliamentary elections in order to ensure the stability of his power, even the triumph of his religious program. And yet in the signal victory of party politics, Whigs and Tories banded together for bloodless revolution. This itself might be seen as a triumph of party, though here the parties drew together in order to precipitate the removal of a monarch who aimed at the reduction of Whig and Tory interests alike in the name of another party, Roman Catholicism.[27] It was following the demise of James at the hands of Whigs and Tories that we see the real blossoming of party politics. Even the interests of the expatriate monarchy are represented in the spectrum of parties in the 1690s. For to Whig and Tory we must add nonjuror and Jacobite, and to do justice to the complexity of party politics in the 1690s we must acknowledge such terms as "Old Whig" and "New Whig" and "Court Whig" and "Country Whig."[28] Under the aegis of party politics we see the growth in the 1690s of clubs and associations, of political bribery and electioneering at a new level. As the legitimacy of party grew, so did the apparent complexity of political machinery—or at least the complexity of that machinery seems more democratized, more public, more liable to visible manipulation. And the openness of manipulation is expressed in the 1690s and after by the growth of the machinery of corruption and the literature of political persuasion—that is, by the growth of party propaganda. So we come to the beginnings of a story to which I referred at the opening of this essay, the story of political pluralism and the gradual emergence of parties at the close of the century.

My interest in this essay is not to construct a narrative of this history, or to suggest its causal implications for literary study. My aim is not to argue the influence of party over literature but, rather, to suggest how party gathered definition through polemical writing and how such writing explored the meaning of centrist and opposition politics while seeking for itself legitimation and authority through stylistic, canonical, and totemic means. Nowhere can such study be better conducted than in the major literary careers of the Restoration,

in which self-consciousness about language and politics is paradig-
matically expressed. And no career suggests a higher awareness of
politics and rhetoric than that of Andrew Marvell. Yet at those points
where the intersection of polemic and art are most completely exposed
in Marvell's career, critical attention has been the most diffident.[29]

II

Marvell's Restoration career has proved something of a threshold for
literary critics. Once we cross from lyric to satire we encounter a
sensibility so utterly different that the satires, until recently, have
been all but cleared from the canon. And true to generic expectation,
the satires are polemical rather than disinterested, reductive rather
than complicating, abusive, harsh, denunciatory, indifferent to lyric
fluency, expansive and accretive rather than syllogistic and lapidary.
The distance between lyric and satire is not simply puzzling; it seems
defeating, especially when it is bridged at the most distant points in
the career or addressed in terms of "literary development." There
seems little indication that Marvell was concerned with his writing
career in the ways suggested by modern criticism; he could hardly
have been interested in such issues as literary coherence or development when the urgent matter after 1660 was legitimation. Political
credibility was a problem that both court and country interests would
have to face in working toward polemical self-definition in the 1660s,
a decade in which the mix of cultural and political claims and interests
were diverse, at points contradictory and bewildering.

For no group were the problems of self-definition more acute than
for those who had written on behalf of the republic—perhaps even
in defense of regicide—in the 1650s. Such men had to come to terms,
professionally and politically, with the restoration of Stuart monarchy.
In 1660, Marvell had a significant writing career behind him, having
published under his own name not only an elegy but as well a powerful and polemically sensitive celebration of protector and protectorate.[30] After 1660, he faced the problem of continuing to write when
the basis of the political culture he had celebrated had been abruptly
terminated and, in great part, discredited. John Wallace has argued
that the idea of loyalism provides a way of studying the political
continuity of Marvell's career, but such a term does not explain the
literary maneuvers of that career. The rhetorical issue that Marvell
faced after the Restoration was the creation of a style and cultural
identity that would allow him a position within the political discourse
of the 1660s. He would need, in this decade, to appropriate a stance

and a manner that would enable him to claim loyalty to the king and simultaneously to strike against the court. He would need to clear space for opposition. Of course, such tropes as the king's evil ministers were standard to parliamentary maneuvers against more than one Stuart monarch. In the opposition literature of the Restoration, however, more than a single trope would be necessary. In creating such a stance Marvell quarried the conventions and materials of literary satire: the roughness of manner, the posture of disinterestedness, the insistence on the patriotic, the inversion and burlesquing of the heroic. And there were materials close to hand that required parody and redress. Out of court panegyric, especially out of the ill-timed celebrations of English naval victories in 1665, tumbled a set of highly exposed generic issues and rhetorical topoi. But the creation of an opposition stance and rhetoric was not solely a matter of retrieving through inversion the materials of courtly panegyric or simply turning to the ancients for satiric models. There was more to the forging of an opposition poetics than such amalgams, and Marvell's *Third Advice* is an important text for addressing the matter of poetics because it openly and significantly deals with narrative and rhetorical problems of praise and blame administered from a position well outside the bounds of court.[31]

Edmund Waller had set the instructional terms with a series of imperatives to visualize the verbal in his *Instructions to a Painter* (1665); the *Second Advice* follows suit, though with invective and revelatory rhetoric. The *Third Advice* begins, however, not with anger but in mockery. The painterly directions are given to one Richard Gibson, a dwarf who himself painted miniatures: an ideal figure for Marvell's purpose of inverting and miniaturizing, for praise through deflation. And it is this last term that proves central to the rhetoric of the *Third Advice:*

> Thou, Gibson, that among thy navy small
> Of marshaled shells, commandest admiral
> (Thyself so slender that thou show'st no more
> Than barnacle new-hatched of them before)
> Come mix thy water-colours and express,
> Drawing in little, now we do yet less.[32]

The last line provides a key to this invocation, for Marvell describes but does not deride the painter's miniature art. Miniature is, in fact, the correct medium for the heroism of this court; mismanagement, corruption, and venality are gargantuan, but the poet's rhetorical circumstance does not allow the high road of denunciation. And the invocation of Gibson the miniaturist anticipates that crucial passage later in the *Advice* when Marvell turns to Nan Clarges, Duchess of Albermarle:

> Stay, Painter, here awhile, and I will stay,
> Nor vex the future times with nice survey,
> Seest not the monkey duchess all undressed?
> Paint thou but her, and she will paint the rest.[33]

The narrator and Gibson withdraw from the poem; not until the envoy will the narrator return in his own voice. He cedes the poem to the "monkey duchess," turns the narrative from the miniature to the grotesque, and shifts from visual to verbal materials in a passage that raises the central issues of stance and style. The duchess' narration raises important issues of decorum, tone, and allusion; in a passage in which the duchess is cast as Penelope, Monck as Ulysses, and the journey home is played against the Ulyssian experience at Troy and Ithaca, questions of literary and political style are centrally and repeatedly addressed. Marvell's poem burlesques epic pretension; his target is initially literary device, and he aims to deflate through inversion. The deflation seems not only to cut against Waller and Dryden but also to hamper those figures whom Marvell would invest with authority and authenticity. And it is centrally this problem of wresting authority from the court and enabling and legitimating a position distinct from, even in opposition to, that court, which this poem addresses.

For the deflation in this scene is meant simultaneously to ridicule and to enable. The mock-epic materials seem to reduce friend and foe alike, yet in this landscape of cowardice and venality it is the duke and duchess of Albermarle who stand alone with honor intact. The duchess climbs about her rooms pinning her coarse decorations to the wall; monkeylike, she is a four-footed beast in dirty smock, careless of posture and appearance. And yet it is this mock Penelope who is cast as prophet after Marvell excludes all possibility of pretension and pretense. Marvell invests her story with urgency and authority by stripping her of pretense; clothing and art are ancient metaphorical twins. The duchess may be no Penelope, Monck no Ulysses, but the failure to approximate epic theater is not a failure of faithfulness or heroism on their part. The epic reversal is commentary on the world they inhabit. For in such a story as the one the duchess must tell, she must be rendered a character and voice utterly devoid of those motives and passions that drive her courtly contemporaries:

> The sad tale found her in her outer room
> Nailing up hangings not of persian loom,
> Like chaste Penelope that ne'er did rome
> But made all fine against her George come home.
> Upon a ladder, in her coat much shorter,
> She stood with groom and porter for supporter,
> And careless that they saw or what they thought,
> With Hony Pensy honestly she wroute.[34]

The passage insists on plainness and honesty; the aim is to couple style and content. Pretension in art and voice are damning categories; this figure is a masterpiece of the low style,[35] and it is not genre alone that dictates voice and stance. This narrator, at once plain dealing and prophetic, is something other than the Horatian gentleman; indeed, the curious and awkward internal rhymes, the multisyllabic couplets, the coarsening of voice and manner are calculated to define a truly prophetic voice. In the context created by Restoration panegyric which had linked court and epic, quarried Roman myth and history for figures and tropes, Marvell needed to separate his literary voice and civic motives from such falsehood. The monkey duchess is such an act of definition. Marvell chose to occupy a space not devoid of the heroic and prophetic, but he needed to reclaim those modes, to re-define the character of epic and prophetic rhetoric by cleansing such rhetoric of false identity. So Marvell's heroes begin as caricature; rather than elevate hero and heroine, Marvell reduces them to true exemplars of virtue and heroism. The qualities that this court has found in such short supply—virtue and chastity, honesty and hero-ism—are asserted not as outsized acts but as the simplest of human characteristics. And the utterly plain is elevated in this narrative into prophecy by a narrator who has heard and observed the duchess:

> . . . she began a story
> Worthy to be had in *momento mori*
> Arraigning past, present, and futuri
> With a prophetic (if not spirit) fury.
> Her hair began to creep, her belly sound,
> Her eyes to startle, and her udder bound.
> Half-witch, half prophet, thus she-Albermarle
> Like a Presbyterian sibyl, out did snarl.[36]

We return to the introduction of this narration; the arts of praise and prophecy in this part are arts of reduction and caricature. Min-iaturists and Presbyterian sibyls are needed in the 1660s to act as truth tellers; the claim is rhetorically and politically complex, one issue linking with and complicating the other. For this low style, this concentration upon the grotesque, is a counterbalance to the harshness of satiric thrust in the poem and a means of legitimation. No false efforts of praise and elevation are to be found here; truth is discovered by reduction to simplicities, almost absurdities. And the conjuring of this particular poetic and prophetic voice is essential for Marvell; there is an effort here almost to deny the literary and artistic. Homer and Lely might provide models for artists faced with other tasks and other worlds, for heroic poetry and high portraiture; Marvell's particular task is to cultivate a voice and stance that might be allowed as loyal and dispassionate while denouncing and disallowing court politics and court poetics. It is not simply the plain style that Marvell seeks here, but something closer to the burlesque: the comic that is allowed access to truths too difficult and embarrassing otherwise to utter. The duchess of Albermarle is not exactly a court jester, but the epithets and apparel give her special dispensation; the poetics are, I think, claimed for similar purpose.

Of course, there are other and more conventional gestures of definition and alignment within the poem. It displays a wide range of conventional satiric techniques and an envoy voiced in a fluent panegyric manner:

> Great prince, and so much greater as more wise,
> Sweet as our life, and dearer than our eyes,
> What servants will conceal and couns'lers spare
> To tell, the painter and the poet dare;
>
> . . . .
>
> Hark to Cassandra's song ere Fate destroy,
> By thy own navy's wooden horse, thy Troy.[37]

The language of concealment and revelation is obvious for this genre; the colors of Philomela's sad embroidery are "loud revealed." But the most telling passages in this poem are not to be found in the conventional denunciations of evil ministers or in the fluent invocation of the king. The formulation of a poetic voice at once plain dealing and penetrating and the creation of a country position in literary terms are aims and achievements of this poem, which acts as an important precedent in the expression of literary authority for the opposition stance early in the Restoration.

The declamation and definition in the poem had some immediate effect, for the "Answer to Mr Waller's New Advisers" is quite explicit on the significance of travesty and on the meaning of low style as political insolence: "shapes that bespeak contempt."[38] What the "Answer to Mr Waller's New Advisers" does not allow is that the manner that the *Third Advice* cultivates not only bespeaks contempt, it also attempts legitimacy. That legitimacy emerges more fully in the rhetoric of country politics in the 1680s and 1690s. The model for the country figure is sketched in Marvell's *The Last Instructions*. This is the only one of the *Advice* poems of uncontested canonical authority; it is an epic version of the *Advice* turned against its original subjects of praise, and it shows us Marvell in the full exercise of this genre. There is little in the satiric literature of the Restoration quite so brilliant as the closing scene in the poem, which makes a daring and subtle attempt on the character of the king. Moreover, *The Last Instructions* again insists on the propriety of the miniature, on the microscopic perspective as the appropriate angle from which to inspect the politics of court corruption. The miniaturizing allows a sort of epic concentration on physical detail; the terms are borrowed from painting, but sign-daubing and antic mastery are paradigms for this literary endeavor that marshals style in the interests of political authority and polemical denunciation. Moreover, the stylistic definitions here are openly linked with the matter of party:

> Draw next a pair of tables op'ning, then,
> The House of Commons clatt'ring like the men,
> Describe the court and country, both set right
> On opposite points, the black against the white.[39]

Marvell makes some claims of disinterestedness—the elevation above faction and party—yet there can be no doubt that the enormous energies of this poem are focused on the steady debasement of court policy and politics and on the legitimation of the country interest. The opening two hundred lines are a brilliant and breathless catalogue of gross bodies and grosser minds, of luxury, of sexual appetites and improprieties, of political mismanagement and deception, of venality and greed. The portrait of Excise is a startling politicization of Milton's allegory of sin and death;[40] but it is the mock battle, the romance brigades of court and country forces, that draws out the full contrast between the politics and poetics of court and country. The Roman models of courage and propriety are summoned for country politics, but it is the portrait of the nearly anonymous English gentry that most fully renders the connection between opposition politics and the idealized country tradition:

> A gross of English gentry, nobly born,
> Of clear estates, and to no faction sworn;

> Dear lovers of their king, and death to meet,
> For country's cause, that glorious think and sweet;
> To speak not forward, but in action brave,
> In giving gen'rous, but in counsel grave;
> Candidly credulous for once, nay twice,
> But sure the devil cannot cheat them thrice.
> The van and battle though retiring, falls
> Without disorder in their intervals,
> Then closing, all in equal front, fall on,
> Led by great Barroway and great Littleton.
> Lee, ready to obey or to command,
> Adjutant-general was still at hand.[41]

Plain and loyal, credulous and generous, these stout-hearted gentry whose estates ensure independence and hence political virtue are the center of the country party. The portrait argues that they are above interest, for such a delineation of party turns on the explicit denial of faction. "Country" politics at this moment in the Restoration explicitly denies program, combining rural simplicity and virtue with patriotism; the meanings of *rus* and *patria* mingle in this portrait of Georgic manners and civic virtue. It is not only rhetorical commonplaces, however, that provide political definition in this portrait, but is as well and as importantly style itself. The balance and composure of the passage are remarkable in the midst of the grotesque, the inflated, and the monstrous. The orderliness of closure in the passage, the undefended character of the writing, the complete obedience to the dictates of heroic couplet, the lack of run-on, chiasma, and disorder are central to the political argument of the program; indeed, they define the stance of loyal opposition.

The argument of style is clarity and simplicity; the politics of the country party is above interest, above avarice, above corruption and passion—indeed, above personality. And the style in which the country party is celebrated is perfectly clear of such motives and passions. The English gentry are rendered as nearly nameless models; compared with the battery of name and personality at the beginning of the poem, the impersonality of this passage makes its own powerful assertion. The contrast is replayed a hundred lines later in the juxtaposition of Hyde and Monck; the first portrait swarms with complex, degrading, cramped, and disgusting detail; the rendering of Monck argues the same connection between style and politics that we find in the *Third Advice:* the general is plain and fearless, balanced and virtuous; he resembles the upright couplets through which he is marched.

A similar dialectic governs the celebration of Archibald Douglas, which is cast as panegyric and elegy and played against a portrait of the Speaker, Sir Edward Turner. It is only in the elegy on Douglas that Marvell dares the high style, and it is a breathtaking passage in its invocation of heroism and its visualization of Douglas's fiery death. The passage brings together the complex pastoral materials from the earlier part of the elegy with details of Douglas's immolation, and the play of pastoral elements—cool limbs, chill ash, virginal modesty— against this fiery though sublimely composed immolation gives the whole an unusual range of feeling and precision. Here alone Marvell seems to put aside the management of verse for political argument;[42] and although there are dialectical issues in the conduct of the portrait (it will soon be answered by a political counterpart as base and in-glorious as this is sublime), the aim in the elegy is to elevate memory and name above the ranks of party, above even the disinterested and virtuous models of country gentry.

But Marvell's poem is essentially and characteristically satire; and the poet does not slacken the pursuit of those interests for long. The most brilliant satirical passage in the poem, though not the one with the most immediate polemical energy—some of its effects are achieved through a subtle manipulation of classical texts—comes at the end of the poem in the portrait of Charles in his bedchamber, startled from sleep by an apparition of virgin England. The passage precedes the envoy and allows Marvell to argue that envoy with a new polemical exactness:

Paint last the king and a dead shade of night,
Only dispersed by a weak taper's light,
And those bright gleams that dart along and glare
From his clear eyes (yet these too dark with care).
There, as in th' calm horror all alone
He wakes and muses of th' uneasy throne,
Raise up a sudden shape with virgin's face,
(Though ill agree her posture, hour, or place),
Naked as born, and her round arms behind
With her own tresses interwove and twined;
Her mouth locked up, a blind before her eyes,
Yet from beneath the veil her blushes rise,
And silent tears her secret anguish speak;
Her heart throbs and with very shame would break.
The object strange in him no terror moved:
He wondered first, then pitied, then he loved
And with kind hand does the coy vision press
Whose beauty greater seemed by her distress,
But soon shrunk back, chilled with her touch so cold,

> The airy picture vanished from his hold.
> In his deep thoughts the wonder did increase,
> And he divined 'twas England or the Peace.[43]

The portrait of the king is a daring and subtle gesture; the choice of the bedroom scene and the initial posture imply criticisms that would run throughout his reign: indulgence, luxury, dalliance. It is the vision, at first misinterpreted, of the bound virgin that provides the most striking accusation. The vision arises in the king's sleep, and he misunderstands its meaning. His first impulse is to regard the imperiled state as fit material for the satisfaction of sexual desires. The charge is quite similar to that laid against the gallery of knaves and lechers at the opening of the poem; it seems to replay the initial themes but in subtler orchestration. Impelled by appetite, Charles reaches forth to touch the vision; its coldness startles him from sleep. Only on reflection does he understand the vision, that the bound virgin has appeared not to serve appetites but to act as prophetic signal. The king cannot distinguish between matters of state and erotic fantasy. This is exactly the charge that Rochester laid against the king, and it is the issue that Dryden chose to address and allay at the opening of *Absalom and Achitophel*.[44]

This vision is followed by another in which the gallery of ghosts and royal demise frighten Charles into new political resolve; the king is now shown to determine on Clarendon's fall, and the poem closes with an envoy in which court and country are truly united: Bacchus is wine, the country is the king. The vision of reconciliation combines the languages of court and country in a true pastoral celebration of "country" virtues and generosity. Marvell seeks and discovers in traditional pastoralism a new political authority for country politics.

The recruitment of style to serve polemical and, more broadly, political matters is central to the purpose of the *Advice* poems, in which the cultivation of literary and cultural manners invests generic issues with political urgency. Marvell's pamphleteering of the 1670s gives additional evidence of the pervasive cross between stylistic and polemical interests. The attack on Archbishop Parker which Marvell conducted through the two long books called *The Rehearsal Transpros'd* repeatedly turns on the relations of politics and manners, party and style.[45] One of Marvell's central charges is that Parker has cultivated a falsely elegant manner; the crossing of Parker with Dryden through the name Bayes is a stylistic and political argument. The luscious and effeminate style, the manner of high romance, the elevation of court poetry: these are categories consistently used to deride the stance of Anglican polemic. Moreover, in making the attack on high style, Marvell throws into familiar opposition honesty and praise; he advises us on the punctuality of history; he denies art. As in the *Advice* poems, Marvell repeatedly argues the cultural and moral authority of style, the authenticity of satiric bluntness, the irreproachable "punctuality" of plain dealing and truth telling. Truth telling is, of course, a claim that all polemicists want to make for their position, but the particular manner of Marvell's assertion, the denial and degrading of eloquence and inflation, the equation of immorality and stylistic excess, the harshness of tone and roughness of meter, these are at once general characteristics of satire and particular political claims in the Restoration. Marvell's attempts after the Restoration in both prose and verse to cultivate a voice at once legitimate and politically empowered turn on the creation of an opposition poetics; and such a poetics would flourish in the years to come.

III

What we witness in Marvell's Restoration satire is the first act in the creation of a distinctive country poetic. What, in such terms, are we to make of Milton's poetry? Marvell and Milton alike were published and republished under party auspices within a decade of their deaths;[46] they would be perceived—and correctly so—as totemic figures for a Whig literary canon.[47] The first edition of Marvell's collected poems was issued at an opportune moment in the creation of that canon—1681; and of course Milton was even more central to such a quest for cultural authority.[48] He was the great figure in the creation of Whig polemical standards for the 1690s, and even though one might suspect that his Whiggish publisher Jacob Tonson did not quite know what to make of *Paradise Lost*—the editions and annotations of Hume and Addison suggest the need for considerable help in reading this "Whig" masterpiece—Tonson understood, in claiming Milton for the cause, the enormous prestige that Milton's literary fame and the poet's erudition might lend to Whiggery.[49] The formation of a Whig literary canon argued the convenience—indeed, the necessity—of cultural legitimation, a necessity to which Marvell had addressed himself in the claims on the reclamations of Roman literary authority for his satiric and self-defining purposes.

If the country position demanded forthrightness and simplicity, a poetics that prized the raw edge of plain-dealing, truth-telling satire, then we must perform a rather complicated maneuver to attempt literary and political alignment between poems such as *The Last Instructions* and *Paradise Lost*—contemporary publications. Nor is it sufficient to bridge the gap by noting the powerful generic directives and constraints under which Milton composed his poem. Few poets were better stocked with generic sensitivities than Milton or with fuller understanding of their obligations to compete—indeed, to outstrip—once committed to generic choice. And yet if we are to seek a meaning for *Paradise Lost* within the polemicized landscape crossed by the Dutch wars, the attack on and dismissal of Clarendon, and the denunciation of the poet himself, we must attempt to understand *Paradise Lost* as Restoration epic, perhaps even as opposition epic.[50]

And yet the idea of *Paradise Lost* as opposition poetry feels too narrow for the enormous range of the epic. The notion of opposition poetry seems better suited to the sharply purposeful satires of the 1660s, to Milton's *Samson Agonistes* with its clear political self-definition,[51] even to the poet's brief epic, with its stricter and more unified poetics, a poem in which style, spiritual authority, and political directives are clearly linked in the common denial of eloquence. Yet it is the very grandeur, the sublimity of *Paradise Lost* that must be addressed if we are fully to recognize the polarizing force of Restoration politics and the politicized character of literary authority in these years. It is one kind of argument to suggest that poems that announce themselves as political betray their origins in and directives as polemical argument; it is a broader and, I think, more important argument to suggest that even those works that studiously or programmatically, even ostentatiously avoid the political or subdue the political to the spiritual not only must grapple with polemical directives and political circumstance but in fact are shaped by that engagement. In Marvell's satires such positioning takes place in a fully public and self-conscious way; the stylistics are part of a program. Marvell denies himself eloquence, even fluency at points; such can no longer be his manner in defining a style appropriate to his politics. But we see little of this kind of self-conscious positioning in *Paradise Lost*. Indeed, it looks quite the contrary in this poem composed of every style. *Paradise Lost* is after all a masterpiece of the high style: it insists on sublimity; eloquence is its metier. It is not solely a masterpiece of that style, however. Milton performs in every style in this poem; he claims as his own pastoral, allegory, and satire; he invokes prophecy and visionary poetics; he denounces and condemns; he practices romance and narrative history; he uses hymns, psalms, and prayers. *Paradise Lost* is indeed a compendium of Renaissance styles and forms. The great models that *Paradise Lost* subsumes and outgoes are the Bible, the *Odyssey*, the *Iliad*, and the greatest epic of the high style: Virgil's *Aeneid*. And it is, of course, partly to outgo these models that Milton wields the enormous stylistic range and sophistication of his poem.

Any attempt to determine *the* style of *Paradise Lost* and to fix its polemical meaning is impossible.

And yet if we turn the problem differently, if we would see the
situation of poet and poem in political terms, we might gain a different
perspective on the problem of polemical meaning and style in *Paradise
Lost*. There is a biographical tradition in Milton criticism that argues
the poet's withdrawal from politics with the restoration of Stuart monarchy, a turn away from the matter of pamphlet and polemic to the
consolation and wisdom of poetry.[52] Exhausted by battle, blind and
alone among enemies, Milton courts his muse. Yet obloquy and exile
may not entirely have dispelled politics from this literary intelligence;
and we might see the poem itself—the great epic of spiritual consolation—as an act of defiance and appropriation. We might consider
the whole of *Paradise Lost*, not just those moments of most striking
political resonance, as an act of polemical self-definition, an assertion
of cultural authority. Milton had been disenfranchised by the Restoration, deprived of office and place, threatened and hunted; his
reflex was to heap scorn and opprobrium on both the politics and the
culture of Stuart restoration. But scorn was not wide enough a palette
for Milton. The writing of *Paradise Lost* was not only an appropriation
of spiritual truths—erectness and probity in the politicized stances of
this poem—but it was an appropriation of all the instruments of
literary culture. Everything is essayed in this poem; and the com-
pendiousness, the encyclopedic character of the poem is its central
polemical argument. Milton was scorned and denounced; he suffered
reversal and humiliation; and although elsewhere he celebrates passivity, the recoil, the thrust of *Paradise Lost* was not passivity. Out of
humiliation and political displacement, out of the need to assert the
authority of his own voice came the epic scope of this poem, an act
of greater erudition, complexity, and freedom than his contemporaries had ever witnessed. The poem displays the vectors of a number
of genres, but it is truly *sui generis*; its fundamental stylistic impulse
is to outgo, to own all styles and all learning.

Paradise Lost is Milton's polemical answer to disenfranchisement
and exile. It is a justification and idealization of his role in a political
cause now defeated. The poem is the moment toward which the whole
life and career would seem, retrospectively, to point. But the life and
career are made to point here with a particular urgency, a need to
own. There is something in this poem of the exile who, having been
denied what is rightfully his, aims to own all that should belong to
him, if not in real property, then in the properties of spiritual and
cultural authority. *Paradise Lost* at times defines itself in political and
more broadly civic terms, borrowing ancient wisdom to argue its

politics and civics, but its polemical gestures are not confined to particular passages or specific styles and stances. The polemical gesture of *Paradise Lost* is the whole poem, not all of which aims at denunciation or commentary, but all of which proclaims an indefatigable superiority of vision and knowledge. The learning of this poem is assembled, Milton claims, to instruct and to console; it serves also to humiliate, to silence, to baffle, even to insult. It is gathered to render the poem inaccessible to a culture debased and degraded. And there are passages within *Paradise Lost* that argue exactly this question of language and audience, that insist on the discriminating powers of the verse. Indeed, such positioning, such arguments about territory and ownership begin in the prefatory note on verse which so insistently couples style and culture:

> The measure is English heroic verse without rhyme . . . rhyme, the invention of a barbarous age, to set off wretched matter and lame metre—graced indeed since by the use of some famous modern poets, carried away by custom, but much to their own vexation, hindrance, and constraint to express many things otherwise, and for the most part worse than else they would have expressed them. . . . This neglect then of rhyme so little is to be taken for a defect, though it may seem so perhaps to vulgar readers, that it rather is to be esteemed an example set, the first in English, of ancient liberty recovered to heroic poem from the troublesome and modern bondage of rhyming.[53]

Acts of territorial defense and aggression surround this passage; it is strikingly similar to the headnote to *Samson Agonistes* which so insistently couples style and civics.[54] The topic is poetics, but the gestures argue more broadly; the passage is endowed with a cultural and moral defensiveness and urgency that seem to overload the ostensible subject. The alignment that Milton claims here is with Homer and Virgil, an alignment that vindicates a poet against the barbarous past and vulgar present. The denial of rhyme is an act of moral and political reclamation; this poem is "the first in English"—the emphasis on primacy and patriotism is characteristic and telling—to recover ancient liberty, to set aside hindrance, constraint, and bondage.[55] The poem is an act of true restoration that defines itself against the political restoration of Stuart monarchy, the bondage of foreign tyranny against ancient and English liberties. *Paradise Lost* is a countermeasure to the restoration of kingship.

And restoration—the "true" restoring, raising, and supporting—is the claim that issues from the invocations of *Paradise Lost*.[56] These are crucial passages for understanding the self-definition and territorial claims that the poem makes. The invocation to book 1 enfolds us in the language of restoration; its directives are to restore and regain, to soar, raise, and support; its language lays claim to a variety of stylistic, mythic, and historical territories. The pressure at the opening of this poem is on vastness and multiplicity; this invocation covers all bases, all sources for inspiration and knowledge. The aim is to own those sources, to argue cultural exhaustiveness and exclusivity. For how else are we to understand its failsafe schemes, the odd coupling of vastness and contingency: "Sing heavenly Muse, that on the secret top / Of Oreb, or of Sinai . . . or if Sion hill / Delight thee more, and Siloa's brook. . . . And chiefly thou O Spirit, that dost prefer / Before all temples the upright heart and pure, / Instruct me."[57] Cornucopia and syncretism might be part of this scheme, but the tripling of invocations and imperatives, the vastness of landscape, the stretch of spiritual and historical territories is part of Milton's steady effort to lay claim. The oddly conditional "or" clauses suggest uncertainty, but such unsteadiness characterizes nothing in *Paradise Lost*. The conditional phrases here are a method of enlargement; they signal vastness of knowledge: Oreb, Sinai, Siloa, Aonian mount, the vast abyss: "Say first, for heaven hides nothing from thy view."[58]

The method at the opening is steady elevation; the perspective is . . . well, even the word "Olympian" is not fully appropriate. The opening invocation would situate poet and poem, poetics and spirit, on insurmountable heights. And the insistence on spiritual probity and moral height plays directly against the opening of book 2, Satan fixed in the depths of monarchical splendor: "High on a throne of royal state, . . . Thus high uplifted . . . aspires / Beyond thus high."[59] Satanic aspiration might raise a throne of royal estate in Hell, but moral and spiritual heights are the exclusive property of the godly. We do not have to read very subtly here to discern the confrontation between spiritual and political restoration; and the issues of positioning and propriety—what belongs to whom—are folded into the several invocations of the epic.

Book 3 begins with reinvocation, a preparation to ascend from satanic to heavenly geography. It argues the same topics of inspiration, the same authority, as the opening invocation, but this invocation is shaded with more daring autobiographical materials.

> . . . Yet not the more
> Cease I to wander where the Muses haunt
> Clear spring, or shady grove, or sunny hill,
> . . . nor sometimes forget
> Those other two equalled with me in fate,

> So were I equalled with them in renown,
> Blind Thamyris, and blind Maeonides,
> And Tiresias and Phineus prophets old.[60]

The invocation solicits guidance in the face of spiritual and intellectual journey, in the face as well of mortal limitation. But Milton's limitation becomes a means of appropriation: he treats physical blindness as an emblem of spiritual vision. The topic drew Milton's attention more than once, nowhere more openly than in Sonnet 14 or in *Samson Agonistes*, where it is invested with powerful and poignant spiritual meaning. This episode begins by working in the same manner. What others might interpret as a sign of God's displeasure is in fact special marking; the loss of sight is answered by the invocation of true vision. What is peculiar in line 33 is the "error" in numbers that leads to a strange gesture within the passage: ". . . nor sometimes forget / those other two equalled with me in fate" produces, in fact, four analogues. The doubling is a slight matter, but it is complicated by Milton's parenthetical, "So were I equalled with them in renown." The force of this aside might be paraphrased, "Having been blinded like Homer or Tiresias, would it were so that I had been given a renown equal to theirs." The invitation seems unguarded, but Milton waits within this passage, not only multiplying names and examples of his erudition but also suggesting his utter familiarity with and command over the inventory. "So were I equalled with them in renown"; this works well enough for blind Maeonides, though perhaps the choice of Homer's placename is mystifying. Thamyris was not a famed bard, and while Tiresias does fit Milton's description, Phineus does not. In the catalogue of blind poets and prophets, the climactic figure is very obscure indeed. The gesture that Milton makes out of this autobiography is double-edged; we might be able to follow Milton some of the way, but there are difficult steps in this digression, and I think that they were meant to test erudition, to match name for obscure name under the rather misleading rubric of renown. There was no other poet who had practiced the arts of polemical writing as had Milton in the 1640s; and positioning in relation to an audience was a lesson that he had mastered. There are very few unguarded moments in *Paradise Lost*, and just as Milton seems to expose a vulnerability— the blindness for which he was taunted, which would seem to mark God's disfavor—he engages in a contest for which his preparation and erudition are unmatched. The technique is used repeatedly; the aim is mastery and authority. It is a political aim, though no longer engaged for the sake of program or party. After 1660, the political had become deeply, perhaps exclusively personal for Milton; the poet took on the spiritual character of godly politics in his suffering and humiliation, and he strikes blow after blow for the authority of that cause in his poem.

The autobiographical gestures are repeated in the invocation to book 7.[61] Again the references are classical. The muse is Urania; Milton dismounts Pegasus and turns with pride and contempt to the subject of his own political humiliation:

> More safe I sing with mortal voice, unchanged
> To hoarse or mute, though fallen on evil days,
> On evil days though fallen, and evil tongues;
> In darkness, and with dangers compassed round,
> And solitude; yet not alone, while thou
> Visit'st my slumbers nightly, or when morn
> Purples the east: still govern thou my song,
> Urania, and fit audience find, though few.
> But drive far off the barbarous dissonance
> Of Bacchus and his revellers, the race
> Of that wild rout that tore the Thracian bard
> In Rhodope, where woods and rocks had ears
> To rapture, till the savage clamour drowned
> Both harp and voice; nor could the Muse defend
> Her son. So fail not thou, who thee implores.[62]

Exile and humiliation are turned to mythic triumph in this fantasy that fits Milton's struggle to the history of Orpheus; invocation works again as defense and superiority. Milton lends—indeed, insists on— epic dignity for his enemies so that he might triumph in this story of victimized inspiration. In this passage the learning is accessible; Milton invites comprehension. He controls the range of reference; the syntax is lucid and linear; for the drama here, the positioning, depends on understanding rather than mystification.

The most polemically tilted of the invocations, the one with most explicit literary investment, opens book 9:

> No more of talk where God or angel guest
> With man, as with his friend, familiar used
> To sit indulgent . . . I now must change
> Those notes to tragic; foul distrust, and breach
> Disloyal on the part of man, revolt,
> And disobedience: on the part of heaven
> Now alienated, distance and distaste,
> Anger and just rebuke.[63]

The tragic matter of the closing books of *Paradise Lost* is human history, but the vision and prophecy of books 11 and 12 are replete with polemical gestures, and even the stylistic positioning of this invocation deserves attention. Milton's claim is "unpremeditated verse," and while there is a lowering of tone in these books, the matter of this invocation is hardly unpremeditated. Milton has a score to settle with romance and with contemporary epic:

> . . . hitherto the only argument
> Heroic deemed, chief mastery to dissect
> With long and tedious havoc fabled knights
> In battles feigned; the better fortitude
> Of patience and heroic martyrdom
> Unsung; or to describe races and games,
> Or tilting furniture, emblazoned shields,
> Impreses quaint, caparisons and steeds;
> Bases and tinsel trappings, gorgeous knights
> At joust and tournament; the marshalled feast
> Served up in hall with sewers, and seneschals;
> The skill of artifice or office mean,
> Not that which justly gives heroic name
> To person or to poem. Me of these
> Nor skilled nor studious, higher argument
> Remains, sufficient of it self to raise
> That name, unless an age too late, or cold
> Climate, or years damp my intended wing
> Depressed, and much they may, if all be mine,
> Not hers who brings it nightly to my ear.[64]

The argument is familiar enough; it is the same argument, though here more fully revealed, that Milton makes at the opening of *Paradise Lost* "that with no middle flight intends to soar above the Aonian mount." He returns to the lists here—competition is his aim. And while Milton claims ignorance of "joust and tournament," "marshalled feast," "artifice and office mean," in fact, the invocation itself is at once a delicate and contemptuous evocation of romance and chivalric epic. Milton's aim is to acquire subject and style and then to dismiss them as unworthy. The appropriation and dismissal depend on tonal mastery, for Milton intends neither burlesque nor caricature; he aims to evoke the chivalrous and romantic, to show mastery of technique, "to describe races and games, / Or tilting furniture, emblazoned shields, / Impreses quaint, caparisons and steeds." This is, the very matter of book 2, the epic games that provide amusement in Hell, and in fact the tilting furniture of mountaintops and chariots is the matter and decor of the War in Heaven. Having displayed and turned these materials to his own use, Milton now turns against them; they are "Not that which justly gives heroic name / To person or to poem. Me of these / Nor skilled nor studious." The powerful caesura in the line and the reflective accent that falls on the blunt monosyllable suggest at least the peculiarity if not the dishonesty of argument being conducted here. Heroic name to person or to poem is certainly what Milton aims to achieve, but the argument that he lacks skill and knowledge in degraded matters of romance is quite false and in this poem demonstrably so. Milton raises nothing over which he does not have mastery.

The invocation argues dominance and control; Milton inscribes personal history over epic intention, but that is, after all, part of the convention of invocation. If Milton is here more complete and relentless in the personalizing, in the intermixing of biography and cosmic history, it is in part the imprint of personality, but it is not that alone. And Michael's vision and prophecy offer a striking confirmation of the argument that I have made about the politicization of literary and cultural properties in this poem. For the history in book 11 and the prophecy in book 12 are controlled by a political program.[65] The structure of book 11 is a dialectic between tyranny and the single just man. Despite the breadth of this history, its central argument is that the just are in perpetual battle with the forces of debauched kingliness. It is an issue not sufficiently marked in the critical literature that Michael's great history lesson begins with a review of monarchy.[66] Monarchy is a subject demanded by neither theology nor drama, and yet what follows the ascent of Michael and Adam, the very first argument, is "all Earth's kingdoms and their glory." The rest of this book unfolds from the initial statement of terms, though not until Milton displays his remarkable catalogue:

> . . . the destined walls
> Of Cambalu, seat of Cathaian Khan
> And Samarchand by Oxus, Temir's throne,
> To Paquin of Sinaean kings, and thence
> To Agra and Lahor of great mogul
> Down to the golden Chersonese, or where . . .[67]

Earthly kingship, we are made to appreciate, is a subject that Milton and Michael—the great archivists of kingship—have made their own.

The narrative makes a number of interconnected arguments, the most obvious of which is set by the introduction: the history of kingship is a narrative of false splendors and carnal appetite. Milton's statement of this motif is governed by the typological scheme that links Adam and Christ, the temptation in the garden and in the wilderness, but the temptation of kingship is neither the initial nor the climactic temptation in Milton's orchestration of Luke in *Paradise Regained*. Of course, the King of Kings is hardly tempted by the vanities of earthly monarchy. And yet the importance of this theme to book 11 and to the whole vision of history in *Paradise Lost* is established in these lines, for the rejection of kingship is crucial to the poet's confrontation with Restoration monarchy. Milton had not said his last word on kingship in *The Readie and Easie Way* . . . ; the poet's unrivaled knowledge of history and monarchy enables him to reject kingship with the privilege of history. He is archivist—indeed, anthropologist—of human monarchy. Cultural multiplicity is the theme of this history, and the long roll call—Almansor, Fez, Sus, Morocco, Algiers, Tremisen—gives splendid evidence of Milton's charge. The aim is, surely, subtly and completely to associate all monarchies with one another. They are expressions of the same impulses and excesses; the implicit placement of Stuart absolutism among the primitive cultures is striking. Whitehall may be absent from the catalogue, but Milton need hardly have drawn it out to involve the political behavior of his own country; it fitted all too well into this vision of splendor.

Michael must counsel Adam to lift his eyes to "nobler sights"; he must draw out the meaning of this rather exotic roll call and does so with pedagogic exactness, underpinning the history of mankind with a dialectical vision of virtue and vice, sanctity and pomp.[68] Milton's relationship to his readers is different from Michael's to Adam, however; Michael's wisdom, authority, and politics hardly needed authentication. Milton, by contrast, could not rely on his name to lend authority; and while Michael may be content to amuse and educate Adam in the cultural varieties of monarchy, Milton's lesson is rather more polemical.

Out of the initial statement of terms grows the whole of the vision that follows; the link among the episodes in book 11 is the figure of the just man in the midst of the prideful and intemperate. The theme is pitched with polemical insistence and argued with authority of Scripture, for all the episodes are grounded in the story of Cain and Abel. From the initial encounter Milton argues the history of mankind as a series of encounters between brutish vice and temperance, revelry and piety, sceptered militarism and justice, title and virtue. And everywhere monarchy rears its head. It should hardly be surprising that the tainting of monarchy is so steady, so continuous, but it is a project of this book that needs remarking because it illustrates how powerfully Milton's need for polemical positioning determines the

structure of this epic, cosmic in scope and yet in its own way relent-
lessly topical.

Each of the episodes in book 11 is marked by the same confrontation; the dialectic guides the linked scenes, nor are they left as moral
abstractions and generalizations. The further Milton moves into the
book, the more daring is the presentation of his own history in this
dialectic. Cain and Abel are the most abstracted version—they are
the moral fulcrum Milton used to move the opening survey of kingship toward its dialectical closure—but as the book proceeds the texture becomes more specific to Milton's immediate concerns:

> . . . thence from cups to civil broils,
> At length a reverend sire among them came,
> And of their doings great dislike declared,
> And testified against their ways. . . .
>
> . . . .
> But all in vain. . . .
>
> . . . .
> One man except, the only son of light
> In a dark age, against example good,
> Against allurement, custom, and a world
> Offended; fearless of reproach and scorn,
> Or violence, he of their wicked ways
> Shall them admonish.[69]

It is, finally, for one just man that God relents. The reference is to
Noah, as the references in book 12 are to Enoch and Christ—true
and just prophets and lawgivers who braved the scorn and envy of
Jew and Gentile to give witness to God's word. The rhetorical situation
of this history is complex and defensive. In every gesture of this
dialectic we read simultaneously of sacred history and of Milton
among the Gentiles; the mode is neither allegory nor parallel, it is
neither Spenser nor Dryden but the steady directing of sacred and
secular histories toward Milton's own enactment of these eternal
truths. Of course, Milton does not position himself as the antitype
toward which all sacred history unfolds, but the force of his continuous presence can be felt in the particulars that cross the vision and
narration and in the shaping of these stories to their self-justifying
and self-authorizing ends.

The book has yet another story to tell about the rhetorical circumstance of the poet. Michael raises Adam to the heights of this vision
as a consolation and education. Yet consolation and education as
rhetorical aims in a fallen world are not so easily to be effected. The
condition of narration within the garden after the Fall is an ambivalent

state between language in Heaven and rhetoric in the fallen world.[70] Michael speaks to a yet emparadised though fallen Adam, but those blessed prophets and witnesses who speak after man's exile into history have a more compromised and difficult rhetorical circumstance. Enoch rises against the wicked,

> . . . till at last
> Of middle age one rising, eminent
> In wise deport, spake much of right and wrong,
> Of justice, of religion, truth, and peace,
> And judgment from above: him old and young
> Exploded and had seized with violent hands,
> Had not a cloud descending snatched him thence.[71]

This is the story of the imperiled narrator and prophet; this is at once the Thracian bard and all witnesses and prophets in the fallen world. And Noah is cast into the same imperiled role, "a reverend sire among them came, / And of their doings great dislike declared, / And testified against their ways . . . / But all in vain."[72] What, then, is the function of preaching, witnessing, prophesying among the fallen? The conclusion at each juncture seems to be the same: "Man is not whom to warn." This poem is written in the language of the just, and Milton takes the whole vocabulary of literary civilization as his to wield; but wielding that vocabulary—witnessing, condemning, preaching, and prophesying—is self-defense, vindication. This poem is Milton's "wondrous ark," a blessed vessel, a covenant with God that might just save mankind from the righteous anger and contempt in which Milton holds that world, anger and contempt that he might wield in its destruction.

Book 12 argues themes similar to those in book 11, but the mode turns now from vision to narration.[73] The historical narrative in book 12 begins with the Israelites in pastoral tribalhood, but that state is soon disrupted by Nimrod, whose pride and ambition destroy fraternal equality. There is something in this episode and the next of a juxtaposition of court and country identities, perhaps some partisan alignment in the language, but I do not think that Milton aims, even here, at partisanship in the manner of his contemporary, Andrew Marvell. The moral issues and even the more specific political engagement implied by the linking of reason and liberty, the careful tapestry of arguments against kingship—these have been studiously noted by commentators on *Paradise Lost*.[74] And yet at its deepest level the partisanship is personal rather than programmatic. Beneath the overtly political topics lay a powerful need to justify and to defend.

Paradise Lost is not simply one more round in the polemical battles so often and at times so brilliantly fought in the prose of the 1640s and 1650s. Here Milton makes one final, grand assault, and for it he marshals everything in his arsenal. That making such an assault from the position of humility to which he had been reduced by the Restoration roused the complexity and revealed the vulnerability of the poet is written into the polemical and polemicized character of the poem. I speak specifically of the ways in which the biography of the just man is written through the whole of the poem; the trail of self-justification, of autobiography and idealization, marks more and more powerfully the invocations and then the final books of *Paradise Lost*. In these final books we witness the battle of divine and satanic powers in history turning into the story of just men braving the scorn of wicked masters: of Milton and violent lords, of Milton and monarchy, of Milton and obdurate kings.

The embattled imagination turns the history of scorned prophets into autobiography on the grandest of scales; Milton is written into this poem in a way that separates it from its great literary predecessors. The poet claims that his aim is to console, to instruct, and to elevate, and Milton poses a number of models for such purposes: teacher, prophet, polemicist, mediator. But the efficacy of language for such purposes as instruction and persuasion are cast in doubt at crucial points, and by none other than the poet himself. There are contradictory convictions in *Paradise Lost* about the possibility of meaning in the poem itself. What is not in doubt is its energy as defense and cultural appropriation. The problem for Milton was not composing heroic verse in an unheroic age, I believe, but rather summoning and sustaining the authority necessary to write at all, to command an audience. "Fit, though few," the poet consoles himself within his book. The first was a hope, the latter fear; and his poem is an attempt to demonstrate fitness through demand and to explain few through its self-justifying cosmology. The history lessons of books 11 and 12 go a long distance toward explicating Milton's understanding of and relationship with his audience in 1667.

IV

Summoning cultural authority at the center of power may seem a less daunting project than conjuring such authority from its margins, yet the circumstance of panegyric and satire wrought at the center is not always simpler than that produced from without. Satire takes authority from "honesty"; panegyric from power itself. Yet honesty can be difficult to verify at the center, and although power in the seventeenth century often implied cultural centrality, it also suggested the capacity for persecution and the potential for corruption.[75] I will now look across the year 1667 toward that center and our third poet, John Dryden, who worked from the center and wrote a poem on the Dutch wars and Great Fire that allows us to consider the problems of cultural authority for those writing from within the circle of power. Dryden's *Annus Mirabilis* is not the poet's most sophisticated conjuring of cultural authority, but the poem rather nicely illustrates the circumstance and complexity of praise and courtly apologetic early in the Restoration, before the heightening of party consciousness that took place late in the 1670s had imposed its own more complex patterning on the intersection of politics and cultural authority.

That *Annus Mirabilis* is a defensive and aggrandizing fiction written to rescue a court from humiliating defeats and "providential" judgments is a fact about the poem that has been described with great exactness in the critical literature.[76] What I would like to stress here is the complex circumstance of courtly panegyric and the nature of cultural offense in the poem. The defensive procedures of the poem are clear, but the notion of political embattlement at the center needs some complication, for the court was under siege not only from without—natural disasters, charges of corruption and error, accusations of popery and libertine excess—but divided as well within—the ministry split, and the attack on the most conspicuous figure at court, Lord Chancellor Clarendon, conducted from outside but as well from within the court.[77] Dryden had early aligned himself with Clarendon,[78] and the verses to Clarendon's daughter, the Duchess of York, that preface *Annus Mirabilis* as well as the praise of the Duke of York's heroism at Lowestoft clearly—indeed, boldly—announce Dryden's position within the court, his loyalty to the Yorkist circle.[79] The alignment with Hyde and York must have been an effort to sustain patronage, and although we can observe the poet's generalized defensive procedures in *Annus Mirabilis,* we also should be aware of the degree to which Dryden's maneuvers on behalf of specific clients determine the nature and function of panegyric within the poem. Milton's status in 1667 was much simpler than Dryden's, for Milton could not have written with the idea of place or patronage in mind. Patronage must have been a steady aim for Dryden in the 1660s, and it is with such issues in mind that we can begin asking what languages belonged to whom in these early years of the Restoration.

Annus Mirabilis suggests that one answer to this question is that the languages of cultural authority—Scripture, the classics, scholarship, history, literary learning—were very much on the open market in the early years of the Restoration. Although Dryden does not attempt to claim exclusive ownership in 1667, *Annus Mirabilis* casts a surprisingly large net over these languages. The net is cast to appropriate, to claim on behalf of the court, the languages of prophecy and apocalypse that had been worked so powerfully by what Dryden could assume was now a discredited segment of the polity: dissenters in religion and politics. Yet dissenters still spoke with surprising daring.[80] As Michael McKeon has shown, Dryden's use of apocalyptic materials attempts at once to exert ownership over and to reapply Scripture in order to authorize arguments for commerce that are made at the close of the poem.

Not all is defense, however; the poem is replete with signs of cultural height, from the epigraphs drawn out of Trajan and Virgil, to the self-authorizing "account of the ensuing poem," to the erudition and touches of philological antiquarianism:

> I am apt to agree with those who rank *Lucan* rather among Historians in Verse, then Epique Poets: In whose room, if I am not deceiv'd, *Silius Italicus*, though a worse Writer, may more justly be admitted.[81]

And what follows this display of learning is a discussion of stanza forms replete with its own learned gestures:

> I have chosen to write my Poem in Quatrains or Stanzas of four in alternate rhyme, because I have ever judg'd them more noble, and of greater dignity, both for the sound and number, then any other Verse in use amongst us. . . . The learned languages have certainly a great advantage of us, in not being tied to the slavery of rhyme; and were less constrain'd in the quality of every syllable which they might vary with Spondees and Dactiles, besides many other helps of Grammatical figures, for the lengthening or abbreviating of them.[82]

Dryden follows the history of the stanza through French and Spanish examples and through English translations of Homer and Lucan's *Pharsalia*. Nor does this discussion exhaust the poet's critical erudition. Within the space of a few hundred lines, Dryden supplies example and precept from Virgil and Statius, Juvenal and Horace; he discusses the character of figures; he juxtaposes Ovid and Virgil as poetic models. The polemical intent here is simultaneously clear and complex. Although there are rather pointed efforts to engage the opposition through claims of historical accuracy, there is another simultaneously worked act of polemical address. For written over the whole of the preface to *Annus Mirabilis* are acts of erudition and taste; the poet is attempting to assemble his authority before the poem begins its work. Learned languages, recondite models, epigraphs, examples, allusions, critics, and commentaries are brought forward in the service of a poem that Dryden aims to deliver bristling with equipment.

How much of this work is political and how much of it is personal, and what are the relations between such motives? We can feel both aims, and they need not—and, in fact, cannot—wholly be separated. With Milton we must remember the imagination in danger and exile as we follow the forceful thrust of autobiography and self-justification through the history of righteousness in *Paradise Lost; Annus Mirabilis* is the work of a novice. Milton's erudition is grand, massive, utterly his own; Dryden's was, at this juncture, rather more makeshift. And yet the worked, at times forced, display of learning and the defter polemical arrangements of the preface suggest how Dryden was hoping to combine personal advancement within a court faction with "genuine" political service for the crown. They could work at the same time; and the learning that Dryden displays in this poem is an effort to service a particular client, to match wits with and rise above the court's detractors, to argue the Christic sacrifice of the king, the epic grandeur of naval battle, and the final triumph of a grateful people. The poem aims to reinterpret, to authorize, to aggrandize; at the same time the poet argues his own powers, provides his own aggrandizement, not simply by putting to the service of the court the equipment of culture but by asserting his own mastery over that equipment.

It has not been sufficiently marked in the writing on this poem that Dryden provides us with one of the first examples of a poem bearing its own interpretive apparatus. *Paradise Lost* may be the first poem annotated within the living memory of its author whose grand learning needed such explication, but *Annus Mirabilis* came to its audience ready-made: Dryden supplied literary sources, marks of chronology and digression, notes, and explications of historical material. The apparatus is a claim to cultural authority, and the claim is lodged simultaneously on behalf of the poet and the politics that he hoped would benefit from his muse. The poem is replete with political defense, explanation, and celebration, and it is rather more sophisticated in that service than in its own. The seams of self-authorization in this poem show openly; the political appropriations are more cleverly concealed. The two were to come together later in Dryden's career, nowhere more brilliantly than in the first great party poem of the language, *Absalom and Achitophel*. In *Annus Mirabilis* Dryden is working simultaneously to establish a literary identity, a relation with patrons, and a political ideology, and he is doing so without the structure of party culture to give definition to his languages and schemes. With *Absalom and Achitophel* we have reached a poem and a point in the evolution of political culture at which the issues of style and authority can be addressed from within a party context. The poem argues a program of repressive political measures while it seeks to align the commodities of cultural authority with the campaign against Exclusion. That alignment is sought most obviously in the confrontation of virtues and vices, a drama effected by the portraits. It is also argued, rather more complexly, through the handling of Scripture. But the most daring and original argument for a politics of cultural authority is made in this poem through the laureate's invocation of literary genius.

The characters in *Absalom and Achitophel* need not long detain us; they have been superbly documented in their history and contemporary articulation.[83] Parliamentary records of the early 1680s reveal the infrastructure of party in the Exclusion Crisis, and the pamphlet literature shows us how Whigs and Tories, words that begin simply as condemnation, emerge early in the 1680s as something broader than caricature.[84] Parties, of course, form a basis for a whole political culture in the early eighteenth century, when Whigs and Tories give definition to the style of Protestantism, property, and monarchy. In *Absalom and Achitophel* the images are not so fully developed, but the poem carefully aligns art and learning with Tory loyalism and reverses that alignment in its striking condemnation of political dissent as false wit and perjured morals. Not only the substance but the style of such praise and blame have important political meaning in this poem.

Cultural authority is even more centrally argued in *Absalom and Achitophel* through the handling of Scripture, but the handling of Scripture, unlike the sharp polarities of the character writing, is tonally complex, elusive, and various. To grasp the status of Scripture in the conduct of the poem's polemic, we must understand both the complexity of manner in which Dryden uses Scripture and the range of feeling and association with which that material was freighted. What, to pose the question most directly, is the meaning of Dryden's scripturalism in the face of party politics that had emerged in the Exclusion Crisis? It is, first of all, a bid for cultural authority in a language not usually associated with a libertine court or with the party whose roaring and swearing had already begun to be proverbial in the pamphlet literature on party.[85] To cast the king's authority in scriptural terms was partly a gesture of daring, though neither the king's authority nor the Tory triumph was so assured in this crisis that any instrument of vindication might be turned away. Yet there is a difference between decorating Restoration panegyrics with touches of scripturalism and underpinning the ideals of Tory triumphalism in a language that would hardly have seemed the peculiar property of king and court in 1681.

The decision to cast this poem as scriptural allegory, then, was part of an effort to suggest that a confluence of interests might actually flow between Scripture and Tory politics and that dissenting Protestants could have something to hope for by way of liberty of tender conscience from a monarch whose abundance and ease had already been suggested in the Declaration of Breda and hinted at in the efforts at Indulgence of 1662 and 1672. Perhaps the scripturalism, the insistence on natural piety, and the clever anticlericalism of the poem would have held some appeal for dissenting laity. Although the history of Jewry in this poem is an embarrassment, a political shambles, the elect nation is not proposed as a joke to be dismissed once the characters beneath the biblical names have been discerned. Scripture had authorized politics from time immemorial and had done so with particular urgency from the late 1640s onward; to do so in the 1680s was to effect a complex maneuver, but the basis of the authorization was once a universally shared assumption.

Part of the brightness of the biblical metaphor is then the unsuspected alliance between the court and Protestant quietism hinted at in the very materials of Scripture itself. The parallel between David and Charles no doubt would have offered wrier amusement to a libertine court. But the scriptural appropriation had as well a harsher meaning, for the constant arraignment of past before present was a crucial ploy for Tory polemic.[86] No cry was raised more frequently or more vehemently by court publicists than " '41 is come again." And that is surely central to Dryden's scripturalism. To cast the history of Charles II's reign in the language of II Samuel is to argue parallel and prophecy and, more specifically, to suggest deicide and regicide; it is to excite the memory of fanaticism and republicanism, of political experiment and restless murmuring in the long desert exile of Cromwellian tyranny. Beneath scriptural fantasy and prophecy, lurking in the shadows of this fanciful parallel, is a hostile and realistic argument. The history of republican godliness—neatly excited by a string of references, allusions, and associations—is one of the crucial themes of Scripture in this poem, a theme that Dryden means to exploit to its highest polemical advantage and to do so by an appeal to the collective memory of Scripture in national politics.

There is as well a moral argument suggested by the frame, an argument about the nature of piety. The play of piety against priestcraft in the opening lines of *Absalom and Achitophel* as well as the steady attack on false piety among the "godly" is an effort to identify

Charles's position, his indulgence and generosity, with the true sanctity of Davidic kingship, to center morality in civic rather than clerical institutions. It has not been sufficiently noted that the attack on priest-craft in this poem is at once an exposure of Roman Catholic idolatry, a ridiculing of Puritan fanaticism, and an undercutting of the moral monopoly of Anglican priestliness. Jewish rabbis and Hebrew priests are after all Anglican doctors of divinity and Anglican clergy;[87] and if that slight is not sufficiently clear, Dryden etches his convictions with great clarity in the opening lines of the poem and in that acid remark on clergy that occurs in the middle of the rather sympathetic account of English Roman Catholics, "Priests of all Religions are the same."[88] Polygamy and patriarchalism are authorized by Scripture, and none could deny either the history of patriarchalism or the sanctity of Davidic kingship, a kingship obviously marred by sexual weakness and paternal indulgence. The poem invites dissenters—indeed, the whole of the nation—to consider the benefits of indulgence, but it aims to deprive dissenting politicians of their purported godliness and to counter the moral authority of any clerical group. The argument for Davidic sanctity and natural piety begins with witty analogy; its seriousness of purpose as polemic becomes more clearly defined as Dryden mounts his complex attack on the principles and arguments of Exclusion. The moral argument is broader than such debunking, however; the sly but insistent distinction between piety and priestcraft and the juxtaposition of religious monopoly with civic morality argue the true character of sanctified kingship in *Absalom and Achitophel*. Patriarchalism rather than priestcraft is the key to a morality, economy, and politics of charity and abundance; and the text that lends itself unstintingly to such an arrangement is, of course, Scripture.

The poem excoriates faction; it conducts a serious campaign against party and in so doing it would address all political interests in the universal language of Scripture. But the attack on party is an attack on Whiggery and the campaign against Exclusion is a party campaign concealed in a language simultaneously scarred with political history and above time. This poem uses Scripture to argue the case against Exclusion as a repetition of the politics of the Puritan Revolution and to exalt the claims of Stuart kingship as eternal verity. Dryden was keenly aware of the politicized character of Scripture in the English past; he also understood the contemporary importance of arguments from sanctity and conscience and how tactful and poised their assertion must now be. Central to the claims of witnesses called to testify in the Popish Plot was the moral and political vigilance of Protestantism. The Popish Plot was the instrument of Roman Catholic priests who would, with the aid and abetment of that monster of French

tyranny, Louis XIV, destroy English Protestantism and English property. If Dryden were attempting to position the poem as an answer
to the vindication of the politics of negligence against such claims of
vigilance, then the language of scriptural sanctity was an important
one to assert on behalf of his clients. The issue was not exactly who
would have believed the Davidic sanctity of sexual misconduct, but
rather how the languages and images of court and king could be
managed in such a way as to appropriate the fundamentals of Protestant sanctity, moral authority, and political vigilance. One language
alone could do so for seventeenth-century political argument. Neither
the ancient constitution nor Bodin nor antiquity—nor, alas, the moral
character and conduct of the king himself—would allow the Poet
Laureate entry into the moral universe of Protestantism and property;
the language that could do so was Scripture. It combined the moral
and political authority of the sacred past with the political lessons of
the present, and it did so because of widespread Protestant convictions about the role of Scripture in the civic life of the nation and
because of the history of Scripture in the political discourse of the
seventeenth century. Dryden's choice of Scripture simultaneously elevated the political interests of Tories above politics and enabled the
poet to debunk the claims of Whigs and Exclusionists to Protestant
vigilance and piety. Scripture had still a powerful moral and political
authority, and Dryden means to claim as much of that authority for
the king and court as he might. And yet he seems to claim very little
of that scriptural authority on his own behalf. The situation of the
narrator of both preface and poem is very different from the relation
that Milton and his narrator assume to Scripture in *Paradise Lost*.

Milton's control over Scripture is utter and complete in *Paradise
Lost*; it may have been a language somewhat tarnished for the poet
by its associations with godly republicanism, but Milton had no choice
in standing forthrightly for what he had always stood. He needed to
confront and to exalt Puritan scripturalism. Dryden was forced into
no such position. Although the economy and precision that Scripture
offered for his political needs are obvious after reading his poem,
before its composition he had at his call a large stock of devices and
languages, of plots and parallels, from which to choose. Scripture
offered him an opportunity to address a crisis of witnesses, plots,
and revelations, but the choice of material could hardly have been
forced on the poet. At any rate, Dryden seems to have so little defensiveness about the frame, he seems so willing to yield authority,
that we must conclude that there was little in the choice of the metaphor that made the poet feel vulnerable, although the opening move
in this poem is so daring in the ways it uses Scripture to address and

authorize libertinism, in its off-handed, almost glib engagement with the Holy Spirit, that it is surprising to find no hints of anxiety in these lines. Indeed, part of what is startling about the handling of the initial jokes is the utter suavity and assurance of tone. There is a familiarity and ease with Scripture that suggests something of the power of the laureateship for Dryden.[89] Although the piety and moral seriousness of Dryden's clients may not have induced confidence, *Absalom and Achitophel* is quite a different performance in relation to its language than *Paradise Lost* with its hectoring exclusivity and propriety. Rather than argue dominance over or reveal defensiveness about Scripture, Dryden seems willing to confess vulnerability to its very terms. Scripture would dictate one conclusion to his poem; Dryden would rather not face that imposition and seeks through charity to turn away the inevitable. He seems pleased by his parallel but under no compulsion to its terms. Indeed, the complexity of tone in which he manages the scriptural materials of both preface and poem is dazzling, at times even baffling.[90]

What seems equally baffling—or at least has seemed so in recent critical argument—is the status of the poet's partisanship.[91] It is, I think, crucial to an understanding of the claims for cultural authority in *Absalom and Achitophel* that we remain aware of the climate of intense partisan struggle and personal abuse in which Dryden argued superiority to partisanship. The campaigns of abuse and invective that surrounded the political and literary contests of these years were violent, and Dryden's address to the issues of partisanship and party is central to his quest for authority in *Absalom and Achitophel*. The final set of terms in which I want to discuss this quest is the literary itself.

This, the most brilliant of political poems, begins with an effort altogether to deny the reality of partisanship. The poem is a harsh condemnation of Whig politics and Whig polemic; it is a subtle and assured raid on the arguments and language of Exclusion; it deploys its enormous energies, distortions, smears, and unfair yokings in the interests of party; it seeks to invest with authority and sanctity a monarchy debased in habit and principle; and it seems to allow the fact of party coalescence but conducts its campaign by deploring faction. The whole game begins with an exaltation of disinterestedness in the face of polarity and with a claim for the literary in the face of the political. The preface grants polarization and partisanship; it allows and understands "Whig" and "Tory," papist and fanatic, but it means, despite the powerful currents of polarization and partisanship, to allow as little force to such polarity as possible. That such an aim ill-suits the arguments, the portraits, the scripturalism, and the actual design of the poem is a lesson that *Absalom and Achitophel* teaches subtly and surely. But we need to allow Dryden the terms of his argument in the preface, although to allow such terms is not to acquiesce to them. The aim of the preface is to open the poem to as wide a readership as possible; the aim is to argue the dominance of the literary over the political, to assert the authority and disinterestedness of the literary itself. Throughout the preface the aims and merits of authorship are argued over and above those of partisanship as if they were analogues. The language is of design, of verse, of gentility, of impartiality.

But literary argument has political weight. The spirit of high authorship is aligned with what will emerge as the spirit of Davidic monarchy. Dryden's literary impulse is to extenuate, to palliate, to indulge, to please by art, and this is the spirit in which David has attempted to conduct his kingship, this is the spirit of Stuart indulgence. It is the opposition alone that is responsible for anything other than the high road of the literary and the monarchical. The preface attempts to cast poetry and polemics into opposition, for the literary itself is an important instrument of authority in this poem.[92] Title and subtitle twin these sources of authority from the very onset: "Absalom and Achitophel, A Poem." Dryden manages two arguments for cultural authority from the first gesture of the title page; nor is that quite all that he accomplishes in that text: "Absalom and Achitophel, A Poem / Si Propius stes / Te Capiet Magis."[93] At the close of the long first paragraph, Dryden returns to his artistic epigraph, "The Frame of it, was cut out, but for a Picture to the Wast; and, if the Draught be so far true, 'tis as much as I design'd."[94] The claim of these effects is cultural authority; the poem repeatedly and self-consciously casts itself as a work of art; epigraph and argument suggest the poem as work of art—indeed, of pictorial art; the language of artistic design and frame argues both the poem's concern with that art and suggests that artistry inhabits a realm above politics. It is an irony in the critical reading of this poem that Dryden's claims to artistry should have been so quickly dismissed in the paper war over Exclusion—the Poet Laureate constantly arraigned on charges of political hackwork—and that those very claims once so dismissively treated should be so piously valued by modern critics that we have developed a notion of Dryden as a delicate literary sensibility weighted against his own instincts with the business of partisanship and political duty. The case is in fact different from both responses. The poem exhibits genius and partisanship; they are so completely bound together in this work that only a thorough naivete about the conditions of literary production in the Restoration would see these issues as contradictory.

The final argument that I want to make about the polemic in this

poem, about the force of partisanship and Tory politics, is the service
of genius in the lists of party. For I think that genius was a property
that Dryden fully recognized in himself. It is a conviction that has
interesting biographical implications that cannot be explored here but
whose force we must recognize—like that of prophecy and inspiration
in *Paradise Lost*—as cultural authorization. I choose the word *genius*
with an awareness that the way we now use this term as an accolade
would not come into wide acceptance until the middle of the eighteenth century.[95] The term in the seventeenth century that seems to
cover this quality is "wit," and Dryden displays his own steady curiosity about this term in the critical prose. I want to insist for a
moment on the word *genius*, however, because it appears in a suggestive connection with the word *authority* in the preface and it suggests
for our ears the very topic of cultural authority itself:

> My Comfort is, their manifest Prejudice to my Cause, will render their
> Judgment of less Authority against me. Yet if a *Poem* have a *Genius*, it will
> force its own reception in the World. For there's a sweetness in good Verse,
> which Tickles even while it Hurts: And, no man can be heartily angry
> with him, who pleases him against his will. The commendation of Ad-
> versaries, is the greatest Triumph of a Writer.[96]

If we abstract this passage for a moment from the preface, it is easy
to recognize that one of the interests of the poem is in genius as we
mean the word, its force and authority, and that the turn between
the meaning of "local spirit" and the modern accolade is taking place
right here. The language of authority, judgment, and artistic power,
the insistence on the literary and the aesthetic, is itself a bid by the
poet for recognition of his genius very much in our sense of the word.
And Dryden's self-knowledge as a poet was quite objective by this
point in his career. Within the argument of the preface, the sentences
are an effort to lodge a claim for the literary against the political, to
claim the purity of literature against the adversary qualities of partisanship. But the claim is also lodged (with the poet's characteristic
show of modesty) on behalf of his own genius, a genius that lay in
defamation: "They who can criticize so weakly as to imagine I have
done my worst, may be convinced, at their own cost, that I can write
severely with more ease than I can Gently, I have but laughed at
some mens Follies, when I could have declaimed against their
Vices."[97] This is, not to put too fine a point on the gesture, a threat
of defamation; it is an argument about power, and the form of the
power is literary, the power to damage, to inflict injury to fame. It is
suggestive that the close of this preface should link satire with surgery;

to propose an act of memory for this hot, distempered state is the necessary remedy. Acts of oblivion may be the king's prerogative, but the prerogative of this poem is naming, and such naming has a particular power when the man wielding the names is a genius and the frame that he is talking about is not only the 1680s but also eternity.

Dryden did not underestimate the cultural authority of traditional sources of legitimation—Scripture, history, literary allusion, scholarly altitude—but he is now keenly aware of the power of his literary genius and aware that one of the long suits of that genius is wit (in our sense of the word) and that praising and blaming are fields in which that genius can flourish. The poet was intent on the identity of his poem as a work of genius, and the abandon and economy of the opening lines, that peculiar and elusive irony in which he casts the piety and abundance of the king, stamp the poem with the identity of Dryden's genius; the lines have few rivals in their ease and complexity. The gallery of rogues again reveals the poet's genius, as does the portrait of the Levites and the little picture gallery that closes the arraignment of the wicked: Balaam, Jonas, Shimei, and Corah. These portraits constitute one of the most entertaining and damaging moments in the poem, and Dryden knew that. He exploited his peculiar genius for defamation in the lists of party politics. His aim was to explode Whiggery, to damage and obliterate; he may have had personal grudges to satisfy in this campaign, but it was a party job, a campaign utterly to deny the personal and political credibility of a political party. And the job is brilliant, a work of genius; it displays all the marks of literary authority, and that authority was galvanized by and functions in the lists of party politics.

Was there finally a higher cultural authority that the poet might summon than his own genius? Certainly there were other gods, but perhaps this one mattered most for the poet, and Dryden must have understood about his own performance in this poem that it displayed his peculiar genius. Perhaps he knew as well that the verse would act as touchstone, as totem for Tory polemic; it certainly became such in the propaganda of succeeding years.[98] In fact, the poem was almost immediately translated into Latin, itself an act of cultural authorization.[99] If the status of classic were rendered by the ancient language, this poem achieved its status almost immediately. The authorizing power of genius is a difficult subject (we use the phrase "self-proclaimed genius" with a heavy edge of irony), but I think that both Milton and Dryden understood the uses of genius and were busy with such hints and self-proclamations. The personalities were very different, but both poets understood the authority of genius and were eager to press its claims. And they did so at a time when others were

prepared to take up those claims on behalf of political aims and programs, as vindication of political party when party sought and needed
all the kinds of authority that could be summoned.

Of course, the idea of panegyric and the institution of patronage
are efforts to convey the prestige and authority of culture through
the attachment of genius to court or patron. Such patronage had
always been and remains an effort to acquire cultural authority. But
the emergence of political parties in the late seventeenth century
brought new clients to the market. It is interesting evidence of the
presence and role of party in the uses of culture that Virgil's great
epic was so insistently read as political and even as party literature
in the late seventeenth and early eighteenth centuries.[100] And it is
further confirmation not only of the politicization of literature but of
the politicization of literary canon that Tonson should have republished *Paradise Lost* on the eve of the Glorious Revolution, that Latin
translations of Milton's masterpiece should have been prepared in
the 1690s, that such important political tracts as *Eikonoklastes* and *A
Defence of the English People* were republished in that decade, and that
the poetical works were enshrined in an edition with copious annotation in 1698.[101] The Milton industry of the eighteenth century takes
us beyond our immediate concerns, but the broader issue of politics
and literary canon helps us to grasp both the situation of literature
in Restoration culture and the role of politics in organizing and de-
ploying the energy, the wit, the styles, and, in some cases, even the
sublimity of art.

11

Fables of Power

Annabel Patterson

ESOPE RESTE ICI ET SE REPOSE. This unusually cogent and even poignant palindrome may serve as my excuse for beginning this inquiry into the politics of fable at the wrong end: so far at the other end of the story that opens, by long-standing tradition, with a Greek slave in the sixth century B.C. that my beginning breaks the chronological boundaries set for this volume and takes us into the eighteenth century. Yet there is a real justification for this procedure, in that by the time Samuel Croxall published his *Fables of AEsop and Others* in 1722, the political history of the fable in England had become so fully understood, so polemically stated, that it renders accessible to us what was implicit or merely potential in earlier phases of the narrative.

It is well known that Croxall was moved to become a fabulist, in part, in reaction against the contributions to the genre that had been made thirty years earlier by Sir Roger L'Estrange. It is equally well known that L'Estrange's *Fables of AEsop and Other Eminent Mythologists: With Morals and Reflexions*, published in London in 1692, were the overt expressions of a political philosophy of which Croxall profoundly disapproved. L'Estrange's philosophy has been called pure Filmerism;[1] but his theoretical affiliations with early Stuart propaganda were surely modified by his experience under the later Stuarts. L'Estrange's political philosophy starts from the premise that society depends on the preservation of its divinely ordered hierarchies, and the long "Reflexions" that he added to his collection of fables are repeated expressions of Jacobitism. These are the principles that Croxall was to repudiate as "coin'd and suited to promote the Growth, and serve the Ends of Popery, and Arbitrary Power."[2] But it must also have been L'Estrange's own observation of the constitutional crises of the 1670s and 1680s, events seen from the peculiar observation point of the Licenser of the Press, that caused him to develop and articulate the power of the fable collection as an oblique medium of political commentary.

The preface to L'Estrange's *Fables* is, like his "Reflexions," strongly ideological, though less transparently so. One of its most revealing impulses is the need to emancipate the fable from its legendary (or historical) origins in the ancient *Life* of Aesop, the apocryphal biography of the witty hunchback, slave, and trickster, of which the earliest version derived from an Egyptian text of the first century A.D. but which was disseminated in the late Middle Ages by the Byzantine Maximus Planudes. L'Estrange's scholarship tells him that "it would be labour lost to Multiply Unprofitable Conjectures upon a Tradition of so Great Uncertainty. . . . For, the Story is come down to us so Dark and Doubtful." And after listing a series of chronological contradictions and impossibilities from the *Life*, he concludes,

> This is enough in All Conscience, to Excuse any Man from laying over-much Stress upon the Historical Credit of a Relation, that comes so Blindly, and so Variously transmitted to us . . . it is not one jot to our Bus'ness . . . whether the Man was Streight, or Crooked; and his Name Aesop, or (as some will have it) Lochman: In All which Cases, the Reader is left at Liberty to Believe his Pleasure. (A1r)

There are two antithetical ways to read this decision. One is to see L'Estrange as a demythologizing rationalist, removing from the fable tradition all that is "Dark and Doubtful" and replacing it with scientific clarity, just as he had attacked the confused textual history of the fable, weeding out repetitions and producing an eclectic text from the collections of "Phaedrus, Camerarius, Avienus, Neveletus, Apthonius, Gabrias or Babrias, Baudoin, La Fontaine, Aesope en Belle Humeur" (B1v). The other is to see him as deliberately suppressing one of the most important controls on interpretation that the fable offered: the memories, however perplexed, of the actual circumstances that gave rise to it. By refusing to recognize the historical existence of Aesop as father of the genre, L'Estrange in effect replaced historical criticism with a principle most familiar to us: "The Reader is left at Liberty to Believe his Pleasure."

In default of Aesop's credibility, the concern of L'Estrange's preface was to establish the credibility of the fable itself. It has, he proposed, three claims on our serious attention. First, it has had a venerable record of success in pedagogy, as an agreeable medium for the indoctrination of children, who will swallow any moral that comes attached to a story about animals. Second, it partakes of the general

antiquity and dignity of symbolic discourse, as in Egyptian hiero-
glyphics and biblical parables. Third, it has an undoubted political
usefulness. Indeed, L'Estrange slides straight from the mention of
Nathan's parable in reproach to David in 2 Samuel 12 to a somewhat
impassioned account of the usefulness of fables as an oblique and
prudent form of rebuke to monarchs:

> Some People are too Proud, too Surly, too Impudent, too Incorrigible,
> either to Bear, or to Mend upon the Liberty of Plain Dealing. Others are
> too Big Again, too Vindictive, and Dangerous, for either Reproof, or Coun-
> cel, in Direct Terms. They Hate any Man that's but Conscious of their
> Wickedness, and their Misery is like the Stone in the Bladder; There are
> Many Things good for't, but there's no Coming at it; and neither the Pulpit,
> the Stage, nor the Press, Dares so much as Touch upon't. . . . This Con-
> trivance of Application, by Hints, and Glances, is the Only way under the
> Heavens to Hit it [Who shall say to a King, What Dost thou?] comes up
> to the very Stress of This Topique. (A2v–B1r)

It is not impossible that this verbal explosion is fired, among other
passions, by a certain ambivalence about the two later Stuarts in
whose cause L'Estrange had served. It may be not only William whose
profile appears among those who are too big or too dangerous to
address directly, or whose "Unaccountable Priviledge" (B1r) puts
them beyond the control of their "Cabinet-Councel"; while his remark
that it is no longer possible to "tell . . . the House of Jacob [James I
and II?] of their Transgressions" may, in its own way, be one of the
very "Hints, and Glances" that comprise the fabulist's political lexi-
con.[3]

This preface is invaluable in defining one of the major premises of
Aesopian tradition, a premise that survives today in the term "Aesopian writing" as a medium of political resistance in eastern Europe.
Yet that it contains both repressions and contradictions was immediately perceived by Samuel Croxall. Croxall was particularly outraged
by L'Estrange's conflation of what his Whig successor saw as incompatible functions for his fables—the education of children and political
suasion; although he might have been less struck by this incompat-
ibility had L'Estrange's views been closer to his own. Croxall noted
that no child could physically handle such a massive volume, and
that no self-respecting child would have anything to do with it:

> What sort of Children therefore are the blank Paper, upon which such
> Morality as this ought to be written? Not the Children of Britain, I hope;
> for they are born with free Blood in their Veins; and suck in Liberty with
> their very Milk. (b4v–b5r)

It was an essential part of Croxall's argument that the *Life* of Aesop represented the father of the fable as a slave; for this was the precondition of the genre. Although slavery was Aesop's own "incidental Misfortune," wrote Croxall, yet he "pass'd the time of his Servitude among the free States of Greece; where he saw the high Esteem in which Liberty was held, and possibly learn'd to value it accordingly" (b6r). He therefore took "all Occasions to recommend a Love for Liberty, and an Abhorrence of Tyranny, and all arbitrary Proceedings." The *Life*, therefore, in Croxall's opinion, renders entirely illegitimate L'Estrange's reading of the fables, as, for example, *The Dog and the Wolf*, which in the text of Phaedrus begins "Quam dulcis sit Libertas" but which, according to L'Estrange, "is to be understood of the Freedom of the Mind." "No body," wrote Croxall, in high indignation, "ever understood it so, I dare say, that knew what the other Freedom was. As for what he mentions, it is not in the Power of the greatest Tyrant that lives to deprive us of it" (b6v). Croxall makes the same point about the role of Phaedrus as mediator of the Aesopian text to the Roman world, or, more specifically, to the imperial culture of Tiberius early in the first century A.D.:

> Phaedrus, whose hard Lot it had once been to be a domestic Slave, had yet so great a Veneration for the Liberty I am speaking of, that he made no Scruple to write in Favour of it, even under the Usurpation of a Tyrant; and at a time when the once glorious free People of Rome had nothing but the Form and Shadow of their ancient Constitution left. This he did particularly in the Fable of *The Frogs desiring a King.* . . . So that we see Lestrange must misrepresent the Sense of his Author, before he can make such a Meaning out of him, as he would have to be written upon the blank Paper of a tender uninformed Child.[4]

Despite his own prejudices, Croxall was correct in seeing dichotomy in the cultural history of the fable, a split between a tradition of moral application that was eminently suitable for pedagogy and a tradition of political functionalism that was not. During the late Middle Ages and early Renaissance the moral, vertical, or generalizing axis of this system was dominant, pulling the curve of fabulist interpretation upward; but by the last quarter of the sixteenth century there were created in England the conditions that promote Aesopian writing—political repression, combined with the existence of an educated elite with a stake in the power structure but no direct access to it. The result was a steadily increasing gravitational pull of the horizontal or topicalizing axis of interpretation, a pressure reinforced both by the course of events in the seventeenth century and by the particular lines drawn or points plotted on this graph of significance by translators or adapters of Aesop. By the time Dryden published *The Hind and the Panther* in 1687, for instance, Edmund Spenser had become as influential a model for the English fabulist as Aesop himself; and no one did more to set up the terms that were taken for granted by L'Estrange and Croxall than John Ogilby, whose several collections of fables were definitive markers of both civil war and Restoration culture. The essential point to grasp, however, is that the principles disputed by L'Estrange and Croxall—the nature of political liberty, how it is to be understood and how supported—were both latent in the fable tradition from the beginning *and* made peculiarly manifest in the lived history of seventeenth-century England.

If we go back, then, to the beginning of the fable's story, there are two ways to proceed. One is to repeat the demythologized account of Aesopian tradition that has resulted from two centuries of scholarship, an account from which, like L'Estrange's, the idea of Aesop himself has been largely erased. What we now know is that Aesop's historical existence is supported only by one brief mention in Herodotus; that there is only one fable that with any certainty can be attributed to him, that of *The Fox, Hedgehog, and Dog-Ticks*, as it was so attributed by Aristotle in his *Rhetoric*; that the medium by which "Aesopian" fables (that is, ancient Greek folk tales) survived was by way of two much later collections, the Latin verse fables of Phaedrus and the Greek verse fables of Babrius, from the middle of the third century A.D.[5]

The extent to which that transmission was of a genre rather than a specific set of texts was rendered a problem by Phaedrus himself, who gave several different accounts of his debt to "Aesopus auctor" in the separate prologues to his first four books of fables. The first simply expressed a debt to the master; the second noted that his model gave him freedom to make pleasing additions ("aliquid interponere / dictorum sensus ut delectet varietas"); the third that where Aesop had made a footpath he had constructed a highway—"ego illius pro semita feci viam, / et cogitavi plura quam reliquerat"; and the fourth that his fables should really be called not Aesop's but Aesopian, since while he followed an ancient genre he was also an innovator:

> (quas Aesopias, non Aesopi, nomino,
> quia paucas ille ostendit, ego plures sero,
> usus vetusto genere, sed rebus novis)[6]

These two collections of late antiquity were themselves transmitted to the Middle Ages through two further intermediaries, the "Rom-

ulus" prose redaction of Phaedrus and Avianus's Latin verse translation of Babrius. In the fifteenth century Italian humanists rediscov-
ered Phaedrus and Babrius, along with the oriental Bidpai fables; but
in the meantime Aesopian tradition had been accreting material from
all directions. In 1484, William Caxton published the first English
version of "Aesop," which contained 167 items, combining fables
thought to be Aesop's from several sources with later additions ranging in date from the fourth century to the mid-fifteenth, and including
two that were apparently original compositions of Caxton's own.[7] By
the standards of textual scholarship, then, "Aesopus auctor" was
merely a convenient fiction, a form of generic nomenclature.

The second procedure, however, is to assume instead that there
was something more than mere convenience in the tenacity of the
fiction of Aesop as author. And on this point Joseph Jacobs, the nine-
teenth-century editor of Caxton's *Aesop* and one of the greatest de-
constructors of "Aesopus auctor," is surprisingly bold. Jacobs asked
himself the question why, despite the characteristic anonymity of folk
tales everywhere, the Greek beast fable was connected from a very
early stage with a specific personality and name. The answer that
Jacobs gave to his own question was as follows:

> His [Aesop's] was the epoch of the Tyrants, and I would conjecture that
> his connection with the Beast-Fable originally consisted in its application
> to political controversy under despotic government, and that his fate [as
> recorded by Herodotus] was due to the influence of one of the Tyrants
> with the Delphic authorities. . . . The Fable is most effective as a literary
> or oratorical weapon under despotic governments allowing no free speech.
> A tyrant cannot take notice of a Fable without putting on the cap that fits.
> Much of our ancient evidence points this way. Jotham's fable (Judges ix,
> 8–15) was directed against Abimelech, the Israelite *tyrannos*. In our list of
> genuinely ancient Greek Fables, one is connected with the name of Theog-
> nis who was ruined by a Tyrant, Solon made use of his for political pur-
> poses, and Archilochus was Satire personified. The only extant Fable that
> can be attributed to AEsop with any plausibility [*The Fox, Hedgehog, and
> Dog-Ticks*] was used by him for political purposes. Our evidence is of course
> scanty, but it all points one way. AEsop could not have been the inventor
> or introducer of the Beast-Fable into Greece, as we find it there before him.
> The only way therefore we can explain the later identification of his name
> with it is to suppose some special and striking use of the *fabellae aniles*
> familiar to all Greek children. Considering the age he lived in and the
> death he died . . . AEsop's name was associated with the Fable, because
> he made use of it as a political weapon. . . . AEsop was not the Father of
> the Fable, but only the inventor (or most conspicuous applier) of a new
> use for it, and when the need for that use no longer existed under out-
> spoken democracies, his connection with the Fable was still kept up as a

convenient and conventional figurehead round which to gather a special-
ised form of the Greek jest.[8]

In other words, the specialized form of the fable that both ensured
its survival and demanded adult respect was a subversive one, empowered by an ancient association with a slave culture and capable
of application to any later circumstances, such as those of Phaedrus,
which required a discourse of resistance to and analysis of political
oppression. The effect of these ancient "authorial" structures was,
first, to permit political interpretations of the fable tradition when
political circumstances demanded them. Certain fables, such as *The
Dog and the Wolf* or *The Frogs desiring a King*, inevitably carried with
them their ancient historico-political context, which allowed them to
become both exemplars of how to construct a topical fable and permanent tropes in the public or constitutional discourse of early modern Europe. Others, particularly those that featured the lion, quickly
became metaphors for the strengths and limitations of monarchical
government. And in certain circumstances the entire genre could
become politicized, either explicitly, as was the case with L'Estrange's
translations of 1692 and their "Reflexions," or in Ogilby's midcentury
"paraphrases" with their inferential application to the civil war and
its aftermath. One might even argue that after a certain point in the
seventeenth century in England—that point being marked by the first
edition of Ogilby's *Fables* in 1651—not even the most literal translation
of Aesop, naked of commentary, could have appeared to its readers
as totally innocent of topical meaning.

Because Aesop's transmission in seventeenth-century England has
been systematically described by Mary Pritchard,[9] I shall instead follow the trajectory of a few central fables and investigate some of the
salient moments in what might be called the fable's *literary* history;
that is, moments in which fable tradition, rather than being merely
recapitulated (usually for schoolchildren), is both galvanized and rendered introspective. What both branches of investigation ought to
show (and they will be conducted concurrently) is a peculiarly potent
collaboration between Aesop as model and history—lived political
history—as innovator, a collaboration the terms of which are perhaps
more precisely and visibly inscribed than most generic systems allow.

The convergence in the fable of literary and political impulses began
in England, as I have suggested, in the last decades of Elizabeth's
reign. It was clearly manifest in Spenser's *Shepheardes Calendar*, where
three eclogues contain fully developed political fables, supported by
a series of allusions to fabulist tradition. This essay is not the place
to explore how and why Spenser reworked, for his own purposes,

the ancient fables of the *Fir and the Bramble* and the *Wolf and the Kid;* but it is fair to say that he set a precedent both for innovative adaptation of the fabulist tradition in general and for its topical potential specifically—in this instance the situation of the Protestant activists in Elizabeth's court. And more important for at least one later fabulist, John Dryden, was Spenser's massive narrative expansion of the fable form in *Prosopopoia. Or Mother Hubberds Tale.* This story of how the ape and the fox conspire to take over the kingdom of beasts while the true ruler, the lion—"sleeping lay in secret shade, / His Crowne and Scepter lying him beside, / And having doft for heate his dreadfull hide"—was clearly an emblem of royal negligence that permits knaves to take over the government. Unlike the majority of Aesopian fables, this one ends well, with the lion recalled to his duty by Mercury and the fox and the ape (who has been wearing a lion's skin) captured and punished.

But there is an earlier phase of the narrative which does not offer the same optimism. The fox and the ape, who will do anything to avoid work, have been begging, the ape got up like a wounded veteran of the wars. They encounter a "simple husbandman," whose Georgic ethos is the reverse of theirs and who offers the ape the opportunity to work on his farm. When the ape submits that his wounds rule out manual labor, the "honest man" gives him instead the undemanding job of shepherd, with the fox as his sheepdog. Not surprisingly, the rogues ravage the flock, eating the lambs as fast as they are born; and when the time comes that they should "render up a reckning of their travels / Unto their master" they simply flee the area. "So was the husbandman left," concludes Spenser of this episode, "to his losse." The effect is of two parallel fables of governance by false deputy, the first a tragedy whose tone matches those of the fables within *The Shepheardes Calendar* and the second a satirical comedy. Also illustrated are two contrasting models of the lawful monarch: the good but naive husbandman and the supreme but slothful beast of prey. It was not an encouraging pair of alternatives nor, for all the summary justice of its conclusion, a respectful representation of the Elizabethan state; but it was one that encouraged Dryden, almost a century later, to rethink the relationship between lion and husbandman and to reshape it to somewhat more constructive ends.

If Elizabeth's reign was, for all its strategic successes and overall stability, occasionally vulnerable to the subversive critical analysis that fables made possible, we would expect the same to be even more true of the first half of the seventeenth century, when the first two Stuarts were considerably less accomplished in having their own theories of monarchy taken for granted. If we can take parliamentary history as an index of constitutional theory and practice, the records show a series of disruptive confrontations between the king and the people's representatives in Parliament, and an even more telling series of discontinuities in the records. Of these, the most definitive, obviously, was the 1628–29 struggle over the Petition of Right and the resulting decision by Charles I to rule without Parliament indefinitely. And in the records of the House of Commons for 22 May 1628 there appears an instance of fabulist discourse that is almost too good to be true, in its making explicit the procedure by which an old metaphor was reappropriated and reinterpreted in terms of the current crisis.

The context of the discussion was whether the Petition of Right should be circumscribed by a proviso proposed by the Lords excluding the king's "sovereign power" from the terms proposed. In opposing the Lords' amendment, Sir Henry Marten (father of the regicide) spoke with unusual forcefulness and color:

> Horace dislikes the painter that *humano capiti* would join a horse's neck. Yet if he made a horse's neck alone it was good. The King may not require money but in parliament. It is a man's head; but add this clause, "unless it be by sovereign power," then it is a lion's neck, and it mars all. . . . It implies the King is trusted with a power for the destruction and also for the safety of the people. It admits also he may use "sovereign power," and if he do we may not refuse it, for it is for our protection. So it bounds up my mouth that I cannot but say that is for the good of the people. "Sovereign power" is transcending and a high word. There is a tale in *Aesop's Fables*, the moral whereof shall be that when actions are regulated by law you may guess at the proportion, but if it be regulated by the prerogative, there is no end. The ass, the lion and the fox agreed to go on hunting, and they found good prey, and the ass was willing to make a division, and so he did, laying all into three heaps, and said to the lion, "It is your prerogative to choose." The lion took it ill and said, "It is my prerogative to choose," and he tore the ass and did eat him up. He said to the fox, "Divide you," so he took a little part of the skin, and left all the rest. The lion asked him what he meant. He answered him, "All is yours." The lion replied, "This is my prerogative," and he asked the fox who taught him that. Said he, "The calamity of the ass."[10]

There could hardly be a more telling demonstration of where the fable stood in relation to the culture. First, its use in this official context implies that the political history of the genre was taken for granted and that no barriers divided political and literary discourse. Second, it is clear that Marten both depended on a preexistent fabulist plot and took certain liberties with it, some of which were articulated and some left to the audience to grasp for themselves. The moral of his fable is not predetermined but "shall be" arrived at. The lion is bound by convention to be recognized as the king; but by retelling an ancient tale of "might makes right" in terms currently "hot," especially the central and ironically repeated "prerogative"—the immediately topical application is secured. And what makes the episode most complex, perhaps, is the subtheme of censorship ("it bounds up my mouth that I cannot but say that it is for the good of the people") and the possibility that the very tale that should permit the mouth that is bound to be opened contains its own logic of accommodation. The fox learns by the calamity of the ass to let the prerogative alone. What other roles than lion, ass, and fox (tyrant, fool, and cynic) were, in fact, available in early Stuart England? I have found nothing to rival this remarkable speech in Jacobean and Caroline texts, of whatever kind; although there may very well be both contemporary meaning and prophetic force in Philip Massinger's play, *The Emperor of the East*, which, though supposedly exploring the nature of rule in a merely fictional setting, reentered the ancient fable of *The Frogs desiring a King* in the form of a royal complaint:

> . . . O the miserable
> Condition of a Prince! who though hee varie
> More shapes then Proteus in his minde, and manners,
> Hee cannot winne an universall suffrage,
> From the many-headed monster, Multitude.
> Like AEsops foolish Frogges they trample on him
> As a senselesse blocke, if his government bee easie.
> And if he prove a Storke, they croke, and rayle
> Against him as a tyranne.[11]

Given the appearance of this play in 1631–32, at the opening of Charles I's eleven years of prerogative rule without recourse to Parliament, the fable would have been unlikely *not* to have been perceived as a comment on the aftermath of 1628–29. And although within the dramatic statement its moral is clearly stated, its valence, as compared to Henry Marten's fable of prerogative power, remains veiled without further knowledge of the dramatist's own position and intentions.

By the first years of the civil war, however, signs began to emerge that writers of all kinds and persuasions were rediscovering the fable as a way of venting the tensions of the time. In the *Reason of Church Government* (1641), Milton developed a spirited adaptation of Avianus's fable of *The Ass in the Lion's Skin* to serve as a metaphor for the way the English bishops, in his view, were encroaching on powers that belonged to the state.[12] In *Of Reformation* he did much the same with the fable of *The Belly and the Members* attributed to Menenius Agrippa, applying it lightheartedly, and with a pun on "Members," to the proceedings of the Long Parliament:

> Sir the little adoe, which me thinks I find in untacking these pleasant Sophismes, puts mee into the mood to tell you a tale ere I proceed further; and Menenius Agrippa speed us. Upon a time the Body summon'd all the Members to meet in the Guild for the common good (As Æsops Chronicles averre many stranger Accidents). (1.583)

There is no little irony to be seen in the fact that at this stage of his career Milton still assumed that the rightful governor of the body politic, the head, was the king, whose preeminence has been challenged not by the hands and feet but by the monstrous wen or tumor of prelacy. Nor apparently did he realize that whereas the original function of the fable was to pacify rebellious troops, he was effectively converting it to the service of a national revolution.

Lesser writers would also recall the fable to political duty. In 1640, the anonymous *Pleasant History of Cawood the Rooke* appeared, an imitation of the medieval *Reynard the Fox*, with the rook in place of the fox and the royal eagle in place of the lion. There is, however, a strong topical inference in the fact that the assembly of birds called by the eagle before his departure to another country coincided with the calling of the first English Parliament since 1629; although the fable actually focuses less on the trickster rook than on Rapax the Hawk, appointed regent in the king's absence, a plausible analogy for the role of Thomas Wentworth during the first months of 1640. In the following year was published John Hepwith's *Calidonian Forest*, where there appeared a lion, clearly the king, a usurping dragon, and an elephant as leader of the parliament of beasts, who calls for reform of the forest. James Howell, in 1640, produced the first installment of his *Dodona's Grove: or the Vocall Forrest*, a massively extended tree fable dealing with English history from the reign of Elizabeth through the war with the Scots, which asserts as one of its final morals that "subjects should be willowes and not Okes."[13] Mildmay Fane, himself a Royalist "willow" who lay extremely low, included in an unpublished manuscript a Latin fable, presumably of his own invention, about a hunter who disturbs a hollow oak tree full of wasps, and how his attempts to disperse them with a slender wand only incense them more.[14] Its dating (22 January 1642) reveals it as a critique of the king's inefficacy in dealing either with the Scots or with his own Parliament. Among the broadside ballads of this period was *A Madrigall on Justice*,

which marshalled a series of fables to demonstrate how the old values
had been inverted by the revolution:

> The world is chang'd, and we have Choyces,
> Not by most Reasons, but most Voyces,
> The Lion's trod on by the Mouse,
> The lower is the upper House:
> . . . .
> The feet, and lower parts, 'tis sed,
> Would trample on, and off the head,
> What ere they say, this is the thing,
> They love the Charles, but hate the King;
> To make an even Grove, one stroke
> Should lift the Shrubb unto the Oake.[15]

No such allusions were more telling than one by Charles himself, a
reminder to his subjects of Jotham's parable in Judges against the
tyrant Abimelech, which was published in a letter to his eldest son
along with the *Eikon Basilike* in 1649, immediately following his execution:

> The sweetness of the vine and the fig-tree is not to be despised, though
> the brambles and thorns should pretend to bear figs and grapes, thereby
> to rule over the trees.[16]

In this Charles both blended the biblical fable with his father's Solomonic typology[17] and weirdly anticipated what was to follow. For in
1654, to celebrate the first anniversary of the Protectorate, Andrew
Marvell would turn Jotham's fable into a compliment to Cromwell for
refusing the crown, as well as a critique of the Levellers:

> Thou with the same strength, and an Heart as plain,
> Didst (like thine Olive) still refuse to Reign;
> Though why should others all thy Labor spoil,
> And Brambles be anointed with thine Oyl,
> Whose climbing Flame, without a timely stop,
> Had quickly Levell'd every Cedar's top.
> Therefore first growing to thy self a Law,
> Th'ambitious Shrubs thou in just time didst aw.[18]

Such instances are interesting primarily for their ironies, for the
way in which they jump from hand to hand, and from one ideological
side to the other. They may also be indicators (although this would
be impossible to prove statistically) of certain shifts and developments

in the national political vocabulary. But what they point to are rather habits of mind and the consequences of a certain type of education than any profound rethinking of the fable and its political uses. For this we need to turn to John Ogilby and his *Fables of Aesop Paraphras'd in Verse*, first published in 1651 with illustrations by Francis Cleyn. Ogilby's interpretations of Aesop stand at the midpoint of both the century and the revolution, and they significantly altered the status of the fable in English political thought for the second half of the century. We need to read them carefully to understand why this was so.

In Mary Pritchard's study of the political fable, Ogilby is given ample credit for his pioneering approach to the fable, his large-scale conversion of it into a medium of historical representation for his own time. She makes the point that this system was signaled to the seventeenth-century reader by "politically charged" language, unmistakably referring to specific persons and events:

> There are, for example, several references to covenants and covenanters (Fables 3, 8, 42) and one to the "Solemn League and Cov'nant" (32). Civil war is likewise mentioned in four fables (6, 21, 40, 72) along with a multitude of references to various kinds of rebellion. Cromwell's cavalry regiment, Ironsides, is alluded to in Fables 8 and 27, while the term "malignants," a common epithet used by the Parliamentarians to describe the Royalists, occurs in Fables 13, 17, 22, 39, 40 and 71 as both adjective and noun. Two fables, 29 and 72, mention sequestration, and four, commonweal or commonwealth (32, 47, 75 and 77). Reference is made to two issues with which Cromwell was particularly concerned during his Parliamentary career: the draining of the fens (15) and the Root and Branch bill (40, 42 and 67).[19]

This careful analysis is useful confirmation that Ogilby's *Aesop* is indeed as topical as it feels. Nor would one wish to quarrel with Pritchard's larger conclusion, that the theme of the volume as a whole is a principle of order and hierarchy, which war and rebellion subvert. But in order to substantiate a claim that Ogilby significantly altered the *status* of the fable, we need to go further than this; and one can hardly do better than begin where the seventeenth-century reader began, with the commendatory poem by William Davenant that preceded the 1651 edition. It was certainly part of the effect intended that Davenant addressed himself to the reader "From the Tower Sep. 30. 1651," underlining the condition of many Royalists after the battle of Worcester that very month. His poem on Ogilby's paraphrases is an elegant play on ideas of imprisonment, updating the tradition of the fable as the political language of slaves and connecting both an-

cient and recent styles of bondage to the freedom with which Ogilby
has treated his material. Davenant begins by praising Aesop for having rescued from Egyptian priests the ancient system of hieroglyphs,
by which animal symbolism conveyed knowledge of the divine, and
for having restored it to "the Laitie," a challenging application of
Reformation imagery to one who clearly opposed the current "re-
formers." He then proceeds to praise Ogilby for having performed a
comparable act of rescue for Aesop:

> Blest be our Poet too! whose fire hath made
> Grave AEsop warme in Death's detested shade.
> Though Verses are but Fetters deem'd by those
> Who endlesse journys make in wandring Prose,
> Yet in thy Verse, methinks, I AEsop see
> Less bound than when his Master made him free:
> So well thou fit'st the measure of his mind,
> Which, though the Slave, his body, were confind,
> Seem'd, as thy wit, still unconstraind and young. (A5v)

And he concludes with a classic defense of poetry as moral suasion,
an argument already associated with anti-Puritan ideology but here
expressed in a language with strong political undertones:

> Laws doe in vain with force our wils invade;
> Since you can Conquer when you but Perswade. (A6r)

What Davenant's poem suggested, everything that we know about
Ogilby's career confirms, from his early service in Wentworth's household in Ireland, through his lost Royalist epic, the *Carolies*, to his
remarkable prestige and privileges at the Restoration.[20] This was to
be a Royalist collection of fables, speaking to a social and cultural elite
of their own urgent concerns; and to that end the classical fable was
to be "paraphrased"; that is, renovated. The old and familiar was to
be reinscribed in the contemporary (which was familiar in a different
way). The element of surprise that the reader was therefore to experience prohibited stock responses and required considerable interpretive work; whereas the *tone* of Ogilby's fables, in its mixture of
comic form and tragic insight, was often genuinely profound. As time
went on Ogilby himself acquired an even higher sense of his own
achievement. In 1665, he brought out the *Fables* in a handsome new
folio edition, using the more prestigious printer Thomas Roycroft,
and replacing the eighty-one etchings by Francis Cleyn with larger
illustrations by Wenceslaus Hollar. And in the 1670 preface to his

Africa he spoke of Aesop as "the most Antient and Wisest of the Grecian Sages," "the Prince of Mythologists," claiming in his paraphrases to have raised his "voice to such a height, that [he] took [his] degree amongst the Minor Poets" (C1v).

Several of the *Fables of Aesop Paraphras'd* also connect to earlier moments in the story of literature's debt to politics. For instance, in Ogilby's version of the fable of the body, applied by Milton in reforming high spirits to the parliamentary attack on episcopacy, there is a similar application to the dealings of the Long Parliament, a similar pun on "Members," a similar assumption that the head of the body is (or was) the king. Yet in Ogilby's *Of the Rebellion of the Hands and Feet* (Fable 47) the decapitated head lies, in the striking illustration, at the feet of the militant but doomed body, while the language of the fable's opening is uncompromisingly Royalist:

> Reason, once King in Man, Depos'd, and dead,
> The Purple Isle was rul'd without a head:
> The Stomach a devouring State swaid all,
> At which the Hands did burn, the Feet did gaule;
> Swift to shed blood, and prone to Civill stirs,
> These Members were, who now turn Levellers.

When the hands and feet (the revolutionary activists) grumble at the body's indolence and refuse to supply it with food, the reconciliation promised in the classical version of the fable is not available; all must starve:

> . . . pale Death her cold approaches made,
> When to the dying Feet the weak Hands said;
> Brethren in evill, since we did deny
> The Bellie food, we must together die.
> All that are Members in a Common-wealth,
> Should more than Private, aim at Publick Health:
> The Rich the Poor, and Poor the Rich must aide:
> None can protect themselves with their own shade.
>
> . . . .
> But the chief cause did our destruction bring,
> Was, we Rebell'd gainst Reason our true King.

This may seem only by accident to be a response to Milton; but there can be no doubt about the Spenserian recall in Ogilby's Fable 36, *Of the Husband-man and the Wood*, one of two in which the influence of Spenser's fable of the oak and the briar is recalled and updated. The other, Fable 62, *Of the Gourd and the Pine*, selects out the youth/

age theme from Spenser's fable for discrete treatment; but in his tale of how the misguided husbandman destroyed the wood on which his welfare depends, Ogilby apparently recognized the political character of Spenser's "February" while delivering a still more complex message. Instead of a case of rivalry between two trees, one with a long history and one an upstart, Ogilby develops the premise of an ancient forest system, "Neer a vast Comons," in which the oak is only one element:

> This wealthy grove, the Royal Cedar grac'd,
>> Whose head was fix'd among the wandring stars,
>> Above loud Meteors and the elements Wars,
> His root in th'Adamantine Center fast;
>> This all surpast
> Crown'd Libanus; about him Elmie Peers,
> Ash, Fir, and Pine, had flourish'd many years,
> By him protected both from heat and cold.
> Eternall Plants, at least ten ages old,
>> All of one mind
>> Their strength conjoyn'd,
>> And scorn'd the wind;
> Here highly honour'd stood the sacred Oke,
>> Whome Swains invoke,
> Which oracles, like that of Dodon, spoke.

Likewise, the rivalry between trees is here only one of the causes that bring the wood to destruction—the presence of "the under cops (that did complain / Their Soveraign / A Tyrant was)," as well as some "rotten-hearted Elms, and Wooden Peers," who support the husbandman's plans for chopping down some of their colleagues in order to give themselves more room. Central to the tragedy is the short-sightedness of the royal cedar, who is persuaded to give the husbandman the wood he needs for a handle to his axe, thus enabling his own destruction and that of his entire kingdom; while the husbandman himself is both villain and victim, who weeps to behold "the havock his own hands had made." What Ogilby offers, in other words, is a polytropic explanation of the causes of the civil war, in which there can be no simple apportionment of blame and for which the final moral, that kings should not put weapons into their subjects' hands, seems (as do several of his formal "morals") reductive when compared with the fable's own narrative inferences.

The tragic tone established here is continued (and darkened with pathos) in another Spenserian recall, Ogilby's version of *The Wolf and the Kid*, which Spenser had adapted to the purposes of anti-Catholic propaganda for an Elizabethan audience. Ogilby returned in his version (*Of the She-Goat and Kid*, Fable 72) to the wolf of the classical original, but the psychological details of his account, in which much is made of the goat's widowhood and her devotion to her only child, "her comfort and her care," are unmistakably derived from Spenser's "May" eclogue. They are equally unmistakably adapted to the new historical circumstances of 1651:

> A She-Goat Widowed by Civill War,
> (As many other woful Matrons are)
> Although her sequestration a small fine
>   Had taken off,
>   Had little cause to laugh,
> For when she rose, she knew not where to dine . . .

Like Spenser's, Ogilby's fable dwells on the death of the kid's father at the hands of the wolf and the mother's fears for her son, whom she must leave alone to go foraging for food. But what the wolf brings with him to the door in 1651 is not the grab-bag of religious superstition but the allure of a political loyalty that is bound to destroy its adherent. Disguising himself as "the King and Father of the Heard," the wolf addresses the kid in the language of those who attempted to drum up military support for Charles II for the abortive campaign that ended on the field at Worcester:

> I live, whom Fame reported dead, and bring
> Good tydings, never better was the King.
> The Lyon now is fourty thousand strong,
>   Enumerous swarms,
>   Both old and young, take arms,
> And he will thunder at their Gates ere long,
> Changing their tryumph to a dolefull Song.
>   And now the Conquering Boar,
>   Of those subdu'd before,
>   Doth speedie aid implore,
> But the dissenting Brethren in one Fate,
>   Too late,
> Shall rue they turn'd this Forrest to a State.

The result, for the kid, is a situation in which all of the most sacred values of his culture are invoked to lure him to his doom: "Whom Pan, his Parents, and his King obey'd, / Duty, Belief, and Piety betraid." Likewise, the situation for the Royalists after Worcester was one in which what once would have seemed a complete betrayal of their cause (taking the Engagement) might actually have become a sounder loyalty. As even Charles II and his senior advisers agreed, the task during the 1650s was to maintain solidarity for the king's cause *without* provoking the revolutionary government to further action against Royalists or their estates.[21]

At such a moment the fable of *The Oke and the Reed* (67) acquired for Ogilby a meaning quite different from that discovered in it by James Howell at the end of *Dodona's Grove*. It reassumed, in effect, its more conventional meaning, sharpened by the experience of those who were trying to survive the revolution with the Restoration as their ultimate goal. As Ogilby's final moral put it,

> Though strong, resist not a too potent foe;
> Madmen against a violent torrent row.
> Thou maist hereafter serve the Common-weale,
> Then yield till time shall better days repeale.

But while his own later career amply confirmed the wisdom of Ogilby's position, it was not merely a rationalization of time serving. The ancient fable of the bat in the war between the birds and the beasts (29) now becomes a way of distinguishing a loyal temporizing from actual collaboration:

> The treacherous Bat was in the battell took:
> All hate the traitors look,
>   He never must display,
>   Again his wings by day,
> But hated live in some foul dustie nook,
> Cause he his Country in distresse forsook.

And the formal moral points specifically to those who compounded with the new government in order to save their estates: "Or King or State their ruin they'l indure, / May they from Sequestration be secure."

One needs this survey of Ogilby's message to the nation in order to appreciate the tone and direction of *The Frogs desiring a King* (12), a fable at first sight utterly at odds with the Royalist position. The classical matrix of the fable was explained by Ogilby himself in the 1665 edition of his *Fables*, where a marginal comment states, "Phaedrus will have this Fable to have been made by Aesop, upon occasion of Pisistratus his seising of the Port of Athens, and taking the Supreme Power into his own hands, as Tyrant." His version opens, however, with the voices of the frogs, speaking from the position of those who

have once enjoyed a king but are now experiencing, and negatively,
a republic:

> Since good Frogpadock Jove thou didst translate,
> How have we suffer'd turn'd into a State?
> In severall interests we divided are;
> Small hope is left well grounded peace t'obtain,
>   Unlesse again
>   Thou hear our prayer
> Great King of Kings, and we for Kings declare.

It continues with considerable charm to describe the two sovereigns,
neither of whom would have suggested, in 1651, an exact political
correlative. First comes the log, with a huge splash:

> At last all calm and silent, in great State
> On silver billows he enthroned sate,
> Admir'd and reverenc'd by every Frog:
> His brow like fate without or frown or smile
>   Struck fear a while;
>   . . . .
> But when they saw he floated up and down,
> Unactive to establish his new Crown;
> Some of the greatest of them without dread
> Draw neerer to him; now both old and young
>   About him throng,
>   On's Crown they tread,
> And last, they play at Leap-Frog ore his head.
>
> Streight they proclame a fast, and all repair
> To vex Heavens King again with tedious prayer,
> This stock, this wooden Idoll to remove;
> Send them an active Prince, a Monarch stout
>   To lead them out,
>   One that did love,
> New realms to conquer, and his old improve.

The result, of course, is the appearance of the stork, a "cruell Prince
that made his Will a Law," and the condemnation of the frogs to
everlasting repentance for their folly in rejecting "a peacefull Soveraign."

The 1665 version also added a reminder of Aesop's final address
to the Athenians, with Ogilby's own translation: "To you, O Citizens,
bear this, he said, / Lest you a greater mischief do invade." Ogilby
thereby encouraged his readers to notice the difference between the

conditions in Athens in the mid-sixth century B.C. and England in
the mid-seventeenth century; the "again" inserted into the frogs' appeal suggests the endless repeatability of this scenario. And in 1665
the prophetic nature of Ogilby's retelling of the fable would have
become fully apparent, not only in light of the Restoration but also
as a result of the repeated requests made to Cromwell during his
Protectorate that he should assume the crown. Ogilby's final moral
is emphatically not a translation of Aesop's advice to the Athenians
to endure the current tyranny without complaint or resistance, but
rather a general observation of the fickleness of the nation:

> No government can th'unsetled vulgar please,
> Whom change delights think quiet a disease.
> Now Anarchie and Armies they maintain,
> And wearied, are for King and Lords again.

The moral assumes an objective distance from both Royalist and republican sentiment; but it rests nevertheless on the deformation, delicately achieved but absolute in import, of the fable's traditional reading.

It is, I suspect, one of the signs of Ogilby's influence on the rest
of his century that this fable, so strongly reanimated here, entered
the political coinage of the Restoration. In 1656, as that event drew
irresistibly nearer, John Milton responded in fury to a sermon delivered in March by the Royalist divine, Matthew Griffith, which had
featured *The Frogs desiring a King* in an argument similar to Ogilby's.
Milton's response, in *Brief Notes upon a late Sermon, Titl'd, the Fear of
God and the King*, attacked Griffith for having distorted the moral of
the fable:

> The frogs (being once a free Nation saith the fable) petitioned Jupiter
> for a King: he tumbl'd among them a log. They found it insensible: they
> petitioned then for a King that should be active: he sent them a Crane (a
> Stork saith the fable) which straight fell to pecking them up. This you
> apply to the reproof of them who desire change: wheras indeed the true
> moral shews rather the folly of those, who being free seek a King; which
> for the most part either as a log lies heavie on his Subjects, without doing
> ought worthie of his dignitie and the charge to maintaine him, or as a
> Stork is ever pecking them up and devouring them.[22]

When the Stuarts were reinstalled, this republican interpretation remained available. Two of Marvell's verse satires assume its immediate
intelligibility. One of the predictions of *Nostradamus's Prophecy* remarks
of Charles II that "The Frogs shall then grow weary of their Crane /

And pray to Jove to take hime back againe"; and in *The Dialogue between the Two Horses*, itself formally related to the animal fable, one of the horses asks the other, "What is thy opinion of James Duke of York?" "The same that the Froggs had of Jupiters Stork,"[23] is the by now predictable answer. In 1674, John Freke's ballad, *The History of Inspids*, was more outspoken still, completely abandoning the fable's classical statement:

> Then, farewell, sacred Majesty,
> Let's pull all brutish tyrants down!
> Where men are born and still live free,
> There ev'ry head doth wear a crown.
> Mankind, like miserable frogs,
> Is wretched, kinged by storks or logs.[24]

Yet almost two decades later it was still possible for Sir Roger L'Estrange to reinvoke the Royalist interpretation suggested by Ogilby while at the same time giving it a tendentiousness that Ogilby had scrupulously avoided:

> This Allusion of the Frogs runs upon All Four . . . in the Resemblance of the Multitude, both for the Humour, the Murmur, the Importunity, and the subject-Matter of the Petition. Redress of Grievances is the Question, and the Devil of it is, that the Petitioners are never to be pleas'd. . . . They Beg and Wrangle and Appeal, and their Answer is at last, that if they shift again, they shall be still Worse; By which, the Frogs are given to Understand the very truth of the Matter, as we find it in the World, both in the Nature, and Reason of the Thing, and in Policy, and Religion; which is, that *Kings are from God*, and that it is a Sin, a Folly, and Madness, to struggle with his Appointments. (Pp. 20–21)

It was this extension of Ogilby into pure Filmerism that Croxall still thought worthy of reprimand, as a distortion of the fable's "true" meaning, in 1722.

Perhaps because *The Frogs desiring a King* had become so explicitly partisan, it did not appear to Dryden a useful medium for debating the political and religious issues of 1687. Yet because *The Hind and the Panther* anticipates and attempts to avert the revolution of 1688, as Milton had anticipated and attempted to avert the Restoration, Dryden does in fact allude in a single line to *The Frogs desiring a King*, as well as to the episode in 1 Samuel 8 with which Sidney had already collated it. When the doves, in their rivalry with the chickens, summon the buzzard from abroad to be their "Potentate" and one who, Dryden's fable warns, will ultimately make them his prey, the allusion to the stork (or crane) of the classical fable is not only plausible, it is authorially encouraged; for the buzzard is, among many other alarming and reprehensible characteristics, described as "A King, whom in his wrath, th'Almighty gave." Yet the warning against those who would once more disrupt the political system by displacing James II and bringing over William of Orange to restore a Protestant dynasty is, of course, only the last item in Dryden's ambitious polemical program.

It may seem superfluous to discuss once again what Dryden did with the fable medium, considering the profound and detailed accounts of this topic already provided by Earl Miner and augmented by Steven Zwicker. Miner demonstrated conclusively how Dryden combined the Aesopian fable with biblical typology and sacred zoology; and also that the two long fables-within-a-fable that constitute most of the third part of the poem each derive from Ogilby's *Fables*. That told by the panther, the story of the martin's prophecy of disaster to the swallows, their failure to heed it, and their fatal refusal to fly south before winter, is a rewriting of Ogilby's Fable 40, *The Parliament of Birds*. That told by the hind, the story of the rivalry between the pigeons ("a sort of Doves") and the "Domestick Poultry" on an estate, derives from Ogilby's Fable 20, *Of the Doves and Hawks*, in which the doves, engaged against their will in a defensive war with the kites, call in the hawks to assist them but then become the victims of their own mercenaries. Miner showed us how the essentially political premises of Ogilby's fables were adapted, by fusion with the biblical typology of dove, swallow, and cock, to Dryden's more complex subject, more complex because the politics of both church and state were involved.[25] What Zwicker added to this already intricate account of the poem was a postmodernist recognition. Dryden saw in the fable genre itself, the genre he designated a "mysterious writ," a formal correlative both to the theological position he newly espoused, that the true religion consists of mysteries "darkly writ" which require one central and infallible interpreter, and to the apparent indeterminacy with which all language is infected. In line with his argument that ambiguity was itself one of Dryden's subjects, Zwicker suggests that the extraordinary obscurity of the interpolated bird fables in part 3, and in particular the apparent confusion between William and Gilbert Burnet as alternative prototypes for the buzzard, was fully intentional, part of Dryden's chosen disguise, a way of speaking his mind without being fully held to account.[26]

Yet a study of the fable's politico-literary evolution, such as I have attempted here, may still have something to tell us about *The Hind and the Panther*. In the first place, we may fairly assume that Dryden would never have entrusted to the fable such a vital topic, matters so close to his heart as his own conversion to Catholicism, if Spenser had not initiated its use as a vehicle for the discussion of the national religion and church polity (although from the counterposition) and if Ogilby had not already given the genre a significant dignity. It is typical of Dryden, whose own rivalry with Ogilby as a translator of Virgil made him less than objective, to omit his competitor in that arena from his list of "great examples" in this one; but it is important to note the place of Spenser in that list, and therefore to quote once more the famous passage with which Dryden opened the third part of his poem:

> Much malice mingl'd with a little wit
> Perhaps may censure this mysterious writ,
> Because the Muse had peopl'd Caledon
> With Panthers, Bears, and Wolves, and Beasts
>   unknown,
> As if we were not stock'd with monsters of our own.
> Let AEsop answer, who has set to view,
> Such kinds as Greece and Phrygia never knew;
> And mother Hubbard in her homely dress
> Has sharply blam'd a British Lioness,
> That Queen, whose feast the factious rabble keep,
> Expos'd obscenely naked and a-sleep.
> Led by those great examples, may not I
> The wanted organs of their words supply?[27]

Second, these lines themselves deserve more exposition,[28] especially of the peculiar attention they direct to *Mother Hubberds Tale*, a model to which Miner's commentary gives little space. It was not, surely, just the nationalization of the fable in which Dryden was here interested but rather the particular form in which the monarch was both represented (as a lion) and criticized for her behavior. The fact that Dryden read *Mother Hubberds Tale* as criticism of Elizabeth (and corrected the lion's sex accordingly) is not without interest as a piece of Spenserian criticism in its own right; but it is more to our purpose here to recall that in Spenser's fable (the obscurity of which for later readers matches Dryden's) there were two alternative representations of the monarch, and that Dryden's fable repeats and inverts this strategy. The sleeping lion of *Mother Hubberds Tale* is matched, in *The Hind and the Panther*, by the royal "Lyon" who lurks in the background of the bestiary. Dryden presents his lion as not only awake and alert but also merciful, pacific, a creature of courage and integrity, and "injured" by the panther (1.335). Yet because of his species it is impossible to separate him absolutely from previous lions in the dynasty, specifically from Henry VIII, "A Lyon old, obscene, and furious made by lust" (1.351) who is linked by the word "obscene" to Spenser's critique of Elizabeth, and whose role in bringing about the English Reformation is the first cause in the long chain of events that has brought the nation to its current dilemma. And indeed, at the very moment that Dryden makes explicit his identification of the lion with James II,

> So when the gen'rous Lyon has in sight
> His equal match, he rouses for the fight;
> But when his foe lyes prostrate on the plain,
> He sheaths his paws, uncurls his angry mane;
>
> . . . .
>
> So James, if great with less we may compare,
> Arrests his rowling thunder-bolts in air . . . (3.267–274)

he also admits into his portrait of the monarch-as-lion some of the problems inseparable from power. The hind asserts her own innocence by stating that her sons "Pay small attendance at the Lyon's court / . . . Attendance is a bribe, and then 'tis bought" (3.239–240). Where Spenser had made his first representation of the monarch a Georgic figure, the honest husbandman whose sheep farm is ravaged by the fox and the ape, in contrast, Dryden makes his final representation of James the "Plain good Man" of the hind's own fable, a figure whose social status, as a landowner with three "lineal" estates, is higher than Spenser's husbandman but whose connection with farming and the simple life is carefully designated:

> Another Farm he had behind his House,
> Not overstock't, but barely for his use;
> Wherein his poor Domestick Poultry fed,
> And from His Pious Hands receiv'd their Bread. (3.993–996)

Freed from the traditional inference that the monarch is the greatest beast of prey of all, Dryden was therefore able to develop an image of James more in keeping with his fable's implied plea for toleration, as well as with a benign interpretation of the Declaration of Indulgence:

> He therefore makes all Birds of ev'ry Sect
> Free of his Farm, with promise to respect
> Their sev'ral Kinds alike, and equally protect. (3.1244–1246)

Although both representations were purged of the negative inferences (tragic naivete in the husbandman, reprehensible sloth in the lion) found in *Mother Hubberds Tale*, they nevertheless offered a view of the king's conduct that was, precisely because of its binary structure, ambiguous. Was the king a lion or a careful farmer, the Declaration of Indulgence an act of beneficence or an unconstitutional exertion of the prerogative? In the line of the best political fables, *The Hind and the Panther* remained discreetly evasive on this, the central political point; the very presence of its "great examples," as subtexts and counterexamples, was theoretically capable of teaching the reader another kind of lesson—that of the dependence of innovation upon tradition. As Dryden, one of whose major themes was linearity, had undoubtedly noticed, linearity in literature as in politics is seldom the shortest distance between two points but rather an amazing pattern of reprises (and surprises).

Finally, there is one postscript to be added to the subject of Dryden's choice of the fable *Of the Doves and Hawks* as the hind's final message. In 1666, a version of Aesop appeared that I have not yet mentioned, a polyglot edition brilliantly illustrated by Francis Barlow. And in connection with *Des Colombes et du Faucon leur Roy*, a fable even in its title closer to Dryden's tale of the pigeons and the buzzard than was Ogilby's, there appears a most interesting and provocative French moralization:

> Mais d'imiter les Colombes de cette Fable en elisant leur Ennemy pour leur Roy, c'est, à mon advis, une Faute insupportable, et digne de toute Reprehension. Cela soit dit seulement pour les monarchies electives; car quant à celles qui ont authorisé d'age en age le droict de succession il est absolument necessaire de n'en pas sortir, à Cause des grands Inconveniens qui s'y rencontrent, et de Zele devotieux que les peuples ont à certaines Familles; comme l'eurent anciennement les Romains aux Descendans d'Auguste . . . ; Et de nostre temps les Anglois, à la Royal Tyge de STUARTS.[29]

I cannot imagine that Dryden failed to discover this Restoration response to Aesop, with all its ironies; ironies he would have seen redoubled during the Exclusion Crisis and which now, with the shadow of the "Glorious Revolution" appearing on his horizon, he decided to face by making this fable his own.

In conclusion, then, the story of the fable in England in the seventeenth century is one that can teach us more than moral commonplaces. It helps to explain how ideology finds expression and how cultural formations appear and disappear in response to historical circumstances. As seventeenth-century writers relearned, from their own varying perspectives, the hard lessons embedded in the ancient fable between liberty and political stability, they left behind them the textual traces of that experience, which, taken in the aggregate, themselves constitute a new historical phenomenon. Indeed, in the last decade of the seventeenth century and the first years of the eighteenth, political fabling became ubiquitous, and Aesop himself took on a new fashionable identity, appearing at court and at Bath and at Tunbridge Wells. But his origins were not forgotten, as we can tell from the preface of the anonymous author of *Aesop at Tunbridge* (1698). Although in 1695 the government had failed to renew the Licensing Act, *Aesop at Tunbridge* continues in the assumption that the fable has a genetic relationship to the concept of freedom of speech:

> But should it be granted that one or two Fables are a little too old and angry, yet since there is some Foundation for such sort of Mutterings and Complaints, from whence can our Rulers learn these Truths more inoffensively, than from such little Stories? They will not, perhaps, attend so easily to wise and good Men as they will to Foxes and Asses; and wise and good Men will not, it may be, dare to tell those Truths these Beasts deliver, which yet our Government should know.

Notes

1. INTRODUCTION

1. Professor J. G. A. Pocock opened up this subject. See Pocock, *The Ancient Constitution and the Feudal Law* (Cambridge: Cambridge University Press, 1957); idem, *Politics, Language and Time,* (New York: Athenaeum, 1972). And see Q. Skinner, "Some Problems in the Analysis of Political Thought and Action," *Political Theory,* 11 (1974): 277–303; idem, "The Principles and Practice of Opposition: The Case of Bolingbroke v. Walpole," in *Historical Perspectives,* ed. N. McKendrick (London: Europa, 1974), pp. 93–128.

2. The common culture and languages of Renaissance letters have been studied by B. Weinberg, *A History of Literary Criticism in the Italian Renaissance* (Chicago: University of Chicago Press, 1961); W. S. Howell, *Logic and Rhetoric in England, 1500–1700* (Princeton: Princeton University Press, 1956); W. J. Ong, *Ramus: Method and the Decay of Dialogue* (Cambridge, Mass.: Harvard University Press, 1958).

3. Cf. Radzinowicz, chap. 9.

4. Cf. Norbrook, chap. 5; Radzinowicz, chap. 9.

5. Pocock, chap. 2.

6. Shakespeare on the Restoration stage can be followed in Brian Vickers, *Shakespeare, The Critical Heritage, Vol. 1 1623–1692* (London: Routledge and Kegan Paul, 1974), and in C. Spencer, *Five Restoration Adaptations of Shakespeare* (Urbana, Ill.: University of Illinois Press, 1965). All known productions of Shakespeare in the Restoration are listed in W. Van Lennep, ed., *The London Stage, 1660–1800, Pt. 1, 1660–1700* (Carbondale: Southern Illinois University Press, 1965).

7. For examples of the study of such words and their changes in meaning over time, see H. T. Dickinson, *Liberty and Property* (New York: Holmes and Meier, 1977); W. H. Greenleaf, *Order, Empiricism and Politics* (London: Oxford University Press, 1964); J. A. W. Gunn, *Politics and the Public Interest in the Seventeenth Century* (London: Routledge and Kegan Paul, 1969); idem, *Beyond Liberty and Property* (Montreal: McGill/Queens University Press, 1985); J. Gough, *Fundamental Law in English Constitutional History* (Oxford: Oxford University Press, 1955). Professor J. H. Hexter has recently advocated the need for a study of the idea of liberty in the Atlantic world; see "Power Struggle,

Parliament and Liberty in Early Stuart England," *J. Mod. Hist.* 50 (1978): esp. 46–50.

8. McKeon, chap. 3.

9. S.v. *Oxford English Dictionary* [*OED*] "Culture."

10. C. Robbins, *The Eighteenth-Century Commonwealthman* (Cambridge, Mass.: Harvard University Press, 1959); Robbins, ed., *Two English Republican Tracts* (Cambridge: Cambridge University Press, 1969).

11. S.v. *OED* "Commonwealthsman."

12. McKeon, chap. 3; Zwicker, chap. 10.

13. S.v. *OED* "Politic: political affairs or business."

14. Below, p. 230.

15. For a perceptive discussion of the coexistence of the old unitary language of country with the nomenclature of party, see D. Hayton, "The 'Country' Interest and Party System, 1689–c. 1720," in *Party and Management in Parliament, 1660–1784*, ed. C. Jones (Leicester: Leicester University Press, 1984).

16. W. A. Speck, *Tory and Whig* (London: Macmillan, 1971).

17. R. J. Allen, *The Clubs of Augustan London* (Cambridge, Mass: Harvard University Press, 1933); J. R. Jones, "The Green Ribbon Club," *Durham Univ. Journ.*, XLIX (1956): 17–20.

18. P. Zagorin, "The Court and the Country: A Note on Political Terminology in the Earlier 17th Century," *EHR*, 77 (1962): 306–311; idem, *The Court and the Country* (London: Routledge and Kegan Paul, 1969).

19. J. G. A. Pocock, "The Commons Debates of 1628," *J. Hist. Ideas*, 39 (1978): 329–334.

20. S.v. *OED* "Party."

21. K. Sharpe, *Sir Robert Cotton: History and Politics in Early Modern England* (Oxford: Oxford University Press, 1979), chap. I.

22. A. Barton, *Ben Jonson, Dramatist* (Cambridge: Cambridge University Press, 1984), chap. VIII.

23. In their emphasis upon the godly politics of the Puritans, historians have paid too little attention to the Royalists' conviction that they fought God's as well as the king's war. See Radzinowicz, chap. 9.

24. Below, pp. 261–264.

25. See H. H. Erskine-Hill, *The Augustan Idea in English Literature* (London: Edward Arnold, 1983).

26. Z. S. Fink, *The Classical Republicans* (Evanston, Ill.: Northwestern University Press, 1945); B. Worden, "Classical Republicanism and the Puritan Revolution," in *History and Imagination*, ed. H. Lloyd-Jones, V. Pearl, and B. Worden (London: Duckworth, 1981), pp. 182–200.

27. J. P. Kenyon, *Revolution Principles* (Cambridge: Cambridge University Press, 1977); J. G. A. Pocock, *The Machiavellian Moment: Florentine Political Thought and the Atlantic Republican Tradition* (Princeton: Princeton University Press, 1975), chap. XIII.

28. F. Raab, *The English Face of Machiavelli* (London: Routledge and Kegan Paul, 1964).

29. See McKeon, chap. 3.

30. See J. Goldberg, *James I and the Politics of Literature* (Baltimore: Johns Hopkins University Press, 1982), E. Miner, *The Cavalier Mode from Jonson to Cotton* (Princeton: Princeton University Press, 1971), and K. Sharpe, *Criticism and Compliment: The Politics of Literature in the England of Charles I* (Cambridge: Cambridge University Press, forthcoming).

31. On the rise of the literary career, see R. Pinkus, *Grub St. Stripped Bare* (Hamden, Conn.: Archon, 1968); Pat Rogers, *Grub Street* (London: Methuen, 1972).

32. S.v. *OED*, "Literature: literary work or production."

33. McKeon, chap. 3; Ian Watt, *The Rise of The Novel* (Berkeley and Los Angeles: University of California Press, 1957).

34. But see Worden, chap. 7.

35. See R. Colie, *The Resources of Kind: Genre Theory in the Renaissance* (Berkeley, Los Angeles, London: University of California Press, 1973); A. Fowler, *Kinds of Literature: An Introduction to the Theory of Genres and Modes* (Cambridge, Mass.: Harvard University Press, 1982).

36. B. K. Lewalski, *Protestant Poetics and the Seventeenth Century Religious Lyric* (Princeton: Princeton University Press, 1979), chap. 2.

37. H. T. Swedenberg, Jr., *The Theory of the Epic in England, 1650–1800* (Berkeley and Los Angeles: University of California Press, 1944); J. E. Spingarn, *A History of Literary Criticism in the Renaissance* (2nd edition New York: Columbia University Press, 1938).

38. Patterson, chap. 11.

39. See G. R. Hibbard, "The Country House Poem of the Seventeenth Century," *J. Warburg & Courtauld Inst.*, 19 (1956): 159–174; W. McClung, *The Country House in English Renaissance Poetry* (Berkeley, Los Angeles, London: University of California Press, 1977); James Turner, *The Politics of Landscape* (Cambridge, Mass.: Harvard University Press, 1979).

40. A. Patterson, *Marvell and the Civic Crown* (Princeton: Princeton University Press, 1978), pp. 113–166.

41. L. S. Marcus, "Masquing Occasions and Masque Structures," *Research Opportunities in Renaissance Drama*, XXIV (1981): 7–16; Sharpe, *Criticism and Compliment*, chap. 5.

42. For a splendid example of the Whigs' attempt to claim texts for their cause, see A. B. Worden, ed., *Edmund Ludlow. A Voyce from the Watch Tower* (London: Camden Soc. 21, 1978), esp. the introduction.

43. See the valuable collection of essays in G. F. Lytle and S. Orgel, eds., *Patronage in the Renaissance* (Princeton: Princeton University Press, 1981).

44. Lewalski, chap. 4.

45. S. J. Greenblatt, *Renaissance Self-Fashioning* (Chicago: University of Chicago Press, 1980).

46. In the study of patronage scholars have too often emphasized the dependence of artist on patron, rather than the interdependence and even equality of the relationship and the author's reinforcement through patronage of his own independent views.

47. S. Orgel, *The Illusion of Power* (Berkeley, Los Angeles, London: University of California Press, 1975); S. Orgel and R. Strong, eds., *Inigo Jones:*

The Theatre of the Stuart Court, 2 vols. (Berkeley, Los Angeles, London: University of California Press, 1973) I: chap. IV.

48. The same argument might well be extended to the work of Thomas Hobbes in exile in Paris and Clarendon after his impeachment and flight to France. We hope to develop in a separate study the politics of exile in Civil War and Restoration texts.

49. S. N. Zwicker, Politics and Language in Dryden's Poetry: The Arts of Disguise (Princeton: Princeton University Press, 1984), chap. I.

50. See D. Norbrook, Poetry and Politics in the English Renaissance (London: Routledge and Kegan Paul, 1984), pp. 109–110, 117, 158–159.

51. S. Orgel, The Jonsonian Masque (Cambridge, Mass.: Harvard University Press, 1965), chaps. 4, 5.

52. See Worden, chap. 7.

53. For an incisive comment on this problem, see Annabel Patterson, Censorship and Interpretation (Madison: University of Wisconsin Press, 1984).

54. Earl Miner reminds us that the borders between fiction and fact are themselves culturally determined: see chap. 8. Since this essay was written Professor Lauro Martines has published a manual for the historical reading of poetry, Society and History in English Renaissance Verse (Oxford: Basil Blackwell, 1985).

55. Worden, chap. 7.

56. On the "Protestant tradition" in English Renaissance literature, see J. N. King, English Reformation Literature (Princeton: Princeton University Press, 1982); Norbrook, Poetry and Politics; and Barbara K. Lewalski, Protestant Poetics and the Seventeenth-Century Religious Lyric (Princeton: Princeton University Press, 1979).

57. See F. Yates, "Queen Elizabeth as Astraea," J. Warburg & Courtauld Inst., X (1947): 27–87, reprinted in idem, Astraea: The Imperial Theme in the Sixteenth Century (London: Routledge and Kegan Paul, 1975), pp. 29–87. Cf. R. Strong, Portraits of Queen Elizabeth (Oxford: Clarendon Press, 1963); idem, The English Icon (London: Routledge and Kegan Paul, 1969); idem, Art and Power (Woodbridge, Suffolk: D. S. Brewer, 1984). Also see D. Bergeron, English Civic Pageantry, 1558–1642 (London: Edward Arnold, 1971); J. Wilson, Entertainments for Elizabeth I (Woodbridge, Suffolk: D. S. Brewer, 1980). Recently the "new historicist" critics have investigated the relations between culture and power in Elizabethan England. See S. Greenblatt, ed., "The Forms of Power and the Power of Forms in the Renaissance," Genre, XV (1982); L. A. Montrose, " 'Eliza, Queene of Shepheardes' and the Pastoral of Power," Eng. Lit. Renaissance, 10 (1980): 153–182; idem, "A Poetics of Renaissance Culture," Criticism, 23 (1981): 349–359.

58. See F. F. Madan, An New Bibliography of the Eikon Basilike of King Charles I (Oxford: Oxford University Press, 1950); Kenyon, Revolution Principles, chap. 5.

59. On the reception of Paradise Lost, see W. R. Parker, Milton, A Biography, 2 vols. (Oxford: Oxford University Press, 1968), I: 602–603; on the Tonson edition, see K. Lynch, Jacob Tonson, Kit-Cat Publisher (Knoxville: University of Tennessee Press, 1952), pp. 126–129.

60. Pocock, "Time, History and Eschatology in the Thought of Thomas Hobbes," in *Politics, Language and Time*, pp. 148–201.

61. On the millenarianism of *The First Anniversary*, see J. Wallace, *Destiny His Choice: The Loyalism of Andrew Marvell* (Cambridge: Cambridge University Press, 1968), pp. 118–122; S. N. Zwicker, "Models of Governance in *The First Anniversary*," *Criticism*, 16 (1974): 1–12; and D. Hirst, "Marvell's Cromwell in 1654," in *The Golden and the Brazen World*, ed. J. Wallace (Berkeley, Los Angeles, London: University of California Press, 1985), pp. 17–53.

62. Radzinowicz, chap. 9.

63. Below, p. 132.

64. Norbrook, chap. 5.

65. For a recent study, see R. S. Peterson, *Imitation and Praise in the Poems of Ben Jonson* (New Haven: Yale University Press, 1981).

66. Pocock, *The Machiavellian Moment*.

2. TEXTS AS EVENTS

1. Quentin Skinner, *The Foundations of Modern Political Thought*, 2 vols. (Cambridge: Cambridge University Press, 1978), 1: x–xiv.

2. Ibid., xiii.

3. A list of his critical and methodological writings may be found in the bibliography appended to ibid.

4. J. G. A. Pocock, *The Ancient Constitution and the Feudal Law: English Historical Thought in the Seventeenth Century* (Cambridge: Cambridge University Press, 1957; New York: W. W. Norton, 1967; reprinted with retrospective material added, Cambridge University Press, 1987).

5. J. G. A. Pocock, "Time, History and Eschatology in the Thought of Thomas Hobbes," in *Politics, Language and Time* (New York: Atheneum, 1971), chap. 5.

6. James H. Tully, *A Discourse on Property: John Locke and His Adversaries* (Cambridge: Cambridge University Press, 1980).

7. J. G. A. Pocock, "Burke and the Ancient Constitution: A Problem in the History of Ideas," in *Politics, Language and Time*, chap. 6; "The Political Economy of Burke's Analysis of the French Revolution," in *Virtue, Commerce and History: Essays in Political Thought and History, chiefly in the Eighteenth Century* (Cambridge: Cambridge University Press, 1985), chap. 10.

8. J. G. A. Pocock, *The Machiavellian Moment: Florentine Political Thought and the Atlantic Republican Tradition* (Princeton: Princeton University Press, 1975).

9. David Hollinger, "Historians and the Discourse of Intellectuals," in John Higham and Paul Conkin, eds., *New Directions in American Intellectual History* (Baltimore: Johns Hopkins University Press, 1979).

10. See, provisionally, J. G. A. Pocock, "The History of British Political Thought: The Creation of a Center," *J. Brit. Studies*, XXIV, 3 (July 1985): 283–310.

11. Leo Strauss, *Thoughts on Machiavelli* (Chicago: University of Chicago

Press, 1978); Harvey C. Mansfield, *Machiavelli's New Modes and Orders* (Ithaca, N. Y.: Cornell University Press, 1979).

12. Pocock, *Politics, Language and Time,* chap. 7.

3. POLITICS OF DISCOURSES AND THE RISE OF THE AESTHETIC IN SEVENTEENTH-CENTURY ENGLAND

1. *The New Organon* (1620), I: lxv, cxxiv, in *The Works of Francis Bacon,* ed. James Spedding, Robert L. Ellis, and Douglas D. Heath (London: Longmans, 1870), IV: 66, 110.

2. *Areopagitica* (1644), in *Complete Prose Works of John Milton,* II, ed. Ernest Sirluck (New Haven: Yale University Press, 1964), p. 550.

3. *A Modest Plea for an Equal Common-wealth Against Monarchy . . .* (1659), p. 81 (place of publication of seventeenth-century works is London unless otherwise noted).

4. *The True Picture of a Modern Whig . . .* (1701), p. 34. The charge was developed more fully by Bolingbroke. For example, see *Craftsman,* no. 59, 19 August 1727; *A Dissertation upon Parties* (1735).

5. *Interest Mistaken, or the Holy Cheat . . .* (1661), pp. 6–7.

6. *A Discourse of Toleration . . .* (1668), p. 26.

7. *The Late Apology In behalf of the Papists Re-printed And Answered, In behalf of the Royallists* (1667), p. 40. The author of the *Apology* is Roger Palmer, Earl of Castlemaine.

8. "R.T.," *A Discourse concerning Liberty of Conscience. . . .* (1661), pp. 16, 19–20.

9. See W. K. Jordan, *The Development of Religious Toleration in England* (London: Allen & Unwin, 1940), IV: 9, 343.

10. *A Discourse of the Forbearance or the Penalties Which a Due Reformation Requires* (1670), p. 165.

11. For example, see Russell Fraser, *The War Against Poetry* (Princeton: Princeton University Press, 1970), chap. 7 and passim; Margot Heinemann, *Puritanism and Theatre: Thomas Middleton and Opposition Drama under the Early Stuarts* (Cambridge: Cambridge University Press, 1980), chap. 2.

12. For attempts to enunciate a "Protestant poetics" that would establish the utility of rhetorical figures to mediate sacred truth, see Annabel Patterson, "*Bermudas* and *The Coronet:* Marvell's Protestant Poetics," *ELH,* 44, 3 (Fall 1977): 478–499; and Barbara K. Lewalski, *Protestant Poetics and the Seventeenth-Century Religious Lyric* (Princeton: Princeton University Press, 1979), chap. 7. For a fuller account of the "problem of mediation," see my "Pastoralism, Puritanism, Imperialism, Scientism: Andrew Marvell and the Problem of Mediation," *Yrbk. Eng. Studies,* 13 (1983): 46–65.

13. William Whitaker, *Disputatio Sacra Scriptura* (Cambridge, 1588), quoted in Lewalski, *Protestant Poetics,* pp. 120–121.

14. William Perkins, *A Commentarie or Exposition upon the Five First Chapters of the Epistle to the Galatians* (Cambridge, 1604), p. 346, quoted in Lewalski, *Protestant Poetics,* p. 121.

15. Critics have observed a more general tendency in Dryden's figures for the determinant relationship between signifier and signified to be weakened or even reversed. For example, see Earl Miner, "Some Characteristics of Dryden's Use of Metaphor," in *Dryden: A Collection of Critical Essays*, ed. Bernard N. Schilling (Englewood Cliffs, N.J.: Prentice-Hall, 1963), pp. 115–124. On the later history of typology, see Steven N. Zwicker, "Politics and Panegyric: The Figural Mode from Marvell to Pope," in *Literary Uses of Typology from the Late Middle Ages to the Present*, ed. Earl Miner (Princeton: Princeton University Press, 1977), pp. 115–146; Paul J. Korshin, *Typologies in England, 1650–1820* (Princeton: Princeton University Press, 1982).

16. *The First Anniversarie* (1611), lines 278–282.

17. Sermon preached at St. Paul's, Easter Day 1624, in *The Sermons of John Donne*, ed. Evelyn M. Simpson and George R. Potter (Berkeley and Los Angeles: University of California Press, 1953), VI: 62.

18. For a reading of Herbert's poetry that is particularly sensitive to his manipulation of material and historical "story," see Barbara L. Harman, *Costly Monuments: Representations of the Self in George Herbert's Poetry* (Cambridge, Mass.: Harvard University Press, 1982).

19. *The Pilgrim's Progress*, Part I (1678), "The Conclusion."

20. *Fire in the Bush . . .* (1650), in *Winstanley: The Law of Freedom and Other Writings*, ed. Christopher Hill (Harmondsworth: Penguin, 1973), pp. 214, 216–217, 224, 231, 233–234, 264.

21. *A Door of Hope: or, A Call and Declaration for the gathering together of the first ripe Fruits unto the Standard of our Lord, King Jesus* (1661), pp. 4–5.

22. See *Censorship and Interpretation: The Conditions of Writing and Reading in Early Modern England* (Madison: University of Wisconsin Press, 1984), pp. 4, 10–11, 17–18, 197–198, and passim.

23. See *Poetics* 1451[a–b], 1460[b]. The text of the *Poetics* became available in Latin and Greek in 1498 and 1508, respectively.

24. The range of experimentation is very broad. See Bernard Weinberg, *A History of Literary Criticism in the Italian Renaissance* (Chicago: University of Chicago Press, 1961), chaps. 1 and 2 and pp. 516, 521, 542–543, 574–575, 639–640, 673, 709–710, 792; on the Renaissance interpretation of the *Poetics* see generally chaps. 9–14. On Sidney, see J. A. Van Dorsten, ed., *A Defence of Poetry* (1595) (London: Oxford University Press, 1966), pp. 35–38, 52–53. Sidney refutes the Platonic charge of falsehood but affirms Horatian pedagogic criteria.

25. *The Works of John Dryden* (Berkeley, Los Angeles, London: University of California Press, 1966, 1956, 1972), ed., respectively, John Loftis and Vinton A. Dearing; Edward N. Hooker, H. T. Swedenberg, Jr., and Dearing; and Swedenberg and Dearing, IX: 25, I: 50, II: 4. Despite appearances, Dryden's "Account" of *Annus Mirabilis* alludes here not to Aristotle but to the *Satyricon* of Petronius. See ibid., I: 270.

26. See my *Politics and Poetry in Restoration England: The Case of Dryden's Annus Mirabilis* (Cambridge, Mass.: Harvard University Press, 1975), introduction.

27. *Poetics* 1447[b], trans. Ingram Bywater, in *Introduction to Aristotle*, 2d ed.,

ed. Richard McKeon (Chicago: University of Chicago Press, 1973), p. 671. See also 1451[a–b] (pp. 681–682).

28. Compare Lionardo Salviati, *Risposta all' Apologia di Torquato Tasso* (1585), p. 15: "Imitation is the genus of poetry, narration that of history. The former has the verisimilar for its subject, the latter the truth. The first is made in verse, the second by its nature in prose" (trans. by and quoted in Weinberg, *History of Literary Criticism*, p. 1017). Some critics, using the example of Boccaccio, made ambivalent attempts to assimilate the prose novella to the category "poetry." See ibid., pp. 538–541, 751. The problem arises also in the case of comedy, where prose is becoming increasingly common. See ibid., pp. 552–554, 617, 706–708. For other denials of the status of "poetry" to prose works see ibid., pp. 443, 448, 463, 510, 514, 554, 586, 608, 637, 710, 736, 758, 944. Sidney is unusual in refusing to make verse a condition of poetry: See *A Defence of Poetry*, pp. 27–28, 50.

29. Printed at the end of *The Annals of Love, Containing Select Histories of the Amours of divers Princes Courts, Pleasantly Related* (1672), sigs. Dd7[v]–Ee4[v].

30. *A Catalogve of The most vendible Books in England . . .* (1657).

31. E.g., see *The Famous and Delectable History of Don Bellianis of Greece . . .* (1673), "To the Reader," sigs. A2[r–v]; *The History of Prince Erastus . . .* (1674), sigs. A2[r]–A3[v].

32. For example, see [Madeleine de Scudéry], *Ibrahim. Or the Illustrious Bassa . . .*, trans. Henry Cogan (1652), "The Preface," sigs. A3[v]–A4[r]; *Artamenes, or The Grand Cyrus . . .*, trans. F. G. (1653), "To the Reader," sig. A4[r]. Compare Roger Boyle, Lord Broghill, *Parthenissa, A Romance . . .* (1655), "The Preface," sig. B1[v], in *Prefaces to Four Seventeenth-Century Romances*, ed. Charles Davies, *Augustan Reprint Society* (Los Angeles), no. 42 (1953); Sir George Mackenzie, *Aretina; Or, The Serious Romance . . .* (Edinburgh, 1660), "An Apologie for ROMANCES," pp. 6–7 (a conscious attempt to extend Sidney's neo-Aristotelian analysis to romance), in ibid.; [Mary de la Rivière Manley], *The Secret History of Queen Zarah, and the Zarazians . . .* ([1705] 1711), "To the Reader," sigs. A4[r–v].

33. *The Certainty of the Worlds of Spirits . . .* (1691), sigs. A3[v]–A4[r].

34. E.g., see *ENIAYTOS TERASTIOS. Mirabilis Annus, or the Year of Prodigies and Wonders . . .* (1661), "Preface," sigs. A2[r], A2[v], A4[r]; Joseph Glanvill, *Saducismus Triumphatus: Or, Full and Plain Evidence Concerning Witches and Apparitions . . .* (1681), sig. Aa2[v], p. 117; Moses Pitt, *An Account of one Ann Jefferies, Now Living in the County of Cornwall . . .* (1696), pp. 5–6, in *Seventeenth-Century Tales of the Supernatural*, ed. Isabel M. Westcott, *Augustan Reprint Society*, no. 74 (1958); William Turner, *A Compleat History Of the Most Remarkable Providences . . .* (1697), sig. b1[v].

35. See the observations of Jacob Viner, *The Role of Providence in the Social Order*, Jayne Lectures for 1966 (Philadelphia: American Philosophical Society, 1972), p. 8.

36. Aubrey L. Williams, *An Approach to Congreve* (New Haven: Yale University Press, 1979), p. 40.

37. See Keith Thomas, *Religion and the Decline of Magic: Studies in Popular*

Beliefs in Sixteenth- and Seventeenth-Century England (Harmondsworth: Penguin, 1973), pp. 90–132, 765.

38. Hugh de Quehen, ed., *Prose Observations* (Oxford: Oxford University Press, 1979), pp. 71–72.

39. *Miraculum basilicon: or the Royal Miracle* . . . (1664), sig. B4ᵛ.

40. See D. P. Walker, *The Decline of Hell: Seventeenth-Century Discussions of Eternal Torment* (Chicago: University of Chicago Press, 1964), pp. 4–5, 69.

41. "Postscript" to *Clarissa* (4th ed., 1751), VII: 350–351.

42. *Of the Dignity and Advancement of Learning* (1623), II: xiii, in *Works*, IV: 316.

43. *The Tragedies of the last Age consider'd* . . . (1677), in *The Critical Works of Thomas Rymer*, ed. Curt A. Zimansky (New Haven: Yale University Press, 1956), p. 27.

44. Sidney, *A Defence of Poetry*, p. 37.

45. On "history-likeness" see Hans W. Frei, *The Eclipse of Biblical Narrative: A Study in Eighteenth and Nineteenth Century Hermeneutics* (New Haven: Yale University Press, 1974), pp. 11–14.

46. The rise of the aesthetic and of aesthetic value can be seen as analogous to and coextensive with the rise of capitalist ideology and exchange value. For an attempt to describe the theoretical nature of this analogy with general reference to the culture of the Greek Enlightenment, see my "The Origins of Aesthetic Value," *Telos*, no. 57 (Fall 1983): 63–82.

47. *The King's Two Bodies: A Study in Mediaeval Political Theology* (Princeton: Princeton University Press, 1957), p. 235.

48. See Eliot, "The Metaphysical Poets" (1921), in *Selected Essays: 1917–1932* (New York: Harcourt, Brace, 1932), pp. 247–248; Kermode, "Dissociation of Sensibility" (1957), in *Essential Articles for the Study of John Donne's Poetry*, ed. John R. Roberts (Hamden, Conn.: Archon, 1975), p. 73.

49. See "Cowley," in *Lives of the English Poets* (1779), ed. G. Birkbeck Hill (Oxford: Clarendon Press, 1905), I: 20.

4. LUCY, COUNTESS OF BEDFORD: IMAGES OF A JACOBEAN COURTIER AND PATRONESS

1. See Franklin B. Williams, Jr., *Index of Dedications and Commendatory Verses in English Books Before 1641* (London: Bibliographical Society, 1962). Excluding royal ladies, the entry for the Countess of Bedford is matched only by that for the Countess of Pembroke.

2. The State Papers Domestic, (PRO SP), especially the letters of Sir John Chamberlain to Sir Dudley Carleton, ambassador to Venice and then to The Hague, provide some indication of her activities, role at court, and influence during the years 1603–1625. My references are to volume and item from the reign of James I.

3. The familiar story is reviewed and supplemented from family records

in Margaret M. Byard, "The Trade of Courtiership: The Countess of Bedford and the Bedford Memorials; A Family History from 1585 to 1607," *Hist. Today* (January 1979): 20–28. The earl's statement disclaiming any treasonous activity is in BL, Add. MS 4160 [Birch MSS], art. 70. Lady Bedford and her father were active in pleading his case: see Lord Harington's letter to Robert Cecil (Hatfield House, Cecil MS 180/37, 11 March 1600–01).

4. Stephen Greenblatt, *Renaissance Self-Fashioning* (Chicago: University of Chicago Press, 1980).

5. Byard, "The Trade of Courtiership," p. 26. The contributions of several friends and relatives (including Lord Harington) and Lady Bedford's sale of part of her jointure (£2000) enabled him to pay almost £7000. James I forgave him the remaining £3000 shortly after his accession. The growing impoverishment of the aristocracy in these years is documented by Lawrence Stone, *The Crisis of the Aristocracy, 1558–1641* (Oxford: Oxford University Press, 1965).

6. See J. H. Wiffen, *Historical Memoirs of the House of Russell,* 2 vols. (London, 1833), pp. 66–68, 102–103; Carola Oman, *Elizabeth of Bohemia* (London: Hodder and Staughton, 1938), pp. 93–96, 152–153.

7. R. C. Bald, *John Donne: A Life* (Oxford: Clarendon Press, 1970), pp. 172–179. For the Goodyere relationship, see Lady Bedford's letter to Cecil, June 1605, Hatfield House, Cecil MS 111/96. See also Arthur Gorges, trans., *Lucan's Pharsalia* (London, 1614), epis. ded. For discussion of her relations with John Burges, see Patricia Thomson, "John Donne and the Countess of Bedford," *MLR* 44 (1949): 329–340.

8. Donne's correspondence mentions various visits to Twickenham. See *Letters to Severall Persons of Honour* (London, 1651), pp. 53–54, 117, 139, 143. Michael Drayton was no longer a client during the Twickenham years.

9. PRO SP (James I) 74/49, 1 August 1613, John Chamberlain to Dudley Carleton; PRO SP (James I) 109/80, 109/89, 8, 12 June 1619, Sir Edward Harwood to Carleton; PRO SP (James I) 109/133, 15 July 1619, Chamberlain to Carleton.

10. *Works of Sir William Temple,* 2 vols. (London, 1720), 1: 170.

11. The *Bedford Memorials* record that a son, John Russell, was born to her on 19 January 1602, but died a month later and was buried at Chenies on 19 February 1602 (Byard, "The Trade of Courtiership," p. 26). Robert Sidney wrote to his wife on 5 September 1610, of another such tragedy: "Upon Monday my Lady of Bedforde was brought to bed of a doughter, but it dyed within two howers. Shee herself is very weake and much greeved for the loss of the childe." Rowland Whyte reports the rumor of an earlier pregnancy in his letter to Sir Robert Sidney on 5 November 1595 (Kent Archives Office, Maidstone, Penshurst Papers, F. 43/182).

12. V. Sackville-West, ed., *The Diary of the Lady Ann Clifford* (London, 1923), p. 8.

13. Hatfield House, Cecil MS 114/130. In 1617, she took an active part in promoting the marriage of Lord Hay and Lady Lucy Percy, youngest daughter of the Earl of Northumberland (Chamberlayne to Carleton, 22 February 1617, PRO SP [James I] 90/79); and in 1619 between Sir John Smith and Lady Isabella

Rich (BL Add. MS 4176 [Birch MSS], T. Larkin to Sir T. Puckering, 5 January 1619)—in both cases over parental opposition.

14. PRO SP (James I) 103/111, 28 November 1618, John Pory to Carleton.

15. Oman, *Elizabeth of Bohemia*, pp. 201–203, 296–297.

16. PRO SP (James I) 140/57, 28 March 1619. The fact that the queen was rumored to be planning her visit while her brother Prince Charles was in Spain (and perhaps in some danger there) raised suspicion that she wished to be on hand should circumstances call her to the throne. See also the countess' letter urging the Queen of Bohemia to write to her brother Charles indicating what good report she has heard of him from England (to calm suspicions and enlist his support) in BL Add. MS 5503, f. 126, and her letter to Carleton to the same purpose, PRO SP (James I) 130/15, 4 May 1622.

17. *HMC*, *21*, *Suppl.*, *Hamilton MSS* (London: HM Stationary Office, 1932), p. 9.

18. For discussion of this point, see Stephen Orgel and Roy Strong, *Inigo Jones: The Theatre of the Stuart Court*, 2 vols. (Berkeley, Los Angeles, London: University of California Press, 1973), 1: 1–75.

19. See *The Complete Works in Verse and Prose of Samuel Daniel*, ed. A. B. Grosart, 5 vols. (New York: Russell and Russell, 1963), 3: 195. Carleton wrote to Chamberlain on 21 December 1603, PRO SP (James I) 5/20: "We shall have a merry Christmas at Hampton Court, for both male and female maskes are all ready bespoken, whereof the Duke [of Lenox] is *rector chori* of th'one side, and the La: Bedford of the other."

20. Edmund Gosse, *The Life and Letters of John Donne*, 2 vols. (New York: Dodd, Mead; London: William Heinemann, 1899), I: 199: "The King . . . hath left with the Queen a commandment to meditate upon a masque for Christmas, so that they grow serious about that already; that will hasten my Lady Bedford's journey." PRO SP (James I) 14, 90/79.

21. Daniel, *Works*, 3: 188, 190, 197. Andrew Sabol notes, in *Four Hundred Songs and Dances from the Stuart Masques* (Providence: Brown University Press, 1978), pp. 231, 580, that a musical score for one of the dances for this masque (BL Add. MS 10444, fols. 39r, 89v) is entitled "The Lady Lucies Masque," in reference to her role as *rector chori*.

22. Cited in C. H. Herford, Percy and Evelyn Simpson, eds., *Ben Jonson*, 11 vols. (Oxford: Clarendon Press, 1925–52), 10: 448.

23. Ibid., 7: 186–187.

24. Ibid., 7: 218.

25. Herford et al., *Ben Jonson*, 7: 230. See Roy Strong, *The Elizabethan Image* (London: Tate Gallery, 1970), p. 78. The portrait is at Woburn Abbey.

26. At the Fitzwilliam Museum, Cambridge. See Erna Auerbach, *Nicholas Hillard* (London: Routledge and Kegan Paul, 1961), pp. 247–248.

27. Orgel and Strong, *Inigo Jones*, I: 135–136. See also Herford et al., *Ben Jonson*, 7: 306.

28. Orgel and Strong, *Inigo Jones*, I: 140, fig. 16.

29. She does not appear in the cast for Daniel's masque, *Tethys' Festival*, danced by the queen and thirteen ladies on 5 June 1610. She might have been

one of the ten unnamed ladies who dance in *Love Freed from Ignorance and Folly* (3 February 1611), but her serious illness in the winter of 1611–12 makes it unlikely that she took part in *The Lord's Masque*, at the wedding of Princess Elizabeth (14 February 1613).

30. Herford et al., *Ben Jonson*, 1: 143. Jonson told Drummond of Hawthornden "that the half of his comedies were not in Print, he heth a Pastorall intitled the May Lord, his own name is Alkin Ethra the Countess of Bedfoords Mogibell overberry, the old Countess of suffolk ane inchanteress other names are given to somersets Lady, Pembrook the Countess of rutland, Lady Wroth."

31. Chamberlain wrote to Carleton on that date, PRO SP (James I) 90/79. "This night he is solemnly invited by the Lord Hay to the wardrobe, to a supper and a masque where the Countess of Bedford is to be lady and mistress of the feast, as she is of his [Lord Hay's] love to the Earl of Northumberland's youngest daughter, with whom he is far engaged in affection."

32. PRO SP (James I) 74/49, 1 August 1613. See also Thomson, "John Donne and the Countess of Bedford," pp. 333–334.

33. For example, *Prince Henry's Barriers, Oberon, The Golden Age Restored, Mercury Vindicated, Pleasure Reconciled to Virtue.*

34. PRO SP (James I) 109/133, 15 July 1619, Chamberlain to Carleton; 109/89, 12 June 1619, Edward Howard to Carleton.

35. Claudius Desainliens, alias Holiband, *Campo di Fior, or else The Flourie Field of Foure Languages* (London, 1583).

36. John Florio, *A Worlde of Wordes, or Most copious, and exact Dictionarie in Italian and English* (London, 1598), sig. A 3v.

37. John Florio, trans., *The Essays or Morall, Politike and Millitarie Discourses of Lo: Michaell de Montaigne* ([London]), 1603), sigs. A 2–4. Florio dedicated book 1 of the essays to the Countess of Bedford and her mother, Lady Harington; book 2 to the Countess of Rutland and Lady Penelope Rich; and book 3 to the Ladies Elizabeth Grey and Marie Nevill.

38. Letter of John Harington to the Countess of Bedford, Inner Temple, Petyt MS 538.43.14, fol. 303.

39. John Davies of Hereford, *The Muses Sacrifice or Divine Meditations* (London, 1612), sig. 2–2v. He also appended a sonnet to his *Scourge of Folly* (1611), observing that the countess is celebrated by all the poets—"Apollos most refulgent sonnes."

40. George Chapman, *Homer Prince of Poets. Translated According to the Greeke, in Twelve Bookes of his Iliads* (London, [1610]), sig. Ee 2.

41. Epis. ded. to Arthur Gorges, *Pharsalia*, sigs. A 3–A 3v. In the epistle Carew Gorges presents himself as a young attendant upon the countess, his mistress, who found the papers in his father's study and won permission to have them amended and printed with the aid of his schoolmaster, so that he might present them to her. The dedication emphasizes the Sidney blood "wherewith you do so neerely participate." In the same year (1614) Arthur Saul dedicated his *Famous Game of Chesse-Play* to the countess.

42. See epistles dedicatory to William Perkins, *A Salve for a sicke man* (Cambridge, 1595); Thomas Draxe, *The Worldes Resurrection, or The Generall Calling*

of the Jewes (London, 1608); Richard Stock, The Churches Lamentation for the Losse of the Godly [funeral sermon for John Harington] (London, 1614); Clement Cotton, The Mirror of Martyrs (London, 1615); John Calvin, Two and Twenty Lectures Upon the Five First Chapters of Jeremiah, trans. Clement Cotton (London, 1620); John Reading, A Faire Warning, Declaring the Comfortable Use both of Sicknesse and Health (London, 1621).

43. PRO SP (James I) 74/49, 1 August 1613.

44. See Thomson, "John Donne and the Countess of Bedford," pp. 334–335; Thomas Birch, Court and Times of James I, 2 vols. (London, 1949), I: 262. Writing to recommend a preacher to the Queen of Bohemia, she referred to his "good aprobacion from Doctor Burges & Mr Preston," PRO SP (James I) 129/5, 4 April 1622.

45. N. Byfield, Sermons upon the first chapter of the first epistle general of Peter (London, 1617), epis. ded.

46. This image was copied in later portraits, including one attributed to Gerard Honthorst in 1628, now at Woburn Abbey. It is reproduced in Herford et al., Ben Jonson, vol. 8, opposite p. 60. See the note on pp. x–xi.

47. Bernard H. Newdigate, Michael Drayton and His Circle (Oxford: Basil Blackwell, 1941), pp. 25–39, 56–69; Matilda. The Faire and Chaste Daughter of the Lord Robert Fitzwater (London, 1594), epis. ded.; Endimion and Phoebe. Ideas Latmus (London, [1595]), ded. sonnet. This sonnet was reprinted as #57 of his sonnet sequence Idea in 1599.

48. The Tragicall Legend of Robert, Duke of Normandy . . . (London, 1596), epis. ded. This dedication is followed by a dedicatory sonnet to her mother, Anne Harington, later reprinted as #58 of Idea.

49. Mortimeriados. The Lamentable civill warres of Edward the second and the Barrons (London, 1596), ded. poem. The invocations are at lines 260–267 and 2080–2087.

50. England's Heroicall Epistles (London, 1597) has no general dedication. The first pair, Rosamond and King Henry II, is addressed to the Countess of Bedford; another pair, Queen Isabel and Mortimer, is addressed to her mother, Anne Harington; and those of Queen Isabel and Richard II, to her husband, the Earl of Bedford. Other pairs are addressed to other patrons. The fact that the dedications to Lady Bedford were retained when some of these poems were reprinted, to be removed finaily in the collected Poems of 1619, is plausibly explained by Dick Taylor, Jr., "Drayton and the Countess of Bedford," Studies in Philology, 49 (1952): 214–228, as an accommodation to the printer's desires.

51. Included in Poemes Lyrick and Pastorall (London, [1606]), sigs. F 8r–v. The four stanzas are added to the "Eighth Eglog" but omitted in the 1619 Poems. Cerberon was probably Ben Jonson. (See Jonson's references to a rival poet in his "Epistle" to the Countess of Rutland below.)

52. See discussion in Newdigate, Michael Drayton, pp. 124–135, of the difficulties Drayton created for himself at court by his satire on several ministers in The Owle, his tactlessness in failing to take any poetic notice of Queen Elizabeth's death, and his reiterated complaints of neglect from all and sundry.

53. Daniel's primary patrons were the Pembrokes and the Cliffords. He was resident for some years at Wilton and tutor to William Herbert; subsequently he was tutor to Anne Clifford in the household of the Countess of Cumberland. Other patrons were Fulke Greville, Lord Mountjoy, and the Earl of Hertford. See Joan Rees, *Samuel Daniel* (Liverpool: Liverpool University Press, 1964), pp. 43–88, 122–146.

54. See discussion in Pierre Spriet, "Samuel Daniel (1563–1619): Sa Vie— Son Oeuvre," *Etudes Anglaises*, 29 (Paris: Didier, 1968), pp. 134–137. The first installment of the *Civile ·Warres betweene the two houses of Lancaster and Yorke* was published in 1594.

55. *Vision of the 12. Goddesses, The Complete Works of Samuel Daniel*, ed. A. B. Grosart, 3 vols. (London, 1885), 3: 195.

56. "To the Lady Lucie, Countesse of Bedford," in *A Panegyrike Congratulatory Delivered to the Kings Most Excellent Majesty. . . . Also Certaine Epistles. With a Defence of Ryme* (London, 1603), sigs. E 3v–E 4v. The stanza form, *terza rima*, is the first extended use of that form in English poetry.

57. Chiefly, Mary Countess of Pembroke, William Herbert, Earl of Pembroke (the countess' son), Elizabeth Countess of Rutland (Sir Philip Sidney's daughter), Sir Robert Sidney and his wife, Lady Mary Wroth (daughter of Sir Robert) and her husband.

58. Herford et al., *Ben Jonson*, 8: 115. For dating see 11: 41.

59. The letter is reprinted in Herford et al., *Ben Jonson*, 1: 197–198. The addressee is not identified in the manuscript, but the Countess of Bedford's position at court makes it likely that she (rather than the Countess of Rutland) was the addressee. Vigorously protesting his innocence, Jonson compliments the countess by the suggestion that she both can and will respond to this injustice: "I wolde intreate some little of your Ayde, to the defence of my Innocence. . . . The cause we understand to be the Kinges indignation, for which we are hartelye sorie, and the more, by how much the less we have deserv'd it." Jonson's pension of £100 was granted in 1610.

60. In his *Conversations with Drummond*, Jonson claimed that the epigram was "stollen out of his pocket by a Gentleman who drank him drousie & given Mistress Boulstraid, which brought him great displeasur" (Herford et al., *Ben Jonson*, 1: 150). In the covering letter to George Gerrard (expected, no doubt, to be seen by the countess) Jonson proclaims his wish that he had earlier known Bulstrode's great virtue: "Would God I had seene her before that some yt live might have corrected some prejudices they have had injuriously of mee" (ibid., 8: 371–372).

61. The manuscript version, headed "To: L: C: off: B:" is in Bodleian, Rawl. Poets 31, fols. 20v–21. It was published in very slightly revised form as "Ode enthousiastike" along with three other poems which constituted Jonson's contribution to the lyric collection, *The Phoenix and Turtle*, to which Shakespeare, Marston, and Chapman also contributed. The dedication is removed in order to generalize the poem. See Herford et al., 8: 364–365; 11: 40–41.

62. Ibid., 8: 662.

63. Ibid., 8: 54–55. Drummond of Hawthornden reports that this epigram was one of the five Jonson best liked to recite. Ibid., 1: 134–135.

64. Ibid., 8: 60–61.

65. Ibid., 8: 52

66. Gosse, *Life and Letters of Donne,* I: 188–189, 198–199, 216–217, 220, 230; II: 42–43.

67. The verse letters were probably written in the years 1608–10; he also addressed an "Epitaph on Himself" to the countess and an unfinished verse letter sometime after the publication of the *First Anniversary* (1611). See Wesley Milgate, ed., *John Donne: The Satires, Epigrams and Verse Letters* (Oxford: Clarendon Press, 1967), pp. 90–104, 252–274. For discussion of the elegies, see idem, *John Donne: The Epithalamions, Anniversaries, and Epicedes of John Donne* (Oxford: Clarendon Press, 1978), pp. 57–63, 66–74. Quotations from these poems in my text are from these editions.

68. Unavailing, because James I determined that he would advance Donne only in the Church. For discussion of Donne's relation to his various patrons, see Bald, *John Donne,* pp. 155–301; Arthur F. Marotti, "John Donne and the Rewards of Patronage," *Patronage in the Renaissance,* ed. Guy F. Lytle and Stephen Orgel (Princeton: Princeton University Press, 1981), pp. 207–234; and Jonathan Goldberg, *James I and the Politics of Literature: Jonson, Shakespeare, Donne, and Their Contemporaries* (Baltimore and London: John Hopkins University Press, 1983), pp. 210–239.

69. Gosse, *Life and Letters of Donne,* I: 293–295, 314. The anxiety about the *Anniversaries* found poetic expression in a verse letter "Begun in France but never perfected:"

> First I confesse I have to others lent
> Your stock, and over prodigally spent
> Your treasure, for since I had never knowne
> Vertue or beautie, but as they are growne
> In you, I should not thinke or say they shine,
> (So as I have) in any other Mine. (11. 11–16)

He proceeds to explain that his praises of others are only "copies" of the original, which she is, for "low Spirits" to read—but evidently did not complete (or send) this wire-drawn apologia. Milgate, *Satires and Verse Letters,* p. 104.

70. Gosse, *Life and Letters of Donne,* I: 213, 220.

71. Ibid., I: 217–218.

72. Both major editors of the songs and sonnets regard "Twicknem Garden" and "A Nocturnall" as poems for the countess. See H. J. C. Grierson, *The Poems of John Donne,* 2 vols. (Oxford: Clarendon Press, 1912), II: 22; Helen Gardner, *John Donne: The Elegies and the Songs and Sonnets* (Oxford: Clarendon Press, 1965), pp. 249–251. C. M. Armitage in "Donne's Poems in the Huntington Manuscript 198: New Light on 'The Funerall,' " *Studies in Philology,* 63 (1966): 697–707, argues on the basis of some manuscript evidence that "The Funerall" may also have been addressed to her.

73. See discussion in Barbara K. Lewalski, *Donne's Anniversaries and the*

Poetry of Praise: The Creation of a Symbolic Mode (Princeton: Princeton University Press, 1973), pp. 42–70.

74. To the Countesse of Bedford: "Honour is so sublime perfection," lines 44–45, Milgate, *John Donne,* p. 102.

75. To the Countesse of Bedford: "Reason is our Soules left hand . . ." lines 34–38.

76. To the Countesse of Bedford: "You have refin'd me," lines 55–60.

77. To the Countess of Bedford: "T'have written then, when you writ," lines 21–26.

78. See the plausible argument to this effect developed by Thomson, "John Donne and the Countess of Bedford," pp. 331–335.

79. Gosse, *Life and Letters of Donne,* 2:73. Donne's covering letter to her with the elegy on her brother's death refers to "your noble brother's fortune being yours" (ibid., 2:44) indicating clearly enough, even as he denies it, that he hoped for some benefit from that fortune. By the time of this letter, however, he may have realized how encumbered her estate was.

80. Ibid., 2:127. *The Sermons of John Donne,* ed. George R. Potter and Evelyn Simpson, 10 vols. (Berkeley and Los Angeles: University of California Press, 1953–1962), 3:187–205.

81. These letters were published in *The Private Correspondence of Jane Lady Cornwallis, 1613–1644* (London, 1842). Jane Cornwallis (the former Jane Meutys, who was in the countess' entourage at Twickenham) married Sir William Cornwallis; he died in 1611, and in 1614 she married Sir Nathaniel Bacon.

82. Ibid., p. 62 (20 January 1619); pp. 25–26 (9 September 1614).

83. Ibid., pp. 24–25 (September 1614).

84. PRO SP (James I) 122/99, 30 August 1621; SP (James I) 103/41, 18 October 1621; SP (James I) 130/67, 13 May 1622; *Cornwallis Correspondence,* pp. 57–58, 126 (October 1618, 12 April 1625).

85. *Cornwallis Correspondence,* p. 86 (November 1623). In the same vein, she conveys the general anxiety about new court appointments after Charles's coronation: "it is thought he will imploye his owne and dismisse his fathers. . . . [H]e makes his owne determinacions and is very stiff in them; having already changed the whole face of the court very near to the same forme itt had in Queene Elizabeth's tyme." Ibid., p. 125 (12 April 1625).

86. Ibid., pp. 44–45 (May 1617). A little after she reports, "The noble Lady Roxbrough is in Scotland, which makes me perfectly hate the court." Ibid., p. 48 (22 October 1617).

87. Ibid., pp. 28–29 (27 October 1614).

88. Ibid., pp. 61–62, 71–72.

89. PRO SP (James I) 109/102, 19 June 1619. And see discussion in Thomson, "Donne and the Countess of Bedford," pp. 335–340.

90. *Cornwallis Correspondence,* p. 76.

91. Ibid., pp. 73, 144.

92. Ibid., pp. 59–61 (20 January 1619). These letters of consolation customarily end with an invitation to visit the countess for a change of scene and air.

93. Ibid., pp. 65–67 (1 June 1620).

94. Ibid., pp. 118–119 (23 March 1625). A little later she shows herself incensed by the rumors that the marquis died a papist, and disposed at least to entertain the idea that he may have been poisoned. She recounts the physical evidence in graphic detail, but weighs it judiciously: "Being att first . . . as fayer a corse as ever their eyes beheld, in the space of three owres his hoole body, head, and every part swelled so strangely and gangrened so generally as it astonished them all; . . . God only knows the truth, who, if he had any wrong, I trust will in his justice declare it. It is true that, when he was opened in his stomack and head, there appeared nothing to confirm this jealousie, which makes the phisicians confident it could be no poison they are in these parts acquainted with; yett both myselfe and many other of his friends rest not clear of doubt, though, but upon some farder evidence, it is not to be stirred in." Ibid., pp. 128–129 (12 April 1625).

95. Ibid., pp. 88–90 (28 February 1624).

96. Ibid., pp. 47, 57 (4 October 1618; 22 October 1617).

97. Ibid., pp. 50–51 (7 March 1618).

98. The elegy attributed to the countess in several manuscripts is printed and discussed in Milgate, *Epithalamions, Anniversaries, and Epicedes of John Donne*, appendix B, pp. 235–237.

99. Ibid., pp. 59–61.

100. Donne's second elegy on Bulstrode (ibid., pp. 61–63) appears to "correct" the first, in light of the countess' poem.

5. *MACBETH* AND THE POLITICS OF HISTORIOGRAPHY

1. Eustace M. W. Tillyard, *The Elizabethan World Picture* (London: Chatto and Windus, 1943), pp. 7–8 and passim; Lionel Charles Knights, *Further Explorations* (London: Chatto and Windus, 1965), p. 32; Wilbur Sanders, *The Dramatist and the Received Idea: Studies in the Plays of Marlowe and Shakespeare* (Cambridge: Cambridge University Press, 1968), pp. 274, 332–338.

2. Terry Eagleton, *William Shakespeare* (Oxford and New York: Basil Blackwell, 1986), pp. 1–8. I am grateful to Alan Sinfield for letting me see a paper, forthcoming in *Critical Quarterly*, in which he has independently raised the possible significance of Buchanan for *Macbeth*. For a variety of reassessments of the politics of Shakespeare's plays, see Jonathan Dollimore and Alan Sinfield, eds., *Political Shakespeare: New Essays in Cultural Materialism* (Manchester: Manchester University Press, 1985); and John Drakakis, ed., *Alternative Shakespeares* (London: Methuen, 1985).

3. The question of Shakespeare's learning has been reopened by Emrys Jones, *The Origins of Shakespeare* (Oxford: Clarendon Press, 1975), pp. 2–5. Jones notes that the cult of Shakespeare as a spontaneous genius reflects a conservative English intellectual tradition "that—especially after the Cromwellian Interregnum—disapproved of intellect and was suspicious of too much learning" (p. 2).

4. Differing critical interpretations of the political effects of performance

on stage effectively cancel each other out. It can be argued that seeing the royal part played by professional players would arouse skepticism about the divine sanction behind traditional roles; on the other hand, it has been argued that performance reifies a play's political categories by giving them such vivid embodiments. See Harry Berger, Jr., "Text Against Performance in Shakespeare: The Example of *Macbeth*," in *The Power of Forms in the English Renaissance*, ed. Stephen Greenblatt (Norman, Okla.: Pilgrim Books, 1982), pp. 49–79.

5. Kenneth Muir, introduction to the Arden edition of *Macbeth*, corrected ed. (London: Methuen, 1972), p. xxxiii. All quotations from the play will be from this edition. For a fuller account of the sources, see Geoffrey Bullough, *Narrative and Dramatic Sources of Shakespeare* (London: Routledge and Kegan Paul, 1973), VII: 421–457.

6. Stephen Booth, *The Book Called Holinshed's Chronicles* (San Francisco: The Book Club of California, 1968), pp. 40, 43, 71.

7. See, for example, Nancy S. Struever, *The Language of History in the Renaissance* (Princeton: Princeton University Press, 1970); Virginia Stern, *Gabriel Harvey: His Life, Marginalia and Library* (Oxford: Oxford University Press, 1979), p. 152.

8. A revised edition of Boece's *Scotorum Historiae* was published by Giovanni Ferrerio at Paris in 1574, but it took the story no further than the death of James III (Boece had ended with the death of James I).

9. James Emerson Phillips, "George Buchanan and the Sidney Circle," *Huntington Library Q.*, 12 (1948–49), 23–55; Ian D. McFarlane, *Buchanan* (London: Duckworth, 1981), pp. 421–424, 436–438.

10. Raphael Holinshed, *Chronicles of England, Scotland and Ireland*, ed. Henry Ellis (London: J. Johnson, etc., 1808), V: 416, 754, 756. (Hereafter referred to as *Holinshed*.)

11. For full discussion, see James Emerson Phillips, *Images of a Queen: Mary Stuart in Sixteenth-Century English Literature* (Berkeley and Los Angeles: University of California Press, 1964), pp. 121–123.

12. Hugh R. Trevor-Roper, *Queen Elizabeth's First Historian: William Camden and the Beginnings of English "Civil History"* (London: Jonathan Cape, 1971). Camden included new matter about Macbeth in the 1607 editions of his *Britannia*, suggesting that he may have been influenced by Shakespeare's play. See Herbert N. Paul, *The Royal Play of "Macbeth"* (Cambridge, Mass.: Harvard University Press, 1950), p. 407.

13. Arthur Melville Clark, *Murder Under Trust: The Topical "Macbeth" and other Jacobean Matters* (Edinburgh: Scottish Academic Press, 1981), argues that *Macbeth* itself alludes to the Gowrie plot and was written to James's commission soon after the plot, ca. 1601. Although his evidence is not convincing, he does show that members of the King's Men were in Scotland for some time shortly before the king's accession to the English throne, and that James was interested in the drama for political reasons. Lillian Winstanley suggested that the play alluded to the Darnley affair in *"Macbeth," "King Lear," and Contemporary History* (Cambridge: Cambridge University Press, 1922). The most plausible suggestions for topical allusions link the play with the Gun-

powder Plot; I would accept that the play's composition was colored by this event but believe that its concerns are not only so immediately topical.

14. Kevin Sharpe, *Sir Robert Cotton, 1586–1631: History and Politics in Early Modern England* (Oxford: Oxford University Press, 1979), p. 25n.

15. David McPherson, "Ben Jonson's Library and Marginalia: An Annotated Catalogue," *Studies in Philology*, 71 (1974): *Texts and Studies*, pp. 33–34; Thomas I. Rae, "The Historical Writing of Drummond of Hawthornden," *Scottish Hist. Rev.*, 54 (1975): 39. Jonson does not seem to have met Drummond at the time of his first visit to London in 1606, but in any case he had links with Scots in London through his residence for five years with Esmé Stuart, Lord Aubigny, brother of the king's favorite, the Duke of Lennox. The Folger Shakespeare Library has an interesting copy of the first edition of Buchanan's history (copy 1) which contains a note claiming that the very extensive markings and annotations (underlinings occur literally on every page of the text) are by Drummond, but the handwriting does not look like Drummond's, and Robert H. MacDonald, in his *The Library of Drummond of Hawthornden* (Edinburgh: Edinburgh University Press, 1971), p. 49, states that Drummond's copy has not survived. Whomever it belonged to, the copy indicates the crucial ideological significance of the period around the reign of Macbeth: verbal annotations, as opposed to underlinings, begin on fol. 67r, at the reign of Kenneth III, continue through the stories of Duncan and Macbeth, and then peter out for a time before resuming on fol. 105r with the reign of Robert III.

16. The phrase of P. Hume Brown, quoted by McFarlane, *Buchanan*, p. 387.

17. Phillips, *Images of a Queen*, pp. 46–49.

18. Marie Axton, *The Queen's Two Bodies: Drama and the Elizabethan Succession* (London: Royal Historical Society, 1977), pp. 46–47, 89–91.

19. McFarlane, *Buchanan*, p. 415; Matthew Gwynne, *Nero: Tragoedia Nova* (London, 1603); presentation copy, British Library shelfmark 636d4(1), sig. A1r, commendatory verse by J. Sandsbury; *Vertumnus sive Annus Recurrens* (London, 1607), sigs. H3r–v. On Gwynne's links with Sidney and Greville, see John Buxton, *Sir Philip Sidney and the English Renaissance* (London: Macmillan, 1966), pp. 160–164, 176, 232.

20. Hugh R. Trevor-Roper, "George Buchanan and the Ancient Scottish Constitution," *EHR*, Supplement 3 (1966): 13.

21. The following highly simplified account is based in particular on J. G. A. Pocock, *The Machiavellian Moment: Florentine Political Thought and the Atlantic Republican Tradition* (Princeton: Princeton University Press, 1975), pp. 9–48, 333–360, and Arthur H. Williamson's important, ground-breaking study, *Scottish National Consciousness in the Age of James VI* (Edinburgh: John Donald, 1979).

22. Sir Christopher Piggot, quoted by Bullough, *Narrative and Dramatic Sources*, pp. 428–429.

23. John Major, *A History of Greater Britain*, trans. and ed. Archibald Constable, with a life of the author by Aeneas J. G. Mackay (Edinburgh: Scottish History Society, 1892), p. 158. On Major's political thought, see Quentin

Skinner, *The Foundations of Modern Political Thought*, 2 vols. (Cambridge: Cambridge University Press, 1978), II: 45–47, 117–123 (hereafter Skinner, *Foundations*), and Francis Oakley, "On the Road from Constance to 1688: The Political Thought of John Major and George Buchanan," *J. Brit. Studies*, 2 (1962): 1–31.

24. *Holinshed*, V: 26.

25. Ibid., V: 39 ff.

26. *John of Fordun's Chronicle of the Scottish Nation*, trans. Felix J. H. Skene, ed. William F. Skene (Edinburgh: Edmonston & Douglas, 1872), pp. 163–166.

27. J. B. Black, "Boece's *Scotorum Historiae*," in *University of Aberdeen: Quatercentenary of the Death of Hector Boece* (Aberdeen: Aberdeen University Press, 1932), pp. 35 ff.

28. Trevor-Roper, "George Buchanan and the Ancient Scottish Constitution," emphasizes the destructive impact of Lhuyd's writings; but not all of Buchanan's English correspondents accepted Lhuyd's arguments, which are based on an equal though opposite nationalist bias. See G. W. S. Barrow's review of Trevor-Roper's study, *Annali della fondazione italiana per la storia amministrativa*, 4 (1967): 653–655.

29. *Holinshed*, V: 245 ff. ("caecus . . . nimiumque propensus in liberos amor," *Scotorum historiae*, fol. 238v).

30. George Buchanan, *Rerum scoticarum historia* (Edinburgh, 1582), fol. 68v; I quote from the translation by J. Aikman, 6 vols (Glasgow, Edinburgh, and London: Blackie & Son, 1856), I: 318. (Hereafter Buchanan, *History.*)

31. Ibid., I: 331–332.

32. *Holinshed*, V: 269. The idea of Macbeth as a nationalist hero rather than a villain has recently reemerged in Peter B. Ellis, *Macbeth* (London: Muller, 1980); the Scots poet Hugh MacDiarmid once planned a verse play about Macbeth to counter Shakespeare's conservative English version, but the project lapsed (personal communication from Mr. George Bruce).

33. Buchanan, *History*, I: 344.

34. The *"Ius Feudale"* of Sir Thomas Craig, trans. James Aron Clyde, 2 vols. (Edinburgh and London: William Hodge, 1934), I: 99 ff.; cf. John G. A. Pocock, *The Ancient Constitution and the Feudal Law: A Study of English Political Thought in the Seventeenth Century* (Cambridge: Cambridge University Press, 1957), pp. 79–90.

35. Buchanan, *History*, II: 495.

36. Ibid., II: 547 ff. Camden denounced Morton's discourse for its "insolent liberty and sharpness of words" (Trevor-Roper, "George Buchanan and the Ancient Scottish Constitution," p. 6).

37. George Buchanan, *De iure regni apud scotos dialogus* (Edinburgh, 1579), pp. 81 ff.; translation by Charles Flinn Arrowood, *The Powers of the Crown in Scotland* (Austin: University of Texas Press, 1949), pp. 100 ff. Quotations will be taken from this translation (hereafter Arrowood).

38. Ibid., p. 110.

39. Buchanan, *History*, II: 549. Buchanan's friend Nicolas de Grouchy argued that the Roman constitution was essentially democratic (McFarlane, *Buchanan*, p. 404).

40. For different interpretations, see Skinner, *The Foundations of Modern Political Thought*, II: 342–345, and Roger A. Mason, "Rex Stoicus: George Buchanan, James VI and the Scottish Polity," in *New Perspectives on the Politics and Culture of Early Modern Scotland*, ed. John Dwyer, Roger A. Mason, and Alexander Murdoch (Edinburgh: John Donald, 1982), pp. 9–33. Mason argues that Buchanan's writings should be seen as a fairly conventional *speculum principis*, holding up to James an ideal of kingship that is constitutionalist in a specifically Scottish tradition. It is worth noting, however, that James's reaction in the case of the *History* was to break the mirror by having the book called in.

41. Arrowood, pp. 122, 144. Buchanan's "tolli," which Arrowood renders as "put out of the way," is a fairly cool word to describe the assassination of an anointed monarch.

42. Donald J. Gordon, "Giannotti, Michelangelo and the Cult of Brutus," in *The Renaissance Imagination: Essays and Lectures by D. J. Gordon*, ed. Stephen Orgel (Berkeley, Los Angeles, London: University of California Press, 1975), p. 236.

43. Trevor-Roper, "George Buchanan and the Ancient Constitution," p. 15; cf. *History*, II: 549.

44. See, for example, Thomas Dempster, *Apparatus ad Historiam Scoticam* (Bologna, 1622), p. 49: Buchanan was "vir improbus, sed bonus poeta."

45. Adam Blackwood, *Adversus Georgii Buchanani dialogum . . . pro regibus apologia* (Poitiers, 1581), pp. 63 ff., 84, 159–95; Ninian Winzet, *Flagellum sectariorum . . . accessit velitatio in Georgium Buchananum* (Ingolstadt, 1582), pp. 160, 239–255; *Minor Prose of King James VI*, ed. James Craigie and Alexander Law (Edinburgh: Scottish Text Society, 1982), pp. 70–71, 73, 76 ff. On Buchanan's admiration for Venice see McFarlane, *Buchanan*, p. 414.

46. For a reassessment of James's rule in Scotland, see Jennifer M. Brown, "Scottish Politics 1567–1625," in *The Reign of James VI and I*, ed. Alan G. R. Smith (London: Macmillan, 1973), pp. 22–39; and also the same author's more recent study; Jenny Wormald, "James VI and I: Two Kings or One?" *History*, 68 (1983): 187–209.

47. Rae, "The Historical Writings of Drummond of Hawthornden," p. 44; John Hall, *The Grounds and Reasons of Monarchy, Considered and Exemplified out of Scottish History* (Edinburgh, 1651), pp. 24 ff.; "Eutactus Philodemius," *Genesis kai telos exousias: The Original and End of Civil Power* (London, 1649), p. 24; compare "Eleutherius Philodemius," *The Armies Vindication* (London, 1649), pp. 34, 53.

48. Lionel Charles Knights, "How Many Children Had Lady Macbeth?" in *Explorations* (London: Chatto and Windus, 1933); Maynard Mack, Jr., *Killing the King: Three Studies in Shakespeare's Tragic Structure* (New Haven: Yale University Press, 1973), p. 190; Sanders, *The Dramatist and the Received Idea*, pp. 253–307. The fact that the unified worldview they analyze helped to sanction such activities as witch-burning fails to trouble some commentators. Stuart Clark, "Inversion, Misrule and the Meaning of Witchcraft," *Past and Present*, 87 (1980): 98–127, draws on Knights's reading of *Macbeth* among other sources in order to make any "doubt" a liberal-minded modern reader might have

about what he terms the "felicity" of demonological arguments "simply disappear" (p. 200). Dismissing the notion that the ideology motivating the persecution of witches was obscurantist, he argues that, after all, it provided "ideal material for the literary imagination" (p. 126).

49. Michael Hawkins, "History, Politics and *Macbeth*," in *Focus on "Macbeth*," ed. John Russell Brown (London: Routledge and Kegan Paul, 1981), pp. 155–188. Anomalies in the play are sometimes accounted for by cuts, revisions, and passages by Middleton or other authors; in the absence of any conclusive evidence, I have abstained from speculation on these points. See J. M. Nosworthy, *Shakespeare's Occasional Plays* (London: Edward Arnold, 1965), pp. 23 ff.

50. Hawkins, "History, Politics and *Macbeth*," p. 178. In his diary Simon Forman reported that in the performance he saw, Macbeth—not Malcolm— was nominated, and it has been suggested that revisions of the play revealed Shakespeare's knowledge of and unease about the tanistry issue. For opposing views, see Elizabeth Nielsen, "*Macbeth*: The Nemesis of the Post-Shakespearean Actor," *Shakespeare Q.*, 16 (1965): 193–199; M. J. C. Echeruo, "Tanistry, the 'Due of Birth,' and Macbeth's Sin," *Shakespeare Q.*, 23 (1972): 444–450; reply by Nielsen, *Shakespeare Q.*, 24 (1973): 226–27. Hawkins, "History, Politics and *Macbeth*," n. 21, is justly skeptical of Nielsen's claim that "all England" would have been conscious of Scottish history; but he seriously underestimates the possibility that Shakespeare may have known about it.

51. Axton, *The Queen's Two Bodies*, pp. 21–22, 79–80, 101–115.

52. Sir Thomas Craig, *Scotland's Sovereignty Asserted*, ed. G. Ridpath (London, 1695), pp. 4–6, 47, 88, 92–93.

53. Sir George Buc, *Daphnis Polystephanos* (London, 1605), sigs. A3r, H2r. (Buc's source here is Buchanan, not Holinshed.) The question of the succession to Edward was itself controversial, but it is impossible to follow up this point here.

54. Skinner, *Foundations*, II: 286.

55. Hawkins, "History, Politics, and *Macbeth*," pp. 177–179.

56. David Harris Willson, *King James VI and I* (London: Jonathan Cape, 1956), p. 290.

57. Jean de Schelandre, *Les deux premiers livres de la Stuartide* (Paris, 1611), pp. 144–145. Schelandre's use of the word "incarnation" (p. 109) might suggest an echo of Shakespeare. There is a draft or "modelle" of this poem addressed to James in the British Library, MS Royal 16Exxxiii. For biographical information, see the edition of his *Tyr et Sidon* by Jules Haraszti (Paris, 1908). Schelandre was patronized by the Duke of Lennox, brother of Jonson's Scottish patron, addressing him as "my-party de l'Escosse à la France" (*Stuartide*, p. 14).

58. Skinner, *Foundations*, II: 283.

59. McFarlane, *Buchanan*, pp. 433, 436; John Florio, *The Essays of Montaigne*, ed. G. Saintsbury III (London: David Nutt, 1893), p. 154 ("Of the Incommoditie of Greatnesse").

60. Pocock, *The Machiavellian Moment*, pp. 3–8 and passim.

61. Williamson, *Scottish National Consciousness*, p. 46.

62. Frank Kermode, *The Sense of an Ending: Studies in the Theory of Fiction* (New York: Oxford University Press, 1967), pp. 83–87.

63. Paul, *The Royal Play of "Macbeth,"* pp. 215–216, agrees that Shakespeare drew on Buchanan's portrayal of Kenneth but ignores the political issues and instead bizarrely suggests that Macbeth's guilty sleeplessness may have been intended as a compliment to the insomniac James I.

64. Buchanan, *History*, II: 553.

65. Cf. Williamson, *Scottish National Consciousness*, p. 11.

66. See Gordon Schochet, *Patriarchalism in Political Thought: The Authoritarian Family and Political Speculation and Attitudes Especially in Seventeenth Century England* (Oxford: Basil Blackwell, 1975), pp. 87 ff.

67. Boece, *Scotorum historiae*, fol. 257v ("tres ... muliebri specie"); *Holinshed*, V: 268; Buchanan, *History*, I: 338.

68. Christina Larner, "James VI and I and Witchcraft," in Smith, *The Reign of James VI and I*, pp. 74–90; see also her full-length study, *Enemies of God: The Witch-Hunt in Scotland* (Oxford: Basil Blackwell, 1983). Peter Stallybrass discusses "*Macbeth* and Witchcraft" in Brown, *Focus on "Macbeth,"* pp. 189–209.

69. Dennis Biggins, "Sexuality, Witchcraft, and Violence in Macbeth," *Shakespeare Studies*, 8 (1975): 255–277.

70. For an important analysis of the role of witchcraft in Scottish political thought, see Williamson, *Scottish National Consciousness*, pp. 53 ff.

71. For a discussion of *Macbeth* in relation to these ideas, see T. McAlindon, *Shakespeare and Decorum* (London: Macmillan, 1973), pp. 132–166.

72. *Holinshed*, V: 277; Buchanan, *History*, I: 349.

73. Williamson, *Scottish National Consciousness*, pp. 88 ff., 112, 124–125.

74. Richard Hooker, *Works*, ed. John Keble, 7th ed., rev. R. W. Church and F. Paget (Oxford, 1888), III: 263.

75. On the question of the play's "Scottishness," see Clark, *Murder Under Trust*, pp. 7–42.

76. C. H. Herford and Percy and Evelyn Simpson, ed., *Ben Jonson* (Oxford: Clarendon Press, 1941), VII: 288; cf. Clark, "Inversion, Misrule and the Meaning of Witchcraft," pp. 121–124, 126.

77. Harry Berger, Jr., "The Early Scenes of *Macbeth*: Preface to a New Interpretation," *J. Eng. Lit. Hist.*, 47 (1980): 1–31.

78. William Camden, *Remaines of a Greater Work, Concerning Britaine* (London, 1605), p. 33.

79. Buchanan, *History*, I: 344.

80. For a late example of this tradition, see Nicholas R. Jose, "*Samson Agonistes*: The Play Turned Upside Down," *Essays in Crit.*, 30 (1980): 124–150. The comparison between Buchanan and Shakespeare which I am making could be extended to Milton and Dryden, although in the latter case the contrasts are still sharper.

81. G. Xylandrus, ed., *Euripidis Tragoediae* (Basel, 1554), preface, pp. 423–424. Buchanan's translation of Euripides' *Medea* was included in some editions of Euripides along with translations by Erasmus; Jones, *The Origins of Shakespeare*, pp. 96–97, argues that Shakespeare must have known the latter trans-

lations. On the performance of Buchanan's *Alcestis* translation at Elizabeth's court (ca. 1563–65), see McFarlane, *Buchanan*, pp. 236–237.

82. Buchanan, *De iure regni*, p. 104 (not in Arrowood's edition); G. Neilson, ed., *George Buchanan: Glasgow Quartercentenary Studies* (Glasgow: Maclehose & Sons, 1907), p. 463. On the political influence of Seneca's plays, see Julius W. Lever, *The Tragedy of State* (London: Methuen, 1971).

83. Peter Sharratt and Peter Walsh, eds., *George Buchanan Tragedies* (Edinburgh: Scottish Academic Press, 1983), pp. 115, 122.

84. The most recent comparison is by Joost Daalder in his edition of Heywood's translation of Seneca's *Thyestes* (London: Ernest Benn, 1982), pp. xxxiii–viii; specific parallels with *Thyestes* are noted by Emrys Jones, *Scenic Form in Shakespeare* (Oxford: Clarendon Press, 1971), pp. 211, 215.

85. Jones, *The Origins of Shakespeare*, pp. 268 ff.

86. Inga-Stina Ewbank, "The Fiend-Like Queen: A Note on *Macbeth* and Seneca's *Medea*," *Shakespeare Survey*, 19 (1966): 82–94. In the period of the "first wave" of feminism, before the increasing insistence on natural hierarchy and degree noticeable in subsequent Shakespeare criticism, Euripides was sometimes contrasted favorably with Shakespeare for his presentation of women, and passages from his *Medea* (which Buchanan translated) were recited at suffragette meetings. Dr. Oliver Taplin has pointed out to me that this tradition has been revived by Tony Harrison in his *Medea: a sex-war opera*, which includes extracts from Buchanan's translation. Tony Harrison, *Dramatic Verse 1973–1985* (Newcastle-upon-Tyne: Bloodaxe Books, 1985), pp. 373, 447.

87. Arrowood, pp. 48–51; James VI, *Minor Prose*, p. 75.

88. Buchanan, *History*, I: 343.

89. Arrowood, pp. 105–107, 145–150; Stewart R. Sutherland, "The Presbyterian Inheritance of Hume and Reid," in *The Origins and Nature of the Scottish Enlightenment*, ed. R. H. Campbell and Andrew S. Skinner (Edinburgh: John Donald, 1982), pp. 141–143. On Hume and Buchanan, see also Williamson, *Scottish National Consciousness*, pp. 128–136; and on political analogies generally, Michael Walzer, *The Revolution of the Saints: A Study in the Origins of Radical Politics* (Cambridge, Mass.: Harvard University Press, 1965), chap. 5. Major attacked "proof from similars" and the metaphor of the body politic in his *History* (p. 220).

90. On discipline, see Milton's *Reason of Church Government*, I: i, and on the 1643 translation (issued as propaganda for Parliament and once, though dubiously, attributed to Milton), see McFarlane, *Buchanan*, pp. 391–392. Milton and Buchanan were posthumously associated with each other when some of their works were publicly burned at Oxford in 1683 (ibid., p. 415). Milton's view of Buchanan varied according to whether he was using Scottish history to justify the regicide in *The Tenure of Kings and Magistrates* or adopting an English viewpoint against the Scots in the *History of Britain*.

91. Cf. McAlindon, *Shakespeare and Decorum*, pp. 15–17.

92. Conventional histories of Shakespeare criticism have not developed these political aspects, but see Roy Pascal, *Shakespeare in Germany* (Cambridge: Cambridge University Press, 1938), pp. 24–36, 153–163, and cf. Marilyn Butler, *Romantics, Rebels, and Reactionaries: English Literature and Its Background*

1760–1830 (Oxford: Oxford University Press, 1981), pp. 45–46 on the rival political associations of Shakespeare and Milton in the 1790s, and pp. 88 f. on Coleridge's political outlook in the period of the *Biographia Literaria*.

93. G. P. V. Akrigg, *Shakespeare and the Earl of Southampton* (London: Hamish Hamilton, 1968), p. 179.

94. A nightmare in 1622 in which Buchanan foretold James's death caused much public discussion, *Calendar of State Papers, Venetian, 1621–1623*, p. 444. During the English republic it was cited as an instance of the inevitable doom marked out for the Stuart monarchy. William Lilly, *Monarchy or No Monarchy in England* (London, 1651), pp. 38–39.

6. CAVALIER CRITIC?

1. P. Zagorin, "The Court and the Country: A Note on Political Terminology in the Earlier 17th Century," *EHR*, 77 (1962): 306–311; idem., *The Court and the Country* (London: Routledge and Kegan Paul, 1969).

2. L. Stone, *The Causes of the English Revolution* (London: Routledge and Kegan Paul, 1972), p. 106.

3. R. Ashton, *The English Civil War, 1603–1649* (London: Weidenfeld and Nicholson, 1978), pp. 22, 29, 30.

4. P. Thomas, "Two Cultures? Court and Country under Charles I," in *The Origins of the English Civil War*, ed. C. S. R. Russell (London: Macmillan, 1973), pp. 168–196; cf. P. Thomas, "Charles I: The Tragedy of Absolutism," in *The Courts of Europe*, ed. A. G. Dickens (London: Thames & Hudson, 1977), pp. 191–212.

5. G. Parry, *The Golden Age Restor'd: The Culture of the Stuart Court 1603–1642* (New York: St. Martin's Press, 1981), pp. 189, 191, and passim. Parry offers only superficial readings of Caroline literature.

6. Thomas, "Two Cultures" pp. 185–191; Parry, *Golden Age Restor'd*, p. 265.

7. See Parry, *Golden Age Restor'd*, passim.

8. A. Harbage, *Cavalier Drama*, 1st ed. (London: Oxford University Press, 1936), 2d ed. (New York: Russell, 1964).

9. G. Parfitt, "The Poetry of Thomas Carew," *Renaissance and Mod. Studies*, XII (1968): 56–68.

10. See, for example, Parry, *Golden Age Restor'd*, chap. 9; Thomas, "Two Cultures."

11. There are two book-length studies of Carew: E. I. Selig, *The Flourishing Wreath: A Study of Thomas Carew's Poetry* (Hamden, Conn.: Archon, 1970), was the first to argue for a recognition of the irony and ambivalence in his verse; L. Sadler, *Thomas Carew* (Boston: Twayne, 1979) is marred by preconceptions about "Cavalier culture." The best short life is to be found in the introduction to R. Dunlap, ed., *The Poems of Thomas Carew* (Oxford: Oxford University Press, 1949). See also BL Add MS 24489 (Hunter's Lives).

12. Dunlap, *Carew*, p. xxxv. For the importance of this post at the court of

Charles I, see my "The Court and Household of Charles I" in *The English Court*, ed. D. Starkey (forthcoming).

13. E. Hyde, Earl of Clarendon, *The Life of Edward, Earl of Clarendon* (Oxford, 1761), p. 36.

14. Ibid., p. 36.

15. T. Carew, *Coelum Britannicum* (London, 1634). See the remarks of S. Orgel and R. Strong, *Inigo Jones: The Theatre of the Stuart Court*, 2 vols. (Berkeley, Los Angeles, London: University of California Press, 1973), I: 66–70. I hope to show the ambivalent, ironic dimension to this masque in a forthcoming study of Caroline literature.

16. See *The Great Assizes Holden at Parnassus by Apollo and his assessours* (1645); J. E. Ruoff, "Thomas Carew's Early Reputation," *Notes and Queries*, 202 (1957): 61–62; Dunlap, *Carew*, pp. xlvi–lii.

17. K. Sharpe, "The Court and Household of Charles I"; Dunlap, *Carew*, pp. xxi–xxvii.

18. Ruoff, "Carew's Early Reputation," p. 62; *Coelum Britannicum* lines 62–65 in Dunlap, *Carew*, p. 157.

19. E. Miner, *The Cavalier Mode from Jonson to Cotton* (Princeton: Princeton University Press, 1971), offered fruitful suggestions toward a reevaluation of the morality and politics of Cavalier poetry. Since this essay was drafted, Lauro Martines has published a manual for the historical reading of poetry, *Society and History in English Renaissance Verse* (Oxford: Basil Blackwell, 1985).

20. "Ingratefull beauty threatned," lines 15–16; Dunlap, *Carew*, p. 18. See below, pp. 135–136.

21. I. Selig, in *The Flourishing Wreath*, distinguishes the singing and speaking voices in Carew's poetry: "the singing voice of the poet in Carew's songs derives a certain vitality from its being forced at all times to contend with the speaking voice, with the recalcitrant world of statement" (p. 59).

22. Dunlap, *Carew*, p. 4.

23. "Good Counsel to a young Maid," lines 10–13; ibid., p. 13.

24. See another poem of the same title, "Good Counsell to a Young Maid," ibid., p. 25.

25. "To A.L . . .," lines 55–60; ibid., p. 5.

26. "To her againe, she burning in a feaver," lines 11–12, ibid., p. 35.

27. "Incommunicabilitie of Love," lines 1–3, ibid., p. 62. See note p. 244.

28. *The Royal Slave*, lines 1003–1014, 1029–1045 in G. Blakemore Evans, ed., *The Plays and Poems of William Cartwright* (Madison: University of Wisconsin Press, 1951), pp. 231–232.

29. Several playwrights of the Caroline period satirize Platonic love as a mask for promiscuity. See, for example, W. Davenant, *The Platonic Lovers, in The Dramatic Works of Sir William D'Avenant*, 5 vols. (London, 1872–74), vol. II.

30. "Incommunicabilitie of Love," lines 4–6, Dunlap, *Carew*, p. 62.

31. "Eternitie of love protested," lines 7–8, ibid., p. 23.

32. "A Rapture," lines 4, 6. For a recent discussion of this little-discussed poem, see P. Johnson, "Carew's 'A Rapture': The Dynamics of Fantasy" in *Studies in Eng. Lit.*, 16 (1976): 145–155.

33. "A Rapture," lines 111–112, Dunlap, *Carew*, p. 52. Cf. Miner, " 'A Rapture,' depended precisely on everything happening in Elizium," *The Cavalier Mode*, p. 199.

34. "A Rapture," lines 108–109.

35. "A Rapture," lines 115–116, 131–135.

36. Ibid., line 26.

37. Cf. Miner, *The Cavalier Mode*, pp. 80, 200.

38. "A Rapture," lines 111–112.

39. Ibid., line 163. Dunlap, *Carew*, p. 53. See below, p. 142.

40. "The Second Rapture," line 9, ibid., p. 103.

41. See 1 Kings 1:1–5; Sadler, *Carew*, p. 69.

42. "Second Rapture," lines 17, 26. The rearousal of sexual passion is related to ideas of renewal.

43. "On the Mariage of T.K. and C.C. the morning stormie," lines 21–24, Dunlap, *Carew*, p. 80.

44. Ibid., lines 31, 32, 36.

45. Cf. the poem, "A Married Woman," included in the 1642 edition of Carew's poetry; on marriage see lines 11–14:

> For in habituall vertues, sense is wrought
> To that calme temper, as the bodie's thought
> To have nor blood nor gall, if wild and rude
> Passions of lust and Anger, are subdu'd;

46. Sadler found it "strange that in some of his amorous lyrics to women not his wife, Carew tries to Platonize the erotic while in most of his celebrations of marriage, he blatantly declares for sexual fulfilment" (p. 115). This is to fail to appreciate the central place of marriage in Carew's morality.

47. Dunlap, *Carew*, p. xxxii; Sadler, *Carew*, p. 15.

48. The correspondence is printed as an appendix in Dunlap, *Carew*, pp. 211–212. T. Clayton suggests that the "Answer" to Suckling is not by Carew but also by Suckling himself. T. Clayton, ed., *The Works of Sir John Suckling: The Non Dramatic Works* (Oxford: Oxford University Press, 1971), pp. lxxxvi, 332. There can be no final conclusion because manuscript copies are found subscribed "T.C." as well as "J.S." If Carew did not write the letter, evidently Suckling thought it a representation of views held by Carew, quite at odds with his own.

49. "A Letter to a Friend," lines 35, 44, Dunlap, *Carew*, pp. 211–212.

50. "An Answer to the Letter," lines 21–23, Dunlap, *Carew*, p. 211.

51. "An Answer," lines 13–16, Dunlap, *Carew*, p. 211; cf. "Eternitie of Love Protested," p. 23.

52. "An Answer," lines 31–32.

53. Ibid., lines 44–45.

54. Ibid., lines 24–25.

55. The phrase is B. King's, "The Strategy of Carew's Wit," *Rev. Eng. Lit.*, 5 (1964): 42–51, esp. p. 51.

56. "A Song" ("Aske me no more . . ."), lines 1–4; See Dunlap's com-

mentary, p. 265. The poem employs the conceit of the phoenix dying in the woman's bosom in order to depict the mistress as the home of nature herself.

57. "The Comparison," lines 1–3, Dunlap, *Carew,* p. 98; cf. Shakespeare's sonnet 130.

58. "The Complement," lines 9, 20, 21, 55, Dunlap, *Carew,* pp. 99–100.

59. Cf. "Epitaph on the Lady S.," p. 55.

60. "The Comparison," lines 13, 24, 25, Dunlap, *Carew,* pp. 98–99. "On a Damaske rose sticking upon a Ladies Breast," line 6, Dunlap, *Carew,* p. 108.

61. "To A.D. unreasonable distrustfull of her owne beauty," line 35, Dunlap, *Carew,* p. 85; cf. "Incommunicabilitie of Love," lines 10–15, ibid., p. 62.

62. "To A.D.," lines 54, 60.

63. "Epitaph on the Lady S.," lines 7–10, Dunlap, *Carew,* p. 55.

64. "The Comparison," lines 25–29, Dunlap, *Carew,* p. 99. A classic illustration of "that wrenching final couplet for which Carew should be better known," Sadler, *Carew,* p. 52.

65. "A Rapture," line 1, Dunlap, *Carew,* p. 49. See Johnson, "A Rapture," p. 149; "Song Persuasions to enjoy," lines 5–6, Dunlap, *Carew,* p. 16.

66. "A Pastorall Dialogue," line 19, Dunlap, *Carew,* p. 43.

67. Ibid., lines 21–22.

68. Ibid., line 45, ibid., p. 44. Cf. "*Nym.* Then let us pinion *Time* and chase / The day for ever from this place." "A Pastorall Dialogue. *Shepherd Nymph Chorus,*" lines 29–30, ibid., p. 46.

69. "A Pastorall Dialogue," lines 46–48, Dunlap, *Carew,* p. 44.

70. The two poems share the same title.

71. Several of Carew's poems, including "A Rapture," are concerned with appropriate time. See, for example, "The Spring," Dunlap, *Carew,* p. 1; A. Long and H. Maclean, " 'Deare Ben', 'Great DONNE' and 'my Celia': The Wit of Carew's Poetry," *Studies in Eng. Lit.* 18 (1978): 75–94. Miner observes that in Cavalier poetry the remedy against time is not the enjoyment of the happy life as much as the virtue of the good life, *Cavalier Mode,* p. 154.

72. "Mediocritie in Love rejected," lines 1–2, Dunlap, *Carew,* p. 12; cf. "The Spring," ibid., p. 1; "A Looking-Glasse," line 16, ibid., p. 19.

73. "Boldnesse in love," Dunlap, *Carew,* p. 42; cf. "A Prayer to the Wind," p. 11.

74. "A Rapture," lines 35–40, ibid., p. 50.

75. Ibid., lines 66–69, ibid., p. 51.

76. "Song. *Celia* singing," lines 3–4, ibid., p. 38.

77. "To the Queene," lines 13–16, ibid., p. 90.

78. Ibid., lines 20, 22, 28, ibid., p. 91.

79. For example, "Loves force," line 1, ibid., p. 116; "Song. *Celia* singing," line 3, ibid., p. 38; "Incommunicabilitie of Love," line 9, ibid., p. 62; "To my friend G.N. from Wrest," line 7, ibid., p. 86.

80. "Disdaine returned" ("Hee that loves a Rosie cheeke, . . ."), line 8, Dunlap, *Carew,* p. 18; "To one that desired to know my Mistris," lines 3–6, ibid., p. 39.

81. See, for example, G. R. Hibbard, "The Country House Poem of The Seventeenth Century," *J. Warburg & Courtald Inst.,* 19 (1956): 159–174; W.

McClung, *The Country House in English Renaissance Poetry* (Berkeley, Los Angeles, London: University of California Press, 1977), passim; M. A. C. McGuire, "The Cavalier Country House Poem: Mutations on a Jonsonian tradition," *Studies in Eng. Lit.*, 19 (1979): 93–108.

82. Dunlap points out that the manor of Wrest Park, Bedfordshire "with the title of the Earl of Kent, had passed in 1631 to Anthony de Grey who died in 1643." This is erroneous. The title passed in 1624 to Henry de Grey, who died in 1639, succeeded by Anthony.

83. "To my friend G.N. from Wrest," lines 1–3, Dunlap, *Carew*, p. 86. For an interesting discussion of this poem, see M. B. Parker, " 'To my friend G.N. from Wrest': Carew's Secular Masque," in *Classic and Cavalier: Essays on Jonson and the Sons of Ben*, ed. C. T. Summers and T. Larry Pebworth (Pittsburgh: University of Pittsburgh Press, 1982), pp. 171–192.

84. Dunlap, *Carew*, p. xli.

85. Compare Carew's opening lines with the first scene of *Salmacida Spolia*, Davenant's masque, performed amid the Scots war on 21 January 1640. "A curtain flying up, a horrid scene appeared of storm and tempest. No glimpse of the sun was seen, as if darkness, confusion and deformity had possessed the world . . .," lines 111–114 in Orgel and Strong, *Inigo Jones*, II: 731; cf. fig. 401, p. 743.

86. "To . . . G.N. from Wrest," lines 15, 19; Dunlap, *Carew*, pp. 86–87.

87. Ibid., lines 9, 11–12.

88. Ibid., lines 28, 34.

89. Ibid., lines 35–46.

90. Ibid., line 54.

91. Ibid., lines 65–68, ibid., p. 88.

92. Ibid., lines 69–80.

93. Ibid., lines 19–20, 42.

94. Ibid., lines 93–96. See A. B. Giametti, *The Earthly Paradise and The Renaissance Epic* (Princeton: Princeton University Press, 1966).

95. "To . . . G.N. from Wrest," line 107.

96. The bucks and stags chased by Carew's friend are the "embleme of warre" and may too signify that war on the borders from which Carew has just escaped to nature's haven. See lines 107–110. Cf. below, pp. 143–144.

97. "To Saxham," lines 18–19, 22, Dunlap, *Carew*, p. 28. Cf. "To Penshurst," lines 30–34.

98. Ibid., lines 23–26.

99. Ibid., lines 35, 38.

100. McGuire, "The Cavalier Country House Poem," pp. 93–94.

101. "To Saxham," lines 49–52, Dunlap, *Carew*, pp. 28–29; compare the implied "open house" at Wrest, "To . . . G.N. from Wrest," lines 34–45, 60. Cf. "To Penshurst," line 48.

102. See Giametti, who points out the connections between the Garden of Eden tradition and that of the secular garden of love, nicely combined in "To . . . G.N. from Wrest," *Earthly Paradise*, chap. VII.

103. For incisive comment on the interdependency of the realms of love and government, see J. Goldberg, *James I and the Politics of Literature* (Baltimore

and London: Johns Hopkins University Press, 1982), pp. 55, 85, 107, and passim. I am extremely grateful to Jonathan Goldberg for several informative and stimulating discussions on this subject. Also see Martines, *Society and History*, pp. 4, 12, 68–76.

104. "My Mistris commanding me to returne her letters," lines 5–6, Dunlap, *Carew*, p. 9.

105. Ibid., lines 15, 24, 70, ibid., pp. 9–10.

106. "A deposition from Love," lines 27–30, ibid., pp. 16–17.

107. "My Mistris commanding . . .," line 28, ibid., p. 9.

108. Orgel and Strong, *Inigo Jones*, I: chap. iv.

109. Parry, *Golden Age*, p. 211; Parfitt, "Poetry of Carew," p. 56; Sadler, *Carew*, p. 85.

110. "To the King at his entrance into Saxham, by Master Jo Crofts," Dunlap, *Carew*, pp. 30–31; for suggested dates of the poem, see ibid., p. 226.

111. "To the King," line 25; "To . . . G.N. from Wrest," line 15.

112. "To the King," lines 3, 4, 6.

113. Ibid., lines 37–39. There is almost a tone of reciprocity in the language and structure of the poem.

114. "To . . . G.N. from Wrest," lines 29–32, Dunlap, *Carew*, p. 87.

115. See below, p. 145, for Carew's attitude to the plastic arts.

116. "Obsequies to the Lady Anne Hay," lines 1–5, Dunlap, *Carew*, p. 67.

117. "To the Countesse of Anglesie upon the immoderatly-by-her lamented death of her husband," lines 57, 65. Like Jonson, Carew turns an epitaph to an individual into a critique of courtly society.

118. Ibid., lines 55–56, 66–67. Cf. "himselfe" with "my selfe" of "To . . . G.N. from Wrest," line 107.

119. The very words "courteous" and "court" (meaning "to woo") come from a society that believed that as the center of virtue the court should prescribe manners to men in public and private life. Hence the best-selling courtesy book remains Castiglione's *The Courtier*. I shall be developing this theme in a book on the politics of literature in the England of Charles I.

120. "A Rapture," lines 4–6.

121. "Feminine Honour," lines 16–18, Dunlap, *Carew*, p. 61.

122. Ibid., lines 19–22. Dunlap suggests the date was 1633.

123. J. Jacobs, ed., *Epistolae Ho-Elianae* (London, 1890), p. 317.

124. Miner, *The Cavalier Mode*, p. 220.

125. Above, p. 127.

126. "Disdaine Returned," lines 7, 12 of a stanza carefully balanced to enfold them both.

127. "To my Mistresse in absence," lines 32–35, Dunlap, *Carew*, p. 22. Once again, the final couplet forcefully turns the sense to an anticipated *physical* union.

128. See, for example, "Separation of Lovers," lines 21–22, ibid., p. 62.

129. Ibid., p. 244.

130. Walter Montagu's *The Shepheards' Paradise* (London, 1659) was acted on 10 January 1633 at Somerset House, Beaulieu to Puckering, 10 January 1632–33, T. Birch, ed., *The Court and Times of Charles I*, 2 vols. (London, 1848),

II: 216. For the court reaction see J. Jacobs, ed., *Epistolae Ho-Elianae* (1890), p. 317.

131. Dunlap, *Carew*, p. 224.

132. "Ingratefull beauty threatned," lines 15–16, ibid., p. 18.

133. "A Divine Mistris," line 16. Once again note the almost subversive final line.

134. For a useful discussion, see Orgel and Strong, *Inigo Jones*, I: chap. IV.

135. "Upon the Kings sicknesse," lines 19–22, Dunlap, *Carew*, p. 35. See notes on ibid., p. 229. The date must remain uncertain. I incline to 1633.

136. Ibid., lines 25–26. The parallel perfectly illustrates the unity of Carew's ethical and political attitudes.

137. Ibid., lines 41–42.

138. Ibid., line 17. Cf. the "government tyranicall / In loves free state . . ." cited below, p. 139.

139. Ibid., line 1.

140. Ibid., line 37.

141. "My Mistris commanding me to returne her letters," lines 31–32, ibid., p. 9. This is a nice reminder that divine right theory involved a responsibility to God, as well as power derived from Him.

142. "To T.H., a Lady resembling my Mistresse," lines 16–24; ibid., p. 27.

143. See above, p. 132.

144. "A deposition from Love," line 30, ibid., p. 17.

145. Ibid., pp. 83–84.

146. Ibid., lines 2–3; "An Elegie on the La: Pen: . . .," line 1, ibid., p. 19.

147. "Upon my Lord Chiefe Justice . . .," lines 8–14. We have seen how Carew uses the term "milde" to describe the havens of nature and the condition of true love.

148. Ibid., lines 19–21. The "deformed shape" of the froward evokes the antimasques of the 1630s, and especially those of the depraved lovers in *Tempe Restored.*

149. Ibid., lines 22–23.

150. See W. H. Terry, *The Life and Times of John, Lord Finch* (London, 1936); *A Complete Collection of State Trials* (London, 1771), VII: 506–719.

151. "To Saxham," lines 57–58, Dunlap, *Carew*, p. 29.

152. "Upon my Lord Chiefe Justice," line 12. It is this optimistic belief in the intrinsic and potential good of human nature that is central to Carew's ethics and politics. It differentiates him sharply, of course, from the Puritans.

153. "Upon my Lord Chiefe Justice," line 10.

154. See F. Yates, *Astraea: The Imperial Theme in the Sixteenth Century* (London: Routledge and Kegan Paul, 1975).

155. "A New-Yeares gift to the King," Dunlap, *Carew*, pp. 89–90.

156. "To the Queene," ibid., pp. 90–91. Perhaps significantly the 1640 edition of Carew's poetry has this poem follow "A New-Yeares gift to the King."

157. The idea that virtue lay in the mean, the text of Aristotle's *Ethics*, was evidently of importance to Carew. Cf. his lines by way of an epilogue to a court play, included in the 1642 edition of his poems: "The pleasure lyes, not

in the end, but streams / That flowe betwixt two opposite Extreames" (Dunlap, *Carew*, p. 127).

158. See above, p. 123.

159. "My Mistris commanding me to returne her letters," lines 37–38, ibid., p. 10.

160. "A deposition from Love," ibid., pp. 16–17; "Truce in Love entreated," ibid., p. 41.

161. "A Rapture," lines 97–99, 110.

162. Dunlap, *Carew*, pp. 74–77; Townshend's "Elegy on the death of the King of Sweden: sent to Thomas Carew," in *The Poems and Masques of Aurelian Townshend*, ed. C. Brown (Reading, 1983), pp. 48–49.

163. See C. V. Wedgwood, *Poetry and Politics Under the Stuarts* (Cambridge: Cambridge University Press, 1960), p. 44.

164. "In answer of an Elegiacall Letter . . .," lines 45–48. The recognition of the obduracy of Charles I's subjects indicates a greater awareness of political reality in Carew than Wedgwood and others have allowed. See below, p. 144.

165. "In answer . . .," lines 52–58. Carew refers to "The beauties of the SHEPHERDS PARADISE"; but it is clear that the masque of Townshend he is describing is *Tempe Restored*.

166. Ibid., lines 2–3, 96–97. Cf. the "drowsie eyes" with the "slumbers" and "amorous languishment" of "A Rapture," lines 41, 52.

167. "In answer . . .," lines 5, 9.

168. Ibid., lines 15–18.

169. Ibid., lines 35–38.

170. Cf. Carew's masque, *Coelum Britannicum*, lines 684–760, in which fortune presents an antimasque, "the representation of battle." Orgel and Strong, *Inigo Jones*, II: 576.

171. "In answer . . .," lines 52, 60, 63–64.

172. Ibid., lines 75–76.

173. Ibid., line 96; cf. "A Rapture," line 92.

174. "In answer . . .," line 97. For an interesting but different interpretation of this poem, see M. B. Parker, "Carew's Politic Pastoral: Virgilian Pretexts in the 'Answer to Aurelian Townshend,' " *John Donne J.*, I (1982): 101–116.

175. "(The Wits) (A Sessions of the Poets)," lines 35–36, Clayton, *Works of Sir John Suckling*, p. 73.

176. "An Elegie upon the death of the Deane of Pauls, Dr. John Donne," lines 4, 69, Dunlap, *Carew*, pp. 71–73.

177. "To Ben Johnson," lines 45–46, Dunlap, *Carew*, p. 65.

178. Ibid., lines 22, 23–25, 44.

179. "Ingratefull beauty threatned," lines 1–6, ibid., p. 17.

180. "To a Lady that desired I would love her," line 31, ibid., p. 82.

181. "To Ben Johnson," line 12; "An Elegie," line 23.

182. "To the Painter," lines 12–14, 43–50, ibid., pp. 106–107.

183. "To Ben Johnson," lines 47–48. The poem exemplifies the capacity for frank criticism within the context of praise.

184. "An Elegie . . .," lines 95–96.

185. "A Fancy," lines 16–18, ibid., p. 117. This poem was included in the 1642 edition.

186. Ibid., lines 15–18.

7. ANDREW MARVELL, OLIVER CROMWELL, AND THE HORATIAN ODE

1. The poem is reproduced by permission of Oxford University Press from *The Poems and Letters of Andrew Marvell,* ed. H. M. Margoliouth, 3d. ed., 2 vols. (Oxford, 1971), 1: 91–94. This essay is an amended version of my article "The Politics of Marvell's Horatian Ode," *Historical J.,* XXVII (1984): 525–547. I am grateful to the editors of that journal for allowing me to reproduce it here. Having had help beyond the ordinary in the preparation of the article, I wish particularly to thank (but not to implicate) Miss Susan Brigden, Mrs. Elsie Duncan-Jones, Mr. Michael Gearin-Tosh, Mr. John Morrill, Professor Quentin Skinner, and Mr. Peter Thomas. Marvellians will recognize my debt to Miss Barbara Everett's essay, "The Shooting of the Bears: Poetry and Politics in Andrew Marvell," in *Andrew Marvell: Essays on the Tercentenary of his Death,* ed. R. L. Brett (Hull and Oxford: Oxford University Press, 1979), pp. 62–103. I gratefully acknowledge the influence of the works by Susan Shrapnel and John Wallace cited below.

2. The Royalism of *Lachrymae Musarum,* the collection in which the Hastings poem appeared, is established by Michael Gearin-Tosh, "Marvell's 'Upon the Death of the Lord Hastings,' " *Essays and Studies,* XXXIV (1981): 105–122. Mr. Gearin-Tosh does not take Marvell's poem itself to be an unequivocally Royalist one, however.

3. For this paragraph see my *The Rump Parliament 1648–1653* (Cambridge: Cambridge University Press, 1974), chap. XI, esp. pp. 224–226.

4. A. R. Waller, ed., *The English Writings of Abraham Cowley,* 2 vols. (Cambridge: Cambridge University Press, 1905–06), II: 345.

5. See e.g., *The Man in the Moon* 9 January–14 February 1650; *Mercurius Pragmaticus* 8–15 January, 30 April–7 May 1650; *Mercurius Elencticus* 6–13 May 1650.

6. W. C. Abbott, ed., *Writings and Speeches of Oliver Cromwell,* 4 vols. (Cambridge, Mass.: Harvard University Press, 1937–47), II: 193, 221, 237, 253–255; and the sources cited there.

7. See my *The Rump Parliament,* pp. 357–358.

8. Abbott, *Writings and Speeches of Oliver Cromwell,* II: 38–39. My italics.

9. Historical Manuscripts Commission Report, *De L'Isle and Dudley,* VI (1966): 472.

10. B. Whitelocke, *Memorials of the English Affairs,* 4 vols. (London, 1853), III: 183.

11. J. Sutherland, ed., *Memoirs of the Life of Colonel Hutchinson* (Oxford: Oxford University Press, 1973), p. 202.

12. Abbott, *Writings and Speeches of Oliver Cromwell,* II: 231–235.

13. *Perfect Diurnal* 27 May–3 June 1650.

14. Abbott, *Writings and Speeches of Oliver Cromwell*, II: 261–262.

15. Ibid., II: 38–39.

16. *A Brief Relation* 18–25 December 1649; R. Elton, *Complete Body* (London, 1650), pp. 8, 12, 132, 181; *A Speech or Declaration of the Declared King of Scots* (London, 1650), pp. 4–5. Cf. *Perfect Diurnal* 10–24 June 1650; *Impartial Scout* 12–19 July 1650. For the recruitment drive of 1650, see Henry Reece, "The Military Presence in England 1649–1660" (D.Phil. thesis, University of Oxford, 1981), a thesis that I cite with Dr. Reece's permission.

17. Cf. Marvell's *The Rehearsal Transpros'd*, ed. D. I. B. Smith (Oxford: Oxford University Press, 1971), p. 120.

18. J. M. Wallace, *Destiny His Choice: The Loyalism of Andrew Marvell* (Cambridge: Cambridge University Press, 1968), chaps. 1, 2; Q. Skinner, "Conquest and Consent: Thomas Hobbes and the Engagement Controversy," in *The Interregnum: The Quest for Settlement*, ed. G. E. Aylmer (London: Macmillan, 1972), pp. 99–120. One pamphlet with a bearing on the Engagement Controversy, published on or about 20 May 1650, was *An Answer to the Vindication of Dr. Hammond*, which contains (p. 1) an interesting use of the term "particoloured"; cf. line 106 of the ode.

19. Cf. *Perfect Diurnal* 20–27 May, 3–10 June 1650; Hull Corporation Bench Book, V: 842; my *The Rump Parliament*, p. 83. For glimpses of Marvell's relations with Hull in the years 1648–59, see Hull Corporation Bench Book, VI: 274; British Library, Add. MS 21, 427 (Baynes Papers), fol. 262ᵛ (concerning Marvell's election to Parliament in 1659); Bodleian Library, Tanner MS 57 fols. 167, 169 & ᵛ; and Northumberland Record Office, Berwick Borough Records, B9/1 (Berwick Letter Guild Book, 1640–1729), letters of Robert Overton and John Oxenbridge, January 1649 (evidence involving William Popple which suggests that Marvell may have first known John Oxenbridge at Hull rather than at Eton). I am grateful to Mr. Henry Reece for introducing me to the manuscript evidence here cited. For Oxenbridge see also A. G. Matthews, *Calamy Revised* (Oxford: Oxford University Press, 1934), pp. 377–378.

20. E. E. Duncan-Jones, "The Erect Sword of Marvell's Horatian Ode," *Etudes Anglaises*, XV (1962): 172–174.

21. Helen Darbishire, ed., *The Early Lives of Milton* (London: Constable, 1932), pp. 44, 74.

22. Here (as often) I must dissent from Joseph Frank, *Cromwell's Press Agent: A Critical Biography of Marchamont Nedham* (Lanham, Md.: University Press of America, 1980), p. 128. For glimpses of Nedham in 1649–50, see D. Gardiner, ed., *The Oxinden and Peyton Letters 1642–1670* (London: Constable, 1937), and *The Historical and Miscellaneous Tracts of the Reverend and Learned Peter Heylyn, D.D.* (London, 1681), p. xix. In the second edition of *Lachrymae Musarum*, Marvell's poem appears next to that of the very forward youth John Hall, whose career Marvell's often paralleled and who followed Cromwell's army to Scotland in 1650, where he contributed to Nedham's newspaper *Mercurius Politicus*.

23. See my "Classical Republicanism and the Puritan Revolution," in *History and Imagination. Essays in Honour of H. R. Trevor-Roper*, ed. H. Lloyd-Jones,

V. Pearl, and B. Worden (London: Duckworth, 1981), pp. 182–200. Cf. Edward Williams, *Virgo Triumphans* (London, 1650), p. 2. Livy is quoted from Philemon Holland's translation in *Andrew Marvell: The Complete Poems*, ed. E. S. Donno (Harmondsworth: reprint, Penguin, 1981), p. 240.

24. Nowell Smith, ed., *Sir Fulke Greville's Life of Sir Philip Sidney* (Oxford: Oxford University Press, 1907), pp. 44–45, 104. Greville recalled the Earl of Leicester's description of his nephew Sir Philip Sidney as "a forward young man" (ibid., p. 29); and the epistle dedicatory of the translation, which Sidney had begun, of Philippe du Plessis-Mornay's *A Work concerning the Trueness of the Christian Religion* (London, 1587) recalled that Sidney had "died not languishing in idleness, riot and excess . . . but of manly wounds received in the service of his prince, in defence of persons oppressed." (Cf. Leicester's own use of "languish" quoted by R. C. Strong and J. A. Van Dorsten, *Leicester's Triumph* [London: Oxford University Press, 1964], p. 57.) There was much interest in Sir Philip Sidney in the early 1650s, Greville's *Life* being first published in 1652.

25. Algernon Sidney, *Discourses concerning Government* (London, 1772), pp. 86, 134, 224–225, 386, 459–460.

26. Christopher Hill, *The World Turned Upside Down* (London: Maurice Temple Smith, 1972), pp. 77–78. Cf. Hill's *Antichrist in Seventeenth-Century England* (London: Oxford University Press, 1971), pp. 102–103; C. V. Wedgwood, *Poetry and Politics under the Stuarts* (Cambridge: Cambridge University Press, 1960), p. 21.

27. A. Macfarlane, ed., *The Diary of Ralph Josselin* (London: Oxford University Press, 1976), pp. 219–220, 264, 268–270, 289, 300–301. On 3 June 1650, when the returning Cromwell was being received in London, a congregation of Kent declared that God would make the Cromwellian army "further instrumental to carry on God's work in these nations (if not elsewhere) to destroy and bring down any whoever that shall engage" for the Royalist cause: Worcester College Oxford, Clarke MS xviii, fol. 42ᵛ (cf. ibid., cxiv, fol. 171ᵛ).

28. *Royal Diurnal* 14–23 April 1650; *Mercurius Elencticus* 22–29 April 1650. Cf. *The Man in the Moon* 6–13 May 1650; *Mercurius Elencticus* 6–13 May 1650; *A Brief Relation* 9–16 July 1650; *Several Proceedings in Parliament* 11–18 July 1650; *Merlinus Anglicus* (London, 1650), preface.

29. M. Nedham, *The Case of the Commonwealth of England Stated*, ed. P. A. Knachel (Charlottesville: University Press of Virginia, 1969), p. 13.

30. *Mercurius Politicus* also portrayed England's invasion of Scotland as a campaign of liberation from oppression. It may be significant that Marvell omits Spain, the traditional butt of English Protestant jingoism, from those prospective victims of Cromwell whom it names: the government hoped to do business with Spain, whom it treated tenderly in its propaganda; venom was reserved for France.

31. *A Brief Relation* 9–16 July 1650; cf. *Several Proceedings in Parliament*, 11–18 July 1650.

32. J. A. Mazzeo, "Cromwell as Machiavellian Prince in Marvell's 'Horatian Ode,' " *J. Hist. Ideas*, xxi (1960): 1–17; reprinted in Mazzeo's *Renaissance and*

Seventeenth-Century Studies (New York: Columbia University Press, 1964), pp. 166–182.

33. See especially Felix Raab, *The English Face of Machiavelli* (London: Routledge and Kegan Paul, 1964); J. G. A. Pocock, *The Machiavellian Moment* (Princeton: Princeton University Press, 1975).

34. The long list is recorded in Anne Barton, "Livy, Machiavelli and Shakespeare's *Coriolanus,*" *Shakespeare Survey* (forthcoming).

35. Raab, *The English Face of Machiavelli,* pp. 130–154.

36. P. Cruttwell, *The Shakespearean Moment* (London: Chatto and Windus, 1970), pp. 189 ff.

37. I have followed the datings that accompany the text of the commonplace book in volume 1 of the Yale edition of Milton's prose works. For the Vane poem, see J. Carey and A. Fowler, eds., *The Poems of John Milton* (London: Longman, 1968), p. 328n.

38. J. G. A. Pocock, in his edition of *The Political Works of James Harrington* (Cambridge: Cambridge University Press, 1977), pp. 4–5, treats this story of the inspiration and composition of *Oceana* with healthy but, in my view, excessive skepticism. We do not know when the friendships mentioned in this paragraph were formed. For a possibility that Milton and Harrington were close in 1648, see W. M. Evans, *Henry Lawes. Musician and Friend of Poets* (New York, Modern Language Assoc., 1941), pp. 179–181. We know that Milton and Marvell were friends by 1653.

39. Pocock, *The Political Works of James Harrington,* pp. 322–323, 329–332, 456.

40. Raab, *The English Face of Machiavelli,* pp. 146–154. Clarendon describes Cromwell's character in the *History,* X: paras. 169–173, and XV: paras. 147–156.

41. See also Cruttwell, *The Shakespearean Moment,* pp. 194–195. Students of Clarendon will be aware that the terms quoted from him in this paragraph were not applied by him to Cromwell alone.

42. The metaphors were not exclusively Machiavelli's, but they were often particularly associated with him: e.g., see J. Spedding et al., eds., *The Works of Francis Bacon,* 14 vols. (London, 1864–74), III: 345; Raab, *The English Face of Machiavelli,* p. 143; *Mercurius Politicus* 1–8 August 1650, p. 137; British Library, Add. MS 28,013 (Oxinden MSS), unfol.

43. G. Bull, ed., *The Prince* (Harmondsworth: Penguin, 1963), p. 131; B. Crick, ed., *The Discourses* (Harmondsworth: Penguin, 1970), p. 430.

44. For Marvell and time see particularly Susan Shrapnel, "The Poetry of Andrew Marvell in Relation to his Contemporaries and to Contemporary History" (Ph.D. diss., University of Nottingham, 1972), p. 133.

45. Bull, *The Prince,* p. 133.

46. Ibid., pp. 130, 134, 138.

47. Crick, *The Discourses,* p. 159.

48. Bull, *The Prince,* pp. 133–134.

49. Crick, *The Discourses,* p. 485.

50. Bacon, *The Essays* (Menston: Scholar Press, 1971), p. 105; Sidney, *Discourses concerning Government,* pp. 152, 400; H. C. Foxcroft, ed., *Life and Letters*

of Sir George Savile, First Marquis of Halifax, 2 vols. (London, 1898), II: 290; Caroline Robbins, ed., *Two English Republican Tracts* (Cambridge, 1969), p. 248 (for Moyle); J. Toland, *The Works of James Harrington* (London, 1700), preface. Cf. Nedham, *The Case of the Commonwealth,* p. 90; *Perfect Diurnal* 24–30 June 1650; Albertus Warren, *The Royalist Reform'd* (London, 1650), p. 4; T. Birch, ed., *Thurloe State Papers,* 7 vols. (London, 1742), V: 608–609.

51. Pocock, *The Political Works of James Harrington,* p. 352.

52. R. I. V. Hodge, *Foreshorten'd Time. Andrew Marvell and Seventeenth-Century Revolutions* (Cambridge: Cambridge University Press, 1978), pp. 117–118 (although there are dangers in regarding a poem by one Presbyterian clergyman, Robert Wild, on the death of another, Christopher Love, as Royalist). See also the quotation from Cleveland in Wedgwood, *Poetry and Politics,* p. 100. It is hard to know whether to draw inferences from resemblances between individual lines in the ode and lines in *Somnium Cantabrigiense . . . by a Post to the Muses* (London, 1650)—not a Royalist work.

53. Quoted by Wedgwood, *Poetry and Politics,* p. 108.

54. J. Dury, *Considerations concerning the Present Engagement* (London, 1650), p. 25; *Two Treatises concerning the . . . Engagement* (London, 1650), pp. 9, 37; Nedham, *The Case of the Commonwealth,* p. 13.

55. *Philo Regis* (London, 1649–50), pp. 4–5.

56. *Discolliminium* (London, 1650), p. 14; *An Exercitation concerning Usurped Powers* (London, 1650), p. 5; *Mercurius Elencticus* 29 April–6 May 1650; *The Man in the Moon* 2–9 May 1650; cf. Isaac Penington, *A Word for the Commonwealth* (London, 1650), p. 2.

57. For Royalist incitements to arms, see especially *The Declaration of Major General Massey* (London, 1650), and *A Declaration of . . . Lord Hopton* (London, 1650). The latter document appeared on 27 May and suggested that England, once a flourishing kingdom, was now a "languishing" one (p. 3).

58. Earlier in the year Royalist newspapers had laughed at the "fear" of the regicides, who "start at their own shadows," and had predicted that the republic's leaders would "show us a clean pair of heels, if O brave Oliver come not to relieve them." *Mercurius Pragmaticus* 25 December 1649–1 January 1650; *The Man in The Moon* 9–16 January 1650.

59. *Traytors Deciphered* (The Hague, 1650), p. 86.

60. Ibid., p. 47.

61. See, for example, *The Declaration of Major General Massey,* p. 6; "An Elegy . . ." (Thomason, E594(10)); *An Apologetick for the Sequestered Clergy* (London, 1649), p. 13

62. *Traytors Deciphered,* pp. 82, 86.

63. On the authorship see Joseph Frank, *The Beginnings of the English Newspaper 1620–1660* (Cambridge, Mass.: Harvard University Press, 1961), p. 194.

64. Nedham, *The Case of the Commonwealth,* p. 79.

65. Miss Everett writes beautifully about the meter in "The Shooting of the Bears," pp. 74–75, 82.

66. Ibid., p. 76.

67. Quoted by Dame Helen Gardner in her edition of *The Metaphysical Poets* (reprint, Harmondsworth: Penguin, 1972), p. 16.

68. Eliot, *Selected Essays* (London: Faber and Faber, 1932), p. 289.

69. The polarization is sensitively described in Cruttwell, *The Shakespearean Moment*, chap. 7; Shrapnel, "The Poetry of Andrew Marvell," chap. 1; P. W. Thomas, *Sir John Berkenhead* (Oxford: Oxford University Press, 1969).

70. The panegyrical properties of the Cromwell poems are discussed by Ralph Nevo, *The Dial of Virtue* (Princeton: Princeton University Press, 1963). (It is conceivable that Cromwell inflicts rather than suffers the "Scars," although the line would still be inaccurate.)

71. *News from Ireland* (London, 1650), p. 22.

72. Whitelocke, *Memorials*, I: 182, 196. Cf. *Perfect Diurnal* 27 May–3 June 1650. In June 1982, when defeated Argentine troops were being shipped back to the mainland, reports reached Britain of the tributes paid by them to the courage, the humanity, and the skill of their British conquerors. No one seemed surprised.

73. Remembering Marvell's scorn for the "Romane-cast similitudes" of Tom May, we may wish to resist attempts to make Marvell's parallels too precise; for this point see John S. Coolidge, "Marvell and Horace," *Mod. Philology*, LXIII (November 1965): pp. 112–113. Machiavelli (Bull, *The Prince*, pp. 132–133) had praised Hannibal's *virtù*—as was remembered during the Puritan Revolution. Raab, *The English Face of Machiavelli*, p. 143.

74. *The Man in the Moon* 26 December 1649–2 January 1650. The same issue of the newspaper referred to the "Westminster hunters" who "laid such a snare for the king" (cf. line 50).

75. See, for example, *The Lawfulness of Obeying the Present Government* (London, 1649), p. 7; *A Combat between Two Seconds* (London, 1649), p. 7; Wallace, *Destiny His Choice*, p. 98.

76. There may be a comparable achievement in Marvell's treatment of the King's execution. Lines 69–70 ("A bleeding Head where they begun, / Did fright the Architects to run") seem to carry an allusion that would have been clear within a week of Cromwell's return to England and that silently bridges the sixteen months since the regicide. On 3 June 1650, a government newspaper brought the news of the beheading of the Royalist Earl of Montrose by the Scottish Presbyterians (*Perfect Diurnal* 27 May–3 June 1650; with which cf. *A Brief Relation* 21–28 May 1650, *Several Proceedings in Parliament* 13–20 June 1650, and *Mercurius Politicus* 5–12 September 1650, p. 224). Dying in the manner of the king he had served, Montrose carried himself on the scaffold, said the report, with a "comely" dignity ("But bow'd his comely Head"). Accounts of the campaign that had preceded Montrose's death had often remarked on the banner beneath which he led his troops "with streams of blood from it" ("A bleeding Head where they begun"): *A Brief Relation* 9–16 April 1650. Cf. *A Full Relation of . . . the Late Great Victory* (London, 1650), p. 1; *Royal Diurnal* 25 February–4 March 1650; Thomason, E594(10). If Marvell is alluding to the death of Montrose, however, in whose cause is he doing so? That of the government, which stressed the dignity of Montrose's bearing in order to denigrate his Presbyterian murderers, and which, although it had taken fright at the bleeding head of Charles I, was now moving toward the creation of a new Roman empire? Or that of Montrose himself?

77. The apparent difficulty of reconciling the Marvell of the ode with the Marvell of "Tom May's Death" has led some critics to question or to postpone Marvell's authorship of the latter poem. There is no need to do so. Marvell retains his anger at the execution of the king—and May's death, unlike Cromwell's return earlier in the year, gives the poet no counterweight to that event. May, the butt of Marvell's anger, had prostituted his calling in the later 1640s, when Marvell's sympathies had lain with Royalists. Cf. Gerald Reedy S.J., " 'An Horatian Ode' and 'Tom May's Death,' " *Studies in Eng. Lit.*, XX (1980): 137–151.

78. *The Life of Edward, Earl of Clarendon* (London, 1759), p. 25. See also Richard Helgerson, *Self-Crowned Laureates* (Berkeley, Los Angeles, London: University of California Press, 1983), chap. 1. Perhaps the lines about "the Poets time" in "Tom May's Death" point to a comparable preoccupation on Marvell's part.

79. Pocock, *The Political Works of James Harrington*, pp. 662, 666, 682 ff.

80. J. Carey, *Milton* (London: Evans Bros., 1969), p. 12.

81. Margoliouth, *Poems and Letters of Andrew Marvell*, II: 166.

82. Ibid., pp. 93, 175, 312; Smith, *The Rehearsal Transpros'd*, pp. 136, 241; A. Grosart, ed., *The Complete Works in Verse and Prose of Andrew Marvell*, 4 vols. (London, 1872–75), III: 115.

83. Smith, *The Rehearsal Transpros'd*, p. 135; Margoliouth, *Poems and Letters of Andrew Marvell*, II: 324.

84. Margoliouth, *Poems and Letters of Andrew Marvell*, II: 177.

85. Ibid., II: 313.

86. Ibid., II: 312, 383–384.

87. Everett, "The Shooting of the Bears," p. 80.

88. Cf. C. H. Sisson, *The English Sermon 1650–1750* (Manchester: Carcanet Press, 1976), p. 15: "The great poem of the 1650s is Marvell's "Horatian Ode," which looks backwards to the Metaphysicals and forwards to the clarities of the Augustan age . . ."

89. H. R. Trevor-Roper, "The Elitist Politics of Milton," *Times Literary Supplement*, 1 June 1973.

90. See Shrapnel, "The Poetry of Andrew Marvell," pp. 15–16.

91. Margoliouth, *Poems and Letters of Andrew Marvell*, II: 2.

92. On the limitations of Royalist elegies, see Shrapnel, "The Poetry of Andrew Marvell," chap. 1.

93. Cf. C. H. Wilkinson, ed., *The Poems of Richard Lovelace* (Oxford: Oxford University Press, 1930), p. 3 (line 1 of Jephson's poem).

8. MILTON AND THE HISTORIES

1. Although I know of no nominalist view of history for the seventeenth century, for recent times see Hayden V. White, *Metahistory* (Baltimore: Johns Hopkins University Press, 1973) and his *Tropics of Discourse* (Baltimore: Johns Hopkins University Press, 1978). Among the Marxist views, the most distin-

guished and pertinent to Milton are those of Christopher Hill. See Hill, Margaret James, and Edgell Richmond, *The English Revolution, 1640* (London: Lawrence, 1940) and in particular Hill's *Milton and the English Revolution* (London: Faber and Faber, 1977). In the interval between the writing and publication of this essay, a new historical study has emerged for Renaissance literature. For example, see the fine study by Thomas M. Greene, *The Light in Troy* (New Haven: Yale University Press, 1982). The same is more or less true of studies of later English literature but, as far as I am aware, none affects the thesis here.

2. Hugh G. Dick, ed., *Selected Writings of Francis Bacon* (New York: Modern Library, 1955), p. 165.

3. George Watson, ed., *John Dryden: Of Dramatic Poesy and Other Critical Writings*, 2 vols. (London: Everyman, 1962), 2: 5; hereafter cited in the text or labeled Dryden. Dryden later terms the third species "biography," the first usage recorded in the *Oxford English Dictionary*.

4. Watson, *John Dryden*, 2: 5.

5. Michael Oakeshott, ed., *Leviathan* (Oxford: Basil Blackwell, 1960), p. 467.

6. Dryden, 2: 6. Although Dryden has his reservations about them, the historians he praises are Thucydides and Polybius, Livy and Tacitus, Guicciardini, Avila (y Zuñiga), Comines, and Buchanan.

7. *Institutes*, 2, 4. For fuller citation and other classical sources, see my *Dryden's Poetry* (Bloomington: Indiana University Press, 1967), pp. 290, 345.

8. Don M. Wolfe et al., eds., *Complete Prose Works of John Milton*, 8 vols. (New Haven: Yale University Press, 1953 ff.), 5: 1. Hereafter cited as *Yale Prose*. The quotations from Milton's poems are from Frank Allen Patterson et al., eds., *The Works of John Milton* (New York: Columbia University Press, 1931), vols. 1–2 in four parts.

9. Ibid., p. 3.

10. Ibid. See also Fogle's note, *Yale Prose*, 5:7 n. 3.

11. *Yale Prose*, 5: 39.

12. Ibid., 5: 391, 402. I owe the awareness of Milton's stress on Christmas to a seminar paper by Mark Patterson of the University of Washington. If, as Fogle thinks, the *History* was written in 1648 ff., it was done after the parliamentary ordinance of 3 June 1647: "That the Feasts of the Nativity of Christ, *Easter* and *Whitsuntide* and all other festivall dayes commonly called holy dayes be no longer observed as Festivall or Holy dayes." Christmas became "the Lord's birthday," and so on. Milton's stress on "Christmas" is therefore difficult to interpret.

13. *Yale Prose*, 5: 13, italics in original.

14. Ibid., 1: 801–823.

15. Ibid., 4: pt. 1, 684.

16. Ibid., 1: 806.

17. Ibid., 1: 807.

18. Ibid., 1: 808.

19. Ibid., 1: 813–815. This appears to be the first English division of literature into the three genres, probably after the example of Minturno. See my "On the Genesis and Development of Poetic Systems," *Critical Inquiry*, 5 (1979): esp. pp. 347–348.

20. *Yale Prose,* 1: 820.

21. Ibid., 1: 821–823.

22. Ibid., 4: pt. 1, 684, 685. As the editors say, the "monument" may recall Horace, "Exegi monumentum aere perennius" (*Odes,* 3, 30,1). Coming as it does, however, at the close of a work and dealing with the great personages of his time, the closer analogy would seem to be with the ending of Ovid, *Metamorphoses,* 15.

23. *Yale Prose,* 4: 685.

24. Ibid., 5: pt. 1, 444–451.

25. Patterson et al., *Works of John Milton,* 2: 235 (8.5–8).

26. Ibid., I:2.

27. Lowry Nelson was (I believe) the first to observe the erratic tenses of verbs in *On the Morning* and in *Lycidas:* in *Baroque Lyric Poetry* (New Haven: Yale University Press, 1961), pp. 41–52, 64–76.

28. Lines 965–974, changed from italics to roman.

29. The English translation is taken, with a little adaptation, from Merritt Y. Hughes, ed., *John Milton: Complete Poems and Major Prose* (New York: Odyssey, 1957), pp. 132–139.

30. The fullest study of *Lycidas* is that by Joseph Anthony Wittreich, Jr., *Visionary Poetics: Milton's Tradition and His Legacy* (San Marino, Calif.: Huntington Library, 1979). His emphasis is on prophecy.

31. One of the best studies of pastoral in *Lycidas* remains Rosemond Tuve, *Images and Themes in Five Poems by Milton* (Cambridge, Mass.: Harvard University Press, 1967), pp. 73–111. For a more recent view of pastoral, among other matters, see Wolfgang Iser, "Spenser's Arcadia," in P. Steiner et al., eds., *The Structure of the Literary Process* (Amsterdam and Philadelphia: John Benjamins, 1982), pp. 211–241.

32. *Yale Prose,* 6.

33. Ibid., chap. 30, p. 585.

34. Ibid., chap. 30, p. 587.

35. Ibid., chap. 30, p. 583; see also Maurice Kelley's note 23.

36. Ibid., chap. 30, p. 581. Kelley shows that Milton draws here, as so often in the work, on Wollebius. The correct "two senses" of what is a "single sense" involve the complex or inconsistent Protestant conception of the "literal" sense. Protestants emphasized, as appropriate to their doctrine of "sola fides," what Nicholas de Lyra termed the "quid credas," what we are to believe in typology as opposed to the Catholic stress on works, "quid agas."

37. Ibid., chap. 28, pp. 547–548.

38. No one can prove when *Samson Agonistes* was written, but its artistry surely qualifies it for the label "mature."

39. I am indebted here to a summary of a paper by Masataka Shiratori in *MCJ News* (Kyoto: Milton Center of Japan), 5: 2–6.

40. "Thus a sort of 'historical' Satan looms before us" (ibid., pp. 2–3).

41. *Paradise Lost* is at once so well known and so complex in these matters that I shall curtail discussion of it here.

42. *Yale Prose,* 5: pt. 1, 1.

43. Ibid., pp. 2–3; however, recall *fabula* as in Quintilian.

44. Ibid., p. 3.

5. Haller, *The Rise of Puritanism* (New York: Harper, 1938), pp. 150–161.
6. S. Johnson, *Lives of the English Poets*, 2 vols. (London: Dent, Everyman's Library, 1925), 1: 160.
47. Ibid., 1: 173, 174; italics added.
48. Ibid., 1: 100, 102, 104, 107–108.

9. THE POLITICS OF *PARADISE LOST*

1. Samuel Taylor Coleridge, Lecture X, *Literary Remains* (London, 1836), quoted from James Thorpe, ed., *Milton Criticism: Selections from Four Centuries* (London: Routledge and Kegan Paul, 1951), p. 97.
2. "Politics, Milton's" by Michael Fixler in vol. 6 of *A Milton Encyclopedia*, gen. ed. William B. Hunter, Jr. (Lewisburg, Pa.: Bucknell University Press, 1979).

For perhaps the most extreme statement of this position, see Hugh M. Richmond, *The Christian Revolutionary: John Milton* (Berkeley, Los Angeles, London: University of California Press, 1974), passim. Richmond argues that political defeat leading to Milton's abandonment of idealist Platonic political thought was the very precondition for the creation of the great poem. Similarly, in *Milton the Puritan* (London: Macmillan, 1977), A. L. Rowse writes, "The Restoration was the best thing that could have happened to Milton. It forced him to drop dealing with the ephemera of politics, back upon his own true genius, the life of the imagination and its expression in poetry" (p. 215). Finally, one might note that although Charles R. Geisst—in the most recent study of *The Political Thought of John Milton* (Cambridge: Cambridge University Press, 1984)—finds that Adam's fall was a fall into political experience (p. 46), he does not specify what in that fallen location Adam or Milton or the reader would find political experience to be.

Jackie DiSalvo notes that "in quest of [a] political Milton one has had to turn mainly to historical studies focused primarily upon his prose, by Arthur Barker, Edgell Rickword, William Haller, Don Wolfe, Zera Fink, A. S. P. Woodhouse, George Sensabaugh, and Florence Sandler." See *War of Titans: Blake's Critique of Milton and the Politics of Religion* (Pittsburgh: University of Pittsburgh Press, 1983), p. 9.

3. "The Marriage of Heaven and Hell," in *The Poetry and Prose of William Blake*, ed. David V. Erdman, rev. ed. (New York: Doubleday, 1970). Christopher Hill adds, "the young Wordsworth recalled Milton the libertarian, Shelley recalled Milton the defender of regicide." See "A Bourgeois Revolution?" in *Three British Revolutions, 1641, 1688, 1776*, ed. J. G. A. Pocock (Princeton: Princeton University Press, 1980), p. 133.

4. DiSalvo, *War of Titans*, pp. 15, 10, 12, 42. She points to support for her analysis in Malcolm Ross, *Milton's Royalism: A Study of the Conflict of Symbol and Idea in the Poems* (Ithaca, N. Y.: Cornell University Press, 1943), pp. 75–119; Christopher Hill, *Milton and the English Revolution* (New York: Viking, 1978); and Edgell Rickword, "Milton, the Revolutionary Intellectual," in *The*

English Revolution, ed. Christopher Hill (London: Lawrence and Wishart, 1940).

5. Herman Rapaport, *Milton and the Post Modern* (Lincoln: University of Nebraska Press, 1983). Rapaport conceives his task in examining "Milton and the State" to be "to counter the Anglo-American reception of Milton as a great humanist in the democratic tradition" (p. 171). He notes, "I stress, not Milton's resistance, but his complicity with the most repellent aspects of fascist, or totalitarian action" (p. 172). He speaks of Milton's "mind harboring a darker fascination with dictatorial takeover, with what amounts to another absolutism much bleaker and calculating than the foppery of Charles I and the grand schemes of the Anglicans under Archbishop Laud" (p. 176).

6. *The Reason of Church Government,* in *Complete Prose Works of John Milton,* ed. Don M. Wolfe et al. (New Haven: Yale University Press, 1953–82), I: 816. All quotations of Milton's prose will be taken from this edition, noted hereafter as *Yale Prose.*

7. *An Apology Against a Pamphlet call'd A Modest Confutation of the Animadversions upon the Remonstrant against Smectymnuus, Yale Prose,* I: 890.

8. I am very far from proposing that one read the course of political education performed in *Paradise Lost* as a kind of "Surprized by Ideology," by analogy to the way in which Stanley Fish handles ethical and other ideas in *Surpriz'd by Sin: The Reader in "Paradise Lost"* (New York: St. Martin's Press, 1967). Milton did not, by my reading, calculate a magnificent plot to entrap his readers into such misinterpretations and corrections as would lead him to salvation. His political paideia is overt and historical; it results in progressive enlightenment as to the very slowness and difficulty involved in human arrangements within fallen history. Where Henry James is Fish's tutelary genius, Socrates is Milton's.

9. *The Readie and Easie Way to Establish A Free Commonwealth,* 2d ed., *Yale Prose,* VII: 443.

10. *Yale Prose,* VII: 427. The addition to the first edition of the material "neither . . . Lord" interprets Proverbs 6:6–8 as supporting from nature Milton's argument for a commonwealth.

11. See Michael Lieb, *Poetics of the Holy* (Chapel Hill: University of North Carolina Press, 1981), pp. 121–127, on the influence of Ezekiel, and Alastair Fowler, *The Poems of John Milton* (London: Longmans, 1968), p. 713, on the influence of Daniel on Milton's portrayal of God as king. See Ross, *Milton's Royalism,* p. 105, for a clear picture of Milton's Spenserian characterization of Heaven.

12. That Milton urges meritocracy has been noted by a number of writers on Milton's politics, one of the most recent and interesting being Andrew Milner, *Milton and the Puritan Revolution* (Totowa, N.J.: Barnes and Noble, 1981), pp. 147–166. I do not think that point has been associated with my two other points here, however—that Milton relieves God from the exercise of personal power and that he so thoroughly insists on praising heavenly institutions in terms of their rationality that he removes the political argument of their precedence.

13. *Christian Doctrine, Yale Prose,* VI: 389.

14. See Claes Schaar, *The Full Voic'd Quire Below: Vertical Context Systems in "Paradise Lost"* (Lund: Gleerup, 1982), pp. 217–226, for a discussion of all the literary strands brought together in the scenes of Satan's enthronement. See Merritt Y. Hughes, "Satan and the 'Myth' of the Tyrant," in *Ten Perspectives on Milton* (New Haven: Yale University Press, 1965), pp. 169–171, for an analysis of the aspects of the tyrant Milton emphasizes.

15. Merritt Y. Hughes, ed., *John Milton: Complete Poems and Major Prose* (New York: Odyssey Press, 1957), pp. 454–455; and Hughes, "Satan and the 'Myth' of the Tyrant," passim. Alastair Fowler, ed., *Paradise Lost* in *The Poems of John Milton* (London: Longmans, 1968), pp. 1028–1032.

16. *The Readie and Easie Way . . .*, 2d ed., *Yale Prose*, VII: 421

17. *A Treatise of Civil Power*, *Yale Prose*, VII: 262. The corresponding words in *The Readie and Easie Way . . .* are used again and again severally.

18. *Yale Prose*, VII: 462.

19. The pun is argued for and explained in E. A. J. Honigmann, ed., *Milton's Sonnets*, (New York: St. Martin's Press, 1966), pp. 32–33.

20. Robert Burton, *The Anatomy of Melancholy*, ed. Holbrook Jackson (London: J. M. Dent and Sons, 1932), III: 415.

21. I have in mind the ceremonial honoring of the patriarch as well as the thoroughly centralized and hierarchicalized scientific establishment. Burton's own skeptical Utopia is another case in point. He weighs giving his Utopia a republican form of government but rejects that. His Utopia cannot improve on the social arrangements of his own day; for it is made of men like those he knows, and "men are partial and passionate, merciless, covetous, corrupt, subject to love, hate, fear, favour, etc." (I: 103).

22. *Yale Prose*, VII: 409, 421, 444.

23. Ibid., p. 462.

24. Ibid., pp. 422–423.

25. It should be noted, however, that having made his reasonable argument, Milton is not above throwing in a touch of his former searching for biblical precedent as well as biblical reason: "a free Commonwealth [is] not only held by the wisest men in all ages the noblest, the manliest, the equallest, the justest, government, the most agreeable to all due libertie and proportiond equalitie, both human, and civil, and Christian, most cherishing to vertue and true religion, but also (I may say it with greatest probabilitie) planely commended, or rather enjoind by our Saviour himself, to all Christians, not without remarkable disallowance, and the brand of gentilism, upon kingship" (ibid., p. 424).

26. Ibid., p. 426. See also, "Wheras a king must be ador'd like a Demigod, with a dissolute and haughtie court about him . . ." (ibid., p. 425).

27. *Areopagitica*, *Yale Prose*, II: 514–515, 527.

28. Ibid., p. 543.

29. *The Reason of Church Government*, *Yale Prose*, I: 746. See also *Eikonoklastes*, *Yale Prose*, III: 338–339.

30. *Animadversions . . .*, I: 702, "that long use and custome . . . hath been nothing else but . . . superstitious devotion"; *Reason of Church Government*, I: 746, "not of custome and awe, which most men do."

31. See *inter alia A Defense of the People of England, Yale Prose,* IV: i, "this king was a tyrant" (p. 338); "[who would] ravage the whole realm with fire and sword, since he is so little subject to the laws as to be permitted what he wills" (p. 347); "He had long planned to turn the government of England into a tyranny, but he thought he could not carry out his plans unless he had first done away with the best part of the citizens' military strength" (p. 529); "an embittered king who acknowledges no master, and who from his earliest days has been taught to think that law, religion, and his own oath are but his vassals" (p. 532).

32. *A Defense of the People of England, Yale Prose,* IV: i, 425–426.

33. *A Defense of the People of England, Yale Prose,* IV: i, 467, 521.

34. *Reason of Church Government, Yale Prose,* I: 752. I am indebted to Robert Hodge, ed., "John Milton, Paradise Lost, Book V," in *The Cambridge Milton for Schools and Colleges,* gen. ed. John Broadbent (Cambridge: Cambridge University Press, 1975), p. 30.

35. *Christian Doctrine, Yale Prose,* VI: 160.

36. *Paradise Lost,* variously from IV: 469–498; my emphasis added.

10. LINES OF AUTHORITY

1. *The Art of Governing by Parties* (London, 1701) is John Trenchard's polemical account of Stuart monarchy; it is interesting to note that the history of party politics should have begun to be self-consciously recorded as early as the first year of the eighteenth century. The current literature on party politics in the first half of the eighteenth century is very large; but, see Basil Williams, *The Whig Supremacy,* 2d ed. (London: C. H. Stuart/Clarendon Press, 1962); Geoffrey Holmes, *British Politics in the Age of Anne* (New York: St. Martin's Press, 1967); J. H. Plumb, *The Growth of Political Stability in England, 1675–1725* (London: Macmillan, 1967); W. A. Speck, *Tory & Whig: The Struggle for the Constituencies 1701–1715* (London: Macmillan, 1970); E. P. Thompson, *Whigs and Hunters* (New York: Pantheon, 1975); Linda Colley, *In Defiance of Oligarchy: The Tory Party 1714–1760* (Cambridge: Cambridge University Press, 1982).

2. See, for example, Isaac Kramnick, *Bolingbroke and His Circle* (Cambridge, Mass.: Harvard University Press, 1968); Michael Foss, *The Age of Patronage* (Ithaca, N.Y.: Cornell University Press, 1971); W. A. Speck, "Politicians, Peers, and Publication by Subscription 1700–1750," in *Books and Their Readers in Eighteenth-Century England,* ed. Isabel Rivers (Leicester: Leicester University Press, 1982).

3. Robert Walcott, *English Politics in the Early Eighteenth Century* (Oxford: Oxford University Press, 1956); J. P. Kenyon, *Revolution Principles, The Politics of Party 1689–1720* (Cambridge: Cambridge University Press, 1977); Henry Horwitz, *Parliament, Policy, and Politics in the Reign of William III* (Newark: University of Delaware Press, 1977); Speck, *Tory & Whig;* Holmes, *British Politics in the Age of Anne.*

4. The major exception is to be found in the work of J. R. Jones, *The First Whigs* (London: Oxford University Press, 1961); *Country and Court: England 1658–1714* (Cambridge, Mass.: Harvard University Press, 1978).

5. The organization of standard literary histories that separate the genres and the topics of literature, culture, and politics discourages an understanding of the relations among these genres and topics; see, for example, James Sutherland, *English Literature of the Late Seventeenth Century* (New York: Oxford University Press, 1969). Recent work on Marvell and Milton by, among others, John Wallace, Annabel Patterson, Barbara Everett, Christopher Hill, and Mary Ann Radzinowicz has given us a much more exact understanding of the relations between polemic and art in the later seventeenth century.

6. See Kramnick, *Bolingbroke*, and Foss, *Age of Patronage*. More specialized study of the literary clubs and their political influence can be found in Robert Allen, *The Clubs of Augustan London* (Cambridge, Mass.: Harvard University Press, 1933); Kathleen Lynch, *Jacob Tonson: Kit-Cat Publisher* (Knoxville: University of Tennessee Press, 1971); and Philip Pinkus, *Grub St. Stripped Bare* (Hamden, Conn.: Archon, 1968).

7. See, for example, Earl Miner's conclusions about *Don Sebastian* and political allegory in H. T. Swedenberg, Jr., *The Works of John Dryden*, ed. Earl Miner (Berkeley, Los Angeles, London: University of California Press, 1976), 15: 394; or John Loftis's distinction between history and politics in Restoration drama, *Restoration and Early Eighteenth Century*, ed. H. T. Swedenberg, Jr. (Berkeley, Los Angeles, London: University of California Press, 1972), pp. 39–42.

8. The classic study of Marvell's political career is the unpublished doctoral dissertation by Caroline Robbins, "A Critical Study of the Political Activities of Andrew Marvell" (University of London, 1926); recent contributions to our knowledge of Marvell's politics include John Wallace, *Destiny His Choice: The Loyalism of Andrew Marvell* (London: Cambridge University Press, 1968), and John Kenyon, "Andrew Marvell: Life and Times," in *Andrew Marvell, Essays on the Tercentenary of his Death*, ed. R. L. Brett (Oxford: Oxford University Press, 1979), pp. 1–35.

9. See Don M. Wolfe, *Milton in the Puritan Revolution* (New York: Columbia University Press, 1941), and Christopher Hill, *Milton and the English Revolution* (New York: Viking Press, 1977).

10. Classic studies of Puritan stylistics are found in William Haller's *The Rise of Puritanism* (New York: Columbia University Press, 1938), chap. 4, and Perry Miller's *The New England Mind: The Seventeenth Century* (1939; reprint, Boston: Beacon Press, 1961). The most comprehensive recent work is Barbara Lewalski's *Protestant Poetics and the Seventeenth-Century Religious Lyric* (Princeton: Princeton University Press, 1979); the influence of dissenting traditions on prose style has been examined by Christopher Hill, "Radical prose in Seventeenth-Century England," *Essays in Criticism* 32 (April 1982): 95–118, and C. Horne, "Hard Words as Contentious or Violent Talk," *Durham University J.* LXXV (1983): 31–42. See also Michael Heyd's survey, "The Reaction to Enthusiasm in the Seventeenth Century: Towards an Integrative Approach," *J. M. Hist.* LIII (1981): 258–280.

11. Marvell's role as opposition publicist was seen, I suspect, as a contra-

diction to his earlier poetic; hence Hugh MacDonald writes of his exclusion of the Restoration satires from the Muses' Library volume of Marvell's poems (Cambridge, Mass.: Harvard University Press, 1952), "It has not been possible to include Marvell's political satires in this edition, although they were printed by G. A. Aitken in the original series of the Muses' Library. They have no relation to his lyrical poetry, and they contain so many allusions that they require a great deal of annotation to make them intelligible."

12. John Wallace's chapter on *The Last Instructions* in *Destiny His Choice* and Annabel Patterson's work on the *Advice* poems in *Marvell and the Civic Crown* (Princeton: Princeton University Press, 1978) are very helpful in establishing the relationship between the poet's political sympathies and the rhetorical program of the satires.

13. Edmund Hickeringill, *The History of Whiggism* (London, 1682), p. 8.

14. On this theme, see J. G. A. Pocock, *The Machiavellian Moment* (Princeton: Princeton University Press, 1975), and the conclusion to Michael Walzer's *The Revolution of the Saints* (Cambridge, Mass.: Harvard University Press, 1965).

15. The origin of the English civil wars is one of the most comprehensively debated topics in political history, and I do not mean to engage the entire range of interpretive issues here.

16. See R. S. Bosher, *The Making of the Restoration Settlement* (London: Adam and Charles Black, 1957); D. R. Lacey, *Dissent and Parliamentary Politics in England, 1661–1689* (New Brunswick, N.J.: Rutgers University Press, 1969); and Keith Feiling, *History of the Tory Party, 1640–1714* (Oxford: Oxford University Press, 1924).

17. See Peter Laslett's edition of Locke's *Two Treatises of Government* (Cambridge: Cambridge University Press, 1960), pp. 92 ff.

18. See J. H. Plumb, *The Growth of Political Stability*, pp. 83 ff.; B. W. Hill, *The Growth of Parliamentary Parties, 1689–1742* (London: Allen and Unwin, 1976), "Introduction" and chaps. 1–4; and Henry Horwitz, "Parties, Connections and Parliamentary Politics, 1689–1714," *J. Brit. Studies*, VI (1966)

19. The phrase is Dryden's and comes from *Absalom and Achitophel*; all quotations are from and citations to James Kinsley's edition, *The Poems of John Dryden*, 4 vols. (Oxford: Oxford University Press, 1958), I: 218, line 72.

20. See the language of the Act of Indemnity and Oblivion, *The Stuart Constitution*, ed. J. P. Kenyon (Cambridge: Cambridge University Press, 1966), pp. 365–371.

21. See, for example, the account of the proceedings against Lord Clarendon in William Cobbett, *Parliamentary History of England*, 36 vols. (London, 1806–20), IV: 381 f.

22. See R. Willman, "The Origins of 'Whig' and 'Tory' in English Political Language," *Historical J.* XVII (1974): 263–264.

23. See J. R. Jones, "Parties and Parliament," in *The Restored Monarchy* ed. idem (London: Macmillan, 1979), pp. 50–54.

24. On the Restoration settlement, see R. Bosher, *The Making of the Restoration Settlement;* and Anne Whiteman, "The Re-establishment of the Church of England," *Transactions of the Royal Historical Society* (5th series, 1955), 5:111–131.

25. See Jones, *Country and Court,* chap. 11, "The Tory Reaction."

26. See C. Hill, *Antichrist in Seventeenth-Century England* (London: Oxford University Press, 1971), pp. 145 ff., and Hill's recent *The Experience of Defeat* (New York: Viking, 1984), passim.

27. On James II's courtship of dissent, see Jones, *Country and Court*, chap. 12; and John Miller, *Popery and Politics in England, 1660–1688* (Cambridge: Cambridge University Press, 1973), chaps. 10 and 11.

28. On the complexity of party politics in the 1690s, see Horwitz, *Parliament, Policy and Politics*, and Kenyon, *Revolution Principles*, chaps. 1–6.

29. The recent work of Patterson in *Marvell and the Civic Crown*, and Barbara Everett, "The Shooting of the Bears: Poetry and Politics in Andrew Marvell," *Andrew Marvell: Essays on the Tercentenary of His Death*, ed. R. L. Brett (Oxford: Oxford University Press, 1979), pp. 62–103, have helped to correct the imbalance of attention between the lyric and the political Marvell. It is interesting, however, to note that in a review of the newest work on Marvell's political poetry, Warren Chernaik's *The Poet's Time: Politics and Religion in the Work of Andrew Marvell* (Cambridge: Cambridge University Press, 1983), Hilton Kelliher should still argue, "Unfortunately no one has yet been able to provide a wholly convincing portrait of the writer who on the one hand was a fine craftsman producing perfect, if ambiguous private poems and on the other a political activist the formal qualities of whose satires elicit unflattering comparisons with the work of Dryden and Pope." See *Notes and Queries* CCXXX (March 1985): 126.

30. The most comprehensive account of *The First Anniversary* is by Derek Hirst, " 'That Sober Liberty': Marvell's Cromwell in 1654," in *The Golden and the Brazen World, Papers in Literature and History, 1650–1800*, ed. John M. Wallace (Berkeley, Los Angeles, London: University of California Press, 1985), pp. 17–53.

31. See Patterson on the rhetoric of the *Third Advice*, particularly its relation to contemporary Royalist panegyric, in *Marvell and the Civic Crown*, pp. 143–152.

32. Quotations are from George deF. Lord et al., eds., *Poems on Affairs of State*, 7 vols. (New Haven, Conn.: Yale University Press, 1963–75), vol. I, edited by Lord, p. 69.

33. Lord, *Poems on Affairs of State*, I: 75.

34. Ibid., I: 75.

35. Ibid., I: 75–76. See also Lord's notes on the duchess, and see as well Patterson on Marvell's handling of this figure, *Marvell and the Civic Crown*, pp. 153–157.

36. Lord, *Poems on Affairs of State*, I: 75–76.

37. Ibid., I: 87.

38. Ibid., I: 154.

39. Ibid., I: 105. Wallace sees some irony in the handling of the House of Commons (lines 107–112 and 267–276) in *Destiny His Choice*, pp. 174–175; cf. Patterson, *Marvell and the Civic Crown*, p. 166.

40. Patterson notes the echoes of Milton's allegory in *Marvell and the Civic Crown*, p. 163; cf. Lord, I: 106.

41. Lord, *Poems on Affairs of State*, I: 114.

42. Wallace makes the interesting suggestion that the elegy on Douglas had political meaning in the context of Scottish politics. See *Destiny His Choice*, p. 180 n. 1.

43. Lord, *Poems on Affairs of State*, I: 136.

44. Wallace seems to ignore this long and damaging attack on Charles II when he argues, "On Charles's one appearance in the narrative he is the 'lov'd *King*' (327), but the envoi to Charles, personally addressed to him, contains the state of Marvell's respect for his rights. . . ." See *Destiny His Choice*, p. 178.

45. Both Wallace and Patterson write extensively and helpfully on *The Rehearsal Transpros'd*; on stylistics, see especially Patterson, *Marvell and the Civic Crown*, pp. 180 ff.; and Raymond Anselment, "Satiric Strategy in Marvell's *The Rehearsal Transpros'd*," *Mod. Philology* LXVIII (1970): 137–150. D. I. B. Smith describes the reception of *The Rehearsal Transpros'd* and remarks on Marvell's calculation of audience in his edition of that work (Oxford: Oxford University Press, 1971), pp. xiii–xx.

46. On the contents and circumstances of publication of Marvell's *Miscellaneous Poems*, see Pierre Legouis, ed., *The Poems and Letters of Andrew Marvell*, rev. ed., 2 vols. (Oxford: Oxford University Press, 1971), I: 241–242, and L. N. Wall, "Marvell's Friends in the City," *Notes and Queries* CCIV (June 1959): 204–207. Also see Patterson, *Censorship and Interpretation* (Madison: University of Wisconsin Press, 1984), p. 125. On the publication of Milton after 1688, see William Riley Parker, *Milton, A Biography*, 2 vols. (Oxford: Oxford University Press, 1968), I: 662–666, and II: appendix I, 1205–1208.

47. See Zera S. Fink, *The Classical Republicans* (Evanston, Ill.: Northwestern University Press, 1962), p. 175; and Bernard Sharratt, "The Appropriation of Milton," *Essays and Studies* (London: English Association, 1982), collected by Suheil Bushrui.

48. On Toland as biographer and editor of Milton, see Stephen H. Daniel, *John Toland, His Methods, Manners, and Mind* (Kingston and Montreal: McGill University Press, 1984), pp. 60–63, 212–213.

49. On the history of Milton scholarship, see Ants Oras, *Milton's Editors and Commentators from Patrick Hume to Henry John Todd, 1695–1801* (London: Oxford University Press, 1931).

50. We do not know, of course, what portion of *Paradise Lost* was composed after the Restoration of the king, and the Trinity MS gives evidence that Milton contemplated a tragedy on *Paradise Lost* as early as 1640. The early biographies date the composition of the poem approximately between 1658 and 1663; see Parker, *Milton, A Biography*, I: 508–509; II: 1064–1065.

51. On the politics of *Samson Agonistes*, see Hill, *Milton and the English Revolution*, pp. 428–448, and Mary Ann Radzinowicz, *Toward Samson Agonistes* (Princeton: Princeton University Press, 1979), pp. 167–179.

52. See Hugh M. Richmond, *The Christian Revolutionary: John Milton* (Berkeley, Los Angeles, London: University of California Press, 1974), passim.

53. John Carey and Alastair Fowler, eds., *The Poems of John Milton* (London: Longmans, 1968), pp. 456–457. All quotations from *Paradise Lost* will be given by page number followed by book and line numbers.

54. See Zwicker, "Politics and Literary Practice in the Restoration," *Harvard Eng. Studies*, 14, ed. Barbara K. Lewalski (Cambridge, Mass.: Harvard University Press, 1986).

55. Cf. the remarks on rhyme and the swipe that Marvell takes at Dryden in the commendatory verse that he wrote for the 1674 edition of *Paradise Lost, The Poems of John Milton*, pp. 455–456.

56. On the invocations in *Paradise Lost*, see Walter Schindler, *Voice and Crisis: Invocation in Milton's Poetry* (Hamden, Conn.: Archon, 1984).

57. *The Poems of John Milton*, pp. 459–461. 1:6–19.

58. Ibid., p. 462. 1:27.

59. Ibid., p. 509. 2:1–8.

60. Ibid., p. 562. 3:26–36.

61. Cf. Schindler, *Voice and Crisis*, pp. 86–87.

62. *The Poems of John Milton*, pp. 776–777. 7:24–38.

63. Ibid., pp. 851–853. 9:1–10.

64. Ibid., pp. 855–857. 9:28–47.

65. On the structure of books 11 and 12, see B. K. Lewalski, "Structure and the Symbolism of Vision in Michael's Prophecy," *Philological Q.*, XLII (1963): 25–35.

66. On the catalogue of tyrants at the opening of book 11, see Stevie Davies, *Images of Kingship in Paradise Lost* (Columbia: University of Missouri Press, 1983), pp. 86–88.

67. *The Poems of John Milton*, pp. 999–1000. 11:387–392.

68. On Adam's education by history, see Hill, *Milton and the English Revolution*, pp. 380–390.

69. *The Poems of John Milton*, pp. 1018–1019. 11:718–726, 808–813.

70. See Stanley Fish, *Surprised by Sin* (New York, 1967), pp. 107–130.

71. *The Poems of John Milton*, p. 1016. 11:664–670.

72. Ibid., pp. 1018–1019. 11:719–726.

73. See Lewalski, "Structure and the Symbolism of Vision," pp. 25–35.

74. The crucial linking between reason and liberty in *Paradise Lost* occurs in book 12, pp. 97–101; on the role of reason in politics in Milton's thought, see Wolfe, *Milton in the Puritan Revolution*, pp. 355–362; and Fink, *The Classical Republicans*, pp. 90–99.

75. On the relation between power and corruption in the 1680s, see *The Medal Revers'd*: "See her true badge, a prison or the Tower; / For Persecution ever sides with power. / . . . In tyrants' courts she ever doth abide, / Accompan'd with Power, with Lust and Pride" (*Poems on Affairs of State*, ed. Howard Schless, III:63).

76. See Michael McKeon, *Politics and Poetry in Restoration England* (Cambridge, Mass.: Harvard University Press, 1975); and Patterson, *Marvell and the Civic Crown*, pp. 144–147.

77. See Jones, *Country and Court*, pp. 161–163; Clarendon's own account can be consulted in *The Life of Edward Earl of Clarendon*, 3 vols. (Oxford, 1759), III: 906.

78. Most obviously in the panegyric, "To My Lord Chancellor," published in 1662; see also Hugh Macdonald, *John Dryden, A Bibliography* (Oxford, 1939),

p. 10 n. 2; and George McFadden, *Dryden, The Public Writer* (Princeton: Princeton University Press, 1978), pp. 41–48.

79. On the relation between Dryden and York, see McFadden, *Dryden, The Public Writer*, pp. 89–94.

80. On the attack from dissenters, see McKeon, *Politics and Poetry in Restoration England*, pp. 79–98, 190–204.

81. Kingsley, *The Poems of John Dryden*, I: 44.

82. Ibid., I: 44–45.

83. See notes and commentary by H. T. Swedenberg, Jr., *The Works of John Dryden*, ed. Swedenberg et al., 20 vols. (Berkeley and Los Angeles: University of California Press, 1956—), II:209–285.

84. See R. Willman, "The Origins of 'Whig' and 'Tory' in English Political Language," *Historical J.* XVII (1974): 263–264; the pamphlet literature on party in the Exclusion Crisis is very large, but some useful examples are Roger L'Estrange, *The Observator*, no. 29 (London, 1681); *The Character of a Tory* (London, 1681); *The Character of a Good Man, Neither Whig nor Tory* (London, 1681); *Some Remarkques Upon a late Popular Piece of Nonsence Called Julian the Apostate* (London, 1682); *The Tory-Poets: A Satyr* (London, 1682); *A Congratulatory Poem on the Whigg's Entertainment* (London, 1682); George Hickes, *A Discourse of the Soveraign Power* (London, 1682); *The Character of A Disbanded Courtier* (London, 1682); *The Recanting Whigg* (London, 1683); *A Parallel of Times: Or a Memento to the Whiggs* (London, 1683). See, as well, vol. 2 and 3 of Lord, *Poems on Affairs of State*.

85. See, for example, *The Medal of John Bayes*, vol. 3, *Poems on Affairs of State*: "If anything could dishoner him, it would be the bloody violence of your (Tories') spirits, your unpunished exorbitancies and breach of laws; your huzzaing, roaring, quarreling, and damning by much the greater part of the nation."; *The Tory-Poets: A Satyr* (London, 1682), A2ʳ, "To talk Bawdy, whore, Lye, &c. are your natural accomplishments; but those more solid endowments that beautifie a rational Creature, viz. Learning and Exercise of right Reason, are of little value to you, who can speak Nonscence by Patent, Slander by Prerogative, and Lye by Commission."; *The Character of a Tory* (London, 1681), p. 2, "He pretends high for the Church of *England;* but as he understands not her Doctrin, so he Dishonours her by his Lewd Conversation: What a pretty Pious Confession of Faith is it, to hear a *Bully* Cry,—*God-Dam-Mee, I am of the Church of* England, *and all the Presbyterians* are Sons of Whores. Indeed, the only proof both of his *Religion* and *Courage*, is, That he Swears most frequently by that *Tremendous* Name, at which, lesser Devils tremble, and his Christianity consists in *Cursing* all those that he is pleased to call Phanaticks. . . . His *Tongue* is always Tipt with Dam-Mee, and *Forty one;* and so *hot* (being set on Fire of Hell) that he is fain to drink *Healths*, (sometimes to the *Pope*, and sometimes to the *Devil*,) Sixty times an Hour to quench it; and then Belches out *Huzza*'s as fast, as Mount *Strombulo* does Fire and Brimstone." Cf. *Poems on Affairs of State*, III: 256, 350.

86. For the rhetoric of the civil wars in Exclusion Crisis politics, especially in Tory propaganda, see Zwicker, *Politics and Language in Dryden's Poetry* (Princeton, 1984), chap. 1; Jones, *Country and Court*, chap. 10; idem, "Parties

and Parliament," in *The Restored Monarchy*, 65–70; and follow the entries under "Civil War" in vols. 2 and 3 of *Poems on Affairs of State*.

87. Cf. *Poems on Affairs of State*, II, ed. Elias F. Mengel, Jr., II:461, 462.

88. Kingsley, *The Poems of John Dryden*, I: 219.

89. Despite the long biographical tradition that links the king and his poet laureate in the composition of this poem, we know very little of their relations during the Exclusion Crisis; see Macdonald, *John Dryden, A Bibliography*, pp. 18–20.

90. There seems to be little consensus among students of this poem on the tone and intention of the opening lines and on the larger question of the poem's scripturalism; on that large and difficult issue, critics seem to occupy an entire spectrum of positions from those who see Dryden's aim as one of debunking Scripture to those who credit the serious political and prophetic resonance of Scripture in the poem.

91. Cf. Zwicker, *Politics and Language in Dryden's Poetry*, pp. 85–90, 218–220.

92. For an interesting variation on this argument, see *The Second Part of Absalom and Achitophel*, lines 441–456, in Kingsley, *The Poems of John Dryden*, I: 283.

93. Ibid., I: 215.

94. Ibid., I: 216.

95. See *Oxford English Dictionary*, s.v. "genius."

96. Kingsley, *The Poems of John Dryden*, I: 215.

97. Ibid., I: 215.

98. Cf. Macdonald, *Dryden, A Bibliography*, p. 18 n. 2.

99. Ibid., p. 25.

100. See Zwicker, *Politics and Language in Dryden's Poetry*, p. 233 n. 16.

101. See Parker, *Milton, A Biography*, II: 1189–1204; on the politicization of Milton's works and reputation in the 1690s, see John Toland's *Amyntor; Or, a defence of Milton's Life* (London, 1699), and *Remarks on the Life of Mr. Milton, as publish'd by J.T. with a Character of the Author and his Party* (London, 1699), p. 2: "It is storied of the Italian Painters, That they Compliment their Mistresses by drawing the blessed Virgin according to their Features; and in truth I am of Opinion that the Author design'd the like Compliment to himself in forming Mr. Milton's Character; for his natural and acquired Parts, Estate, Publick Post, Great Reputation and Universal Esteem excepted, the Parallel seems to be drawn as near as may be."

11. FABLES OF POWER

1. George Kitchin, *Sir Roger L'Estrange: A Contribution to the History of the Press in the Seventeenth Century* (London, 1913), p. 397.

2. Samuel Croxall, *Fables of AEsop and Others, Newly done into English, With an Application to each Fable* (London, 1722), b4r.

3. A similar inference might be drawn from L'Estrange's allusion to Ec-

clesiastes 8:4, its immediate context being a king who does whatever he pleases, as James I had chosen to identify himself with Solomon. The same text was adduced by Charles I, in the speech prepared for his trial, as a defense of the prerogative. See Charles Petrie, ed., *The Letters, Speeches and Proclamations of King Charles I* (London, 1968), p. 259.

4. Croxall, *Fables*, b7r. Much of Phaedrus' biography remains conjectural. One of the principal manuscripts of his fables states that he was made freedman by Augustus, and various autobiographical hints in his fables place him as living under Tiberius (and Sejanus). See Ben Edwin Perry, ed., *Babrius and Phaedrus*, Loeb edition (Cambridge, Mass.: Harvard University Press, 1964), pp. lxxiii–lxxxii.

5. See Joseph Jacobs, *The Fables of Aesop*, 3 vols. (New York, 1889, reprint 1970), 1: 1–43; and the introduction to Perry, *Babrius and Phaedrus*.

6. Perry, *Babrius and Phaedrus*, pp. 190, 232, 254, 298.

7. R. T. Lenaghan, ed., *Caxton's Aesop* (Cambridge, Mass.: Harvard University Press, 1967), pp. 4–9.

8. Jacobs, *The Fables of Aesop*, 1: 38–40.

9. Mary H. Pritchard, *Fables Moral and Political: The Adaptation of the Aesopian Fable Collection to English Social and Political Life, 1651–1722* (unpublished Ph.D. diss., University of Western Ontario, Canada, 1976). This contains an extensive bibliography.

10. Robert Johnson et al., eds., *Commons Debates 1628*, 5 vols. (New Haven and London: Yale University Press, 1977), 3: 532.

11. Philip Massinger, *The Emperor of the East*, in *The Plays and Poems of Philip Massinger*, ed. Philip Edwards and Colin Gibson, 5 vols. (Oxford: Oxford University Press, 1976), p. 428.

12. John Milton, *Complete Prose Works*, ed. Don M. Wolfe et al., 8 vols. (New Haven, Conn.: Yale University Press, 1953–80), 1: 583–584, 834.

13. James Howell, *Dodona's Grove: or the Vocall Forrest* (London, 1640), p. 215. A second part appeared in 1650.

14. Mildmay Fane, from *Fugitive Poetry*, Harvard MS Eng. 645, described and excerpted by Eleanor Withington, *Harvard Library Bull.* (1957), 11: 47.

15. *Rump; or, an Exact Collection of the Choycest Poems and Songs Relating to the Late Times*, 2 vols. (1662, reprint London, 1874), 1: 36.

16. Petrie, *The Letters*, p. 270.

17. The Solomonic text is 1 Kings 4:24 ("And Solomon had . . . peace on all sides round him. And Judah and Israel dwelt safely, every man under his vine and his fig-tree"). James I had cited this text in a defensive address to the Lords: *His Majesties Speech in the Upper House of Parliament, on Monday, the 26 of March, 1621* (London, 1621), B3v; and Charles had recycled it in his equally defensive Declaration of 10 March 1629, in which he stated his reason for dissolving Parliament. See Petrie, *The Letters*, p. 78.

18. Andrew Marvell, *The Poems and Letters*, ed. H. M. Margoliouth, rev. Pierre Legouis, 2 vols. (Oxford: Oxford University Press, 1971), 1: 115.

19. Pritchard, *Fables Moral and Political*, pp. 36–37.

20. For Ogilby's biography, see Katherine Van Eerde, *John Ogilby and the Taste of his Times* (Folkestone, Kent: Dawson, 1976); and see also Marion

Eames, "John Ogilby and His Aesop," *Bull. of the New York Public Library,* 65 (1961): 73–78; Earl Miner's facsimile edition of the 1668 *Fables* (Los Angeles: Augustan Reprint Society, 1965), pp. i–xiv; Margret Schuchard, *John Ogilby, 1660–1676; Lebenbild eines Gentelman mit vielen Karieren* (Hamburg: P. Hartaag, 1973).

21. For Engagement politics, see David Underdown, *Royalist Conspiracy in England, 1649–1660* (New Haven: Yale University Press, 1960), pp. 30–51, 73–96.

22. Milton, *Complete Prose,* 7: 478.

23. Marvell, *Poems and Letters,* 1: 179, 212.

24. John Freke, *The History of Insipids,* in *Anthology of Poems on Affairs of State,* ed. George de F. Lord (New Haven and London: Yale University Press, 1975), p. 143.

25. Miner's commentary is available both in his *Dryden's Poetry* (Bloomington and London: Indiana University Press, 1967), pp. 144–205, and in *The Works of John Dryden,* vol. 3., ed. Earl Miner and Vinton A. Dearing (Berkeley and Los Angeles: University of California Press, 1969), pp. 326–459.

26. Steven Zwicker, *Politics and Language in Dryden's Poetry: The Arts of Disguise* (Princeton: Princeton University Press, 1984), pp. 123–158.

27. Dryden, *Works,* 3: 161.

28. For instance, the fact that this self-defense does not appear until the opening of part 3 suggests a slight generic shift, toward a more explicitly Aesopian discourse, and hence one that is less theological, more political. The reference to Caledon may recall John Hepwith's *Caledonian Forest.*

29. *Aesops Fables With His Life: in English, French & Latin. The English by Tho. Philipott Esq; The French and Latin by Rob. Codrington M.A.* (London, 1666), pp. 32–33.

Contributors

Barbara K. Lewalski: William Keenan Professor of English and American Literature, Harvard University.

Michael McKeon: Professor of English, Boston University.

Earl Miner: Townsend Martin, Class of 1917, Professor of English and Comparative Literature, Princeton University.

David Norbrook: Fellow of Magdalen College, Oxford and Lecturer in English, University of Oxford.

Annabel Patterson: Professor of English, Duke University.

J. G. A. Pocock: Harry Black Professor of History, Johns Hopkins University.

Mary Ann Radzinowicz: Jacob Gould Schurman Professor of English, Cornell University.

Kevin Sharpe: Lecturer in History, University of Southampton.

Blair Worden: Fellow of St. Edmund Hall, Oxford and Lecturer in History, University of Oxford.

Steven N. Zwicker: Professor of English, Washington University, St. Louis.

Index

353

Designer: U.C. Press Staff
Compositor: Auto-Graphics, Inc.
Text: 10/12 Palatino
Display: Palatino
Printer: Edwards Bros.
Binder: Edwards Bros.